Wisdom With Understanding is Better Than Rubies

Lurine Karon Greenberg
Fine Arts Collection

Rethinking
Social Realism

Stacy I. Morgan

Rethinking
Social Realism

**African American Art and
Literature, 1930–1953**

The University of Georgia Press
Athens and London

© 2004 by the University of Georgia Press
Athens, Georgia 30602
All rights reserved
Set in Ehrhardt by Graphic Composition, Inc.
Printed and bound by Thomson-Shore
The paper in this book meets the guidelines for permanence and durability of the
Committee on Production Guidelines for Book Longevity of the Council on
Library Resources.

Printed in the United States of America
07 06 05 04 03 C 5 4 3 2 1
07 06 05 04 03 P 5 4 3 2 1

Library of Congress Cataloging-in-Publication Data
Morgan, Stacy I., 1970–
Rethinking social realism : African American art and literature, 1930–1953 / Stacy I.
Morgan.
    p.   cm.
Includes bibliographical references and index.
ISBN 0-8203-2564-3 (hardcover : alk. paper) — ISBN 0-8203-2579-1 (pbk. : alk. paper)
    1. African American arts—20th century.   2. Social realism—United States.   I. Title.
NX504 .M67 2004
700'.412'08996073—dc21   2003011153

British Library Cataloging-in-Publication Data available

Contents

Illustrations

Acknowledgments

Despite the seemingly countless hours of isolated work that have gone into the writing of this book, even a few moments of reflection call to mind a host of others who have left their imprint on its development in meaningful ways.

The genuinely helpful and professional staffs at several institutions helped to facilitate the research that made this study possible. The Rare Books and Special Collections staff members at Northern Illinois University's Founder's Memorial Library went out of their way to provide me with access to their vast Willard Motley Collection. The employees of the Department of Special Collections at the University of Wisconsin's Memorial Library allowed me to make use of their Willard Motley papers, Theodore Pierce papers, and Sukov Little Magazines Collection. And the personnel at the Archives of American Art in Washington, D.C., offered expert advice that enabled me to examine a range of their holdings in a manner much more efficient than I otherwise would have managed.

At various junctures, this project also received important financial support from a graduate student summer research grant from the Graduate Institute of Liberal Arts at Emory University and a summer research grant from the Research Advisory Council at the University of Alabama.

Nancy Grayson, Erin McElroy, Jon Davies, and the staff of the University of Georgia Press have my gratitude as well. They have shown considerable patience at points when life intervened and did not allow the expeditious progress that I would have liked; and certainly they have helped to shape this study into a more tightly written and readable book. Jeanée Ledoux provided copyediting advice of the highest caliber. In Tuscaloosa, David Noe provided crucial assistance in reproducing several of the images that appear in this text.

I have been especially fortunate to have had many remarkable academic mentors throughout my education. Richard Long served as the director of an earlier dissertation stage of this project, and any contributions offered by this study are due in no small measure to his expert guidance. I count myself truly lucky to be among the vast number of scholars who have benefited from his incisive intellect and wisdom. Frances Smith Foster, Mark Sanders, Cris Levenduski, Trudier Harris-Lopez, Allen Tullos, Jacqueline Nassy Brown, Gilbert Bond, and David Brown also have aided my work significantly. They have given their time and energy liberally over the years and have offered exemplary models of rigorous scholarship and inspired teaching. Further, Ashraf Rushdy, Sharon Holland, and Cynthia Horan have been among those who have offered valuable advice both during and beyond my years as an undergraduate at Wesleyan University. I only hope that I can emulate the genuine dedication to my own students that all of you have shown toward me.

This project would not have reached fruition, either, without the consideration that I have received from my fellow faculty in the Department of American Studies at the University of Alabama. A junior faculty member truly could not ask for a more engaging, good natured, and generous group of colleagues. Thanks are due, as well, to the office staff members with whom I have worked while toiling on this project: Brenda Crosby, Joy Vodak, and Jennifer Stocking at Emory University; Barb Grueser, Leslie Johnson, Diane Lucas, and Dorothy Anderson at Ohio University; and Beth Goode, Janice Stewart, and Veronica Pruitt at the University of Alabama. You have helped to make the places where I have hung my hat as a graduate student and faculty member a little more like home.

Among the many friends and colleagues who have helped to shape my thinking in this project are Lynne Adrian, Michael Antonucci, Gabrielle Civil, Petrina Dacres, Francis Desiderio, Bobby Donaldson, James Hall, Lovalerie King, Steve Levin, Rich Megraw, Krista Thompson, Jeremy Webster, and Michelle Wilkinson. Ira Dworkin has been a game road trip companion and charitably lent his assistance to my archival research of Willard Motley. Despite distance, Jacqueline Francis has tirelessly offered essential knowledge and advice in my moments of anxiety and befuddlement. Shabnaum Amjad, Shibani Baksi, Jennifer Aliff, Timothy Dodd, Renee Rallos, Billie Jean Crigger, Natalie Collins, Julie Folger, Anil Mujumdar, Amy Harries, Emily Satterwhite, Dave Rainey, Terry Easton, and Theresa Same have given me much-needed doses of perspective and humor more times than I can count. And Pat Wehner has contributed more to this project than he probably realizes, helping me to sharpen my ideas, to keep my shoulder to the proverbial wheel, and to develop a respectable fade-away jumper.

Finally, I offer my heartfelt thanks to my family—especially my parents, Jerry and Betty Jo Morgan, my brother, Ryan, and my grandmothers, Madge Morgan and Leota Smith. Your unconditional love sustains me and your example consistently reminds me of the importance of trying to live as a decent human being in this world.

**Rethinking
Social Realism**

Chapter One

Expressing the Life and Cause of the Masses: Ideologies and Institutions

We can see that the New Negro came of age during the Thirties. He grew away from the status of the exotic, the accidentally unusual Negro, the talented tenth of what the white audience chose to consider an otherwise mentally infantile minority group whose masses were illiterate, disfranchised, exploited, and oppressed. Negroes became members of a new school of writers who were no longer isolated because of their color, who were integrated around the beliefs that created the New Deal. They were the poets of social protest who began to catch a glimmer of a global perspective, who as spokesmen for their race did not beg the question of their humanity, and who cried out to other peoples over the earth to recognize race prejudice as a weapon that is as dangerous as the atomic bomb in the threat to annihilation of culture and peace in the western world.
MARGARET WALKER, "NEW POETS"

Despite a recent efflorescence of scholarship on African American cultural work of the 1930s and 1940s, many readers may find it surprising that the late poet and novelist Margaret Walker would point to the *1930s* as the decade in which "the New Negro came of age," rather than to the more frequently celebrated watershed achievements of the Harlem Renaissance of the 1920s. To be sure, Walker's retrospective evaluation owes in part to the fact that the mid-to-late 1930s were the historical moment in which she herself came of age as a writer. Nonetheless, she is right to assert the emergence of a new movement in African American arts and letters during the Great Depression decade.

The movement that Walker singles out for special praise is one that artists and writers of the day usually called "social realism." As social realists, African American visual artists and writers of the 1930s—like their peers—began to place heightened emphasis on the role of the creative artist as an agent of democratic consciousness raising and social change. While not conceiving of art as strictly a "weapon," almost all of the participants in the movement of social realism seem to have shared a profound faith in the capacity of *cultural* work to leverage transformations in the social and political sphere on behalf of America's poor and working classes. Indeed, what goes unstated in Walker's account here is the fact that her generation was keyed not only to the energetic spirit of the Roosevelt administration's New Deal programs but also to the revolutionary enthusiasm of leftist politics, especially those articulated by the U.S. Communist Party (CPUSA). Consequently, African American social realists of the 1930s increasingly began to call attention to the threat of both race prejudice *and* class inequalities. Throughout the period under study, African American artists and writers evidenced a faith in the ability of their cultural work to serve alternately as an instrument of social criticism, a means of instilling race pride, and an agent of interracial working-class coalition building.

Significantly, Walker rhetorically maps this new course for African American cultural work in explicit contrast to what she glosses as "the exotic, the accidentally unusual Negro" of the Harlem Renaissance era, a generation she all but accuses of pandering to the primitivist impulses of white audiences. Like Walker, many African American artists, writers, and cultural critics adopted an antagonistic tone toward the Harlem Renaissance during the 1930s and 1940s for what they retrospectively perceived as its modernist "decadence." Even now, most major academic studies of the Harlem Renaissance seem to have been profoundly shaped by such works as Wallace Thurman's *Infants of the Spring* (1932), a satirical novel that likens the Harlem literary scene of the 1920s to a debauched cabaret, and Langston Hughes's 1940 autobiography, *The Big Sea*, which offers a jaded account of the renaissance as a fleeting and insincere "vogue for things Negro" (see also Johnson and Johnson 89). Similarly, so-called black Victorians like W. E. B. Du Bois accused African American writers of the 1920s of playing to the basest expectations of white audiences by drawing their subject matter from lower-class black life. Du Bois described the "disastrous results" of such appeals to white patronage in *Dusk of Dawn* (1940): "Most whites want Negroes to amuse them; they demand caricature; they demand jazz; and torn between these allegiances: between the extraordinary reward for entertainers of the white world, and meager encouragement to honest self-expression, the artistic movement among American Negroes has accomplished something, but it has never flourished and never will until it is deliberately planned" (202–3). Even Alain Locke, the most widely heralded of the "midwives" of the Harlem Renaissance, essayed several critical retrospective glances on the work of the 1920s in this vein.

For example, when addressing the 1937 meeting of the labor-oriented National Negro Congress (NNC), Locke termed the "cultural creed and viewpoint" of the Harlem Renaissance generation one of "aesthetic individualism and art for art's sake" and accused the renaissance's writers quite pointedly of "having prostituted their wares and their artistic integrity" ("Resume" n.p.). The following year he accused the writers of the 1920s of going "exhibitionist instead of going documentarian" and getting "jazz-mad and cabaret-crazy instead of getting folk-wise and sociologically sober" (Stewart 272). Indictments of this sort found company with Marxist detractors like African American cultural critic Eugene Gordon, who castigated the Harlem Renaissance for its alleged "middle class nationalism" (Foley 186; Wald, *Exiles* 263–64).

As scholar George Hutchinson has argued, such narratives of disillusionment have exerted a disproportionate influence on subsequent interpretations of the Harlem Renaissance, contributing to the entrenchment of an academic conventional wisdom that is decidedly at odds with the genuine concern for interracialism and for the political efficacy of cultural work exhibited by most of the movement's members, both black and white (14–28). Yet, it does seem true that with the shift toward social realist aesthetics during the early 1930s, many artists and writers—particularly those positioned in locales other than New York City—sought to rhetorically distance themselves from the renaissance. For example, in a 1985 interview with John Edgar Tidwell, Chicago poet Frank Marshall Davis recalled his perception of the Harlem movement during the late 1920s: "By staying in Chicago, I avoided being identified with the New Negro Renaissance. I did not want to be part of the Effete East. . . . Chicago was rugged, possibly brutal, and unsophisticated. . . . New York was over-refined, lacking the raw strength of the Midwest" (Tidwell, "Interview" 106). Especially in light of recent scholarly attention to the homosexuality and bisexuality of several key participants in the renaissance, Davis's disparagement of the 1920s Harlem scene as "effete" now seems rather problematic at best. Nonetheless, such unflattering sentiments regarding the ostensibly "alienated" character of American modernists seem to have been taken for granted as often as not in fledgling social realist circles of the 1930s.

In the course of essaying their respective criticisms, Thurman, Hughes, Du Bois, Locke, and Davis each caricatured the actual content of the Harlem Renaissance (and modernism more broadly) in rather dubious ways, particularly inasmuch as they attributed simplistic, apolitical motives to the artists and writers of the 1920s. After all, the leftist, proletarian terms in which cultural organs such as A. Philip Randolph and Chandler Owen's socialist magazine the *Messenger* (1917–28) initially defined the New Negro movement of the late 1910s and 1920s anticipated the labor-centered concerns of social realist cultural production of the 1930s and 1940s in important ways (Gates xxxv–xxxvi). And scholar William Maxwell's *New Negro, Old Left* (1999) has recently demonstrated that the engagement of African American cultural workers with the Communist Party (CP) extends back to at least the early 1920s in the work of such figures as Claude McKay and Andy Razaf. Obviously, too, given the presence of creative artists such as Hughes, Sterling Brown, and Gwendolyn Bennett, whose work chronologically and thematically bridges conventional Harlem Renaissance and social realism periodizations, one should not juxtapose these two movements in an overly simplistic manner.

Still, however inaccurate or imprecise, the castigation of the Harlem Renaissance to which I have been referring does offer an important indicator of how key figures in the 1930s conceptualized *their own* intentionality as artists, writers, and critics. In other words, these criticisms are significant less for what they reveal about the previous generation of African American artistic and literary production than for the way in which such notions regarding the Harlem Renaissance provided a rhetorical ground against which social realists could articulate their own respective projects.

The Emergence of African American Social Realism

One of the central points articulated by way of these retrospective jabs at the Harlem Renaissance was the juxtaposition of an alleged Roaring Twenties preoccupation with black exotica against social realists' concern with the struggles and experiences of poor and working-class people. Without wanting to reify an overly tidy—and, by now, all too familiar—notion of social realism's advent as a phenomenon spun out of whole cloth by the onset of the Great Depression, one must acknowledge that the "hard times" of the depression did play an important role as a catalyst of many artists and writers' gravitation toward an emphasis on proletarian and underclass themes. Like the rest of America's increasingly visible poor and working classes, artists and writers struggled more than ever to make ends meet in the depression era; many, if not most, even took up working-class and service-sector employment themselves. Willard Motley's 1940 *Opportunity* article, "Negro Art in Chicago," illustrates a representative range of the ways in which aspiring African American visual artists supported their cultural work during this period: "[Charles Davis] worked from eight to eight washing dishes and came home to paint until two or three in the morning every night without fail. At another time he was employed as a pick and shovel man on the WPA at the airport"; Bernard Goss, a University of Iowa graduate, "played in a jazz band, 'hopped' bells, washed dishes, waited on tables at Hull House, worked in commercial studios, ran a poker game, and even taught art"; and Charles White, observed Motley, "has been a newsboy, delivered groceries for the A & P stores, washed dishes for Thompson's restaurants, [and] scrubbed floors at Jack and Jill ice cream parlors," in addition to work as a cook, valet, and houseboy (20–22).

Naturally, artists and writers also observed what was transpiring on a broader scale in the communities around them. In this regard, it bears emphasizing that the depression exerted a particularly detrimental impact on the already bleak prospects of most African Americans for socioeconomic advancement. Not only were black employees typically the first released from the relatively meager number of industrial jobs that they had managed to secure, but downwardly mobile whites displaced many black workers from even those menial service-sector jobs that African Americans previously had monopolized. Consequently, the jobless rate for African American men soared to as high as three times that for white men, while some estimates held that one-third of blacks were unemployed and another one-third were underemployed; and although African American women were employed in higher relative numbers than white women, they found themselves almost exclusively relegated to domestic work and similar service-sector jobs (Cayton and Drake 215–216; Naison 31–32). Moreover, lynchings and other acts of racist terrorism increased precipitously during the early 1930s, not least due to the scapegoating of black men for the prevailing socioeconomic downturn (Biles 180; D. Lewis 284). African American social realism emerged, in large part, directly out of the efforts of artists to come to terms with these harrowing social conditions. In so doing, this new generation of creators felt themselves to be *of* as well as *for* the poor and working-class masses of African Americans, often construing themselves as "cultural workers."

By moving such phenomena as poverty and joblessness, racial violence, and legal injustices firmly into the scope of appropriate subject material, and by reconfiguring the notion of an artist's relationship to his or her audience, social realism gave rise to new ideologies regarding the kind of cultural work that visual art and literature could (and should) perform. And this proved as true for African Americans as for their peers. The thinking of African American social realist artists and writers on this front was influenced primarily by two interlocking strands of cultural criticism: the revamped thinking of two African American intellectuals more frequently associated with the Harlem Renaissance period, W. E. B. Du Bois and Alain Locke; and Marxist cultural criticism, especially as it was articulated in the pages of the period's leftist little magazines.

Du Bois's case offers a useful signpost for the seismic shifts transpiring among the African American left during the early 1930s. In 1934 Du Bois severed his long-standing ties with the *Crisis* (1910–96), the official organ of the NAACP, following a controversy that centered on editorial comments expressing what he perceived as a necessarily cynical pragmatism regarding the short-term prospects of conventional integrationist models for African American racial up-lift. While by no means relinquishing the struggle to end racial discrimination, Du Bois proposed a need for African Americans to work for uplift within the ex-isting institutional constraints of segregation, at least in certain strategic in-stances. Yet, during this same period, Du Bois also pressed his fellow African Americans to consider the applicability of Marxist thought and political organ-izing to their collective situation with a heightened sense of urgency. In one 1930 *Crisis* editorial, he even proposed government ownership as a potential solution to the perennial disfranchisement of African American labor by trade unions and industry management (Aptheker, *Writings* 594–95). These shifts in Du Bois's writing of the early 1930s reflected the growing intensity of his sympathy for *both* socialist/communist politics *and* black cultural nationalism. Seeking simulta-neously to espouse class consciousness and race pride in this way, Du Bois's com-plex and occasionally conflicted sentiments mirror the tenor of several of the artistic and literary pieces discussed in the ensuing chapters of this study.

Although Howard University philosopher Alain Locke is forever tied to the Harlem Renaissance, it is essential to recognize that he remained an observant and consequential cultural commentator during the 1930s and 1940s as well. His landmark catalog *The Negro in Art* (1940) and the annual literature reviews that he penned for the African American little magazines *Opportunity* (1923–49) and *Phylon* (1940–56) between 1928 and 1953 were particularly influential docu-ments. In these prominent venues, Locke espoused a critical agenda that oscil-lated between high art aestheticism and populism, and between integrationism and cultural nationalism. Throughout his critical writings Locke contended that what he termed "cultural racialism" was distinct from "cultural separatism" (Stewart 273). Thus, for Locke, racial self-determination and cultural assimila-tion did *not* comprise mutually exclusive agendas for African Americans, "there being for truly great art no essential conflict between racial or national traits and universal human values" (186); rather, Locke perceived "Americanization" as a process of harmonizing, not melting, ethnic cultural differences (see also Hutchinson 83). Nor was Locke alone in voicing these sensibilities. For example, the mission statement of Karamu House, an interdisciplinary cultural center that supported work in literature, graphic art, dance, music, and drama in Cleveland, stated members' dual concern with "First, the direction of the Negro's creative abilities into the mainstream of American life . . . Secondly, to enable the Negro to tell his own story to the community and the Nation, making directly known his sufferings, his dissatisfactions, his aspirations and his ambitions" (Porter 128). As in Locke's writings, the Karamu mission statement thus presents the two goals of professional integration and forging a self-determined mode of African Ameri-can cultural expression as complementary objectives.

Similarly, the specific injunctions that Locke offered to visual artists and writers regarding matters of craft advocated an art that struck a balance between social commentary and the aesthetic ideals of "beauty," which he held to be essential to the fashioning of "universal" art. On the one hand, then, Locke's continually evolving perspective led him to champion the virtues of "realism" in important essays on visual art and literature as early as the late 1920s. Locke's retrospective literature reviews for *Opportunity* during the 1930s even bore such revealing titles as "The Saving Grace of Realism" (1934) and "God Save Reality!" (1937). Perhaps the most telling moment in this regard was Locke's participation in a session of the second annual meeting of the labor-oriented National Negro Congress in 1937, where he asserted, "Each generation has some such characteristic and representative aesthetic, and I grant that today's is social realism, reaching out to what has been called proletarian art or the expression of the life and cause of the masses" ("Resume" n.p.). On the other hand, Locke at times qualified his enthusiasm for the new turn in African American cultural work of the 1930s by calling for an "enlightened" or "poetic" realism that steered clear of didactic moralizing (Stewart 222, 288–89). For instance, in his 1936 essay "Propaganda—or Poetry?" Locke chastised Langston Hughes's proletarian poetry of the early 1930s for what he perceived as "turgid, smouldering rhetoric, rimed propaganda, and the tone of the ranting orator and the strident prosecutor" (Stewart 57). Like many African American social realist artists and writers themselves, Locke thus eschewed *both* a detached notion of art-for-art's sake *and* overt propaganda. Instead, praising the poetry of Sterling Brown, the fiction of William Attaway, and the graphic art of William E. Smith as exemplary models, Locke called for a brand of realism that would offer social commentary in symbolic, sublime, or even ironic tones (Stewart 288–89; Locke, "Chicago's New Southside" 373).

Perhaps the most systematic articulation of a social realist agenda specific to African American cultural workers was Richard Wright's "Blueprint for Negro Writing," which appeared in the lone issue of *New Challenge* in the fall of 1937. Whereas Locke ultimately remained more interested in the development of a racial aesthetic than issues of social class, the CP member Wright described cultural nationalism as something that artists ultimately should "change and transcend" (58). Arguably, what is more crucial than these differential emphases, however, is the fact that Locke and Wright each posited both race *and* class as central concerns for African American creative expression during the 1930s. Moreover, Du Bois, Locke, and Wright all contended that *cultural* expression could more effectively transform people's social consciousness than could doctrinaire political treatises. So too, intellectuals as diverse as Locke and Wright both affirmed the plurality of aesthetic possibilities through which African American cultural workers might appropriately address politicized issues, with Wright stressing that "Negro life may be approached from a thousand angles, with no limit to technical and stylistic freedom" (62).

Readers familiar with the proletarian literature and Marxist cultural criticism of the depression decade will by now have noted several striking connections with the respective commentaries of Du Bois, Locke, and Wright from this same period. Prior to studies such as Mark Naison's *Communists in Harlem during the Depression* (1983), the consensus narrative of African American encounters with the CP closely mirrored the intrigue and manipulation portrayed in Richard Wright's embittered autobiographical reflections and the fictionalized "Brotherhood" of Ralph Ellison's *Invisible Man* (1952). However, scholars like Naison—and, more recently, William Maxwell, James Smethurst, and Barbara Foley—have helped to reconstruct a more thorough portrait of the interface between black and red constituencies in the period under study. In particular, these scholars have stressed that, notwithstanding the occasionally dogmatic polemics of particular Marxist critics, the overall scope of CP injunctions proffered to cultural workers in leftist little magazines of the 1930s and 1940s allowed social realists considerable leeway with respect to stylistic decisions and even thematic content. Consequently, one might accurately conceive of the official ideology of the CP as an analytical apparatus from which African American artists and writers could borrow somewhat selectively.

And draw on CP theory and practice many certainly did. For example, while issuing a caution against the crafting of formulaic fiction, Wright's "Blueprint" essay nonetheless suggests that a key source of the CP's ideological appeal was the way in which Marxism seemed to offer a method for ordering, or at least deciphering, the socioeconomic chaos of depression-era America. In short, Marxist theory offered what Wright termed a "blueprint" for social analysis, one that he encouraged young African American writers to draw on in fashioning their literary work—asserting that such a vision "creates a picture which, when placed before the eyes of the writer, should unify his personality, organize his emotions, buttress him with a tense and obdurate will to change the world." "When consciously grasped," argued Wright, Marxism "endows the writer with a sense of dignity which no other vision can give" (59–60). Visual artist John Wilson, a social realist who came of age in Boston during the 1940s, has recalled the sense of purpose and clarity of vision offered by Marxist ideology and CP political action in similar terms: "Everyone in the community understood that there was a 'Negro Problem' but they had learned to adjust. They had no real answers besides prayer. No real answers as to how people acquire power [were articulated] except by the socialists. They had a plan. They broke down how wealth and power worked through the free labor of others" (LeFalle-Collins and Goldman 43). Thus, for Wright and Wilson, as for many of their leftist peers, Marxist thought constituted less a source of stuffy gloom and doom pronouncements than a source of hope and a seeming route to progressive social change (see also Peeler 175). This brand of idealism was bolstered by the editorial reports of luminaries such as McKay, Hughes, and Du Bois from the Soviet Union during the 1920s and early 1930s regarding the USSR's apparent support of racial and ethnic democracy (Maxwell 63–93; Aptheker, *Writings* 441–42, 458–60; Hughes, *Good Morning* 71–98). Locke, too, lauded "the cultural minorities art program being consistently and brilliantly developed in the Soviet Federation for the various racial and cultural folk traditions of that vast land" during the mid-1930s ("Resume" n.p.).

On the U.S. front, the counterpart to the Soviet support of minority cultural traditions was to be found in the CPUSA's "Black Belt" thesis. Borrowing from Lenin's and Stalin's statements on "the national question," the official CP thesis during the early 1930s advocated African American "self-determination" in the form of a separate state within the Black Belt region of the southern United States.[1] In this vein, CP spokespeople like Harry Haywood argued that African American cultural expression was to be "national in form, but proletarian in content." Thus, for example, cultural workers might infuse black vernacular forms, such as spirituals or blues music, with new revolutionary lyrics (Foley 173–85). Reading selectively from this CP thesis, social realists were able to identify a validation of African American vernacular culture—one that writers in particular took as instrumental to their cultural work. In this light, it begins to make a good deal of sense that Locke perceived a "considerable harmony" between "cultural racialism" and "the class proletarian art creed of today's younger generation," citing "the expression of Negro folk life" as a common denominator uniting the two ("Resume" n.p.). Notably, in following this path, cultural workers ignored the official CP injunction to African Americans of the urban North—where most social realist artists and writers resided—to subordinate racial agendas to class politics.

This assuredly is a far cry from the paradigms of manipulation and betrayal that have long pervaded scholarship pertaining to the role of the Communist Party in cultural production of the depression era (*especially* vis-à-vis African Americans). Arguably, these older paradigms grossly underestimated the critical intellect of American artists and writers, relatively few of whom ever truly resembled the unthinking dupes or jargon-mongering CP mouthpieces described in the caricatures of subsequent cold war–era evaluations.[2] As a point of comparison, one might consider historian Robin Kelley's *Hammer and Hoe* (1990), which carefully illustrates numerous examples of ways in which African American members and affiliates of the Alabama CP—most of whom were sharecroppers and industrial laborers—routinely recast the "party line" in light of their own distinctive cultural traditions of radical, prophetic Christianity. Not only did Alabama's black communists graft new politically charged lyrics to the tunes of familiar spirituals, but they also often went a step further by replacing references to CP icons such as Lenin with the names of their own local heroes (Kelley 104–8). It would seem axiomatic that studies of cosmopolitan artists and writers of the 1930s and 1940s should grant their similar capacity for critically revising and refashioning CP ideology into a relatively flexible cultural practice.

As the CPUSA shifted its official policy from a radically oppositional "Third Period" politics in the early 1930s to a more broadly inclusive, coalition-minded "Popular Front" strategy in the latter half of the 1930s, African American cultural workers again found much that resonated with their own ideals and objectives. Not least among the reasons for the Popular Front's appeal to African American social realists was the fact that the new directives continued to feature racial justice issues at the forefront of the CP's political agenda. In particular, the CP labored substantively and on multiple fronts during the second half of the 1930s to equate U.S. racism with the fascist rhetoric and practices of Hitler's Germany and Mussolini's Italy; and, as such, the CP consistently called for vigilance regarding the domestic half of this equation—at least until it began to devote greater attention to the international sphere following the Nazi invasion of the Soviet Union in 1941. Among the numerous African American cultural workers to take up this Popular Front ethic in earnest was the poet Melvin Tolson. Although justifiably best known for his later high modernist poetics, early in his career Tolson drew on the language of the Popular Front to announce a new "New Negro"—one with a decidedly leftist shading—in works such as his long poem "Dark Symphony" (1942):

> The New Negro,
> Hard-muscled, Fascist-hating, Democracy-ensouled,
> Strides in seven-league boots
> Along the Highway of Today
> Toward the Promised Land of Tomorrow! (40)

Here, Tolson reflects his sense of African American identity in militant, proletarian terms, forging a new Popular Front style of patriotism: an emphatically workerist brand of "Americanism" whose exponents stand prepared to fight for democratic equality both abroad and on the home front. At the same time, African American social realists sustained an interest in the nationalist politics of the CP's early 1930s Black Belt thesis, even when the party's official directives moved away from this policy's oppositional stance. Richard Wright's "Blueprint" essay, for instance, builds on the Black Belt thesis despite the fact that the party had shifted its official policy toward coalitionist Popular Front politics by the time Wright crafted his essay (Smethurst 43–44). In short, then, African American social realists found that the CP's affirmation of both black nationalism *and* interracial coalition building offered ideologically appealing agendas worth pursuing through their own cultural work.

As a concrete point of reference, I would suggest that if Alain Locke's landmark *The New Negro* (1925) offers a compelling window onto the Harlem Renaissance cultural moment, Nancy Cunard's anthology *Negro* (1934) indexes the cultural politics of social realism in a comparable fashion. Although its limited circulation (only one thousand copies in its original printing) prevents one from arguing an overly widespread influence of Cunard's collection, this massive volume of nearly nine hundred pages, compiled from the work of more than 150 contributors, nonetheless seems representative of the spirit of the early stages of American social realism in at least three important respects. First, Cunard focuses conspicuously on communism as a potential solution to the social problems confronting African Americans. Establishing this premise in the foreword, she writes, "But the more vital of the Negro race have realised that it is Communism alone which throws down the barriers of race as finally as it wipes out class distinctions" (xxxi).[3] And, as I have suggested, the CPUSA was an important contributor to the ideological underpinnings of American social realism through at least the late 1930s, especially in the cultural criticism offered by publications like *New Masses* (1926–48).

Second, although she herself hailed from England, Cunard's volume illustrates the centrality of issues of racial justice in U.S. leftist circles during the 1930s. While cultural exploration of racial justice causes clearly possessed precedents in publications such as A. Philip Randolph and Chandler Owen's *The Messenger* and in the Harlem Renaissance–era cultural work of writers such as Claude McKay and Langston Hughes, these issues attained an unprecedented public visibility and an increasingly forthright articulation in leftist political culture during the depression years. For example, one might consider Jack Conroy's description of the spectacle of "Irish Workers' Clubs brandishing shillelaghs and shouting 'Free Tom Mooney and the Scottsboro Boys!' as they marched just before the resplendent white limousine of Father Divine" as part of the 1935 May Day parade in New York City (Wixson 394).[4] It is, of course, worth recalling that in this same era Cunard could describe her euphoria regarding the interracial unity displayed at a May Day event in New York City's Union Square, only to be harassed and threatened by racist passersby less than two blocks away for walking with a black man on her way home from the event (Cunard xix–xx). Nonetheless, the high profile of racial-justice causes in the leftist cultural work of the depression era cannot be gainsaid: novels like Myra Page's *Gathering Storm: A Story of the Black Belt* (1932), Grace Lumpkin's *A Sign for Cain* (1935), and Josephine Johnson's *Jordanstown* (1937) highlight the extent to which the specific concerns of members of the African American working class occupied the attention of many white authors of proletarian literature (Foley 193–202). Although not wholly devoid of the racial biases they set out to critique, the novels of authors like Page, Lumpkin, and Johnson do encompass an interest in working-class issues and a militant call for sociopolitical reform that markedly distinguish them from white authored works like DuBose Heyward's *Porgy* (1925) and Carl Van Vechten's *Nigger Heaven* (1926) of the preceding decade. The contrast between the cultural politics of the Harlem Renaissance and depression era also becomes apparent when one considers the sizable space that Cunard's *Negro* allots to such highly charged *contemporary* issues as the Scottsboro trials and the exploitation of black prison laborers vis-à-vis the relative absence of such topically specific, class-centered politics in Locke's *New Negro*. Hence, notwithstanding Langston Hughes's jaundiced recollection of a fleeting "vogue for things Negro" during the 1920s, within leftist political and cultural circles interest in African American causes expanded exponentially during the early 1930s—precisely the moment at which conventional wisdom holds that white Americans abandoned interest in African American cultural production.

A third way in which Cunard's *Negro* seems emblematic of the early formations of American social realism is the way in which it brings together such varied materials as photography, journalistic reportage, political treatises, history, musical transcriptions, cultural criticism, biographical sketches, and poetry. The theme of black chain gangs, for instance, receives attention in poetry, a photoessay by muckraking journalist John Spivak, and southern folk songs collected by Lawrence Gellert. In a similar vein, social realist writers like William Attaway, Lloyd Brown, Frank Marshall Davis, Langston Hughes, Willard Motley, Ann Petry, and Richard Wright often examined a given issue in more than one expressive mode. The interest of these African American novelists and poets in such media as personal essays, photography, and nonfiction reportage seems to have owed in part to their profound concern with transforming the contemporary social and political conditions critiqued in their literary work. Toward this end, recognizing the potential limitations of literature as an agent of social change, writers dabbled in these documentary modes as a way of authenticating to readers the experiences presented in their novels and poetry and, perhaps, as a way of reaching audiences not readily accessible through literary media. Moreover, each of these authors drew selectively upon formal conventions associated with the aforementioned documentary genres in fashioning their poetry and novels as well. Thus, even though Cunard's *Negro* contains no examples of prose fiction or graphic art, in other respects it comprises a representative collage of the variety of modes through which radical cultural workers of the depression era pursued a documentary impulse in representing contemporary social-justice issues.

Social realist convictions regarding the cultural work that artists and writers might perform as transformative agents vis-à-vis poor and working-class audiences were facilitated not only by ideological currents and theoretical statements but also by the material assistance of new sources of patronage and the emergence of new venues for the circulation of visual art and literature in the depression era. The appeal of the CP to African American artists and writers, for instance, owed to the ideological precepts discussed earlier and to concrete forms of support provided by CP-affiliated organizational structures. Among the earliest of these organizations were the John Reed Clubs (JRCs), and they helped to establish the basic template for many of the leftist artist and writer groups to follow. During the early 1930s, the JRCs brought together aspiring artists and writers in interracial (and often interdisciplinary) workshop settings in thirty local chapters that stretched from New York to Hollywood. Even more, many of the local chapters of the JRCs organized little magazine publications wherein these cultural workers were encouraged to forge politically engaged work (see also Kalaidjian 47). Most famously, Richard Wright came of age as a writer in the Chicago JRC and published some of his early poetry in the organization's little magazine, *Left Front* (1933–34). What seems especially notable in the case of Wright is not only that this group helped to launch his literary career, but also the fact that the JRC offered Wright a model for literary network building applicable outside of CP circles—as when Wright helped to found the South Side Writers' Group (SSWG) with a group of fellow black Chicagoans in 1936. Further, radical grassroots ventures like *Left Front* served as models for an array of other leftist publications that emerged during the 1930s and 1940s, including Dorothy West's African American–focused *Challenge* (1934–37). Not coincidentally, West soon forged strong ties with Wright, Marian Minus, and fellow members of the SSWG, who collectively assembled the lone issue of *New Challenge* in 1937.

Likewise, in support of the visual arts, the JRCs sponsored Marxist-oriented discussion groups, lectures, journals, art schools, and exhibitions (McCoy 325). In New York City, for example, the JRC chapter organized interracial art exhibits at the ACA Gallery with revealing titles such as *The World Crisis Expressed in Art: Paintings, Sculpture, Drawings, Prints on the Theme Hunger, Fascism, War* (1933–34) and *The Struggle for Negro Rights* (1935)—the latter being an antilynching exhibit.[5] The exhibition and publication opportunities provided by the JRCs were especially appealing to young artists and writers in light of the depression's detrimental impact on the American art world and the publishing industry. (Perhaps needless to say, the collapse of conventional sources of patronage heavily impacted African American cultural workers, despite the fact that their access to many museums, galleries, journals, and publishers was only marginal, at best, even before the onset of the depression.) So too, CP-affiliated publications with a national reach, such as *New Masses* and the *Daily Worker,* served to instill in artists and writers a sense of connection to cultural workers operating in other locales.

The CPUSA captured the imagination of African American artists and writers not only by means of such specifically cultural projects but also through its highly visible program of concerted political action. As in its cultural work, the CP's efforts in the area of direct political mobilization accorded special attention to African American liberation struggles. The CP consciously positioned itself at the forefront of such issues as tenants' rights, antilynching campaigns, the celebrated trials of Angelo Herndon and the Scottsboro Boys, and—later in the decade—a crusade against fascism that condemned Mussolini's military invasion of Ethiopia.[6] While Mark Naison has demonstrated that the masses of working-class African Americans often participated selectively in such CP-affiliated protest campaigns without necessarily subscribing to Marxist ideology per se (although certainly a number did), the Communist Party did gain considerable visibility and even open sympathy in black communities through these depression-era campaigns.

While the CP facilitated the emergence of social realism in crucial ways, in terms of sheer scale the most significant agents in helping to fill the dearth of conventional exhibition and publication opportunities during the depression were the government-sponsored cultural programs created by President Roosevelt's New Deal administration, especially those housed within the Works Progress Administration, later retitled the Work Projects Administration (WPA). Programs initiated under Roosevelt's watch included the Public Works of Art Project (PWAP), the Treasury Department's Section of Painting and Sculpture, and the Federal Art Project (FAP) in the visual arts, as well as the Federal Writers' Project (FWP). To be sure, the hiring practices of these cultural programs were often quite poor in terms of extending employment opportunities to African Americans. The FWP, for instance, hired only a little more than one hundred African American writers, while the FAP employed an even lower number of African American visual artists (Stewart 478; Hutchinson 437). Only in New York City and Chicago were African American cultural workers able to make sizable inroads, and even then only following major demonstrations and picketing by local groups of unionized artists. Yet, many of those African American visual artists and writers who *did* attain WPA employment have described its significance as nothing less than a godsend. Both in statements contemporaneous to the period under study and in subsequent interviews, African Americans (like their peers) have cited four central reasons for the critical importance of the various New Deal cultural programs: (1) they provided artists and writers with a means of earning a livelihood amidst the otherwise crippled art economy of the depression

era; (2) they gave cultural workers an opportunity to pursue substantial enterprises in their own chosen fields of creative expression in the context of regular
interaction with their peers; (3) the workshops, instruction, and equipment made
available through the FAP allowed artists not only to maintain their skills but also
to experiment with new media and techniques; and (4) sociological and historical
knowledge garnered through research for the FWP contributed meaningfully to
the literary work of several social realists.

Fortunately for artists, although the original vision for a government-
sponsored art program involved only the country's most prestigious artists executing mural art for federal buildings, in practice a majority of the WPA cultural
programs more closely resembled the New Deal's other relief programs for the
employment of workers with proven economic need.[7] According to Hale
Woodruff, who worked with the PWAP for a time in the 1930s while teaching at
Atlanta University, "Almost everybody worked on the Project and they'd get
$23.75 a week. That was general pay. It really kept everybody alive, certainly kept
the artist alive. . . . And this helped to create the upsurge in art, for whites and
blacks, throughout the country" (Murray 81). Thus, not least among the reasons
for the appeal of WPA jobs was the simple fact that work on programs like the FAP
or FWP provided a source of economic stability in the midst of depression-era
deprivation. Ironically, as Sterling Brown once reflected, "Negro writers actually
made more money during the Depression than they had made before. Because
they got on WPA, they got a regular check" (Rowell 807). One might note, too,
that Brown himself held the important post of editor of Negro Affairs for the FWP
at the national level (Sanders, *Afro-Modernist Aesthetics* 98).

Individuals involved with the WPA cultural programs of the 1930s and early
1940s almost uniformly have cited a second of the most important accomplishments of these projects as establishing a heightened feeling of community among
fellow cultural workers. In the words of New York City artist Charles Alston,
"One of the very important things of that period was that artists, for the first time,
got some sense of an identity. Things were so bad that you had both artists who
had no reputation as well as artists who had already begun to have a reputation
involved in the thing. So younger artists had an opportunity to talk to the artists
who were prominent."[8] In particular, artists and writers of the period note that
the WPA programs facilitated discussions with fellow cultural workers regarding
the appropriate social function of art and how best to realize their politicized aims
in aesthetic terms. Significantly, the extensive informal networks associated with
institutions like the FAP-sponsored Harlem Community Art Center and the
South Side Community Art Center of Chicago ensured that such discussions
would include cultural critics, politically engaged scholars, artists, writers, and
individuals with talents in a range of other creative media.

A third critical function of the New Deal cultural programs was that they provided many visual artists with their first exposure to the skills and equipment needed to explore new media. Particularly on the Federal Art Project, artists had considerable leeway to use available materials as their own interests dictated. Woodruff recalls that while he worked on the projects in Atlanta, the PWAP and FAP inspectors checked in on an artist "about every two or three months to see how you were getting on" (Murray 81). With this flexibility, commented Alston, "You could experiment. All of the development wasn't out of what was officially done. It was out of the fact that you had a source of materials and you could work."[9] Alston also pointed out that artists could make official shifts by transferring between the various divisions of the FAP in order to do work in several media. In just such a fashion, Chicago artist Charles White switched from the FAP's easel division to the mural department, where he completed some of his earliest work in the latter medium.[10] The Community Art Centers sponsored by the FAP also provided instructors and equipment that contributed substantially to the emergence of graphic arts (especially lithographs, linocuts, and woodblock prints) as the media of choice for many young social realists. Indeed, the resources provided by the WPA programs enabled a number of artists of the 1930s and early 1940s to achieve their goal of a mass production of art, as scholars generally estimate that the graphics division of the FAP produced more than two hundred thousand prints from some eleven thousand original designs (Hills, *Social* 11).

The situation for writers was somewhat different. In the case of the FWP, it is important to note that this program seldom sponsored the literary projects of its employees directly. Rather, assignments generally involved tasks such as the collecting and compiling of information for local and state-based historical guidebooks.[11] Yet, by providing a steady income and a job with relatively flexible hours, FWP employment afforded writers the resources necessary to pursue literary projects on their own time. For instance, it was while working with the Illinois Writers' Project during the mid-1930s that Richard Wright completed most of the novellas that he first published as *Uncle Tom's Children* in 1938. Further, many writers integrated material on local history and contemporary social conditions that they had garnered from work with the Writers' Project into their subsequent literary enterprises. To cite one example, Willard Motley drew extensively upon his early 1940s Illinois Writers' Project research on Chicago's Italian American and underclass neighborhoods in crafting his first novel, *Knock on Any Door* (1947), over the course of the next several years.

By the latter half of the 1930s, the networks of cultural workers developed out of institutional structures such as the CP's John Reed Clubs and the New Deal government projects gave rise to a remarkable range of politically engaged organizations among artists and writers. Particularly after the Communist Party's decision to dissolve the partisan John Reed Clubs in 1935, leftist cultural workers coalesced into more broadly based Popular Front organizations like the Artists' Union (AU), the American Writers' Congress (AWC), and the American Artists' Congress (AAC) to lobby for issues such as the institutionalization of permanent government-sponsored cultural programs, the creation of artist-controlled municipal art centers, and freedom from censorship. As had the John Reed Clubs before them, such organizations formed active chapters that battled for these and other issues not only in New York and Chicago but also in far-flung cities such as Pittsburgh, Cleveland, Los Angeles, St. Louis, and Washington, D.C.[12] Again, the struggle for African American civic and political rights was very much a part of the broad agendas articulated by these leftist organizations. For example, among the resolutions passed by the AAC in 1937 were a condemnation of fascism and war; protests against the attempted censorship of WPA murals by artists like Rockwell Kent and Charles Alston; a demand to end America's discrimination against Negroes and noncitizens; a call for an end to global discrimination against Jews; an affirmation of support for trade unions; a pledge of support for the Spanish Loyalist forces; and a recommendation for the passage of a federal Antilynching Bill.[13] Likewise, Elizabeth Catlett scarcely exaggerated when she described the Artists' Union in 1944 as "one of the greatest forces for the promotion of Negro-white art unity in the history of our country" (5).

Organizations like the AU, AWC, and AAC articulated this wide-ranging brand of Popular Front politics through conference resolutions and petitions and by taking to the streets. Meanwhile, publications such as the Artists' Union's *Art Front* (1934–37) reported and editorialized on the demonstrations of local chapters, including one New York sit-in strike that ended with police attacking and wounding several participants before arresting 219 artist-demonstrators (New York 3). Many artists and writers from this period have stated that such activities helped to engender a seemingly unprecedented sense of common cause among cultural workers. Notably, too, in their campaigns for the creation of permanent federal programs for artists and writers, the AU, AWC, and AAC each took care to recruit the endorsement of labor-based organizations like the newly formed Congress of Industrial Organizations (CIO) and the National Negro Congress. Such a move should not prove surprising. After all, the AU, AWC, and AAC shared with these newly emergent labor organizations an emphasis on class consciousness and the virtues of distinctive ethnic cultures, as well as a commitment to a Popular Front style of interracial coalition building as a means to promote their concerns. As did industrial trade unions, the Artists' Union attended to issues such as wages, working conditions, and steady employment, in addition to striving for a wider distribution of artists' work. In fact, in New York City the Artists' Union even formally affiliated itself with the CIO movement by becoming Local 60 of the United Office and Professional Workers of America in December 1937 (Shapiro and Shapiro 93–94). Such organizations thus signaled the extent to which leftist artists of the depression era not only identified with America's "common man" but also construed *themselves* as being at least adjunct members of the American working class (see also Park and Markowitz 9).

By the same token, the CIO, the International Workers Order (IWO), and the National Negro Congress helped to facilitate a wide variety of cultural work during the latter half of the depression decade, including roundtable discussions by cultural workers, volumes of poetry, works of drama, and mass rallies that featured the music of Popular Front mainstays like Paul Robeson and Josh White.[14] The NNC originated in 1936 as a part of the broader project to reform organized labor along interracial lines that had been signaled by the launching of the CIO the previous year. The congress included among its key members A. Philip Randolph, the preeminent black labor leader of the day (Anderson 229–40). From its inception, the NNC integrated cultural work into the agenda of its influential annual meetings, joining the AAC and AWC in their calls for permanent WPA-style cultural programs. Not coincidentally, then, the organization's first gathering in Chicago helped to catalyze the formation of the aforementioned South Side Writers' Group by NNC participants like Richard Wright and poet Frank Marshall Davis. Further, the pages of the NNC's chief publication, *Congress Vue/Congress View* (1943–46), later featured the graphics of artists such as Charles White during the mid-1940s. Little wonder, then, that leftist cultural workers sometimes directly linked their own campaigns in predominantly white groups like the American Artists' Congress with those of labor-based organizations like the National Negro Congress. "There is more than coincidence in the movement of the Negro people for social and political equality and the movement of artists for the right to function as artists," explained an *Art Front* editorial in 1936. "Fundamentally both Congresses are phases of the same question" ("National" 3).

One can hardly overstate the significance of social realists' forays beyond the bounds of art and literature per se and into the realm of concrete leftist activism. Indeed, the attempt by artists and writers to address social crises through both cultural work and corollary forms of political mobilization, as well as the reciprocity between cultural and labor organizations, comprise two of the hallmarks of the social realist movement. This was, after all, an era in which prominent writers such as Theodore Dreiser and John Dos Passos were visiting the front lines of coal-mining strikes in eastern Kentucky; an era in which numerous artists and writers, both black and white, fashioned a considerable amount of cultural work protesting Jim Crow segregation and the lynching of African Americans; and an era in which many of these same artists and writers added their participation to mass demonstrations organized around causes such as the Angelo Herndon and Scottsboro Boys trials. Likewise, Elizabeth Catlett sought to curtail the practice of lynching both through her graphic artwork and on the steps of Washington, D.C.'s city hall; and novelists William Attaway and Lloyd Brown worked for a time as labor organizers before crafting their signal novels of working-class life, *Blood on the Forge* (1941) and *Iron City* (1951), respectively. In the various strikes and protests organized by groups like the Artists' Union and the American Writers' Congress, artists and writers also engaged in collective political activity along the lines of industrial and trade unions on their own behalf. In short, participation in the sorts of cultural networks I have been describing helped to structure the way in which social realists came to think of themselves as *cultural workers* in a sense spiritually akin and tangibly connected to the nation's working classes.

Granting the ambitions of social realists with respect to extending their art and literature to an audience inclusive of America's working classes, anecdotal evidence suggests that their efforts in this regard did not always meet the reception that they might have expected, or at least hoped for. The extent to which actual working-class audiences embraced the vision of themselves presented by social realist artists and writers is, of course, difficult to determine with any precision. Such evidence of audience reception that does exist suggests that working-class viewers and readers at times greeted social realist work with something less than wholehearted endorsement. For example, Downtown Gallery director Edith Halpert recalled inviting the working-class members of a NYC Sacco-Vanzetti Club to an exhibit of Ben Shahn's *Sacco and Vanzetti* series, only to find that the members found Shahn's depictions "grotesque." As Halpert explained ruefully, "I was so anxious to be able to tell Ben that he had reached the right audience! But it was the rich—whether because of a guilty conscience or a more perceptive taste, who knows?—who bought the pictures" (Shapiro 35).[15]

Yet, in many important respects, the John Reed Club exhibits, the Federal Art Project community art classes, the New Deal murals of the 1930s and 1940s, and the period's leftist little magazines *did* extend the visual art and literature of African American social realists and their peers to a more economically and geographically diverse set of audiences than had been reached in previous generations. To cite one suggestive example, historian Lerone Bennett Jr. aptly eulogized Charles White in a special memorial issue of *Freedomways* by observing, "They loved him, the people did. And they paid him the greatest of all compliments. They tore his paintings out of books and made crude reproductions and hung them on the walls of their kitchens and barbershops and bars" (204). Further, participation in the leftist cultural networks of the depression era afforded African American artists and writers a relatively unprecedented access to the "mainstream" American organizations of their respective fields, as individuals like Hughes, Wright, and Gwendolyn Bennett all held prestigious positions within the AWC and AAC. Aided by such organizations, African American social realists and their peers sought not merely to portray the masses, but in so doing to inspire a transformation of race and class consciousness within this audience.

Whatever the ultimate limitations of the social realist project, the *idea* of the audience toward which artists and writers imagined their work to be directed remains significant. Ironically, as David Peeler points out, a certain optimism regarding the potential for progressive (even radical) social transformation harbored within the hard times of the 1930s generally seems to have tempered the depression-era despair of many young artists and writers. Indeed, social realists embraced their newfound role as political actors, positioning the cultural worker as spokesperson, prophet, or leader of an anticipated mass social movement. For instance, in his "Blueprint" essay, Wright earnestly pronounces, "With the gradual decline of the moral authority of the Negro church, and with the increasing irresolution which is paralyzing Negro middle class leadership, a new role is devolving upon the Negro writer. He is being called upon to do no less than create values by which his race is to struggle, live and die" (59). Clearly, then, much of the appeal of the CP-sponsored John Reed Clubs of the early 1930s, the AU, AAC, and AWC of the Popular Front period, and the more broadly based organizations generated out of the WPA programs pertained to the way in which such organizations posited a newly invigorated role for the creative artist in catalyzing social change. In numerous emerging urban centers of cultural activity, these entities contributed to the ascendancy of social realism within U.S. art and literature by holding out at least the promise of helping artists and writers to reach a mass audience on an unprecedented scale.

The Endurance of African American Social Realism

Thus far, the shape of African American social realism might seem consistent with the contours of U.S. social realism writ large—and, indeed, it was in many respects. In terms of ideology, African American visual artists and writers of the depression decade shared with their peers a sense of participating in a radically new brand of cultural work, one committed—to a seemingly unprecedented degree—to forging vigorous, partisan forms of expression that were most often *about* and *for* the nation's poor and working classes. In its concrete manifestations, specifically African American ventures like Chicago's South Side Writers' Group (c. 1936–38) were modeled after the example of the CP-affiliated John Reed Clubs of the early 1930s, while Dorothy West's little magazine *Challenge* (later *New Challenge*) patterned itself after publications like Jack Conroy's *Anvil* (1933–35). Moreover, African Americans were active in the interracial arenas of social realist cultural activity, featuring prominently in certain of the JRC workshops; the antifascist campaigns of the American Artists' Congress and American Writers' Congress; the pages of little magazines such as Conroy's *Anvil;* and the New Deal programs for visual artists and writers. Indeed, as William Maxwell has persuasively argued in *New Negro, Old Left,* African American participants significantly helped to shape the agenda of cultural work on the American left during the 1920s and throughout the 1930s, not least in terms of amplifying the left's focus on racial justice as a primary point of concern.

Scholars of social realism have tended to date the end of this movement to the very early 1940s—citing leftist disillusionment triggered by the signing of the Nonaggression Pact between Hitler and Stalin in 1939, an impulse among those on the left to "close ranks" in a fight against the fascism of the Axis nations following the U.S. entry into the Second World War, and the relative economic recovery of the war years as the principal contributing factors. However, the careers of African American cultural workers tell a different story, one that extends for at least a full decade beyond the bounds of conventional periodizations. In fact, many of the more striking works of social realism produced by African Americans date from the 1940s and early 1950s. Novelist Ann Petry, artist John Wilson, and poet Robert Hayden were only a few of the African American cultural workers to *debut* an engagement with social realism during these years. And African American creative artists' sustained engagement with social realism did not go unremarked by cultural critics of the day. For instance, although contemporary literary scholars generally construe social realism as a phenomenon of depression-era American writing, it was the African American literature of 1946 that Alain Locke described as "cast in a socially serious vein and a crusading mood" and with regard to the literature of 1947 that he remarked, "Our artists increasingly become social critics and reformers as our novelists are fast becoming strident sociologists and castigating prophets" (Stewart 319, 329). One also might consider that the African American–authored novel most openly sympathetic in its portrayal of the Communist Party, Lloyd Brown's *Iron City,* was published not during the 1930s but in 1951.

Nonetheless, many factors did contribute to a tempering and modulation of politicized cultural work in the United States during the 1940s and 1950s. After all, novelist Willard Motley's assessment of the post–World War II era as one of "lean years" has *not* emerged as the consensus opinion of the age (*We Fished* vii). In many ways, it was precisely those cultural workers on the political left who were uniquely positioned to see the decade as did Motley. For by the late 1940s attacks on leftist artists and writers were pervasive and the McCarthyite anticommunist political movement was in full swing, building in part on FBI files that had been compiled against writers such as Langston Hughes beginning in the 1930s (Folsom 118). In the case of African American cultural workers in particular, one should also note that "agitation" for racial justice was one of the prominent causes for persecution of progressive intellectuals by the House Un-American Activities Committee (HUAC). As Chicago-based artist and poet Margaret Burroughs later reflected of the cold war's impact on social realism's "black and white, unite and fight" ethic, "You know, black and white people were together all the time. We visited each other's homes. . . . The thing that broke that up was the 1950s and the McCarthy scare. The McCarthy period came on and certainly any black person who had a white friend was a Communist."[16] In equally concrete terms, the cold war ethos of red baiting served to dismantle much of the cultural apparatus of radical labor organizations like the International Workers Order, which had played an important patronage role in the Popular Front movement of the late 1930s and early 1940s (Denning 77).

From another angle, Jack Conroy biographer Douglas Wixson has noted a more subtle form of publishing-industry pressure on novelists to abandon politicized social realist fiction as popular tastes gravitated toward "brutal realism without the social commentary that writers like [Nelson] Algren, Motley, and Conroy nurtured" (459). Given the desire of most novelists to support themselves by means of their literary craft, these unspoken commercial incentives to abandon literature of social critique were of considerable consequence; hence, many proletarian writers turned to genres such as detective and mystery fiction during the 1940s (Denning 257). Likewise, as the United States entered the cold war era, it was readily apparent to those in any way affiliated with the American art world that art that paid would be cast either in the vein of Norman Rockwell's homespun national self-imaging or in the terms being established by the new young lions of abstract expressionist painting. In 1949, for instance, a *Life* magazine feature posed the question, "Jackson Pollock: Is He the Greatest Living Painter in the United States?" (Phillips 32). By at least the late 1940s, then, writers and artists faced a considerable confluence of professional incentives and political disincentives militating against an overt engagement with leftist brands of cultural work.

For all of these constraints, however, the very fact that writers like Motley and poet Frank Marshall Davis, along with artists such as John Wilson and Charles White, were still issuing biting social critiques in public statements and cultural work at midcentury attests to the fact that the thematic concerns, formal techniques, and interpersonal networks established in the social realist movement of the depression decade continued to play an important role well beyond the alleged 1930s heyday of U.S. social realism. A brief consideration of two African

American social realists, the artist Charles White and the poet Frank Marshall Davis, can serve to concretize this point. I will delve into the trajectory of White's early development as an artist at length in the following chapter. For now, one might note the continuity between White's heartfelt commitment to the Spanish Loyalist cause as a member of the Chicago chapter of the League against War and Fascism in the mid-1930s, his travels to Mexico for study at the Mexican School of Painting and Sculpture (informally known as the Esmeralda) and the Taller de Gráfica Popular (a leftist graphic arts workshop) in the mid-1940s, and his tour of the Soviet Union in the fall of 1951. Throughout these years, White remained a highly visible advocate of leftist politics and social realist cultural work in the face of an American climate increasingly unsympathetic to such commitments. Settling in New York City following his sojourns to Mexico, White remained extremely active, holding one-man shows and participating in several group exhibits with politically like-minded artists of diverse styles and ethnic backgrounds—all of this despite a series of severe health complications.[17] On the one hand, White continued to circulate in a social milieu in which African American intellectuals and cultural workers from diverse fields regularly interacted. Living in Harlem's Sugar Hill neighborhood, White came to know W. E. B. Du Bois and his wife, the novelist Shirley Graham, Duke Ellington, Harry Belafonte, Jacob Lawrence, Langston Hughes, Lorraine Hansberry, and Paul Robeson (Horowitz 22–23). In the early 1950s, White continued his progressive cultural activism with these and other individuals like actor Sidney Poitier, fellow artist Ernest Crichlow, artist/photographer Roy De Carava, and the young novelist John Oliver Killens in organizations such as the Committee for the Negro in the Arts—a group that, much in the manner of the John Reed Clubs of the 1930s, formed local chapters directed at the training of aspiring African American novelists, dramatists, musicians, and painters (Killens 193; Horowitz 23–24).

Simultaneously, White sustained his contacts with predominantly white radical cultural institutions: by exhibiting in a one-man show at Herman Baron's ACA Gallery; by participating in the American Labor Party's 1949 *Contemporary American Art* show in Brooklyn along with artists such as Crichlow, Yasuo Kuniyoshi, Elizabeth Olds, and Jack Levine; and by contributing prints and illustrations to publications like Paul Robeson's *Freedom,* the CP's *Daily Worker,* and a 1948 Taller de Gráfica Popular portfolio titled *Negro, USA.*[18] Further, in 1946, White began serving as a contributing editor for *New Masses,* joining a board that included white social realist artists such as Philip Evergood, Robert Gwathmey, and Anton Refregier, as well as fellow African American activists like Du Bois and Robeson. These were alliances that White extended into the mid-1950s as a regular contributing editor to the *New Masses*'s successor, *Masses and Mainstream* (1948–56). So too, during his 1951 visit to the Soviet Union, White engaged in a number of memorable activities: visits to schools, where children performed peace songs; participating in an art class at the House of Culture; making a speech to an Antifascist Women's Committee; attending a peace rally with between six thousand and ten thousand participants in the Public Square of Stalingrad; and meeting with African American expatriates to the USSR like the playwright and actor Waylon Rudd, who had resided in the Soviet Union for fifteen years.[19] Affirmed by these experiences on Soviet soil, White held steadfastly to his chosen mode of politicized figurative art during the 1950s, in spite of the heightening cold war assault on progressive cultural expression and the commercial ascendance of abstract expressionism. (Indeed, White pointedly critiqued the latter movement for its "denial of the human element.") "Formerly, at home, striving to give my art a more realistic quality, going so to speak against the tide of what apparently everyone was claiming to be the 'new' and the 'future', I sometimes felt very much alone," White explained of the impact of his Soviet sojourn. "I now realized that the great forward-moving tide of art was realism, and that the majority of creative artists in the world were realists" ("Path" 41).

The range of Frank Marshall Davis's cultural work during the 1940s was equally ambitious and diversely situated. His activities in this period included organizing conferences on black-white unity and legislation for U.S. servicemen; participation on the National Committee to Combat Anti-Semitism; teaching courses on jazz music at Chicago's radical Abraham Lincoln School (an institution once termed the "little Red schoolhouse" by the *Chicago Tribune*); writing at least one major speech for the National Maritime Union leader Ferdinand Smith as part of the 1944 Roosevelt presidential campaign; speaking at the meetings of various CIO unions in Chicago and Gary, Indiana; and cofounding the *Chicago Star*, a labor newspaper, in 1946 (*Livin' the Blues* 278–99). Moreover, in terms of Davis's poetry, John Edgar Tidwell observes of the 1948 volume *47th Street*, "Many of his earlier poems were characterized by an almost black nationalist political sensibility. This volume, however, registers a shift to a more proletarian belief" ("Frank Marshall Davis" 64). *47th Street* poems such as "For All Common People" and "Peace Is a Fragile Cup," for example, call for a multiethnic populace to unite in struggle against not only racism but also capitalist exploitation of the working class, global militarism, and the new perils of life in the atomic age.

What, then, does it mean for our understanding of U.S. cultural history as contemporary readers that many African Americans were still presenting an intensive political critique in works of social realist visual art and literature at the height of the cold war? The fact that Davis's radicalization—like that of contemporaries such as Willard Motley and John Wilson—actually *increased* rather than diminished during the 1940s is significant on at least two counts. First, the cultural work of White, Davis, and their peers supports Cary Nelson's contention that, while the institutional terrain of social realism may have shifted during the Second World War and in the context of the early cold war era, the movement's overarching concern for America's poor and working-class people did not disappear during the 1940s. Clearly, if one is to take the example of figures such as Charles White and Frank Marshall Davis at all seriously, one must begin to call into question the notion that social realism summarily ended with the Hitler-Stalin Nonaggression Pact and the relative alleviation of the depression's socioeconomic crises. As one begins to survey the visual art and literature detailed in the ensuing chapters of this study, it becomes increasingly apparent that one cannot dismiss figures like White and Davis as mere anomalies with regard to the uncowed radicalism of their cultural work and public political activism. Rather, various modes of social realist art and literature remained viable options in the eyes of many African Americans in the early cold war era, in spite of the considerable incentives to pursue less explicitly politicized types of cultural work.

Second, as Nelson recognizes in the case of poetry, one should note that African Americans were at the forefront of this sustained engagement with social realism during and beyond the Second World War. Arguably, it is only the way in which subsequent generations of scholars have treated African American cultural workers almost exclusively under the rubric of race—with "race made a matter of black self-interest rather than a national concern" (C. Nelson 165–66)—that has effected the erasure of this fact. I would suggest that a reconsideration of African American social realists such as White and Davis in the context of work by their fellow artists and writers should challenge those periodizations that would delineate a tidy progression from proletarian forms of cultural work in the depression era to an introspective modernism in the 1940s and 1950s: that is, from the muscular figurative realism of an artist such as Charles White to the abstract expressionism of painter Norman Lewis; or from the "race fiction" of Richard Wright to the "universal" craft of Ellison's *Invisible Man*.

If this is indeed the case, then one must ask: (1) *how* African American social realists were able to sustain such a relatively prolific output vis-à-vis their peers during the 1940s and early 1950s; and (2) *why* so many African American artists and writers chose to do so. The sustained engagement of African American cultural workers with social realism was enabled, in a practical sense, by their ability to find new niches and means of institutional support beyond the scope of those mainstays of depression-era patronage, the CPUSA and the New Deal cultural programs. One such source of patronage that African American artists and writers pursued with notable success in both the 1930s and the 1940s consisted of fellowships from the Julius Rosenwald Foundation. Sponsored by the famed Chicago head of the Sears Roebuck corporation, the Rosenwald Foundation was initiated in 1917 to help finance projects that served the end of furthering the general "well-being of mankind," primarily through an ethic of "self-help" roughly akin to that advocated by Booker T. Washington. Following Rosenwald's death in 1932, however, the fund's executive director, Edwin Rogers Embree, guided it toward an increasingly liberal agenda, turning the fund's resources not only to social science projects but also to a relatively wide array of work in the visual arts and literature, including a major mural by Charles White, *The Contribution of the Negro to Democracy in America* (1943); an important series of linocuts by Elizabeth Catlett, *The Negro Woman* (1946–47); a volume of poetry by Frank Marshall Davis, *I Am the American Negro* (1937); and novels such as William Attaway's *Blood on the Forge* (1941) and Willard Motley's *We Fished All Night* (1951).[20] And although the Rosenwald Foundation primarily targeted its monies for support of projects with a "race relations" focus between the early 1930s and its demise in 1948, in actual practice social realists used this funding to undertake projects that foregrounded themes of both race and class.

Colleges and universities—especially historically black institutions—comprised a second important source of institutional support that extended from the 1930s into the ensuing decade. In the realm of literature, tours of southern colleges and universities provided Langston Hughes with a much-needed source of income at certain junctures during the 1930s, as well as an opportunity to address a relatively broad public with radical cultural work (Berry 131–46). The support of such schools proved even more crucial in the visual arts, especially for work in the mural medium. Most famously, in 1939 Alabama's Talladega College sponsored Hale Woodruff's series of three murals on the famed *Amistad* incident, and this was hardly an isolated case.[21] For example, even though Charles White's *The Contribution of the Negro to Democracy in America* mural was funded principally by Rosenwald money, he turned to a historically black college—Virginia's Hampton Institute—as the site in which to execute his painting. A Hampton student at the time, John Biggers had already executed a mural titled *Dying Soldier* at the school, and he would go on to execute three further social realist murals at Pennsylvania State University, as well as subsequent large-scale works at institutions such as Texas Southern University, Winston-Salem State University, and (again) Hampton University. Perhaps such locales proved appealing to social realists because they offered a quasi-public institutional space in which to position mural paintings yet were subject to somewhat less scrutiny from conservative politicians and bureaucrats than had been the murals fashioned in courthouses and post offices in conjunction with the government-sponsored art programs of the depression era. As I will elaborate in the next chapter, such a supposition is supported by the fact that these college and university murals articulate a more overtly radical brand of politics than the vast majority of those executed under the auspices of the New Deal art programs.

This also seems to have been the case when African American social realists occasionally found themselves turning to black businesses for support, as with Charles Alston and Hale Woodruff's *The Negro in California History* murals for Los Angeles's Golden State Mutual Life Insurance Company (1949). Although such a patronage arrangement possessed a certain irony, given the Marxist orientation of much social realist art, this corporate sponsorship afforded one of the relatively few sources of support for such an elaborate, public-minded visual art project as Alston and Woodruff's by midcentury. Moreover, I will show that Alston and Woodruff were able to articulate the racial-pride theme designated by the Golden State sponsors in ways that spoke specifically to working-class features of African American history. As with the aforementioned Rosenwald projects, the artists forged their murals in this manner not out of duplicity, but simply because most social realists deemed racial justice themes inseparable from a sense of class politics.

The endurance of social realism through the 1940s decade also was bolstered substantially by the continued vitality of leftist little magazines. To be sure, by the early 1940s such benchmark publications as *The Rebel Poet* (1931–32), *Anvil/New Anvil* (1939–40), *Art Front,* and *Challenge/New Challenge* had all passed from the scene. However, new little magazines continued to emerge over the course of the following decade, supplying poets, graphic artists, and short fiction writers with viable venues for the circulation of their work. Among these publications one would have to count African American–focused ventures such as *Negro Quarterly* (1942–43) and *Negro Story* (1944–46), as well as interracial little magazines like *Common Ground* (1940–49). The latter, for instance, included reportage, literature, and visual art centered around themes of racial justice and published work by African American writers such as Margaret Walker, Melvin Tolson, Gwendolyn Brooks, Langston Hughes, Chester Himes, Owen Dodson, Arna Bontemps, Zora Neale Hurston, and Ralph Ellison, as well as graphics by the likes of E. Simms Campbell, Jacob Lawrence, Cleveland's William E. Smith, and radical cartoonist Ollie Harrington. Further, social realists also availed themselves of the continued presence of the Urban League's *Opportunity,* the NAACP's *Crisis,* and the CP-affiliated *New Masses* and its later incarnation, *Masses and Mainstream,* in which African Americans like Charles White and Lloyd Brown became an increasingly visible presence by midcentury. Even the formerly moderate *Chicago Defender* newspaper moved decidedly to the left following the death of founder and longtime owner Robert Abbott in 1940, publishing a noteworthy array of radical graphics, poetry, essays, and reviews through at least the end of

World War II (Mullen 44–74). Perhaps the leftist little magazine movement had faded somewhat in prominence by the 1940s, due in part to the unprecedented proliferation of mass-market periodicals. Yet, taken collectively, the aforementioned publications comprise often-underappreciated institutional points of continuity between the depression decade and the 1940s (Denning 447–53).

An equally significant point of connection between African American cultural work of the 1930s and that of the ensuing decade consisted of the interpersonal networks that united artists and writers with one another in particular locales, often across strict disciplinary boundaries. As Bill Mullen has recently demonstrated in *Popular Fronts* (1999), Chicago was the preeminent site of African American social realism in both the 1930s and the 1940s. With a nod to the exploration of working-class themes by preceding generations of Chicago writers, including Sherwood Anderson, Carl Sandburg, and James T. Farrell, African American social realists fostered what literary critic Robert Bone influentially has termed a "Chicago Renaissance" during the 1930s and 1940s. In fact, African Americans were not the only midwestern social realist writers who identified with their regional environment in terms that intentionally contrasted with what they perceived as the overly intellectual literary culture of New York. Editor and novelist Jack Conroy once quipped, "The ideological tempest raging in New York City coffee pots seemed unreal and remote out in the Midwest, where C. I. O. organizers were getting their heads cracked while organizing factories" (Salzman and Ray 133). In a similar vein, African American poet Margaret Walker commented, "American naturalism seems to have been born in the Middle West. So many of its progenitors lived in Chicago it seemed made for that city—raw, husky, brutal Chicago" (*Richard Wright* 81). In this light, it is hardly coincidental that artist Charles White and writers such as Richard Wright, Willard Motley, William Attaway, Frank Marshall Davis, and Walker all possessed substantial Chicago connections.

In Chicago, the most important African American literary network of the 1930s was the South Side Writers' Group, whose membership included Wright, Davis, Walker, playwright Theodore Ward, and Marian Minus. This group typically met in members' homes and offered aspiring black writers substantial opportunities for peer critique, as participants regularly read from works in progress. The SSWG also had a visible impact on the larger African American literary field through members' collaboration with Dorothy West on the publication of *New Challenge* in 1937 and, later, through former members' contributions to Alice Browning and Fern Gayden's *Negro Story*, a mid-1940s journal of stories, essays, and poetry (Walker, *Richard Wright* 71–80, 91; Bone 446–47, 464–65; Mullen 106–25). Significantly, too, by the late 1930s and early 1940s several writers from this circle interacted extensively with members of Chicago's visual arts scene via the South Side Community Art Center (SSCAC). Founded in part through the sponsorship of the Federal Art Project, the SSCAC remained as an autonomous and vital Chicago institution long after the demise of the New Deal cultural programs, facilitating the endurance of social realism by bringing together cultural workers who were operating across a number of creative disciplines. Writers such as Davis, Willard Motley, and the young Gwendolyn Brooks, as well as the dancer Katherine Dunham and the photographer Gordon Parks, all frequented the South Side Community Art Center. Such figures contributed to the life of the SSCAC not only through the center's exhibits, classes, and residencies but also through their participation in wide-ranging, politicized forums on issues such as the cultural worker's proper orientation to the mass public.

While conventional periodizations mark the demise of the Harlem Renaissance with the 1929 stock market crash (or, for David Levering Lewis, with the 1935 Harlem riots), New York City remained a prominent arena of African American cultural production throughout the era of social realism. In terms of literature, the various cultural circles organized by long-standing IWO member Louise Thompson during the 1930s and 1940s were of special significance.[22] Perhaps most notable was Thompson's Vanguard group, which brought together writers like Langston Hughes and the young Ralph Ellison, as well as cultural and political figures like Paul Robeson and the NAACP's Walter White. Even earlier, it had been primarily Thompson who organized a tour of African American entertainers and intellectuals to the Soviet Union in 1932, with the goal (ultimately unrealized) of producing a film titled *Black and White* about "the exploitation of the Negro in America from slavery to the present" (D. Lewis 288–91). So too, by 1937 Richard Wright—the most acclaimed of Chicago's African American cultural luminaries—was himself in New York, participating in Thompson's Vanguard group, working for the Federal Writers' Project, and writing pieces for the *Daily Worker* as he drafted his landmark novel of Chicago, *Native Son* (1940).

Harlem also retained a special aura for social realists in the visual arts. Although sculptor Augusta Savage was not herself a social realist, she played a key role in bringing numerous African American artists into contact with one another during the 1930s, initially through her work at the Library School at 135th Street with fellow artists Charles Alston, Gwendolyn Bennett, and Aaron Douglas. After the Carnegie Foundation funding for this school was discontinued, she opened the Savage School of Arts and Crafts under WPA sponsorship. Meanwhile, Alston relocated to 306 West 141st Street, where he was joined by already familiar peers like Bennett and young artists like James Yeargens, Vertis Hayes, Ronald Joseph, and Georgette Seabrooke. Here, too, a diverse and interracial group of intellectuals, entertainers, and cultural workers began to frequent informal workshops and social events. Among those who Alston and his peers recall as either regular or occasional visitors to his "306" studio during the 1930s and early 1940s were Savage, Norman Lewis, Romare Bearden, E. Simms Campbell, George Schuyler, Benny Goodman, Countee Cullen, Agnes De Mille, Ralph Ellison, Gwendolyn Knight, Walter White, Alain Locke, Claude McKay, Orson Welles, Charles White, William Attaway, and Richard Wright (Coker 20–21; Jemison 10; Wheat 59). As Alston described the activity that occurred in and around his studio, "We'd meet and have just bull sessions, knockdown, drag out. Some of them were pretty rough. But it was a sort of forum. [At the time] I don't think any of us realized the value of those things, but there was a tremendous exchange of ideas. . . . Practically everything that was done locally was talked over in 306."[23] In a similar vein, Alston's one-time student Jacob Lawrence explained, "At 306 I came in contact with so many older people in other fields of art. . . . Although I was much younger than they, they would talk about . . . what they thought about their art. . . . *It was like a school* (Wheat 30, my emphasis). Further, Lawrence also has recalled black nationalist history club meetings directed by figures such as Joel Rogers, Charles Seifert, and Richard B. Moore as being very much a part of this same Harlem cultural scene (Fax, *Seventeen* 152; Wheat 35).

Bolstered by the support of the African American visual artists loosely grouped around Alston's 306 studio—most of whom were members of the leftist Harlem Artists' Guild—the Harlem Community Art Center opened under the auspices of the Federal Art Project in December 1937. Under the direction of Savage and, later, Bennett, the Harlem Community Art Center compiled a remarkable record of accomplishments that were very much in keeping with the mass-outreach objectives of its social realist participants. By 1939, the Harlem Center averaged a weekly class attendance of five hundred to six hundred students, many of these students the children of working-class parents; offered regular lectures, motion pictures, and public forums on community issues; afforded access to media ranging from ceramics and costume design to lithography and block printing; and served as a meeting site and exhibition venue for the members of the Harlem Artists' Guild.[24] As Langston Hughes described his impressions of the Harlem Center in a letter to the sponsors of Chicago's then fledgling South Side Community Art Center, "I have seen its beautiful galleries filled with constantly changing exhibitions of the best in art brought to Harlem for the first time; and around this Center I have seen a new art consciousness and a new pride in art springing up in our great colored community of Harlem" (J. Baker 78, 80). It was precisely this "new art consciousness" that the Harlem Community Art Center and the members of the Harlem Artists' Guild helped to extend into the 1940s decade. Even after the center's demise, for instance, many of its affiliated cultural workers still shared in outreach to the working classes of Harlem through leftist institutions such as the George Washington Carver School, where Bennett served as director and artists Elizabeth Catlett, Ernest Crichlow, and Charles White all worked as teachers (Herzog 36–40).

Although Chicago and New York City were the preeminent sites of African American social realism, it is worth remarking that similar work transpired in other U.S. cities. In Cleveland, for example, Karamu House served as an inter-disciplinary cultural center, supporting social realist work in poetry, graphic art, and drama, as well as dance and music projects. For its part, Washington, D.C.—and Howard University in particular—played host to an array of talented figures whose work in some measure impacted the development of African American social realism, including James Porter, a practicing artist who authored the landmark art historical volume *Modern Negro Art* in 1943; James Lesesne Wells, a highly regarded painter and printmaker; Elizabeth Catlett, a young graphic artist and sculptor who studied with both Porter and Wells; philosopher and cultural critic Alain Locke; and poet Sterling Brown.

Meanwhile, Atlanta could boast two key developments in the visual arts. First, upon returning from France in 1931, artist Hale Woodruff founded an important art program at Atlanta University, where the students under his tutelage frequently took as their subject poor and working-class black communities in and outside of Atlanta. For this, the group of young artists even gained a collective notoriety of sorts as the "Outhouse School," so called due to the frequency with which an outhouse seemed (at least to one critic) to appear in the rural landscapes of these artists (Stoelting 73; Murray 72).[25] Second, beginning in 1942, Woodruff orchestrated a prestigious series of annual exhibitions at Atlanta University, which featured work by leading black artists from across the nation. While the prizewinners in the Atlanta University annuals varied significantly in theme and style, the juries for these exhibitions generally seem to have been supportive of social realist work. (Social realists John Wilson, Charles White, and Elizabeth Catlett each took prizes on multiple occasions, for example, while White and Woodruff sometimes served as judges.) As the recollections of numerous parties attest, the Atlanta University annuals thus provided important publicity for many young African American artists, as well as affirmation that an artist could produce politically engaged work and still establish a professionally successful artistic career.

Notably, this artistic activity took place while considerable social science research was ongoing at Atlanta University. The school was, after all, home to important scholars such as Ira De A. Reid, Mercer Cooke, and Rayford Logan. Further, it was during Woodruff's tenure that Atlanta University's W. E. B. Du Bois founded *Phylon* as a leading forum of African American literary and cultural criticism. In at least one subsequent interview, Woodruff specifically cited the importance of the sociological issues raised by Atlanta scholars like Reid and Du Bois to himself and his students: "The group of students I had and I used to talk about these problems. Not only talked about them, we experienced them. . . . Also their work reflects our interest in the Negro sociological theme, or scene—therefore there was this awareness" (Murray 78–79).

Perhaps the most intriguing site of social realist network building, however, was not in the United States at all, but in Mexico City. The impact of Mexican mural painting on U.S. social realism extended back to the emergence of the latter movement in the early 1930s. Providing the key inspiration for the New Deal art programs of the depression era, the work of Mexican muralists like Diego Rivera, José Clemente Orozco, and David Alfaro Siqueiros appealed especially to leftist artists and writers in the United States as a model of aesthetically powerful, politically engaged cultural work capable of reaching a mass audience. Certainly, their example was not lost on African American social realists.[26] Alain Locke's essay for the 1939 *Contemporary Negro Art* exhibition catalog noted the influence of Rivera, Orozco, and Siqueiros on African American artists in terms of both technique and the exploration of themes such as "religion, labor, lynching, unemployment, and other human or social document subjects" (Stewart 182). One can well imagine the appeal of these Mexican artists to Locke himself, as they combined demands for social justice with a reverence for the indigenous folk cultures of Mexico's ethnic minorities. Further, as African American social realists undoubtedly noted, Mexican muralists like Rivera and Orozco featured African Americans and other people of color prominently in both their critiques of America's social ills and their prophetic imagery of revolutionary working-class coalitions.

Mexican politics and art figured prominently in the imagination of U.S. social realists, and several African American artists—like their peers—were significantly influenced by direct contact with Mexican artists, both in the United States and in Mexico. To cite a handful of examples: Charles Alston frequently came to observe Rivera as he painted his controversial *Man at the Crossroads* mural at Rockefeller Center in 1933 (Coker 7); Jacob Lawrence met Orozco as the latter worked on his *Dive Bomber and Tank* mural for the Museum of Modern Art in 1940 (Fax, *Seventeen* 158); Hale Woodruff took advantage of a work-study grant to apprentice in the fresco mural technique with Rivera in Mexico in 1936 (Stoelting 213–17); John Wilson resided among and studied with the radical artists of Mexico City from 1950 to 1956, executing a number of graphic artworks and at least one mural of note during his extended residency; and, as noted earlier, Charles White studied at both the Escuela Nacional de Pintura y Escultura and the Taller de Gráfica Popular in Mexico City in the mid-1940s. Although the engagement of writers with their Mexican peers was not quite so substantial, one should note that Richard Wright and Langston Hughes both traveled to Mexico in the period under study, while novelist Willard Motley made Mexico his new permanent residence in 1951. Sculptor and graphic artist Elizabeth Catlett, who first arrived in Mexico City with her then-husband Charles White in 1946 (with the aid of a Rosenwald Fellowship), has enjoyed the most substantial of such interactions. In the course of what is now over fifty years of direct exchange with the artists of Mexico (including her second husband, Francisco Mora), Catlett has worked with Siqueiros; Rivera and his wife, Frieda Kahlo; sculptors José Ruiz and Francisco Zúñiga; and graphic artists like Leopoldo Méndez, in addition to serving as a long-standing member of the Taller collective in her own right (LeFalle-Collins and Goldman 59). While obviously not all of the above cited exchanges were as enduring as Catlett's, each of the aforementioned artists subsequently reflected on the critical contribution of such interaction with Mexican artists to his or her own creative development.

During the 1940s and early 1950s, in particular, the Taller de Gráfica Popular offered artists such as Wilson, White, and Catlett a crucial means of *sustaining* radical cultural work and a spirit of collective enterprise akin to that exemplified by U.S. organizations and institutions such as the John Reed Clubs, the Harlem Artists' Guild, and Chicago's South Side Community Art Center. As Catlett has explained the nature of work at the Taller, "The people were exposed to art because it was placed around as posters and leaflets all over town. People would come to the workshop if they had problems: if students were on strike, or if trade unions had labor disputes, or if peasants had problems about their land, they would come to the workshop and ask for something to express their concerns" (Samella Lewis 21). Especially with leftist cultural work coming under increasing scrutiny on the U.S. home front by the mid-1940s, one can well understand the appeal of the Taller to a social realist such as Catlett. Like the artists of the Taller, many African American social realists of the 1940s and early 1950s strongly believed that it was not enough simply to produce pieces *about* and *from* the perspective of the poor and working classes; as a cultural worker, one also attempted to craft one's art or literature *for* these downtrodden social groups. And this, of course, echoed the ideological precepts that had attended the emergence of social realism as a major movement in U.S. art and literature during the depression era.

The question of *how* so many African American artists and writers sustained their engagement with social realism through the 1940s and into the early 1950s, then, is in large part a question of *where* they strategically positioned such engagements: namely, in projects sponsored by the Rosenwald Foundation; on the walls of black businesses and colleges; in the pages of the black press and new Popular Front–style little magazines; and in the relative safe haven of Mexico

City. And much of this activity was facilitated by the extension of networks of leftist artists, writers, and cultural critics first generated during the 1930s. The decisions made by African American social realists to forge so much of their work through such means was clearly a matter of strategic choice, affording an opportunity for continuing to engage poor and working-class audiences while simultaneously attempting to circumvent the mounting obstacles that confronted politically engaged cultural workers with the rise of cold war conservatism on the American scene.

In terms of examining *why* so many African American visual artists and writers sustained their engagement with social realism for so long, it should by now be clear that one cannot suppose that they somehow simply failed to receive the proverbial memo about social realism's passing from critical vogue with the dawn of the 1940s. African American cultural workers were too intimately involved with the institutions and informal networks of the American left not to know which way the prevailing winds of the nation were blowing during World War II and the early cold war era. Nor would it be correct to suppose that these artists sustained a viable role for social realism merely by distancing themselves from the radical class-based politics of the depression era to focus on a more narrowly race-based "civil rights" agenda (see also Denning 466–67). To be sure, African American social realists were motivated by the fact that while the increased industrial production of the war effort extended some measure of economic recovery to the U.S. working classes, this was the case to a much lesser degree with African Americans, who continued to be victimized by racial discrimination in housing, the job market, and education during and after the conclusion of the war. Meanwhile, in the postwar era, the highly publicized cases of the Trenton Six and Rosa Lee Ingram served to dramatically highlight widespread racial inequalities in the U.S. legal system quite similar to those that had been flagged by the Angelo Herndon and Scottsboro Boys trials of the 1930s.[27] Yet, most of the figures considered in this study made a conscious choice to continue to use their chosen media of cultural expression as a means to examine the interlocking nature of race and class-based oppressions within a Marxist-informed framework, even as the very real teeth of McCarthyite cold war repression of leftist cultural workers and institutions became increasingly apparent. (Again, it bears noting that several of the artists and writers considered in this study actually *initiated* their respective engagements with social realist themes and aesthetic strategies in the midst of the rabid anticommunism of the 1940s and early 1950s.) In other words, it is not simply a matter of racial justice concerns enduring beyond the U.S. entry into World War II. Rather, if African Americans increased their attention to racial justice concerns in the 1940s (a time—at least in the early

1940s—when the official CP policy relegated racial justice issues to a relative back burner), many also continued, quite insistently, to situate their social critiques within a framework that encompassed class dynamics as well. Many, in fact, pointed to class politics as an important (albeit partial) avenue for radical social change with respect to racial justice in the United States.

The most significant among the new contextual factors extant in the 1940s, of course, was the Second World War. And concerns about the war—particularly the terms in which African Americans would participate in the U.S. campaign— marked one of the key divides between black social realists and their peers. I have observed that the dangers of international fascism constituted a well-established theme among the American left by 1941, and the United States's entry into the Second World War brought the impending threat of these forces home with a new sense of urgency. Consequently, many artists and writers on the left quickly moved to "close ranks" with the larger nation by offering their resources to the war effort, as in the case of bastions of depression-era radical graphic art like Hugo Gellert and William Gropper helping to spearhead a collective known as Artists for Victory. The war also drew African American figures such as Langston Hughes and Charles Alston back toward the American mainstream to some degree. Poems such as Hughes's "Freedom Road," for example, openly called for African American participation in the war effort against the Axis powers, while Alston crafted similarly minded illustrations for the Office of War Information. However, it is worth emphasizing that Hughes and Alston did not issue such work without reservations. More so than most of their peers, African American social realists like Hughes and Alston continued to express considerable ambivalence toward African American participation in the war—praising the contribution of black troops or defense workers in a given poem, graphic, or public statement, and then rigorously interrogating the U.S. commitment to democracy within its own borders in their next such output. Even Hughes's "Freedom Road" incorporated the leftist "black and white together, unite and fight" slogan and carried an implicit promise to fight for freedom on the American home front as part of a broader antifascist crusade. Similarly, Alston's *Free Labor Will Win* graphic for Labor Day, 1942 depicts a group of muscular black and white male defense workers joining to leverage a battering ram against a symbolic Axis stronghold, thus envisioning a racially integrated American proletariat as integral to the war effort.[28]

On the whole, whereas the imperatives of the Second World War drew many white social realists back toward the American mainstream, the racial hypocrisies of the World War II experience served as a sustaining motivator and thematic focus in the work of many African American artists and writers. Particularly at issue was the racial segregation that characterized the American defense industries until the issuing of Executive Order 8802 by President Roosevelt in the summer of 1941, and that remained the policy of U.S. military units throughout the war. Novelist and *New Masses* editor Lloyd Brown captured the conflicted sentiments of many African Americans on this front while reflecting on his own military experience: "This was the question which in one form or another was discussed in our barracks bull-sessions, over our PX beer, incessantly and everywhere: would we Negroes still be treated as second-class citizens of America when the war was over?" ("What about It" 14). It was in precisely this context that the *Pittsburgh Courier* first launched the "Double V" campaign in 1942. The idea of this campaign, explained the *Courier* reader who first proposed it, was for African Americans to undertake a dual struggle against fascism both abroad and at home: "For surely those who perpetrate these ugly prejudices here are seeking to destroy our democratic form of government as surely as the Axis forces" ("Double V" 115). Particularly in African American poetry and graphic arts, one could cite numerous examples of this sort of framing of American racism as a domestic brand of fascism during both the 1930s and the 1940s. For instance, Waring Cuney's "Headline Blues" (1942) states, "Just turn to the Negro papers and see what they have to say / Turn to the Negro papers see what they have to say / You'd think they were talking about Hitler's Germany not the U.S.A." After citing a series of widely publicized instances of racist violence and discrimination, Cuney concludes the poem by referencing a notoriously racist southern politician and suggesting that "Hitler and Talmadge look like the same piece of change to me."[29] Thus, to the extent that antiracism on the home front comprised a central component of the larger American antifascist agenda during the 1940s—and likeminded statements did appear with some regularity in such leftist publications as *New Masses*—this fact owes in no small part to the labor of African American social realists like Cuney and Lloyd Brown.

This engagement with the contemporary scene seems particularly significant given the penchant of scholars to position the social realists of the 1940s and early 1950s as something of a historical anomaly, ossified relics of an earlier day in American arts and letters. To cite one example, Jerome Klinkowitz seems to sound the consensus opinion of novelist Willard Motley when he describes him as an author "whose artistic style and political ideology seemed a decade behind the vogue of such authors as Richard Wright and James T. Farrell" (*Diaries* xv). In fact, social realists like Motley, Charles White, John Wilson, and Frank Marshall Davis were—at least at times—quite interested in matters of aesthetic innovation, albeit that their respective brands of formal experimentation did not mirror those of midcentury high modernism. And certainly in terms of thematic content, African American social realists were anything but anachronistic. To the contrary, the social realist work of the 1940s and early 1950s was imminently "on

Chapter One

time"—as longtime St. Louis community activist Ivory Perry might have it—squarely situated in contemporary conditions of crisis and insurgent liberation struggles (Lipsitz, *Life* 269).

The Form of African American Social Realism

As African American social realists joined their peers in partaking of the depression era's new forms of sponsorship and means of circulating their work, and as they extended the legacy of social realism into the ensuing decade, they sought to better serve poor and working-class audiences by positioning their art and literature in new kinds of cultural spaces. Toward these ends, social realists directed much of their output into carefully selected genres of cultural work. In drama, for instance, the 1930s and early 1940s saw the staging of a number of participatory laborist pageants, as well as the emergence of "living newspaper" performances by the Federal Theatre Project—in which performers emulated techniques of contemporaneous "March of Time" newsreels by bringing to life contemporary crises and other events of note in a bold, three-dimensional form.[30] As with these theatrical genres, the media selected by cultural workers in the visual arts and in literature were keyed to the objective of reaching a mass audience that most perceived as being unlikely to seek out the relatively rarified turf of an art gallery or a highbrow literary magazine. Driven by such aims, four media proved particularly appealing to African American social realists: mural paintings, graphic arts, poetry, and novels.

What proves particularly interesting is that one does not find a monochromatic expression of either ideology or aesthetics across these four media. To be sure, certain thematic terrains—especially poverty and joblessness, racial violence, cases of legal injustice, antifascism, and the Second World War—do surface, in one way or another, in examples of African American–authored murals, graphics, poetry, and novels. And the social realist movement in African American art and literature was defined at least as much by this thoroughly pervasive set of politicized issues as by the shaping influence of any of its particular patrons or individual participants—even an artist like Charles White or poets like Langston Hughes and Frank Marshall Davis, whose prolific bodies of work touched on each of these subjects. Yet, it is also the case that the social realism of African American muralists does not precisely resemble the social realism of African American graphic artists, which does not prove exactly congruent with the social realism of African American poets, which itself parts company from the social realism of African American novelists in certain key respects. In essence, African American cultural workers used these respective media to articulate interlocking but distinctive aspects of a broader social realist agenda and sensibility. Even more, this point generally seems to hold true even for figures like Hale Woodruff and Richard Wright, who operated in more than one of the media under consideration.

While the ensuing chapters will offer further detail regarding the nature of projects executed in each of these media and the strategic reasons underlying their use, the special appeal of these four media merits consideration here as a means of understanding how social realists came to envision that their cultural work might play such a socially transformative role. Granting attention to the cultural spaces in which projects of African American social realism appeared can suggest how the material contexts through which contemporaneous audiences would have encountered works in these varied media might have shaped the relative visibility and type of cultural work that such creative projects could hope to accomplish. These issues are of special relevance to a study of social realism, as most cultural expression in this vein clearly aims to *do* something: namely, to sharpen the political consciousness of audiences as a step toward leveraging social and political change on behalf of America's poor and working classes.

If an individual is at all familiar with American visual art of the depression era, such awareness is likely to include an example of mural painting. Through the ambitious series of New Deal mural commissions (particularly the hundreds of post office and courthouse murals sponsored by the Treasury Section of Fine Arts) and such incidents as the heated controversy surrounding the Rockefeller family's destruction of Diego Rivera's *Man at the Crossroads* in New York City, murals gained an unprecedented public visibility on the American scene during the 1930s.[31] In the second chapter, I thus turn to a close analysis of social realist aesthetics and themes in the murals of Charles Alston, John Biggers, Charles White, John Wilson, and Hale Woodruff. In addition to their intrinsic merits as individual works of art, the murals executed by these five artists between 1934 and 1953 also offer a reasonably representative sampling of the diversely situated regional locales (e.g., New York City; Los Angeles; Chicago; Atlanta; Hampton, Virginia; and Mexico) and institutional settings (e.g., colleges and universities, hospitals, libraries, and black-owned businesses) in which African American muralists of this period most frequently exhibited their work. Whether working in New Deal programs or under some other auspices, many social realist artists selected the mural as an expressive medium in an attempt to reach a mass audience through the mural's impressive scale and by positioning their work in relatively prominent public (or quasi-public) settings. Yet, the very public visibility of murals opened such cultural work to a heightened level of scrutiny, and occasionally even censorship concerns. Hence, taking a cue from their Mexican counterparts, African American muralists turned, in the main, to historical themes during the period under study. While many of these artists' respective murals center on an exploration of historic events and personages, I will suggest that the aforementioned artists carefully crafted such works as allegories that remained vitally connected to the contemporaneous concerns of the social realist movement.

The third chapter turns to an examination of social realism in African American graphic arts. More so than the examination of murals in chapter 2, this chapter considers the work of a broad range of artists, including Alston, Biggers, White, Wilson, and Woodruff, as well as Robert Blackburn, Elizabeth Catlett, Ernest Crichlow, Elton Fax, Wilmer Jennings, Hughie Lee-Smith, William E. Smith, Raymond Steth, and James Lesesne Wells. In part, this broadened focus serves to acknowledge just how pervasive social realist styles and themes were among African American visual artists of the 1930s and 1940s, particularly in graphics. Whereas muralists were able to extend their work to a mass audience via their medium's monumental scale and public institutional setting, graphic art forms resonated with leftist ideologies of the social realist era in that they were easily reproducible for relatively large-scale distribution. Depending in part on the graphic medium employed, artists could produce prints in editions ranging from a few dozen to hundreds, rather than one-of-a-kind easel paintings. Consequently, graphics seemed to hold out a potential for affordability such that "they can be bought by the average citizen, not just the wealthy collector" (Olds 142). Moreover, African American social realists frequently contributed their graphics to the leftist little magazines of the day as a way of significantly furthering the reach of their cultural work.

In terms of content, graphic artists seem to have felt considerably more at liberty to explore contemporary themes pertaining to poverty and joblessness, racial violence, cases of legal injustice, antifascism, and the Second World War than were artists operating in the mural medium. Indeed, one might aptly think of social realist graphic artists as chroniclers of the period's contemporary crises. While I will discuss some notable examples of African American graphic art that venture into explicit social analysis, the overriding impulse in this medium seems to have been to document the everyday frustrations, struggles, and heroism of anonymous working-class men and women. This is not to say, of course, that African American graphic artists aimed to craft nonpartisan documentation. Rather, they sought to chronicle social crises in order to transform them—or rather to encourage viewers to work to transform these crises—even if the artists only occasionally essayed to suggest precisely what course of action such a transformation might require.

The fourth chapter focuses on the poetry of important figures such as Gwendolyn Brooks, Sterling Brown, Frank Marshall Davis, Robert Hayden, Langston Hughes, Melvin Tolson, Margaret Walker, and Richard Wright. Poets faced challenges in reaching a broad audience owing to the fact that, even more so than novelists, they bore the brunt of depression-era publishing woes in terms of book-publication opportunities. Of these poets, for instance, only Hughes and Davis managed to publish complete volumes of their work with any consistency during the 1930s and 1940s.[32] However, unlike the novel, the relatively concise form of poetry lent itself to publication in leftist little magazines such as *Challenge, Common Ground,* and *New Masses.* While publishing their work in such dispersed locations has not aided these poets in terms of their subsequent canonical standing (or lack thereof in some cases), this practice did allow them to continue to participate in the forefront of social realist culture in an era of diminished conventional publishing opportunities. Further, as Cary Nelson has so ably illustrated, positioning poetry in this way served to place it in implicit dialogue with the politically engaged graphics, short fiction, and reportage that also occupied the pages of such magazines.

While none of the above named poets produced work exclusively in a social realist vein, such verse did constitute a significant amount of their respective outputs between 1930 and the early 1950s. Sharing thematic concerns with many of their peers in the realms of mural painting and graphic arts, these poets performed important cultural work by calling attention to the often-neglected historical legacy of African American liberation struggles and by chronicling the nature of contemporaneous working-class experience. Yet, these poets also distinguished themselves from their peers by the frequency with which they used their medium as an explicit "weapon" for social change. Alternately extolling and chastising readers somewhat in the manner of activist orators, they used poetry to forge the most forthright calls to present-day revolutionary action to be found in the annals of African American social realism, often exhorting America's poor and working-class masses to radically transform not only their race and class-consciousness, but also the concrete political sphere.

The final chapter considers social realist aesthetics and themes in a selective group of African American novels: William Attaway's *Let Me Breathe Thunder* (1939) and *Blood on the Forge* (1941); Lloyd Brown's *Iron City* (1951); Willard Motley's *Knock on Any Door* (1947) and *We Fished All Night* (1951); Ann Petry's *The Street* (1946); and Richard Wright's *Lawd Today!* (c. 1935) and *Uncle Tom's Children* (1938/1940).[33] Given a context in which many writers of the social realist era were extremely conscious of reaching a mass audience with their work, the novel comprised a vexed and contested medium. Specifically, in light of dwindling depression-era book sales, many critics and writers came to question the efficacy of the novel as a means of social realist expression. Sales figures ranging from twelve hundred for William Rollins's *The Shadow Before* (1934) to twenty-seven hundred for Jack Conroy's *The Disinherited* (1933) seemed drastically inadequate to those who hoped for cultural workers to assume a prominent role in mobilizing a large-scale social movement (Hart 161). The ambivalence toward the effectiveness of the novel expressed by numerous writers and critics of the 1930s and early 1940s even leads Michael Denning to conclude, "[T]he cultural front, the culture of the CIO, was not primarily located in novels, even proletarian ones" (241). While granting the merits of Denning's observations, one should note that the market for social realist fiction improved markedly by the close of the depression decade. Indeed, many prominent black writers continued to use the novel to powerful effect, crafting some of the most widely influential works of African American social realism.

However, in part due to the influence of preceding generations of American naturalist writing, the vast majority of African American social realists offered considerably less cause for revolutionary optimism in novels than what one finds expressed allegorically in murals or more directly in poetry of the period. Instead, the novelists of African American social realism tend to portray a national landscape littered with irreparably fractured American dreams. One does, of course, find a similar pessimism in certain social realist murals, poems, and documentary-minded graphics, but on the whole novelists present far fewer viable avenues for social change than their contemporaries operating in these other media. Put another way, if poets were African American social realism's revolutionary orators, urging America's masses toward liberation through a strategic use of Marxist-inflected, exhortatory oratorical language, novelists were—to borrow Locke's phrase—the movement's "castigating prophets." Indeed, novelists often proved deeply skeptical of the power of *any* social gospel to redeem the American scene, even leftist visions with which they were themselves largely sympathetic. Like their peers, of course, most novelists of social realism did intend their cultural work to serve as a spur to social change, but as often as not they seem to teeter on the brink of outright disillusionment, as if overawed by the sheer magnitude of the revolutionary task at hand in the face of remarkably intransigent social forces—including not only the mechanisms of government and corporate capitalism but also a paucity of vision on the part of America's poor and working classes themselves.

It is to such an analysis of the nuanced distinctions between the varied media of African American social realist expression that I turn in greater detail in the ensuing chapters, using detailed examinations of understudied murals by Charles White, graphics by John Wilson, poetry by Frank Marshall Davis, and novels by Willard Motley as centerpieces for a broader consideration of African American cultural work in these designated genres.

Chapter Two

Articulating History to the Radical Present: Murals

I demand a gut reaction to art.
CHARLES WHITE

In standard art historical narratives, the collapse of government-sponsored art programs and the onset of World War II together served to bring about the demise of both social realism and American mural painting by the early 1940s. For example, in the estimation of George Biddle—the artist whose 1933 letter to President Roosevelt had helped to generate the New Deal cultural programs—this confluence of factors "killed almost overnight" the American mural movement and left social commentary in art "entirely wiped out."[1] Although such an interpretive framework has proven extremely appealing to most scholars of both American mural paintings and social realism, it neglects several of the most important examples of social realist murals by African American artists.

At the outset of the depression era's mural revival in the United States, African American artists found their way to the mural medium through the same routes as their contemporaries—namely, New Deal cultural programs such as the Public Works of Art Project (PWAP), the Treasury Department's Section of Painting and Sculpture, and the Federal Art Project (FAP). Especially in the case of mural painting, most U.S. artists came to the projects with little or no previous opportunity to work in the medium. As Charles Alston explained, "This was the first opportunity that artists had to get a wall. You have to have a wall before you can get a mural."[2] Indeed, Alston, Charles White, and Hale Woodruff all painted their first murals through these government programs, under whose auspices U.S. artists produced a staggering thirty-six hundred murals between 1933 and 1943. Equally important, African American artists turned with vigor to the mural medium in the depression era for many of the same *reasons* as their peers. As part of its overarching agenda of serving a broad U.S. audience with cultural work on a grand scale, the PWAP and its successor programs encouraged artists to explore mural painting because the scale of this medium could capture the attention of a mass audience much more readily than could easel painting. Further, the government art programs encouraged artists to site their murals within public institutional settings—that is, libraries, hospitals, post offices, and courthouses. To artists of various political sympathies, this seemed an especially effective way in which to reach audiences not likely to venture into the gallery and museum exhibition venues of the conventional art world. For their part, social realists embraced this principle due to its congruence with their own interest in effecting a far-reaching transformation of America's political consciousness with regard to matters of class struggle and related campaigns for social justice. As Woodruff succinctly put the matter in a 1936 speech marking his acceptance of a mural commission at Alabama's Talladega College, "Art has been for the few, but it should be for the many. Great periods of art have been those in which some great purpose motivated all the artists" (Stoelting 207–13).

Despite the enthusiasm of politically engaged artists like Woodruff for the mural medium, it is worth keeping in mind that social realists comprised a minority among muralists working on and off the government art projects during the 1930s. After all, depression-era American artists of varying political and aesthetic affinities possessed an interest in democratizing art for the "common man" and turned to readily accessible imagery in the mural medium as a means of doing so (Baigell 18). Formulating what scholar Jonathan Harris has termed a "usable future" out of "a mythic . . . pre-urban and pre-capitalist past," the government-sponsored murals of the Treasury Section, in particular, evidenced a predominantly Regionalist—not social realist—aesthetic. Generally speaking, this Regionalist or "American Scene" aesthetic reflected the optimism of the New Deal administration more so than a spirit of social criticism (113). A fairly representative work in this regard is the painter Thomas Hart Benton's 1936 *Politics and Agriculture* mural for the Missouri State Capitol, which fully projects the type of mythic past described by Harris. Although Benton's mural does include elements of satire and the backdrop of a menacing dust-storm cloud, these features do little to mute the painting's overriding sense of vigorous action as conveyed by the iconic imagery of a Davy Crockett character with hunting dogs, two brawny yeomen cutting wood with a handheld saw, and male farmers threshing rich wheat fields while women prepare plentiful food baskets.[3] Notably, this agrarian landscape is at once remarkably prosperous and relatively unsullied by industrial technology. In short, while photographers such as Dorothea Lange and Arthur Rothstein were consciously rendering graphic exposés of the era's agrarian poverty for the New Deal's Farm Securities Administration and related WPA programs, the majority of U.S. muralists opted for nostalgic local history scenes or wishful projections of economic abundance (see also Marling 112–15). Such was the pervasiveness of this Regionalist aesthetic that even an otherwise radical artist like Joe Jones, much of whose work from this era falls under the rubric of social realism, executed at least two post office mural scenes of pastoral affluence in this same vein.

Nonetheless, while social realists may have comprised a decided minority among depression-era muralists, they still on occasion sought to articulate the mural medium to controversial political causes such as the labor movement, antiracism, and Marxist socioeconomic reform. The PWAP murals of Bernard Zakheim and Victor Arnautoff at San Francisco's Coit Tower, Philip Guston's series of three fresco murals on the Scottsboro Boys trials for the Los Angeles chapter of the John Reed clubs, and Eitaro Ishigaki's *Civil War* murals for the Harlem Courthouse comprise only a handful of the more notable cases discussed by scholars to date.[4] Such selected examples from fellow American artists assuredly provided some measure of affirmation and influence; yet, the *primary* model for African American social realists beginning work on mural projects in the mid-to-late 1930s (Woodruff, Alston, White) and in the 1940s (Biggers, Wilson) was indisputably the Mexican mural movement. Three Mexican muralists—José Clemente Orozco, Diego Rivera, and David Alfaro Siqueiros—exerted particular influence on their American peers from the early 1930s through at least World War II. The story of these muralists and their impact on U.S. artists has been extensively documented elsewhere in studies by scholars such as Laurence Hurlburt and Lizzetta LeFalle-Collins and, hence, does not necessitate retelling in full here. Still, three areas of Orozco, Rivera, and Siqueiros's impact on African American social realist mural painters do require special acknowledgment within the context of this study.

First, these Mexican artists made a compelling ideological case for the mural as a *public* art medium and provided aesthetically impressive examples of such work themselves, both in Mexico and in the United States. (These three artists received fourteen documented U.S. mural commissions among them, which provided U.S. artists ample opportunities to meet with the Mexican masters and witness their work firsthand in sites ranging from Los Angeles to Detroit to New York City—this, in addition to the influence of reproductions of work executed in Mexico.) As early as 1923, these three painters had been part of a syndicate of Mexican artists that issued a manifesto hailing the potential of the mural medium as a means of democratizing art: "We repudiate the so-called easel art and all such art which springs from ultra-intellectual circles, for it is essentially aristocratic. We hail the monumental expression of public art because such art is public property" (Hurlburt 202). The example of the Mexican muralists in this regard served as one of the principal inspirations for the New Deal art programs in the United States. In his oft-cited letter to President Roosevelt proposing such a program, artist George Biddle pointed to the Mexican artists as an exemplary model for a "national school of mural painting" (Marling 31).

In contrast to Biddle's vision of federally sponsored art as a means of building public consensus around liberal New Deal values, however, the Mexican muralists also were insistent that the public medium of the mural comprised a viable vehicle for the articulation of revolutionary political messages. To cite one of the most famous cases in point, Diego Rivera painted a portrait of Lenin joining the representative hands of a multiracial cadre of working-class men in an explicit gesture of proletarian unity as part of his *Man at the Crossroads* mural for New York City's Rockefeller Center in 1933. More broadly, Rivera's *Crossroads* mural pointedly counterpoised the health and vigor of the working classes to the ostensible decadence and even disease of the American bourgeoisie.[5] Likewise, in terms of the operative ideological frameworks that helped to generate such mural projects, Orozco's report on the activities of Mexico's National Assembly of Artists to the 1936 gathering of the American Artists' Congress (AAC) indicates that there existed a remarkable degree of overlap between the respective political agendas of leftist artists in Mexico and the United States by the mid-1930s, as both groups stressed the position of the artist in relation to war and fascism; the economic security of artists; the relationship between artists and labor organizations; and the relationship between form and content in art.[6]

For African American artists, in particular, a second appeal of the Mexican muralists resided in the fact that Orozco, Rivera, and Siqueiros executed epic works that stylistically and thematically dramatized the heritage and contributions of ethnic minority cultures within the larger nations of Mexico and the United States. For example, Rivera's *Zapotec Civilization* mural, from his *Mexico through the Centuries* series, presents a sophisticated and dignified pre-Columbian society whose members are engaged in a range of productive literary, decorative, and industrial arts. In fact, "the exultation of the Indian as the quintessential Mexican" in the art of Rivera and his protégés became so pronounced that it drew criticism from certain leftist art critics and artists (including Siqueiros), on the grounds that it constituted a form of cultural romanticism (LeFalle-Collins and Goldman 45). Yet, in fairness to Rivera, one should note that, like Orozco and Siqueiros, he *also* documented the oppression suffered by Mexico's indigenous cultures with the arrival of European colonial powers—a fact surely not lost on

African American social realists. Artists with even a general awareness of American history could hardly have failed to note the striking parallels between the enslavement, torture, and lynching of indigenous peoples in a work such as Rivera's *Disembarkation of the Spanish at Veracruz* (also from the *Mexico through the Centuries* series) and similar abuses committed against American Indians and African Americans in the United States.[7] As artist Elton Fax has astutely observed, the work of the Mexican muralists "was especially significant to those black artists whose entire life style, from 1619 to the present, was attributable, from their point of view, to the same kind of human oppression that Mexican artists were painting about" (*Seventeen* 26). In short, critiques regarding Rivera's alleged folkish romanticism notwithstanding, his championing of Mexico's ethnic minority cultures resonated with African American artists' interest in producing work that was at once both representatively American *and* emblematic of ethnically distinctive black cultural traditions. In this sense, Rivera's art closely resembled the two-fold agenda advocated by cultural critic Alain Locke throughout the 1930s and 1940s (see also LeFalle-Collins and Goldman 26).

Mexican artists also extended their critique of social injustices confronting ethnic minority cultures by painting instances of racial persecution within the United States. For instance, Rivera's 1934 mural *The New Freedom* documents the contemporary drama surrounding the unjust prosecution of the Scottsboro Boys alongside other leftist-cause célèbres such as Tom Mooney and Sacco and Vanzetti. In a similar manner, echoing a pervasive Popular Front equation, Siqueiros's famous *Portrait of the Bourgeoisie* mural for the Electrician's Union Building in Mexico City (1939–40) expressly poses a lynched black male as the U.S. counterpart to the victims of the fascist military regimes in Germany, Italy, and Japan (LeFalle-Collins and Goldman 75).[8] As most African American artists from this period have attested, the example of such prominent muralists undertaking these controversial themes helped many young social realists to affirm the appropriateness of tackling similar antiracist subject matter in their own work.

In addition to providing a model for use of the mural as a medium for championing the achievements of minority cultures and critiquing racial oppression, a third crucial appeal of the Mexican muralists to U.S. artists was the fact that they offered a particular strategy for realizing these objectives: the use of historical allegory. Like the post office murals sponsored by the U.S. Treasury Department's Section of Painting and Sculpture, Mexican-authored murals routinely addressed sweeping historical themes. However, Orozco, Rivera, and Siqueiros did so from a decidedly more critical perspective, openly attempting to analogize connections between historical scenes and the contemporary socioeconomic crises of the depression as a means of illustrating root causes and, occasionally, proposing solutions. In this vein, following his abrupt dismissal from the *Man at the Crossroads* mural, Rivera executed his *Portrait of America,* a series of twenty-one fresco panels that interpreted American history from the age of colonization and the Revolutionary War through the New Deal era within an openly Marxist framework.[9] As African American artist John Wilson once noted of such works, "You can't look at the great Mexican muralists without being conscious of their expressions of revolution against the evils of existing social orders" (Fax, *Seventeen* 40). Further, one might note that themes of racial justice again feature prominently in Rivera's historical saga of the United States, both in his critiques of violence against American Indians and African Americans *and* in his inclusion of African American figures such as Crispus Attucks, Nat Turner, Sojourner Truth, Frederick Douglass, and an anonymous black participant in Shays's rebellion among his catalog of heroic historical figures who champion democratic causes.

African American muralists of the 1940s and early 1950s did not persist in a sustained engagement with social realism—and the example of the Mexican muralists in particular—out of sheer obliviousness to the pronounced drift of American art writ large away from such forthrightly political subject matter and aesthetics. Rather, artists like John Wilson and Charles White, who chose to work primarily in social realist modes of expression, made a conscious decision to do so out of a number of available aesthetic options, rather than out of ignorance of the formal innovations of their contemporaries. Wilson addressed the matter directly in a 1945 lecture titled "The Role of Negro Art in the Negro Liberation Movement":

> I am well aware of the work of the more abstract painters and the non-objectivists and I understand and appreciate them for what they have contributed. However, being a Negro who grew up during the height of the last depression has made me probably a lot more conscious of the various patterns of life here in America and the relationship of my race to the whole system. . . . Landscapes and still life interest me but I feel that because I seem to have the ability to paint rather well and forcefully I can use this to try to express something maybe more directly functional and concrete as far as it relates to our present social setting.[10]

At least a handful of other important African American artists—including Charles White, Charles Alston, Hale Woodruff, and John Biggers—joined Wilson in citing similar reasons for continuing to use the mural as a medium of politicized cultural expression well into the cold war era.

That they were able to do so in an era of mounting political repression of leftist cultural work owes to at least two crucial strategies. First, during the 1940s and early 1950s, African American muralists only occasionally sited their work in New Deal–style venues such as hospitals and libraries; more often, their locales of choice were in historically black colleges, black businesses and community institutions, and—in at least one instance—outside of the United States entirely, on a wall in Mexico City. All of these latter locales, one might note, fell outside of the direct sphere of authority of the period's anticommunist politicians. Second, between the onset of the depression and the early 1950s, African American muralists most often articulated social commentary of contemporary relevance through the vehicle of historical allegory. And although the artists tended to operate in this allegorical mode, much of their work still evidences thematic and stylistic continuities with the works of social realism in visual media that more consistently addressed contemporary topical issues in direct ways, such as the graphic arts. At this point, I will turn to a consideration of specific murals, beginning with a close examination of the early career of Charles White, in order to concretely illustrate the important and underacknowledged points of contiguity between African American muralists and the broader social realist movement.

The Murals of Charles White

Like many African Americans who participated in the social realist movement, Charles White was a product of the Great Migration of African Americans from the rural South to the urban North, which profoundly reshaped the topography of American life between the First and Second World Wars. In an autobiographical sketch published in the CP-affiliated *Masses and Mainstream* in 1955, White recollected the rationale of his parents' decision to move from Mississippi to Chicago during World War I:

> They had no resentment against the southern land itself. In fact, they were deeply attached to it, for practically everything useful that had come out of the soil was largely a product of their toil. And they had no illusions that the North was a place free from prejudices. But in cities like Chicago factories were growing, and workers were needed, the demand growing with the war production boom. The employers discovered that a Negro's two arms could serve a machine or an open hearth in a steel mill as well as those of anyone else. ("Path" 33)

As White's comments suggest, whereas the vast majority of African Americans previously had lived as southern agricultural laborers, with the onset of these massive migrations blacks entered the ranks of America's industrial proletariat in unprecedented numbers. Thus, like many of his social realist peers, Charles White came from a working-class background. His father worked in the stockyards and steel mills of South Chicago before finding employment with the post office. Unfortunately, White was only eight years old when his father died, leaving his mother, who had been a domestic worker since her own childhood, as the family's sole source of financial support.[11]

Consequently, White grew up with personal experience delivering groceries, sweeping shops, shining shoes, and, later, holding part-time employment as a hotel bellhop and an ice cream parlor counter attendant. White also found occasional work to help support himself and his mother as a professional sign painter for theaters, beauty shops, and other local businesses from the age of fourteen until his graduation from high school some four years later.[12] Even before White was old enough to pursue employment, his mother sometimes had to take him with her to work. In this way, the artist formed vivid memories of his mother scrubbing, cooking, and washing for relatively wealthy white families for only the most nominal earnings. Such personal experiences contributed to his pursuit of political radicalism via participation in Communist Party activities at an early age, as evidenced by a mid-1930s CP pamphlet on racist oppression and an article for the CP's *Young Worker* titled "Free Angelo Herndon," both reputedly authored by White.[13] Likewise, some of White's earliest artwork—including a drawing titled *Laborers* (c. 1936) that depicts a group of young workers bearing the tools of proletarian labor—illustrates the formative stages of what would become a sustained interest in black working-class subject matter. A sensitive youth, White also perceived the way in which prevailing racial ideologies shaped his and his mother's identities as African Americans: "The idea that there were 'differences' was ever present in the attitude of the teachers and in what we were taught. When I learned to read, there it was in the books, as well as in the motion pictures, cartoons, newspapers, 'jokes' and advertisements. The Negro people were portrayed as grotesque stereotypes" ("Path" 34). Hence, White came of age well acquainted with the material and social constraints that race and class could impose on an individual's life possibilities.

Still, White's childhood did possess some counterbalancing influences, particularly books. When White's mother needed to run errands, she often left him at the public library. There, by his own account, White voraciously read works of American authors like Jack London and Mark Twain, as well as historical novels of romance and adventure. Then, almost by accident, he came upon a book that profoundly altered his consciousness as an aspiring African American artist: Alain Locke's anthology of Harlem Renaissance essays, poetry, art, music, and drama, *The New Negro* (1925). Described by White as "a book that fascinated me, and opened up new vistas," Locke's anthology provided White with a crucial window onto African American cultural figures ranging from James Weldon Johnson to Countee Cullen to W. E. B. Du Bois ("Path" 35). More specifically, White explained, Locke held "a particular interest to me because of his own special interest in art, the history of the Negro artist in America."[14] By including both Locke's scholarly work on the significance of African sculpture and the example of a professional black artist in the work of Aaron Douglas, *The New Negro* offered aspiring artists of subsequent generations, such as White, a source of affirmation seldom found in school or other aspects of life—even if social realists of the 1930s and 1940s articulated their own cultural work to more directly political aims than had a Harlem Renaissance artist such as Douglas. Equally important, explained White, "I had never realized that Negro people had done so much in the world of culture, that they had contributed so much to the development of America, that they had even been among the discoverers of the continent" ("Path" 35). In this way, White's reading of *The New Negro* served as a springboard to his own quest for knowledge regarding the heroes of African American history: "Once I found this *one* book, then I began to search for other books on Negroes, which led to Negro historical figures, individuals that played a role in the abolition of slavery."[15]

Yet, in spite of the fact that White's fellow students at Englewood High School included the progressive young artists-in-the-making Margaret Burroughs and Eldzier Cortor, he later recollected his experiences there as stifling to his interests in black history. Frustrated by the lack of available information in his high school textbooks, White undertook several research projects and reports for his classes on figures like Sojourner Truth, Harriet Tubman, Nat Turner, Denmark Vesey, Booker T. Washington, and Frederick Douglass. Unfortunately, White's high school history teachers seemed to share little of his enthusiasm for such topics, responding to his questions about such omissions "smugly and often angrily. . . . When I spoke up about these ignored great figures, I would be told to sit down and shut up" ("Path" 35–36). The militancy of White's emerging racial consciousness was piqued further when he was awarded scholarships to both the Chicago Academy of Fine Arts and Frederic Mizen Academy of Art, only to have the prizes abruptly withdrawn in both cases when the institutions discovered his racial identity (Horowitz 11).

Denied these early opportunities for formal training, White turned to more self-directed modes of furthering his art education. Specifically, he read books on art and regularly visited Chicago's various art galleries. In the course of such visits to the Art Institute of Chicago, White encountered a handful of professional artists who encouraged him in his artistic ambitions. Two white leftist painters, Mitchell Siporin and Edward Millman, even invited White to their respective studios to watch them at work. Also, White received his first training in the mural medium when he enrolled in art classes at Hull House and the South Side Settlement House, including a course in fresco painting taught by Siporin and Millman (Motley, "Negro Art" 20–28).[16] Later, White would cite these two mentors as key influences on his early efforts to paint "objectively" about depression-era social conditions and the impact of these conditions on the lives of everyday people.[17] In fact, the social realist critique articulated by these artists was such that a 1940 *Chicago Tribune* article criticizing the pervasiveness of leftist political influence on the work of local artists singled out Siporin's work as "un-American in theme and design" and shot through with "communist influences." Similar allegations of cultural radicalism led the Lucy Flower Technical School to go so far as to plaster over Millman's six panel mural series *Women's Contribution to American Progress* (McKinzie 110)—a series that may well have planted a seed in White with regard to using the mural medium as a viable means to grant public visibility to the long-neglected cultural contributions of socially oppressed groups. In any event, it is not surprising that both Siporin and Millman were highly influenced by the social realism of the Mexican muralists, an enthusiasm that they helped to pass on to the young Charles White.[18] White's early interest in the politicized Mexican art of the day also was fired by his work with Morris Topchevsky, with whom White took courses at the CP-affiliated Abraham Lincoln School. A member of the Chicago chapter of the John Reed Club, the Artists' Union, and the American Artists' Congress, Topchevsky had spent time in residence with the Taller de Gráfica Popular in Mexico City on several occasions by the early 1940s and provided a further example to White of the possibilities of radical, politicized art (Forhman 10).

For all of White's sense of isolation in striving to acquire knowledge of African American history and culture during his high school years, he did not come of age as a black artist in a vacuum. To the contrary, by the age of fourteen or fifteen, White became aware of an organization known as the Arts and Crafts Guild while working with other aspiring artists as a sign painter and decided to seek out the group. This impressive cadre of young African American artists was anchored by the mentorship of George E. Neal and included talented members such as Charles Sebree, Margaret Burroughs, William Carter, Lawrence Jones, and Bernard Goss.[19] The early successes of these artists seem all the more remarkable given that, due in large part to prohibitive costs, only the somewhat older and more established Neal initially was able to enroll in courses at Chicago's Art Institute. Thus, members of the guild gathered on Saturdays, usually at Neal's studio, so that he might share what he had learned at the Institute, what White termed "the technical aspects of handling paint." For this reason, Burroughs has praised Neal as an underacknowledged "central figure" of the Chicago art world who "inspired and kept together our whole generation of young artists"—at least until his premature death due to tuberculosis in 1938.[20]

When not convening at Neal's studio, often this group simply gathered at one another's homes for discussions that intermingled social, practical, and theoretical concerns. At times, the group held social functions aimed at raising money to support the further artistic activities of its members. Drawing on funds raised in this manner, the Arts and Crafts Guild organized several of its own exhibits. As Burroughs and White each explained in later interviews, due to the marginal position of African American artists vis-à-vis the broader Chicago art world of the 1930s, the primary venues for such exhibitions were local YWCAs and YMCAs, Hull House, the South Side Settlement House, church basements, storefronts, or even a vacant lot on occasion. Mirroring Chicago's mainstream exhibits, on a smaller scale, the guild recruited local community leaders as judges and gave out modest prizes to leading exhibitors. Over time, these prizes came to consist of small scholarships to Chicago's Art Institute, where some dozen guild members eventually enrolled in classes. As Neal had done earlier, these scholarship winners then shared the fruits of their formal art education with the larger guild membership in the group's regular meetings (White, "Path" 37).

The WPA art programs made up a second major institutional framework that united White with other African American artists of Chicago. As in many other locales, New Deal employment opportunities were not extended equally to black artists in Illinois, at least not initially. According to White, the Illinois Art Project employed only one African American artist, Archibald Motley Jr., until White himself and other black artists joined the Artists' Union: "[The Union] went on strike against these discriminatory practices. We picketed the projects, I was arrested a few times by the police, and spent some nights in jail. Finally we won. And so my first lesson on the project dealt not so much with paint as with the role of the unions in fighting for the rights of working people" ("Path" 38). Following this breakthrough, African American artists were able to lobby successfully for the creation of the South Side Community Art Center (SSCAC) in 1940 under the auspices of the Federal Art Project.[21] One of more than fifty such community art centers established around the country, primarily in urban neighborhoods, the SSCAC provided a stable site for the gatherings and exhibitions of the group of artists that formerly had gathered around Neal and the South Side Settlement House. Burroughs, Goss, Eldzier Cortor, and Charles White all taught classes and staged some of their earliest exhibits at the new center, for example. Whereas shortly before the founding of the SSCAC Willard Motley had observed that "Charles White's easel is the back of a chair in a crowded dining room" ("Negro Art" 19–21), White and his peers now had a stable base for their work and a nexus for community building among the city's African American cultural workers. By the mid-1940s, the SSCAC also had exhibited the work of radical white Chicago artists like Si Gordon and African American artists from outside of Chicago, such as Hughie Lee-Smith, William E. Smith, Augusta Savage, Hale Woodruff, and John Biggers (Tyler 35; Fax, *Seventeen* 105).

As Bill Mullen's recent scholarship in *Popular Fronts* serves to underscore, this African American–controlled institutional anchor helped affiliated artists and writers to sustain social realist cultural work in an array of disciplines well into the early cold war era.[22] For despite a temporary disruption of the SSCAC's activities in 1942—when the government converted it into a Wartime Art Service Center that engaged personnel in activities such as map tracing—the SSCAC's relative autonomy enabled it to sustain vitality as a nexus for progressive cultural work well past the demise of the Federal Art Project, which had helped to sponsor its creation (Contreras 230). Gatherings at the SSCAC attracted diverse cultural workers through a vibrant mix of the artistic, the political, and the social. Richard Wright, Willard Motley, and the young Gwendolyn Brooks were all affiliated with the center's writers' forum, for example, while groups like the Nat King Cole Trio played jazz concerts at the center's social events (Tyler 35). As White described the Chicago arts scene of his youth in a 1977 interview with Sharon Fitzgerald:

> I happened to grow up in a time in Chicago when my peer group included Gwendolyn Brooks, Margaret Walker, Katherine Dunham, Richard Wright. . . . The way the community structure was, if you were interested in any of the arts you eventually knew everybody else, every other Black brother and sister who was interested in the arts. We developed a social relationship and a very close-knit one. We formed a theatre group called the Negro People's Theatre which all of us participated in. There was a poetry workshop organized. . . . There were community art centers where dancers performed, where poetry reading groups were formed, writing and art groups. All of us got involved in all of the arts. . . . It was a very exciting period. (159)

At related parties in Dunham's studio, White also conversed with somewhat older figures like playwright Theodore Ward, as well as novelists Nelson Algren and Willard Motley; inspired by the discussions and activity of this circle, White soon tried his own hand at verse, set design, acting, and dance (Horowitz 13). In fact, as White mentions here, the SSCAC helped to initiate the Negro People's Theatre, a group in which White, Burroughs, Bernard Goss, and other visual artists participated as both actors and designers of sets and costumes. Among this group's productions were radical works such as Irwin Shaw's antiwar drama *Bury the Dead.*[23]

While certainly an important locale for the bonding of African American creative artists with one another in interdisciplinary projects, the SSCAC, from its inception until at least the early 1950s, played host to an interracial mix of artists and writers. Significantly, this fact owed little to the vision of federal government sponsors, since, as Richard McKinzie notes, "The FAP, like most New Deal agencies, honored local customs on segregation of races" (145). Rather, the interaction of black and white artists that characterized the early years of the SSCAC resulted from the active commitment of politically engaged artists themselves to the principle of interracialism. For many young African American artists, the center thus provided an otherwise rare chance to interact with white peers, which often proved a profitable opportunity for ideological and aesthetic growth for all parties involved. For example, Margaret Burroughs recalls, as a teenager, going with Charles White to the home of white SSCAC teacher Si Gordon, where Gordon loaned her an illustrated book on Harriet Tubman—thus helping to inaugurate her study of black history. Likewise, Burroughs credits Gordon and Morris Topchevsky as being important sources of information to her and White regarding the writings of Marx, Engels, and Lenin (153). By the same token, the SSCAC granted artists like Gordon and Topchevsky a context in which to interact with a sizable contingent of fellow artists who shared their commitment to working toward racial and economic justice through art—an opportunity all the more valuable with the demise of the New Deal cultural programs and the waning of groups such as the American Artists' Congress by the early 1940s.

The ranks of prestigious artists indebted to the center also include the photographer Gordon Parks, who set up one of his early exhibits in the SSCAC basement. Benjamin Horowitz remarks on the special camaraderie that sprung up between Parks and White, in particular: "Parks had not done much documentary work at that time and he became very interested in White's social documentary of the Negro people of Chicago's south side, a project White was working on at the time. He accompanied White on his tramps through the slums, photographing the same scenes that Charles White painted. As people gathered to watch White paint, Gordon would photograph them" (15). As this anecdote suggests, visual artists and other cultural workers affiliated with the SSCAC scene of the late 1930s and 1940s tended to be interested in social realist projects that involved documenting the lives of ordinary people in a politically engaged manner. By the time of the nationally representative exhibit of visual art in the Chicago Coliseum as part of the 1940 American Negro Exposition, the SSCAC-affiliated contingent of Chicago artists had captured considerable praise from prominent figures such as Alain Locke. Arguably, the most esteemed of these young artists was Charles White, whose charcoal drawing *There Were No Crops This Year* won a first prize award at the exposition (Horowitz 13). Depicting a closely huddled rural couple complete with oversized, rough-hewn hands and weather-beaten, anxiety-ridden facial expressions, White's drawing gave a firm indication that this young artist was an unabashed social realist, one whose work would stand in critical counterpoint to the wishful abundance that typified the depression era's Regionalist paintings.[24]

Concurrent with his efforts in helping to found the SSCAC, White submitted samples of his work and qualified for the prestigious easel painting division of the

Federal Art Project, which granted him a respectable income and freedom to work on themes of his own design. As with other FAP easel painters, this position also enabled White to work without direct supervision, requiring only that he submit one painting every five weeks. Yet, in White's estimation, the significance of the New Deal art programs resided not only in the fact that they provided needy artists with employment but that "they also embraced the principle—one practically unheard of up to then in United States history—that the arts were socially useful work." White especially valued the community-minded orientation of the FAP: "The most wonderful thing for me was the feeling of cooperation with other artists, of mutual help instead of competitiveness and of cooperation between artists and the people. It was in line with what I always had hoped to do as an artist, namely paint things pertaining to the real everyday life of people, and for them to see and enjoy" ("Path" 38–39). Soon, White took advantage of another positive feature of work on the Federal Art Project—the relative flexibility of artists to transfer between departments—in order to pursue work in the medium of mural painting.[25] White had specific reasons for seeking out the mural medium, which related to the democratic ideals that characterized his entire professional career. He explained his special interest in painting black history murals to Willard Motley in 1940:

> I am interested in the social, even the propaganda, angle in painting; but I feel that the job of everyone in a creative field is to picture the whole scene. . . . I am interested in creating a style that is much more powerful, that will take in the technical end and at the same time will say what I have to say. Paint is the only weapon I have with which to fight what I resent. If I could write I would write about it. If I could talk I would talk about it. Since I paint, I must paint about it. ("Negro Art" 22)

Moreover, White shared with many social realist peers a conviction regarding the special communicative power of murals, explaining in a 1943 interview with the CP's *Daily Worker,* "Art is not for artists and connoisseurs alone. It should be for the people. A mural on the wall of a commonly-used building is there for anyone to see and read its message."[26]

For his first mural as a member of the FAP, White began work on a five-by-twelve-foot oil on canvas painting titled *Five Great American Negroes* (1939). According to contemporaneous journalistic accounts and White himself, a survey in a local black newspaper, most likely the *Chicago Defender,* was used to decide who people felt were "the five outstanding Negroes throughout the last 50 years or 100 years or so."[27] The resulting mural consists of four principal tableaus: on the far left of the mural, Sojourner Truth leads a vast procession of African Americans from slavery to freedom; in the center of the mural, Booker T. Washington addresses what appears to be a middle-class black audience from behind a podium, while Frederick Douglass comforts a newly escaped slave, who cries in relief upon Douglass's shoulder; in the upper right, Marian Anderson performs to the delight of two anonymous black concertgoers; and in the lower right, George Washington Carver peers through a microscope.

While this work does not possess the same degree of overarching conceptual unity evidenced in his subsequent murals—perhaps in part due to the newspaper poll's rather arbitrary selection of figures to be included—the topic clearly was extremely well suited to White's already avid interest in black historical heroes, as well as his ability to render such personages with monumental dignity and stature. Further, White's representation of the Sojourner Truth–led procession as a mass of iconic figures marching in a frontal trajectory that seems to lead forward into a more promising future (represented by the achievements of Anderson and Carver) is formally consistent with numerous social realist portrayals of revolutionary working-class action. Likewise, the bulging musculature with which White renders the arms of Booker T. Washington seems to owe much more to the artist's proletarian aesthetic sensibility than to any desire to offer a photographic likeness of this famous orator and racial spokesman. Significantly, after exhibiting this mural in several venues, including Chicago's Savoy Ballroom and the Library of Congress in Washington, D.C., White temporarily installed *Five Great American Negroes* in the South Side Community Art Center.[28]

On the heels of this first mural, White received a prestigious commission from the Associated Negro Press to complete a mural history of the organization for the aforementioned 1940 American Negro Exposition. Remarkably, White completed this nine-by-twenty-foot oil on canvas work within the constraints of a three-week deadline.[29] Although not as overtly radical as his subsequent murals, White's *History of the Negro Press* nonetheless encompasses at least three elements important to the artist throughout his career. First, White's inclusion of Frederick Douglass proves consistent with his interest in historical heroes who struggled for the collective racial uplift of African Americans. In this work, White renders Douglass with one arm thrown around the shoulder of a shirtless black man while presenting the man with a paper of some sort, leading one to imagine that Douglass may be sharing an abolitionist newspaper with a recently escaped fugitive from slavery—that is, a very similar motif to White's depiction of Douglass in the *Five Great American Negroes* mural. In this same vein, on either side of Douglass and the anonymous freedman, White includes two other historic personages of note: John Russworm, who founded the first documented black newspaper, *Freedom Journal*, in 1827; and T. Thomas Fortune, the famed editor of the *New York Age* who, during the 1880s and 1890s, offered influential commentary on issues such as the interlocking nature of racial oppression and capital's exploitation of labor.[30]

Second, like historical personages such as Douglass and Russworm, White certainly was a believer in the liberating power of literacy and the written word. Particularly as a mode of black self-assertion, White thus conceives of the Associated Negro Press and its forebears in black newspaper publishing as crucial agents of liberation for the African American community. And with good reason, as Bill Mullen's recent scholarly work shows the *Chicago Defender* to have been an essential facilitator of and vehicle for African American "Popular Front" cultural activism of the 1940s (44–74). Third, one also should note of this mural that the stated aims of the black press—namely, the documentation of everyday happenings in African American communities—coincided with White's own objectives as an artist. Hence, White highlights the activities of a photographer and a reporter with a notepad who seem to be staring at some event to the fore of the mural frame with intent interest—a tableau that might call to mind the aforementioned collaboration between White and Gordon Parks in documenting life on the streets of Chicago's South Side through painting and photography. Indeed, it hardly seems to overstate the matter to describe much of the social realist art of the 1930s and 1940s as itself comprising a type of cultural reportage or interpretive journalism.

The following year, White received his next major mural commission under the auspices of the Federal Art Project, a painting designated for the George Cleveland Branch of the Chicago Public Library, to which White gave the revealing title *Technique to Serve the Struggle*. In keeping with the aesthetics of the Mexican muralists and White's fellow American social realists, this mural consists of a dense arrangement of human figures positioned in interlocking and thematically interrelated scenes. White uses the architectural constraint of a doorway to make a division in his mural between two thirteen-by-twenty-one-foot oil on canvas panels: in the left panel are events set in the rural South, while the right panel depicts a scene of life in the contemporary urban North (figure 1). In the southern component of the mural White illustrates a range of forces conspiring to sustain African American oppression: in the center of the mural, a black man hangs lynched from a dead and broken tree, facing away from the viewer; also, a well-dressed black overseer or businessman bearing a whip stands with a merciless expression over a chained black man, who kneels with his head bowed, as if on the point of collapse. Notably, White renders the well-dressed man's prominently raised hand in such a manner as to suggest the willingness of the black middle class to keep their less economically secure brethren "under their thumb," so to speak. In this way, White implies that the oppression of African Americans in the rural South owes not only to white racism, but also to intraracial class oppression.

However, White counterbalances these images of race and class oppression by

Figure 1. Charles White (1918–79), *Technique to Serve the Struggle,* 1940–41. Tempera. (Federal Art Project.)

depicting rival forces that contend for freedom: a man and woman hold aloft a book and a writing implement, respectively; simultaneously, John Brown distributes rifles. Notably, White depicts one man accepting a rifle, while another seems to cringe and turn away from Brown's offer. Even the man who accepts a rifle essays a glance over his shoulder to his wife and child, suggesting the difficult but necessary choice he is about to make. In any event, White clearly seems to suggest that *both* literacy and education, on the one hand, *and* militant self-defense or even armed aggression, on the other, have played an important, complementary role in the historic struggle for African American liberation. Meanwhile, the artist seems to leave deliberately ambiguous whether the two men engaged in conversation at the base of a pulpit engraved with the message "God is Love" regard White's preacher as an agent of emancipation or—perhaps reflecting the artist's own Marxist sensibilities—the purveyor of a seductive opiate.

Among scholars of American art history, it is by now axiomatic that such historical scenes tell us as much about depression-era hopes and anxieties as about

the historical epochs ostensibly represented—whether one speaks of Regionalist depictions of heroic and manly labor as an attempted antidote of sorts for depression-era joblessness or, as with White's antebellum South, a not-so-subtly coded commentary on continuing forms of black labor exploitation under southern sharecropping. That is, if White is not precisely invoking depression-era viewers to take up arms in a John Brown–styled armory raid, his mural most certainly *does* highlight a perceived need for some type of militant revolt against contemporary forms of race and class oppression. Moreover, White's mural is relatively nuanced in suggesting that both black and white actors have played a role in perpetuating such oppression, just as both black and white radicals have aided efforts for African American liberation.

I have noted that such a strategic use of historical allegory proved appealing to many politically engaged artists in the mural medium—especially while operating under the scrutiny of government-sponsored art programs. Consider, for instance, Eitaro Ishigaki's *Emancipation of the Negro Slaves* (c. 1938), from his *Civil*

War murals for the Harlem Courthouse, which includes an array of anonymous African American laborers surrounding icons of abolitionism such as Union soldiers (both black and white), Frederick Douglass, an armed John Brown, and Abraham Lincoln.[31] While one shirtless and muscular black man bends under a load of sugarcane, a counterpart has burst his shackles and stands with a clinched fist—a common symbol of labor militancy since at least the 1910s and one that pervaded leftist visual culture during the 1930s. Likewise, scholar Walter Kalaidjian notes that another of the agricultural laborers depicted in the mural carries a sickle, almost surely a coded emblem of proletarian revolution in the context of depression-era iconography (181). As a political progressive who had been active in the John Reed Clubs of the early 1930s and was among the founding members of the American Artists' Congress, Ishigaki clearly intended this provocative, allegorical imagery of abolitionist heroes and dramatically posed African American workers to radicalize the consciousness of his contemporary Harlem audience as much as to serve as a historical document per se.

Given the pronounced penchant for historical allegory among leftist painters of the day, it is all the more striking when White makes explicit the contemporary (and radical) applications of his historical allegory in the right half of his *Technique to Serve the Struggle* mural. In particular, White extends the themes of his multifaceted southern scene into a neo–Marxist vision of contemporary black urban life, which one might take as the artist's symbolic evocation of his native Chicago. In the complex montage of imagery assembled here, White seems to offer little in the way of optimism regarding the contemporary prospects that confront the African American masses: a black orator (either politician, preacher, or both) rants before a cowed, timid audience (minus the notable exception of one markedly unimpressed black worker, who willfully turns his back on the speaker); a large billboard supports the campaign of a white machine politician with the suggestive name of "Honest Joe Goon"; a white policeman attacks a picketing black worker with a club; a line of men and women with downcast heads forms a massive line at a relief station; and a black tycoon, seemingly the counterpart of the overseer in the left half of the mural, smiles smugly as he clutches a bag of money. In the lower right corner of this panel, an African American couple clings to one another as if for solace from the events that surround them—essentially echoing the figuration of the couple in White's aforementioned drawing *There Were No Crops This Year.*

In short, White's *Technique to Serve the Struggle* assembles several motifs prominent in social realist art of the 1930s and early 1940s: antilabor violence against striking workers; the rampant corruption of American politics and organized religion; relief lines of the poor and unemployed; and the corporate exploiter who reaps wealth from the misery of the community of workers. As in his earlier murals, White renders his figures—both male and female—with a highly defined musculature that seems to owe a significant debt to the aesthetics of proletarian social realist art of the 1930s. On a conceptual level, as well, White's choice of the title *Technique to Serve the Struggle* suggests that he seeks common cause with the revolutionary spirit of race and class liberation prevalent in leftist American politics during the late 1930s and early 1940s; in essence, White's own "technique" to serve such struggles is to reveal both patterns of exploitation and exemplars of resistance through a readily legible brand of cultural work. As reviewer Robert A. Davis astutely noted of White in the *Chicago Sunday Bee* in 1940: "He is interested in dramatizing in his work the social problems of his time, particularly those of his own people. However, he cannot be classed as a nationalist painter. He sees the problems of Negroes as differing from those of other workers in degree of intensity rather than in kind. He believes that all working class people have a common interest and that there is a common solution to their problems."

To be sure, this mural (particularly the contemporary urban panel) does not portray unified revolutionary working-class action per se, but rather a prerevolutionary moment—what White termed at the time "the chaotic stage of the Negro, past and present" (W. Carter n.p.). Hence, White wanted to create a mural that would serve to *generate* a radical racial and working-class consciousness in its audience so that his illustration of social evils might, in turn, lead viewers to find ways to combat the most pressing injustices confronting contemporary African American communities. In fact, the way in which White inscribes a musician in each half of the mural—a banjo player on the left and a piano player on the right—subtly points to the artist's conviction that *cultural expression* has a key role to play in the struggle for African American liberation.

Around the time that White was completing these three mural projects, sculptor and social realist graphic artist Elizabeth Catlett entered into the Chicago art scene, albeit briefly. Catlett had studied with the artists James Lesesne Wells and James Porter at Howard University, before entering a graduate art program at the University of Iowa under the mentorship of the famed Regionalist painter Grant Wood. Following the receipt of her master's degree from Iowa, Catlett relocated to Chicago to take summer courses at the Art Institute; while there, Catlett spent time working with the artists of the South Side Community Art Center and stayed with her friend from the University of Iowa, Margaret Burroughs, and poet Rosalie Davis. It was at this time that Catlett and White met one another; the couple wed and relocated to Dillard University in New Orleans in 1941, where Catlett assumed the directorship of the art department and White served as an instructor (Burroughs 153; Fax, *Seventeen* 21; Samella Lewis 16, 159).

The couple soon found themselves relocating again when White received a prestigious Rosenwald Fellowship. Notably, White desired to begin his Rosenwald work with a study of mural techniques in Mexico. However, he was thwarted by complications with his local draft board in this regard and, as an alternative, opted to move to New York City (LeFalle-Collins 39). There, White used part of his Rosenwald money to enroll in courses on tempera and fresco techniques at the Art Students' League in preparation for an ambitious mural on the role of African Americans in their nation's history.[32] He also pursued a course in egg tempera mural painting with Harry Sternberg, a "great, great teacher" whom White credited in large part for the maturation of his own "ideological approach."[33] Much of Sternberg's art from the 1930s and 1940s is expressly political, as in his contribution to the NAACP's 1935 *An Art Commentary on Lynching* exhibit, a chilling lithograph titled *Southern Holiday*. As scholars Marlene Park and Margaret Rose Vendryes have observed, this work depicts a castrated black lynching victim at the forefront of a landscape of phallic forms—pillars, smokestacks, and a church steeple; in a telling detail, Sternberg renders the facade of the pillars—emblematic of civilization—in a state of decay. Sternberg himself later recalled, "I was filled with anger and shame as I worked on this stone and evidently transmitted these emotions through the finished print" (Park 347). White, no doubt, identified closely with Sternberg's sense of personal, emotive engagement with his work.

While White's early murals indicate that he had, in fact, already established a relatively well-defined "ideological approach" to his art prior to his work with Sternberg, one might imagine that White took from this mentor not only technical skills but also an affirmation of the type of politicized cultural work that an artist could call upon his or her craft to perform. White often rendered his figures in emphatically proletarian terms that recall the muscular, worker-heroes of Sternberg's murals and graphics, and he also shared this mentor's concern with issues of social justice that impacted the lives of America's poor and working-class citizens. Further, much as Sternberg lent his talents to the illustration of radical pamphlets such as *They Still Carry On! Native Fascists: How to Spot Them and Stop Them* (Landau 112), White fashioned numerous illustrations and other works of graphic art specifically for leftist pamphlets, journals, and newspapers during the late 1940s and early 1950s—including *New Masses* and its even more emphatically Marxist-oriented successor *Masses and Mainstream*, both of which White served as a regular contributing editor.

Still a mere twenty-four years old, Charles White next traveled with Catlett from New York City to Hampton Institute to execute his Rosenwald Fellowship mural, an epic work titled *The Contribution of the Negro to Democracy in America*. White's choice of locales for this project was far from arbitrary and, I would argue, is extremely suggestive as to the pivotal role of historically black colleges and universities in enabling African American artists relatively autonomous institutional support for the continued exploration of politically engaged themes and aesthetics in the mural medium following the curtailment of government sponsorship for such cultural work by the early 1940s. Indeed, one might make a case that such venues provided artists like White a relative safe haven from the red baiting of the Dies Committee and—in later instances—the House Un-American Activities Committee (HUAC). If not completely beyond the periphery of vision of such anticommunist politicos, attacking works in such locales certainly would have offered them less of a coup than prominent targets such as the Federal Theatre Project, the "Hollywood Ten," or Paul Robeson. In any event, White specifically selected Hampton only after a tour of numerous black colleges and universities; he made his decision in no small part because Hampton's locale and institutional history promised White access to the southern roots of African American folk culture.[34] In addition to its long-standing commitment to higher education for African Americans, Hampton also possessed an exciting new art department under the direction of Austrian political refugee Viktor Lowenfeld, who had fled the incursion of Nazi forces in 1939. Originally hired for his expertise in psychology, Lowenfeld found little support from the Hampton administration for his initial proposal to offer courses in art. However, Lowenfeld's series of night classes drew such an enthusiastic student response that he was soon granted permission to develop an art major at the school. In his courses, Lowenfeld introduced students to the works of a range of artists: socially conscious European modernists like Käthe Kollwitz; American Regionalists like Thomas Hart Benton; social realists like Harry Sternberg and the early Ben Shahn; and the Mexican muralists Orozco, Rivera, and Siqueiros. Further, drawing on Hampton's rich collection of African art, Lowenfeld encouraged students to recognize the importance of this latter body of art to the aesthetics of European modernists and as an aspect of their own cultural heritage (Wardlaw, *Art* 26–28).

Particularly as a refugee who had lost several family members to the Holocaust, Lowenfeld seems to have been quite sympathetic toward the use of art as a form of social protest and African American uplift (Samella Lewis 17). John Biggers, one of the most talented students in Hampton's art program at the time of White and Catlett's residency, recalls Lowenfeld's stance toward the intersection of art and politics in this way: "He taught us that art was a way for all people to speak. There is no censorship in art. Discrimination, restrictions, almost anything could be overcome with art, with self-expression through art" (Biggers and Simms 7). Another way in which Lowenfeld was able to fire the enthusiasm of students and resident artists like White and Catlett was by bringing prominent visitors to Hampton such as Alain Locke, sculptor William Artis, and Atlanta

University's Hale Woodruff (Wardlaw, *Art* 29). Samella Lewis, also a Hampton student at the time, recalls that Lowenfeld even organized a conference on the Mexican muralists at Hampton during White's residency (LeFalle-Collins and Goldman 90–91). Likewise, White later recalled Lowenfeld in extremely laudatory terms and stated that he consulted with Lowenfeld in the preparatory stages of his work on the Rosenwald mural.[35]

While at Hampton, White came to conceive of the black South as embodying the organic roots of the cultural beliefs and lifeways of the vast majority of African Americans. This development in his thinking certainly resonated with the cultural nationalism of the CP's Black Belt thesis of the early 1930s, but it seems to have emerged organically from a sense of deeply felt personal connection. As a Chicago native, born of southern black migrants, White consciously sought out these roots as a way to better grasp the culture and history of the African American masses on the level of lived experience. And, to a large extent, White seems to have found what he was searching for in this respect:

> I also learned to understand and love my people as I had never before. In Chicago I had still tried to defend them against misrepresentation, by showing that we too had our philosophers, our artists, our explorers, our orators, our military heroes. We were just like the white figures told about in the books. . . . And now, in the South, I began to understand the beauty of my people's speech, their poetry, their folk lore, their dance and their music, as well as their staunchness, morality and courage. Here was the source of the Negro people's contribution to American culture, and of the far vaster contribution they could make to the world in the future. ("Path" 39–40)

In this same vein, White likened the new aims of his art in the early 1940s to what "the great Paul Robeson expresses in his singing in a marvelous way, so that he becomes the foremost bard of a whole people, symbolizing their common aspirations" ("Path" 40). Much as Robeson was able to adapt various African American "folk" music traditions—particularly spirituals and labor songs—to the conventionally "high art" milieu of the concert stage, so did White seek to transmute the folk heroes of black history and legend into an accessible brand of public fine art that would offer a representative statement about and for his people.

Executed in egg tempera directly on an expansive twelve-by-eighteen-foot section of wall, White's *The Contribution of the Negro to Democracy in America* resembles his earlier *Technique to Serve the Struggle* mural in its dense layering of compositional elements and dramatic use of gesture. Among the many figures and events depicted are Crispus Attucks falling before the guns of British soldiers; Peter Salem, a Revolutionary War hero of the Battle of Bunker Hill; Nat Turner, holding a torch aloft and pointing the way to freedom for three enchained black men; Denmark Vesey, armed and on horseback; an escaped slave named

Peter Still; Harriet Tubman, shown leading two fugitive slaves toward freedom through a doorway that symbolizes the Underground Railroad; members of the famed Fifty-fourth Massachusetts regiment of the Union Army; political leaders Frederick Douglass and Booker T. Washington; the scientist George Washington Carver at work in his laboratory; National Maritime Union leader Ferdinand Smith; contemporary cultural performers Marian Anderson, Paul Robeson, and Leadbelly; and, in the center of the mural, a self-portrait of the artist kneeling in front of a woman and child, with a blueprint unfurled before him (figure 2). Seeming to preside over this scene are a sword-bearing angel and the hands of a gigantic black male figure wrapped about a section of industrial machinery. In the lower left corner of the mural, notes art historian Lizzetta LeFalle-Collins, "White sets the context for resistance by inserting a white colonial . . . who is destroying a bill of the 1775 Provincial Congress that outlawed the sale and importation of slaves to the colonies," thus establishing the precedent for white America's perpetual deferral of democratic rights to people of African descent (39–40). For White, the tenor of black response to this legacy of disfranchisement from the promises of American democratic rhetoric seems best encapsulated by the flowing red banner held aloft by Peter Still in the upper right corner of the painting, which reads, "I will die before I submit to the yoke." Indeed, this inscription serves as an apt creed for the *Contribution* mural writ large.

This mural encompassed the full range of White's artistic and political concerns to that point in his still blossoming career: an admiration for the black heroes and heroines of American history; an advocacy of revolutionary social change through militant political activism; a concern with the contemporary black working class; and a celebration of African American folk culture (see also LeFalle-Collins 39). In effect, *Contribution* comprises an attempt by the artist to extend the theme of political struggle from his earlier *Technique to Serve the Struggle* mural to a fuller and more triumphant view of African American history. As such, the site of the *Contribution* mural at Hampton again seems significant, for here White could have presumed a primary audience familiar with a majority of the figures included in the painting. After all, instructors like Lowenfeld regularly referenced such historical figures as part of the Hampton curriculum. Even where particular figures proved unfamiliar, the mural stood—potentially at least—to play an educative role, as accompanying wall text could supply a concise tutorial of sorts to the interested viewer.

Precedents for a sweeping historical composition like White's *Contribution* abounded in the social realist murals of the 1930s and 1940s.[36] Like thematically similar mural projects by Mexican and fellow U.S. social realists, White's *Contribution* mural effectively works to collapse historical distance in such a way that nineteenth-century figures such as Nat Turner and Harriet Tubman can occupy

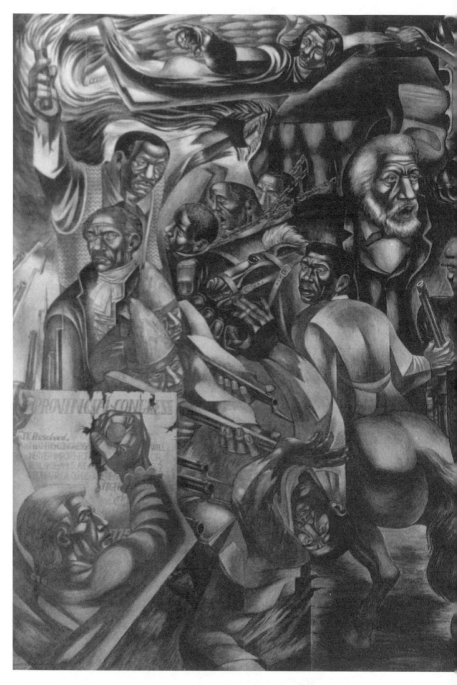

Figure 2. Charles White (1918–79), *The Contribution of the Negro to Democracy in America,* 1943. Tempera, 12 × 18 ft. (Hampton University Museum, Hampton, Virginia.)

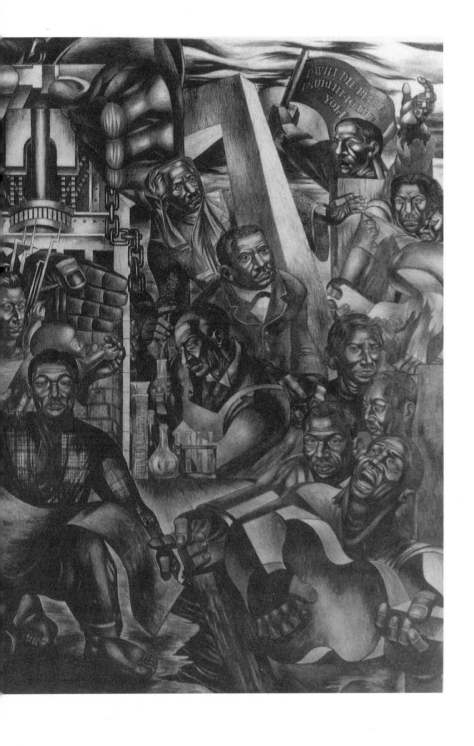

the same conceptual space as contemporary cultural workers like Paul Robeson and Marian Anderson. Even earlier, White stressed the intended function of these kinds of correspondences in a 1940 interview, referring to his sense of "a definite tie-up between all that has happened to the Negro in the past and the whole thinking and acting of the Negro now" (Motley, "Negro Art" 22). In this regard, White's use of history certainly resonates with government administrator Thomas Parker's account of the type of cultural work attempted by the Federal Art Project during the 1930s and early 1940s: "Our worthiness to appreciate the past may be judged, not by scholarship or reverie, but by our ability to use this heritage to develop a significant contemporary movement" (Park and Markowitz 13).

Yet, unlike the government-sponsored murals of the depression decade, the "significant contemporary movement" that White hoped to inspire through an African American history mural like *Contribution* also was articulated against the immediate backdrop of the Second World War. Consequently, early 1940s audiences scarcely could have looked upon White's portrayal of the Massachusetts Fifty-fourth regiment without it in some measure evoking the participation of African American soldiers in the contemporary global military campaign for democracy against the forces of fascism. In addition to expanding the scope of African American contributions to the quest for democracy to a global stage, such implied parallels also served to sustain (or recuperate) the Popular Front's insistence on rooting out agents of fascism on the American home front as well as abroad. As White well knew, the equation of American racism with Nazism was absolutely ubiquitous within the Popular Front speeches, editorials, political cartoons, and music during the late 1930s. (Indeed, figures such as Paul Robeson and Leadbelly, men White features prominently in this mural, played an important role in articulating such Popular Front ideals; and even Marian Anderson, who also appears in the mural, had done some measure of such cultural work in the form of fund-raising benefit performances.) It is in this context, as well, that the white colonial figure mutilating the 1775 Provincial Congress bill that had promised an end to the slave trade would have carried such a powerful resonance among 1940s viewers—it is as if to ask, in effect, whether the heirs of Crispus Attucks and the Massachusetts Fifty-fourth currently laying down their lives in the European and Pacific theaters of the Second World War would see the promises of postwar racial equality and full citizenship redeemed or similarly betrayed. In this manner, White's mural would seem to join the activism of a Paul Robeson in seeking to extend the Popular Front–era demand for antifascist self-scrutiny on the American home front into the World War II era and, if necessary, beyond.

Moreover, if many figures on the left had "closed ranks" with the mainstream of U.S. liberalism following the onset of World War II, White's historical allegory clearly champions *militant* political activism as a means of bringing about radical democratic social change within the United States. White brings home this point most emphatically through his choice of heroes and mode of representation. As LeFalle-Collins notes, although White here portrays educators and scientists as important contributors to the legacy of African American struggles for social justice, "[his] most dramatic portrayals depict individuals who participated in militant armed resistance": that is, Attucks, Salem, Vesey, Turner, Still, and the Massachusetts Fifty-fourth regiment (39). Significantly, these are all African American historical subjects who undertook the considerable risk of a violent death in an effort to defend or attain the personal liberty of themselves *and* their fellow Americans.[37] In White's rendering, Vesey and the soldiers of the Fifty-fourth Massachusetts regiment even visibly take up arms toward this end.

Stylistically, too, it is worth noting that White's rendering of solidly built and assertively gesturing militant activists like Vesey, Nat Turner, and Harriet Tubman seems apropos of a theme pertaining to revolutionary self-liberation. Indeed, this aesthetic parallel with specifically proletarian modes of social realism—including the art of contemporaries such as Mitchell Siporin and Hugo Gellert—suggests a third major theme of the *Contribution* mural: White's concern for the fate of the black working classes of his own era. Emblematic of the centrality of working-class identity to White's vision in this mural is the large machine structure that looms in the top center of the composition within the hands of a towering African American figure, an image almost certainly indebted to Rivera's detailed rendering of industrial technology in his *Detroit Industry* murals of the early 1930s.[38] LeFalle-Collins speculates that this image is "a reflection of [White's] fear that the industrial machine would crush the hopes of African American laborers unless blue-color [sic] workers were protected by trade unions" (40). Indeed, the chains that bind the slaves addressed by Nat Turner extend from one of the giant hands in the top center of the painting, suggesting a historical link between pre–Civil War enslavement and twentieth-century forms of wage slavery. However, as if to counterbalance this pessimism regarding the ability of the African American industrial working class to function as an agent of its own liberation, White presents a self-portrait in the front and center of the mural. This latter tableau depicts White as an artist-worker who holds a blueprint in his hands—presumably, as in depression-era murals such as Orozco's *Allegory of Science, Labor, and Art* or Seymour Fogel's *The Wealth of the Nation*, the blueprint for a better, more just society.[39]

Significantly, like Paul Robeson and other Popular Front mainstays, White sought to connect himself with the pressing concerns of America's poor and working-class masses not only by supporting the cause of organized labor but also through an immersion in folk cultural traditions. Hence, White accords African

American folk culture a degree of militancy in this mural that stands in decided contrast to the romanticized treatments of such material by many of his contemporaries in art, literature, drama, and the academy. For instance, whereas collectors and adapters of African American folklore from the 1920s and 1930s like Roark Bradford, Howard Odum, and even Zora Neale Hurston all sought to highlight the artfulness of vernacular expression, White seems to have been primarily interested in the more explicitly political aspects of such traditions. Consequently, where folklore enthusiasts like Bradford (i.e., *Rainbow Round My Shoulder*) and Odum (i.e., *John Henry*) flirt with the exoticized shadings of minstrelsy by crafting literary representations of black vernacular performers as relatively untutored naïfs, organically rooted in a cultural milieu that is decidedly "other," White's Leadbelly seems a performer of unmistakable gravity. As White was aware from visits to Café Society during his recent residence in New York City, Leadbelly often shared the concert stage with other openly political "folk" singers like Woody Guthrie, Pete Seeger, Josh White, Sonny Terry, and Brownie McGhee. Leadbelly's repertoire ranged from traditional blues and ballads to original compositions like "The Bourgeois Blues," which protested the pretensions of Washington, D.C.'s white and black middle classes with biting astuteness. Moreover, through his participation in the Popular Front Café Society scene, Leadbelly entered a cultural milieu that was interracial and "crossed class lines in the black community, bringing together working-class artists with little formal education like [Richard] Wright, [Billie] Holiday, and [Josh] White, with black intellectuals like Hughes, Robeson, and Waring Cuney" (Denning 359–60). Thus, in White's inclusion of Leadbelly—as well as performers like Robeson and Anderson, who adapted the spirituals to the concert stage with reverence and dignity (and often expressly to raise funds for leftist political causes)—his sympathies place him in much closer company with social realist poets like Margaret Walker and especially Sterling Brown than with a Bradford or Odum.[40]

Another way in which White expresses his concern regarding African American working-class issues is through his inclusion of Ferdinand Smith, a prominent officer in the National Maritime Union. By placing Smith in the *Contribution* mural, White suggests the importance of organized labor to the collective uplift of African American communities, particularly given that the CIO was steadily gaining ground in the battle to eliminate long-standing patterns of racial exclusion within the American labor movement. Notably, too, White positions Smith amidst *cultural* workers Marian Anderson, Paul Robeson, and Leadbelly, an arrangement that seems particularly appropriate given the highly visible involvement of each of these figures—including Smith—in the laborist culture of America's Popular Front at the time White composed the mural. In this way, White's compositional scheme speaks to the profound interpenetration of cultural and political activism that characterized the larger social realist movement of which White was a part. And much like Richard Wright's *Blueprint for Negro Writing*, it is the artist himself who holds the all-important blueprint in the center of the mural. That is, it is precisely the cultural worker (White himself in this case) who is able to synthesize such connections between a Leadbelly or Robeson and a Ferdinand Smith, *and* to substantiate the importance of such connections in American minds through his accessibly sited artistic work. In this sense, the blueprint seems to operate both as an indicator of White's own labor as a kind of social engineer and as a metaphor for the larger mural; that is, the *Contribution* mural itself comprises a kind of blueprint for contemporary heroic activism through its presentation of historical and contemporary exemplars.

Further, White's incorporation of figures such as the scientist George Washington Carver and even the relatively conservative Booker T. Washington among this honor roll of heroes bespeaks a broad-minded inclusiveness that scholars have long noted as a distinguishing feature of U.S. leftist culture during the Popular Front period of the late 1930s. Not least among the distinguishing features of White's mural, in this light, is that it provides a clear case in point of the extent to which African American cultural workers were at great pains to extend such expansive coalition building and interconnections between "cultural" and "political" activism beyond the official demise of the CPUSA's Popular Front policy. Indeed, White's peers carried this task forward into at least the 1950s— even in the mural medium, which scholars have long supposed went into a state of dormancy between the end of the depression and the onset of the mural revivals by Chicano and Black Arts Movement painters during the 1960s.[41]

Muralists as Revisionist Historians

Although Charles White's *The Contribution of the Negro to Democracy in America* does feature the slaying of Crispus Attucks, and although the chains shackling the necks of the three men addressed by Nat Turner serve as a powerful evocation of slavery, it seems striking that his mural does not center on direct portrayals of *contemporary* class struggle or racial conflict—that is, the motifs for which social realist art is arguably best known today. While White voiced expressly radical political sensibilities with respect to art and the broader socioeconomic sphere throughout the period under study, images of phenomena such as lynching and police brutality appear only in *Technique to Serve the Struggle* among White's mural projects. Moreover, a model that would attribute the differential strategies employed by White in his *Struggle* and *Contribution* murals to a matter of periodization (i.e., with the latter mural falling after the supposed heyday of social realism) proves inadequate in light of an examination of the facts of White's career.

Not least, one should note that the exigencies of White's everyday experience as a radical African American man were not appreciably abated by the onset of World War II and the concurrent economic revitalization that so many scholars have long pointed to as principal factors in the unraveling of social realism. Thus, if White's travels in the South as he planned and executed his *Contribution* mural enabled him "to understand and love [his] people as [he] had never before," it is also true that White's experiences in Hampton and New Orleans brought him into contact with the open brutality of southern racism. For example, a group of whites in New Orleans beat him severely for entering a segregated restaurant, and a white streetcar operator in Virginia once pulled a gun on White while ordering him to the rear of the car (Horowitz 16).[42]

So too, it was in the late 1940s and early 1950s that White stepped up his involvement with radical little magazines such as *Masses and Mainstream*, and in the fall of 1951 that he made an affirming sojourn to the Soviet Union. Most telling of all, White's forays in graphic arts media maintained a consistently radical *and contemporary* focus into the early 1950s. By contrast, where White and his peers overtly referenced race and class oppression in their murals, they typically approached such subjects through the vehicle of historical allegory. Where contemporary figures do appear it is often—as in White's *Contribution* mural— within a cadre of heroic figures drawn from the annals of U.S. history. Thus, within the scope of White's overall work as a mural painter during the first two decades of his artistic career, the explicit present-day setting of one half of his *Technique to Serve the Struggle* mural emerges as something of an exception to the prevailing pattern.

As scholars of depression-era murals—including Karal Ann Marling, Barbara Melosh, and Richard McKinzie, among others—have discussed at length, this trend had much to do with pragmatic concerns particular to the mural medium. On the one hand, the monumental scale and public settings of government-sponsored murals of the depression era offered a compelling match with socially minded artists' desire to reach a broader poor and working-class audience in the communal spaces of everyday life. However, this very same confluence of high public visibility and government sponsorship meant that muralists tended to face considerably greater scrutiny—often at both a local and federal level— than did artists working in, say, the easel division of the Federal Art Project. As Charles Alston, an African American muralist with the New York City branch of the FAP, described the matter, "With the Painting projects, there were no holds barred. . . . There wasn't that same freedom in the Mural projects. There were these stop signs and 'you can't do this and you can't do that,' which still exists."[43] The sensitivity on the part of government administrators regarding the content of New Deal murals owed specifically to ongoing campaigns by political conservatives to discredit Roosevelt's WPA programs as sites of boondoggling and subversive political activity. Particularly in this respect, officials in charge of New Deal art programs often felt that they could ill afford much controversy regarding a highly visible medium such as the public mural. It seems telling, for instance, that one of the most intense of the controversies pertaining to government-sponsored murals involved a case where artists working at the Coit Tower site in San Francisco included *contemporary* scenes that depicted workers reading radical literature in a public library and perusing the *Daily Worker, New Masses*, and other CP-affiliated publications from the racks of a street corner newsstand (McKinzie 24–26; Contreras 44–46; Marling 45–49).

Not that dressing one's social commentary in the trappings of historical allegory guaranteed an artist immunity from attempted censorship and suppression, of course—as was revealed by another of the era's most publicized public art controversies, Charles Alston's *Magic and Medicine* murals for the Harlem Hospital. In fact, the simple presence of Alston as a supervisor of a government-sponsored mural project transpired only following the organized protests of groups like the Harlem Artists' Guild regarding the lack of African American representation in such positions.[44] For the project at the Harlem Hospital in 1935–36, Alston directed as many as thirty fellow artists in executing a set of murals with varying styles and themes suited for their respective settings. Among these artists were Beauford Delaney, Georgette Seabrooke, and Vertis Hayes, the latter of whom assumed charge of a mural titled *Growth of Medicine* that depicted a painter and sculptor at work alongside a dignified black hospital staff of surgeons, a nurse, and an administrative professional.[45] Still, for all of this considerable supporting talent, the centerpiece of the Harlem Hospital project clearly was Alston's own *Magic and Medicine,* which consisted of two seventeen-by-six-foot oil on canvas panels.

Even before being installed in the Harlem Hospital, these paintings generated considerable excitement in New York's African American art community when they became the first murals by a black artist to be exhibited at the Museum of Modern Art (Coker 22).[46] Yet, after Alston's designs for the *Magic and Medicine* murals were approved by the Municipal Art Commission and the Federal Art Project administration, white Hospital Superintendent Lawrence Dermondy abruptly rejected Alston's work (and the work of three other African American muralists) on the grounds of what he deemed their excessive black subject matter (Park and Markowitz 51–52). As Alston recalls this dispute, "In the Modern panel, I had a complete integration—racial integration—perhaps with some emphasis on the brown and black people because that was the character of the community. The Superintendent objected to this and said that his wasn't a Negro Hospital—that he wasn't going to have that kind of thing in his hospital, you know."[47] Dermondy's objections proved all the more galling given the fact that "his" hospital was, as an *Art Front* editorial pointed out, "located in the heart of the largest Negro community in the world" ("Harlem Hospital" 3). Nor was Dermondy's case bolstered when he endorsed works by four less-talented white muralists that contained white subject matter. Quite appropriately, then, a statement that Alston drafted on behalf of the Harlem Artists' Guild in protest of the attempted censorship of his mural explained, "Such an action on the part of Mr. Dunwoody and the Department of Hospitals, if allowed to go unchallenged will set a dangerous precedent as far as art production of Negro painters is concerned, and add another pillar to the ever growing structure of discrimination being raised in the Department of Hospitals."[48]

Alston and the Harlem Artists' Guild were joined in their protest campaign—which eventually proved successful—by the major interracial artist organizations of the day.[49] In addition to support from the Artists' Union, a statement of protest against the blatant discrimination involved in the attempted censorship of Alston's *Magic and Medicine* was among the resolutions passed by the League of American Artists in 1936 as a precursor to the first American Artists' Congress ("League" 13). Likewise, the aforementioned editorial in *Art Front* regarding the Harlem Hospital mural controversy emphasized that the "fight for these special demands for the Negro artists must be placed in the forefront of general struggle for higher wages, permanent W.P.A. Projects and freedom of expression" ("Harlem Hospital" 3).

As to the murals themselves, the first of Alston's panels offers his conception of the medicinal traditions of Africa in a work alternately titled *Magic in Medicine* and *Primitive Medicine*. Dominating the upper portion of this mural is a larger than life-sized work of African sculpture—specifically, a Fang reliquary figure—surrounded by four dancers garbed in animal skins and woven cloth performing a ceremonial dance. A row of masked figures, two gazelles, and a semimountainous landscape lie beyond this tableau. Significantly, this mural also portrays both rural and urban African American homeopathic practices derivative of African healing traditions. Before a wooden house and lush vegetation in the lower left of the painting, men employ prayer, an herbal mixture, and drumming in an attempt to heal an ailing community member. In the lower right corner of the mural, Alston depicts a scene of urban folk cultural practice, as signified by a backdrop of tall city buildings. Here, a spiritualist figure in robes and a turban speaks to a small group of seated figures, drawing on the resources of a crystal ball and several books stacked on a nearby table.

In the second panel of his diptych, Alston presents *Modern Medicine* as principally white and Western in origin, but interracial in its contemporary practice. In the center of this panel is a large microscope, which serves as a compositional and conceptual counterpoint to the Fang reliquary figure in Alston's representation of classical African culture (figure 3). Likewise, as a parallel to the African

Figure 3. Charles Alston (1907–77), *Modern Medicine,* 1936. Oil on canvas, 17 × 6 ft. (Federal Art Project.)

imagery of his first panel, Alston fills the upper register of the second panel with images suggestive of the Western historical roots of modern medicine: an acropolis of classical Greek design; a smugly rendered statue of Hippocrates; and the portraits of four noted white scientists. The untamed gazelles of the African scene here seem to have given way to the type of domesticated farm animals used to derive medical serums, while African drums lie symbolically broken in the upper right corner of the *Modern Medicine* panel. Turning to contemporary medical practice, such as that of the Harlem Hospital itself, Alston depicts African Americans engaged in research, nursing, surgery, and medical education alongside white peers. Included in this group of figures in the mural's lower foreground are images of Dr. Louis Wright, the hospital's supervising physician; Alston's future wife, Myra Logan; and a self-portrait (Coker 10–12).

On one level, Alston's *Magic and Medicine* thus traces an implicit arc of progress through which African Americans enter into the narrative of "modern" society, as connoted by the titles most often attributed to its two component murals, *Primitive Medicine* and *Modern Medicine*. Yet, lest one judge too harshly Alston's apparent willingness to relegate African societies to a premodern historical position, it bears emphasizing that this type of narrative imagery—that is, one that traces the historical trajectory of medicine as a path from mythological religious ritual to enlightened and rational scientific practice—comprised something of an established convention in government-sponsored hospital murals of the day. Take, for example, Queens General Hospital medical superintendent Dr. Marcus Kogel's concise description of William Palmer's mural series on the history of medicine: "Mr. Palmer has taken us a long way—from myth through the classical ages of the healing art, the ages of darkness, the Renaissance—to the threshold of the golden age of medicine. In the last mural, we see the triumph of rational medicine over faith—the victory of science over superstition" (Park and Markowitz 50–51). A similar premise underlies Walter Quirt's surrealist *The Growth of Medicine from Primitive Times*, a Federal Art Project mural executed for New York City's Bellevue Hospital (Contreras 190–92). Even an artist as sympathetic to the cultural traditions of ethnic minorities as Diego Rivera rendered a similar theme in his *Aztec Medicine and Modern Medicine* mural, painted for Mexico's Ministry of Social Security in 1929. In fact, given Alston's relatively intimate familiarity with Rivera and his work (recall that Alston had shared in conversations with Rivera as the latter completed his controversial *Man at the Crossroads* mural in New York City in 1933), it seems likely that he derived the general conception of his own *Magic and Medicine* mural from Rivera's Mexican frescoes.

Even more, at least two aspects of *Magic and Medicine* would seem to call into question whether one ought, in fact, to read Alston's paintings as a paradigm of unambiguous cultural progress. First, the dignity with which Alston depicts

Chapter Two

African civilization in the *Primitive Medicine* panel conveys an attitude of respect toward the culture being depicted, rather than an air of disdain or a merely exotic interest. For example, one does not find in Alston's paintings an image of a naked youth bound and hanging upside down, as in Rivera's *Aztec Medicine* mural. Rather, Alston's African ritual dancers exhibit grace and composure, while his homeopathic healers in the rural American tableau seem to evidence genuine compassion for their patient (and perhaps even some measure of efficacy—Alston's painting does not suggest otherwise in the same way as does Rivera's). Second, Alston's seemingly ironic rendering of the statue of Hippocrates suggests that the broken drums in the *Modern Medicine* panel may bespeak a loss of something of value, rather than merely providing an allegory for rationality's displacement of "primitive superstition" (see also LeFalle-Collins and Goldman 36). In short, if Alston's murals ultimately render Western "modern" medicine as an avenue of racial uplift, the artist nonetheless presents African American history as possessing a classical heritage of its own that is rooted in African as well as European cultural traditions.

In this regard, perhaps more so than any other mural of the 1930s, Alston's *Magic and Medicine* evidences a strong element of continuity with the Harlem Renaissance cultural mission epitomized by *The New Negro*, even as it also displays a social realist penchant for the imaging of interracial advancement through cooperative, productive labor. In particular, Alston's work reflected the influence of Howard University aesthetician and *New Negro* editor Alain Locke, whom Alston had known since his days as a student at Columbia University. For instance, the prominent Fang reliquary figure in the first of Alston's *Magic and Medicine* panels almost certainly owes in large part to his exposure to African art via Locke's personal collection, examples of which Alston helped to mount in an exhibition for the 135th Street Public Library in the early 1930s. Alston himself has commented on the significance of this experience: "This was the first time I'd seen any number of examples of African art. I was fascinated with them. And with Locke right there on the scene I probably asked a million questions about them and I had a chance to hold them and feel them."[50] I have suggested that Alston employs the Fang reliquary figure in *Magic and Medicine* as a way of signifying that ancient Africa possesses a classical cultural heritage equivalent to the Western heritage referenced in the classical form of the Acropolis and Greek statuary of the *Modern Medicine* panel. Certainly, this was very much in keeping with Locke's own enthusiastic regard for African sculpture as a form of classical high art. As Locke wrote in his influential essay "The Legacy of the Ancestral Arts" for *The New Negro*, "If even the present vogue of African art should pass . . . for the Negro artist they ought still to have the import and influence of classics in whatever art expression is consciously and representatively racial" (267).[51]

In an important sense, Alston's *Magic and Medicine* comprises an attempt by the artist to resolve his own interest in forging an art that is both "consciously and representatively racial" and consciously and representatively American. On the one hand, like Locke, Alston had grown somewhat suspicious by the mid-1930s of "folk stuff" of the sort found in selected Harlem Renaissance poetry as "the kind of writing about Negroes that appeals to a great segment of the white population."[52] Nevertheless—again, à la Locke—Alston remained interested in articulating a racially specific mode of art, at least at this relatively early stage in his career.[53] Herein lies a further significance of Alston's prominent use of African sculpture. Like Locke, Alston was well aware of the influence of traditional African art on the innovative modernist artists of his own day. Hence, by including the Fang reliquary figure in his mural, Alston implicitly confronts white viewers with their own cultural debt to Africa, even as the murals simultaneously acknowledge the debt of African American health care professionals to predominantly white scientific traditions. (Here, too, it seems telling that, whereas most European modernists proved willing to concentrate exclusively on the formal properties of an object like the Fang reliquary figure, Alston attempts to position this object within what he conceives of as its original cultural context.) Simultaneously, Alston also places dignified African American professionals as active and equal participants in all segments of his representative swath of modern medical endeavors. In so doing, Alston would seem to insist on the right of African Americans to claim a fully integrated position within all phases of American society without necessarily having to disavow themselves of the African aspects of their cultural heritage.

Alston did not undertake another mural project of note until a dozen years later. Between 1936 and 1948, of course, much had changed in the landscape of American art—not least with regard to mural paintings. The WPA mural programs were not only defunct by the late 1940s, but also certain of the government-sponsored murals—particularly those that embraced contemporary subjects, such as Anton Refregier's treatment of the 1934 San Francisco waterfront strike—were being discussed as targets of demolition by anticommunist politicians like California Congressman Richard Nixon (Hills, *Modern* 188–89). However, much as Charles White was able to turn to the Rosenwald Foundation and the auspices of Hampton Institute for his *Contribution* mural in the early 1940s, Alston and Hale Woodruff were able to renew their engagement with the mural medium near the end of the decade by availing themselves of a commission from the Golden State Mutual Life Insurance Company, one of the largest black-owned businesses of its day. Specifically, the Golden State Company enjoined Alston and Woodruff to execute a pair of murals dedicated to the theme of *The*

Negro in California History for the lobby of their new office building in Los Angeles. Following travel to California to see the state's landscape firsthand and to peruse research compiled by African American librarian Miriam Matthews, Alston and Woodruff completed their paintings in 1949 (Coker 12–13).

This is not to suggest, of course, that the Golden State Company discretely sought to sponsor "subversive" art. To the contrary, clippings from the time now gathered in the Archives of American Art's papers of Alston and Woodruff suggest that the company envisioned this project, first and foremost, as an opportunity to celebrate race pride. Nor, for their part, did Alston and Woodruff in this case set out to subtly encode their murals with icons of a proletarian revolution in the manner of Diego Rivera's self-styled "guerilla aesthetics." However, both artists' Golden State murals do use historical allegory in ways clearly intended to address the prevailing racial ideologies of their own era *and* to celebrate the often obscured historical contributions of African American labor in forging the infrastructure of the contemporary American nation.

For his mural, Alston selected the theme *Exploration and Colonization*, treating the period between California's "discovery" by Spanish explorers in 1527 and the mid–nineteenth century. In the manner of many Mexican and U.S. murals of the preceding decade, Alston compresses a number of specific historical personages and events within a single epic landscape (figure 4). Among the distinct elements of the composition are Estevanico, a black guide who accompanied de Vaca, the man credited as the first European to cross the North American continent; an unnamed "Negro priest" who accompanied Coronado's famed expedition of the mid–sixteenth century; Father Serra at the grave of Ignacio Ramirez, a slave who purchased his freedom and later received the first Christian burial in the state; the founding of Los Angeles in 1781 by settlers possessing a motley mixture of Spanish, mestizo, black, mulatto, and Indian heritage; Peter Ranne, a black member of the 1820s expedition of Jedediah Smith, the man credited as the first "American" to enter California by an overland route; William Leidesdorff, a wealthy San Francisco merchant and a U.S. vice consul to Mexico in the first half of the nineteenth century; John Grider, who helped to fashion California's bear flag in 1846; James Beckwourth, a scout, trapper, trader, and U.S. Army veteran who in 1850 discovered Beckwourth Pass, a route by which he guided many early immigrant wagon trains through the Sierra Mountains into California; and Biddy Mason, a woman who came to California as a slave in 1851, but died one of the state's wealthiest women and most noted philanthropists. Even more than a painting such as Charles White's *Contribution of the Negro to Democracy in America*, this is clearly a mural that places demands on its audience. For while the general narrative theme of African American participation in the history of California's settlement is readily apparent, only a state-history buff would likely

Figure 4. Charles Alston (1907–77), *The Negro in California History: Exploration and Colonization,* 1949. Oil on canvas, 9¼ × 16½ ft. (Golden State Mutual Life Insurance Company.)

be able to identify the mural's specific figures. This is, then, a mural that consciously draws in the prospective viewer with bold color and panoramic narrative, inviting the curious to learn more about the historical actors thus depicted. The Golden State Company aided the latter objective by distributing flyers that identified the mural's key personages and the nature of their respective historical contributions.

For the counterpart to Alston's *Exploration and Colonization* mural, Woodruff chose the theme of *Settlement and Development,* picking up with the end of Alston's mural circa 1856 and extending to 1949. Compositionally and stylistically similar to Alston's work, the montage of elements in Woodruff's mural includes an anonymous black miner, receiving a paper that signifies he has purchased his freedom through his work as a prospector (as did several African Americans during the heyday of the California Gold Rush); black cavalrymen guarding Chinese laborers as they build the transcontinental railroad; the 1856 Convention of Colored Citizens of California, which fought to repeal segregation laws and other racist legislation; Mammy Pleasant, a champion of civil rights who helped to supply John Brown with the rifles used in the historic raid on Harper's Ferry; a scene depicting the interior offices of the *Elevator,* an early black-owned and edited newspaper first published by Philip Bell in 1865; an African American "Pony Express" mail carrier; William Shorey, a prominent sea captain and whaler of the late nineteenth century; anonymous black laborers at work on San Francisco's Golden Gate Bridge and the Boulder Dam; and, at the far right of the mural, the construction of the Golden State Mutual Life Insurance Company building itself (figure 5).[54]

In their attention to regional detail and apparent optimism regarding the forward march of history, Alston and Woodruff's murals seem remarkably kindred to many of the local history murals executed under Treasury Section sponsorship during the 1930s. As Karal Ann Marling astutely explains the efficacy of the latter set of murals, they "constitute 'An Article of Faith' in the future of the community. They are psychic bridges, anchored at one end in the local past and vaulting over the present into tomorrow; historical continuity invokes and guarantees a future of dreams come true for those who believe in work and home and neighborly cooperation" (21–22). In a similar vein, Alston and Woodruff intended the historical personages and events depicted in their Golden State murals to stand not only as a source of historical pride for African Americans but also as emblematic of virtues and accomplishments relevant to the contemporary black community. In this regard, there seems at least a general way in which their California history murals share with a work like Thomas Hart Benton's aforementioned *Politics and Agriculture* a certain faith in the rewards of yeoman-like labor and self-reliance. The distinction, of course, is that Alston and Woodruff's choice of subjects suggests that self-reliance—especially for African Americans—has historically necessitated militant political struggles for freedom and civil liberty.

Even more, while the parallels between these California history murals and certain Regionalist works extend to something more than a superficial level, Alston and Woodruff's depiction of black rather than white figures in heroic roles comprises more than a mere surface distinction. Particularly striking in this regard is Alston's rendering of James Beckwourth, who stands majestically in the upper center of the *Exploration and Colonization* mural with raised rifle and conventional frontiersman paraphernalia, complete with coonskin cap. In effect, Alston here positions a historically authentic African American figure within iconographic trappings more often associated with exemplars of white conquest over the American landscape, like Davy Crockett or Daniel Boone. In this vein, Alston's notes for the mural quote researcher Miriam Matthews as stating, "Beckwourth was hardly surpassed in dexterity and skill as a frontiersman by Jim Bridger, Kit Carson, Fitzpatrick, Jedediah Smith, or any others of that masterful band." By illustrating Matthews's conclusions in paint, Alston works to bring African Americans collectively from the marginal position they typically had occupied in white America's mass culture and popular consciousness to the center of a more broadly reconfigured American historical narrative. So too, by including individuals like Estevanico and the anonymous priest who accompanied de Coronado, Alston effectively demonstrates that peoples of African descent have been a part of California's history for every bit as long as people of European ancestry. In fact, Alston's visual narrative points out that black participation in the history of the present-day California region predates any substantial Anglo presence.

As with Alston's use of American frontiersman iconography in his rendering of James Beckwourth, Woodruff's *Settlement and Development* mural presents African American historical figures in the accouterments of several of America's most deeply rooted stock heroes: the vigilant and courageous soldier; the majestic sea captain; the Pony Express rider in cowboy apparel; and the masculine proletarian laborer. Here, one must bear in mind that in 1949 it still constituted something of a radical act to place African American subjects in these types of heroic roles. This was, after all, an era in which white men played valiant movie cowboys, while black actors found themselves relegated almost invariably to subservient, if not comic, roles in the realm of U.S. popular culture. In artist John Wilson's estimation, the stark reality at midcentury was that, "To dare to break out of the stereotyped role assigned to you and assert yourself a fully equal human being meant to risk your life."[55] Hence, for contemporaneous viewers of various races, one imagines that Alston and Woodruff's heroic figures must have proved striking indeed.

Figure 5. Hale Aspacio Woodruff (1900–1980), *The Negro in California History: Settlement and Development,* 1949. Oil on canvas, 9¼ × 16½ ft. (Golden State Mutual Life Insurance Company.)

Even Woodruff's depiction of the proletarian heroes who work on the construction of the Golden Gate Bridge and the Boulder Dam in the upper right quadrant of the *Settlement and Development* mural comprises a significant act of historical reclamation. Woodruff's image of African American laborers at work on two of the American West's most lionized triumphs of civil engineering certainly is a celebration of working-class contributions to American culture, very much in keeping with a proletarian brand of social realism. Yet, it is more than this. It constitutes an assertion of a specifically African American presence at the heart of U.S. labor history. To apply proletarian iconography to these particular instances of African American labor was to validate the interracialism of the CIO and the broader progressive labor movement of the day *and* to suggest something of the larger scope of black labor's essential role in building America's infrastructure writ large.

In another key act of historical revision, Woodruff's rendering of Bell's militant *Elevator,* Mammy Pleasant, the Convention of Colored Citizens, and the miner receiving his writ of emancipation provides a striking array of evidence regarding the role that African Americans played in effecting their own liberation from slavery and postbellum forms of oppression. With the work of patent racists like Ulrich Phillips still holding considerable sway with many U.S. historians at midcentury, to paint African American subjects engaged in militant self-defense constituted a statement every bit as radical as the work that revisionist historians like Du Bois, C. L. R. James, and Herbert Aptheker were performing during the social realist era with studies such as *Black Reconstruction* (1935), *The Black Jacobins* (1938), and *American Negro Slave Revolts* (1943), respectively. This fact becomes particularly apparent when one pairs Woodruff's mural with a work like John Steuart Curry's 1942 mural *The Freeing of the Slaves.* In Curry's painting, a group of African Americans gives thanks to God and an advancing Union Army for an emancipation in which—if one were to judge solely from this image—they apparently had no agency. By contrast, both Alston and Woodruff clearly take special care to render their African American subjects with determined expressions and postures that stand in decided contrast to the racist caricatures of docile and affable blacks that still permeated America's visual culture during the 1940s. One need only contrast Woodruff's militant Mammy Pleasant with a mammy figure from popular culture, like the Hattie McDaniel characters in films such as *Judge Priest* (1934) and *Gone with the Wind* (1939), or with the kneeling mammy figure in the center of Curry's painting to drive home this point.[56] So too, work by African American social realists like Alston and Woodruff dramatically recast the iconography of "kneeling slaves" that art historian Kirk Savage has found to be so pervasive in nineteenth-century American sculptural monuments (70–84). Even in the case of the few kneeling black figures in Woodruff's *Settlement and*

Development, one finds a couple bending to plant a sign in protest of the racial segregation of schools and another man stooping to pick up a gun for the impending raid on Harper's Ferry. Like the history texts of Du Bois, James, and Aptheker, such mural imagery seeks to serve as both historical testament *and* an allegorical injunction to viewers regarding the need for militancy in campaigns for social justice in the contemporary moment.

None of these historically revisionist objectives was entirely new for Woodruff. By the time he completed his *Settlement and Development* mural for the Golden State Mutual Life Insurance Company, Woodruff already had several historically themed murals under his belt. Woodruff's first murals were organized around a more thematic—as opposed to historically specific—basis. As part of his work on the federal government's Public Works of Art Project in 1933 and 1934, Woodruff and his student Wilmer Jennings completed a mural project titled *The Negro in American Life* for David T. Howard Junior High School in Atlanta (Stoelting 67). This four-mural series consisted of a rather placid image titled *Agriculture and Rural Life,* as well as three murals depicting young African Americans at work in the cultural fields of *Art, Music,* and *Literature,* respectively. Frustrated by what he perceived as the aesthetic inadequacies of this initial foray into the mural medium, Woodruff secured a Columbia University fellowship to study fresco painting in Mexico during the summer of 1936. As Woodruff later recalled this experience, "My going to Mexico was really inspired by an effort to get into the mural painting swing. I wanted to paint great significant murals in fresco and I went down there to work with Rivera to learn his technique" (Murray 81).[57] Indeed, Rivera was an ideal mentor for Woodruff, given that the two artists shared not only a political concern for producing art related to issues of social justice but also an interest in aesthetic modes as seemingly diverse as social realism and cubism (McDaniel 5). Significantly, while in Mexico, Woodruff was able to see firsthand several of the important murals by Rivera, Orozco, and Siqueiros sited within various public buildings (LeFalle-Collins and Goldman 33).

Woodruff's study with Rivera soon bore rather remarkable fruit. Building on his apprenticeship with the Mexican master painter and his earlier, unsatisfying mural experience as part of the PWAP, Woodruff completed what remains his most well-known mural project in 1939: the *Amistad* murals for Talladega College's Savery Library.[58] The project, a further example of the crucial patronage of historically black colleges, emerged from something of a collective enterprise. The original conception for this mural project came from Talladega's President Buell Gallagher, who selected the *Amistad* theme as a way of paying tribute to the antislavery struggles of both black and white abolitionists—particularly the American Missionary Association, a group that had provided legal and financial support for the *Amistad*'s African rebels and, not coincidentally, also had founded Talladega College (McDaniel 6). The theme and black college setting of this project meshed nicely with Woodruff's own ideals regarding the historically instructive potential of the mural medium: "Most murals deal with subject matter which is generally known to the public that sees it. . . . It is chiefly narrative. . . . It can be inspirational. A mural is a teaching."[59] Desiring "to paint great significant murals" along the lines of Rivera, Woodruff greeted the epic theme of the *Amistad* incident with enthusiasm from the moment of the project's inception. Here, it seemed to Woodruff, was a project that would afford him the opportunity to present historically documented heroes of the past as allegorical models for contemporary revolutionary values in the manner of his Mexican mentor.

Woodruff began this project by throwing himself like an autodidactic historian into research of the *Amistad* case at the Yale University archives and the New Haven Historical Society (Stoelting 229–30). Secure in his background knowledge of the facts, and having possession of dozens of ambrotypes and etchings from the time of the incident, Woodruff then set about to paint this story in three large oil on canvas panels with the assistance of students like Robert Neal. The first panel, *The Mutiny aboard the Amistad, 1839*, depicts the revolt of the *Amistad*'s slaves against the ship's crew. Most prominently, four pairs of muscular male combatants from these contending factions grapple in life and death struggle for control of the vessel. Woodruff's second panel, *The Amistad Slaves on Trial in New Haven, Connecticut, 1840*, again follows the stylistic lead of Rivera in its complex layering of bodies as Cinque, the leader of the African mutineers, stands to face an accuser from among the surviving crew members in court. Especially given this work's compositional density, it seems all the more remarkable that Woodruff rendered the overwhelming majority of these figures from actual portraits dating to the time of the trial (Stoelting 232). In the final panel, the *Amistad* fugitives "return," free, to Sierra Leone in 1842 with the help of sponsors from the American Missionary Association. The act of books being lifted from a trunk by one of Cinque's compatriots suggests the importance of literacy to the group's newfound empowerment.

As with the historical murals of his mentor, Diego Rivera, and as in his own later collaboration with Alston on the *Negro in California History* project, Woodruff's *Amistad* murals collectively work to challenge received notions of North American history as a simple narrative of discovery and expansion in which peoples of color played a passive and largely marginal role. To the contrary, like Rivera, Woodruff shows this continent's history to involve contested, often violent, struggles for power—struggles in which racial identity often marked a point of distinction between oppressed and oppressor. Specifically, Woodruff's *Amistad* murals depict black heroes who aggressively resist the dehumanization of slavery with strength, intellect, and courage. As I have suggested with reference to Woodruff and Alston's California history murals, to portray *this* kind of black historical subject in the context of the racist caricatures that pervaded "mainstream" historical scholarship and popular culture of the day was to communicate a radical message regarding the dignity and historical rootedness of black freedom struggles. Moreover, this message echoed the insurgent spirit of African American struggles for civil and social equality in Woodruff's own day.

The collective response to the *Amistad* murals expressed in black publications suggests that this type of connection was hardly lost on contemporary viewers. For example, in describing Woodruff's murals in an April 1939 *Crisis* article, Talladega's President Gallagher glossed the *Amistad* incident as "the 'Scottsboro Case' of the past century," lamenting that, "A century ago, the alternative before the Negro was acquiescence or revolt. Despite much real progress in some areas, the situation has not greatly changed" (110). The works also stirred considerable excitement in one of Woodruff's Atlanta University colleagues, W. E. B. Du Bois. As Woodruff proudly recalled in a 1968 interview with Albert Murray, Du Bois was so enthusiastic about the *Amistad* murals that he solicited money especially for the purpose of reproducing the paintings in color in an early issue of *Phylon*, an important journal of literature and culture that Du Bois helped to found in 1940 (78).[60] Alain Locke also singled out Woodruff's *Amistad* murals for prominent display in his important 1940 volume *The Negro in Art.*

Less well known than the *Amistad* works are the three murals on the theme of Talladega College's founding that Woodruff painted to decorate the east side of the Savery Library lobby. In the first of these panels, *Underground Railroad,* Woodruff depicts three generations of African Americans as they receive assistance from the railroad's "conductors" in the form of shelter, a written pass, and transportation across the Ohio River to "free" territory. In keeping with historical accuracy, these heroic fugitives from slavery seem to travel with literally little more than the clothes on their backs. Extending the theme of racial uplift into the postemancipation era, the mural *Opening Day* presents the humble yet dignified opening of Talladega College in 1867. Finally, in *Building the Library,* Woodruff paints the construction of Savery Library itself by an interracial construction crew of muscular black and white laborers, as President Gallagher stands conferring with one of the workers over a set of blueprints.[61] In short, much as Woodruff's rendering of the *Amistad* saga evokes a larger history of militant black resistance to enslavement, he uses this second set of murals to document the collective struggle of African Americans and progressive-minded white allies for black education and institution building, as manifest in the particular example of Talladega College. While vastly understudied relative to their *Amistad* counterparts, these latter murals are significant in their own right—for they suggest that

Woodruff, like Gallagher, perceived *Amistad*-style militant rebellion and black institution building as two coequal and complementary dimensions of the broader struggle for African American liberation.

Even more so than in the case of his later California history mural, Woodruff's Talladega works draw on the work of Rivera as well as the murals of contemporary American Regionalists like Thomas Hart Benton—a point that it would be all too easy to lose sight of in light of the often disdainful rhetoric exchanged between social realist painters and the Regionalist camp (including conservative art critic Thomas Craven). For example, the productive activity engaged in by the brawny construction workers of Woodruff's *Building the Library* comprises a brand of yeoman-like skilled labor of the sort one also finds in many Regionalist murals, such as Benton's *Politics and Agriculture* and *City Building* (1930).[62] Likewise, in the *Amistad* murals Woodruff seems given to a highly dramatic—even theatrical—posing of his figures, as were Benton and many of the Regionalists who helped fashion the Treasury Section murals in post offices and other government buildings across the country. Further, the stagecoach and steamboat in the rear ground of the *Underground Railroad* image add a touch of midwestern frontier flavor that seems very much in keeping with a Regionalist aesthetic. Yet, if Woodruff borrowed from Regionalist peers like Benton, he clearly did so selectively. Whereas Benton's treatment of the black figure often lapsed into melodrama and even racist caricature, Woodruff carefully invested his African American protagonists with qualities of refinement and dignity, even in the midst of the dramatic mutiny scene of the first *Amistad* mural. Perhaps most significantly, while Benton's murals tend to express either a smug satire of human foibles or a certain satisfaction with the world as depicted, Woodruff's murals imply a need for further societal transformation along the lines of the historic struggles of his protagonists.

While Regionalist murals of the New Deal era tended to portray idyllic vistas of agrarian abundance in the face of depression-era dust bowl impoverishment, most African American artists joined the more socially critical of their peers in offering an unambiguous dismantling of American pastoralism. The work of John Biggers is especially significant in this regard. Taken collectively, Biggers's murals from the 1940s depict a rural landscape that is as likely to be characterized by social rupture, loss, and dislocation as by wealth and community harmony. Moreover, his work on this front includes two of the most striking mural projects to step outside of the mode of historical allegory and examine the contemporary scene. The first of these projects paired works titled *Harvest Song* and *Night of the Poor*, which were painted concurrently for the Pennsylvania State University Education Building in 1946. These two murals comprise a direct study in contrasts: in the former work, mothers and children sing to the accompaniment of a guitarist, while other figures engage in intimate conversation as they gather rich harvests of fruit and wheat; in the latter mural, figures in the background grapple in violent conflict amidst decaying brick and wood structures, while others stand emaciated by hunger with nothing but empty sacks to show for their labor.[63] Further, in *Night of the Poor* several figures cover their faces with their hands in shame and despair; a young man begs for alms; and a bald, malnourished child occupies a prominent space at the bottom center of the mural. Although the imagery of these murals was already clear in its own right, Biggers prepared substantial explanatory wall texts as a way of enhancing the didactic power of these contrasting images of deprivation and plenty. These texts merit quoting in full:

> In [*Harvest Song*], as contrasted to the opposite painting, it is shown how people of all lands have learned to cooperate and share in a spirit of creativeness. Their rich life is symbolized by fruit and harvest which have been the historical symbols of fertility and wealth. The singing is indicative of the well-being of people whose happiness has been founded on the education and care they received during childhood as depicted by the group of children of different origin and their teacher.
>
> In [*Night of the Poor*] the effect which lack of education has on people is depicted. It is shown by their inability to get along, their lack of cooperation and knowledge which results in "empty bags" as symbols of poverty, lack of knowledge and starvation. Through such contrasting experiences as seen in the two murals, the artist sought to emphasize that the ultimate goal of education is life. (Greene 99–100)

In this respect, Biggers's murals would seem to echo a theme of many government-sponsored murals of the 1930s: the ability to rehabilitate communities out of poverty through New Deal–style social engineering or specifically, as here, through education. What separates Biggers's murals from most works in the earlier corpus of New Deal murals is his willingness to depict the bitter conditions of poverty prevalent in areas where progressive social engineering remains far from a reality (see also Greene 99).

Biggers further explored the theme of black agrarian poverty in several works of graphic art and at least one other mural during the 1940s and early 1950s. In *Sharecropper Mural,* another work completed for the Pennsylvania State campus in 1946, Biggers offers an image of a tightly huddled black family standing before a humble wooden shack (figure 6). Although flanked by scenes of sympathetically rendered church rituals, which bespeak the spiritual strength of rural African American communities, the coarse dress, gnarled hands, and fatigued posturing of the central sharecropper family nonetheless make their material poverty and its attendant physical and psychic strain readily apparent. In addition, the background of the mural includes an array of densely packed and roughly constructed

Figure 6. John Biggers (b. 1924), *Sharecropper Mural,* 1946. Tempera, 4 × 8 ft. (Paul Robeson Cultural Center, Pennsylvania State University.)

shacks akin to the one directly behind the central family. Particularly in this mural, Biggers's work seems to have much more in common with contemporaneous photojournalism's focus on the deprivations faced by southern sharecroppers than with Regionalist painters' oft-noted romanticization of agrarian labor. Notably, Biggers presents a somber family in full frontal view before a rather dilapidated wooden home, with more children to care for than the family's income would seem to allow—an iconography and manner of framing that depression-era documentary photographers such as Russell Lee, Dorothea Lange, Marion Post Wolcott, and Carl Mydans had employed in various midwestern and southern locales.

Equally significant, as in many such works of documentary photography, Biggers does not explicitly illustrate the factors responsible for the sharecropping

Chapter Two

family's poverty and bitter frustration. Yet, given that Biggers could presume a certain familiarity among most of his viewers with the workings of the share-cropping system—a familiarity that owed in no small part to the work of the aforementioned documentary photographers—one might confidently interpret his *Sharecropper Mural* as an indictment of the way in which corrupt landowners kept sharecroppers in perpetual debt peonage regardless of whether or not the farmers made a good crop. Certainly writers such as Richard Wright, William At-taway, and Sterling Brown issued like-minded literary indictments of sharecrop-ping on precisely this count throughout the 1930s and 1940s. In addition, this expressly politicized interpretation seems to be supported by Biggers's return to this theme in his 1952–53 *Contribution of the Negro Woman to American Life and Education* mural for Houston's Blue Triangle branch of the YWCA, wherein he portrays a despair-ridden male sharecropper as the icon of an oppressive way of life being displaced through assertive campaigns for African American emancipation (figure 7).

Inspired in part by the suggestion of mentor Viktor Lowenfeld that he focus on the legacy of the prominent black heroines Harriet Tubman and Sojourner Truth, Biggers's expansive eight-by-twenty-four-foot commissioned mural for the Houston YWCA resembles the works of White, Alston, and Woodruff in its pronounced focus on the role played by African Americans themselves in the historic struggles for emancipation and racial uplift. As in his Pennsylvania State murals, Biggers here follows the aesthetic of Mexican social realist painters by employing a complex layering of figures as a way of heightening the dramatic tension of the composition (see also Greene 98). In the right half of the mural, the artist's Harriet Tubman guides a massive procession of formerly enslaved African Americans to freedom in an image that looks more reminiscent of a militant cadre of marching workers from the annals of depression-era proletarian art than it does a covert band stealing away via the Underground Railroad. Even more specifically, this segment of Biggers's mural seems to be patterned after the marching phalanx that follows Sojourner Truth in Charles White's *Five Great American Negroes* mural. Significantly, too, Biggers's Tubman bears not only the torch of freedom but also a large rifle, casting her, in Alvia Wardlaw's terms, as "a true flesh and blood 'Statue of Liberty'" ("Strength" 138). Likewise, several of the figures who follow her carry agricultural implements—pitchforks, rakes, and hoes—that, in this context, could easily serve as weapons. As Edmund Barry Gaither notes, a classical column symbolic of the antebellum social order crumbles in the center of the mural before the advance of Tubman's bold procession (85).

In contradistinction to most such proletarian processions from the depression era, however, this Biggers mural depicts revolutionary collective action with predominantly *female* participation and leadership. Tubman's armed procession contrasts dramatically with a mass of kneeling black male figures who face backward, as if in submission to the oppression of enslavement. Tubman, in fact, bears one of these men to his feet with her sturdy supporting right arm, cradling his seemingly semiconscious body between her breast and the rifle in her left hand. This gendered contrast is echoed by an older man in the bottom center of the mural, who is bent forward under the weight of a cotton sack; while Biggers renders this figure's labor with dignity, it seems telling that the man's left arm grasps the very same crumbling classical column that Tubman's procession seems determined to topple.[64] As Wardlaw observes, "The old man's face expresses a deep grief and despair over misspent strength and pain. To gain their freedom, blacks first had to put down the alien monuments of their own labor" ("Strength" 139).

Also symbolic of the dismal past out of which Tubman and the painting's equally heroic anonymous black women lead their people is a scene on the far right of the mural in which two women gather the body of a robed black male from a gallowslike structure—even as smaller children cling to the side of one of these women. In short, women in the right half of this mural play crucial roles as sustainers of black families in conditions of crisis *and* as leaders on the front lines of militant revolt.

Similarly, in the left half of the mural, serving as what Biggers termed "a pioneer teacher," Sojourner Truth addresses a gathering of freedmen, women, and children while standing on a set of railroad tracks in front of a church building; meanwhile, an old man pores over a book by lamplight and a young woman reads to her child from a book of poetry by Phillis Wheatley. On a symbolic level, Biggers uses this imagery to suggest the new opportunities for mobility (the railroad) and community stability (the church) that accompanied the African American quest for education in the postemancipation era (Biggers and Simms 62–63; Gaither 85). Moreover, Biggers acknowledges a complementary role for both the spoken and written word (represented by Truth and Wheatley, respectively) in this ongoing project. Taken as a whole, then, Biggers's painting offers a kind of blueprint for revolutionary social transformation that encompasses a role for both militant mass action and institution building, much as had Woodruff's work at Talladega and Alston and Woodruff's *Negro in California History* murals.

Again, the most striking way in which Biggers's YWCA mural revises the aesthetics predominant in American history murals of the 1930s and 1940s lies in his rejection of the masculinist presuppositions that characterized both Regionalism and proletarian brands of social realism. Indeed, even the most casual survey of this era's murals leaves one with a sense of American artists' nearly unremitting fascination with male workers as protagonists—a trend that seems to hold true across the spectrum of political ideology. Where women do appear in murals of the 1930s and 1940s, it is most often in the role of nurturer or helpmeet to male counterparts (Melosh 43–51, 57–62). By way of contrast, Biggers commented in the program for his YWCA mural's unveiling, "Masculine society has been inclined to place woman in a minority role; yet in the history of our country, no more heroic work has been done than that performed by woman. She has not only organized the family but has had to lead in struggles to build a society in which that family could grow. She has been the leader in public, rural, and informal education" (Biggers and Simms 63). Although perhaps Biggers had not entirely abandoned gendered notions of something like a nurturing female essence, his willingness to cast female protagonists in public roles of militant community leadership—as had Alston and Woodruff in their California history murals—in-

Figure 7. John Biggers (b. 1924), *The Contribution of the Negro Woman to American Life and Education,* 1952–53. Tempera, 8 × 24 ft. (Blue Triangle Multi-Cultural Association, Inc.)

dicates that these three artists envisioned a much broader spectrum of female life possibilities, past and present, than the vast majority of their male peers.

Interestingly, however, Biggers reported that the imagery of this mural proved so forthright that it disturbed many of the middle-class female patrons of the Houston YWCA (Biggers and Simms 62). It may be that viewers recognized and objected to Biggers's open appropriation of proletarian aesthetics in a cold war period that found the radical politics connoted by such imagery increasingly out of fashion. Or else, perhaps more likely, these YWCA patrons simply objected to the fact that the protagonists of Biggers's mural—both the famous Tubman and Truth, and their anonymous compatriots—possess very human scars and frailties. To be sure, these figures are not, in any conventional sense, "pretty." As an essay coauthored by Biggers retrospectively glosses the mural: "Black boys and men are dressed in faded blue overalls. Black girls and women wear gingham

       Chapter Two

and sackcloth. The people have gnarled, calloused, trembling hands. They have bruised feet and bodies and, obviously, bruised minds. But they also have strength, as evinced by the masses rising in number and marching toward freedom" (Biggers and Simms 62–63). In short, if Biggers's African American heroines and heroes possess beauty, it is not a beauty of sweetness and light, but rather a beauty of lives dedicated to a collective struggle for social justice and community uplift.

If certain of the YWCA patrons of Biggers's *Contribution of the Negro Woman to American Life and Education* mural were displeased with his work due to its self-consciously rugged aesthetic sensibility, they almost surely would have been dismayed with the artist's first mural, *Dying Soldier*. Completed in 1942, in the midst of what was only his second year of formal art instruction with Viktor Lowenfeld at Hampton Institute, the *Dying Soldier* mural offers an exceptionally graphic depiction of the violence of war. According to Biggers, this mural originated as part of his response to the news of the Japanese attack on Pearl Harbor on December 7, 1941. As art historian Jeanne Zeidler explains: "In recent lectures at Hampton, Biggers vividly recounted his feelings as he awoke in his dormitory room that Sunday morning and was greeted by the news. He was angry that he and his fellow students faced having their studies cut short by being drafted into the armed services, and that they faced possible death fighting for a country which discriminated against them because they were African Americans" (51). Although the mural is now lost, photographs and Biggers's preliminary sketches for this work allow for a substantial reconstruction of the mural's composition. In the lower third of the mural, Biggers depicts a scene from the front lines of World War I: while a phalanx of soldiers charges forward in the background, an African American army sergeant hangs on a fence of barbed wire, stranded and dying (figure 8). Here, Biggers renders the brutality of war in uncompromising detail: the sergeant's torn uniform reveals a body mutilated by barbed wire, and the fingertips of his right hand have been torn away, while a pile of bones, boots, helmets, and weapons at his feet evokes the larger scale of war casualties. As Alison de Lima Greene has noted, these aspects of Biggers's *Dying Soldier* mural are influenced by artists such as the famous radical German illustrator George Grosz and Mexican muralist José Clemente Orozco, both of whom Biggers had become familiar with through his studies at Hampton with Viktor Lowenfeld (Greene 96–98). Lowenfeld also may have exposed Biggers to the antiwar triptych *War* (1929–32) by the German artist Otto Dix, which contains bodies similarly ravaged by military combat.[65]

Biggers adds considerable compositional and rhetorical complexity to the central battle scene of *Dying Soldier* by painting a wide-ranging series of memories and visions in the upper register of the mural. According to Zeidler, Biggers has described these images as "what he might think about if he were dying" (51). Indeed, it is as if Biggers wants the viewer literally to see the soldier's life flash before his eyes. Toward this end, Biggers not only patterns his work after the social realist examples of Grosz, Orozco, and Dix but also draws on the aesthetics of surrealism and contemporary film. These latter two spheres of influence are not as wholly divergent as they might at first appear. After all, much as cinematic montage "emphasize[d] dynamic, often discontinuous, relationships between shots and the juxtaposition of images to create ideas not present in either one by itself" (Bordwell and Thompson 495), so too did surrealists tend to "rearrange the objects of the real world in order to produce startling, often disquieting conjunctions" (Haskell 327). As with these models, Biggers's juxtaposition of experientially discontinuous memories and visions in the upper register of his *Dying*

Chapter Two

Figure 8. John Biggers (b. 1924), *Dying Soldier,* 1942. Tempera. (Hampton University Museum, Hampton, Virginia.)

Soldier mural serves to divulge a larger meaning that would not be apparent from a presentation of any one of these memories or visions in freestanding isolation: namely, the underlying causes for the dying soldier's disillusionment with his country.

On the one hand, certain of these memories bespeak an earlier state of domestic bliss: the soldier's mother nursing him as an infant before a fireplace; the soldier and his girlfriend walking hand in hand; and young men engaged in sporting activities. Yet, the soldier's memories also include his mother on her knees scrubbing floors as a domestic worker and a black man (presumably either the soldier himself or the soldier's father) in overalls, pushing a broom as a city street sweeper. For Biggers, the black soldier's sacrificial death for his country offers no vision of dramatic change following the war in the restriction of black men and women's employment opportunities to these types of menial service-sector jobs. Clearly, then, one quality that distinguishes Biggers's mural from the work of most of his surrealist contemporaries is that his painting conveys a sense of "entrapment and isolation" (Haskell 323) that is *not only* psychological but also physical and social—indeed, political. In this respect, Biggers articulates the visual language of surrealist dreamscapes toward politically radical ends to a more pronounced degree than even left-leaning "social surrealist" contemporaries such as Peter Blume and O. Louis Guglielmi.

One of the specific ways that Biggers grounds his appropriation of surrealist fantasy in a concrete physical, political reality is by insistently and graphically situating the larger mural in a particular historical context. It is critical to the dramatic impact of Biggers's mural that these scenes flash through the mind of the soldier precisely at the moment that he lies dying on a foreign battlefield, fighting to protect a democracy that he and fellow African Americans do not yet enjoy on the American home front. Hence, an image of a black man nailed to a large crucifix seems to emerge at a diagonal angle directly from the soldier's head, echoing both the dying soldier's formal posture and his symbolic status as a martyr. Even more, a vision of a woman crying out in horror over a lynched black man, whose body hangs from a tree, lies on a diagonal plane that intersects that of the crucified black man. In this juxtaposition of motifs, Biggers followed in what was by then a relatively well-established social realist convention of imagery paralleling lynching victims to the crucified Christ. (Not coincidentally, this same type of black Christ imagery also pervaded the work of social realist graphic artists and poets during the period under study.) In all of these respects, the contemporary poignancy of Biggers's historical allegory seems considerably less veiled than in most of the murals considered in this chapter.[66] And it seems telling that Biggers reached back not to the nineteenth century in the manner of so many muralists of his day, but instead to the still painful sense of betrayal felt among many African Americans regarding the First World War and its aftermath. Driven by his palpable sense of outrage at the prospect of this not-so-distant historical scene replaying itself in his own life, the artist painted the gruesome and fantastic montage of *Dying Soldier* to operate simultaneously as a focal point for historical reflection and as a sobering act of radically disillusioned prophecy. As chance would have it, Biggers himself was later drafted into the segregated navy in 1943, where he became so demoralized that he eventually received an honorable discharge owing to his state of psychological distress in the winter of 1945 (Wardlaw, *Art* 32–33).

Although today it comprises a seldom-discussed part of Biggers's remarkable artistic career, the *Dying Soldier* mural received considerable exposure during the 1940s and was consistent with the social realist tenor of most of Biggers's early work in other media. Following the unveiling of the mural at Hampton, art instructor Viktor Lowenfeld included *Dying Soldier* in *Young Negro Art*, an exhibition of Hampton student works that opened at the Museum of Modern Art in 1943. And while the critical response to Biggers's mural was not uniformly positive—a review in *Art News* complained, "Of the screaming propaganda of John Biggers's picture, the less said the better"—the event did serve to mark Biggers's entry into the art world on a decidedly politicized note (Wardlaw, *Art* 28–29). Further, the mural received a considerably warmer response from viewers more sympathetic to Biggers's radical politics. For instance, when the CIO-affiliated United Transport Services Employees of Chicago acquired and installed Biggers's *Dying Soldier* mural in 1946, it garnered praise from the *Chicago Defender*, representatives of the Art Institute of Chicago, and prominent African American artists like Margaret Burroughs. Notably, *Dying Soldier* achieved this relatively wide circulation and positive reception in leftist circles despite the fact that, like the murals of Orozco, Biggers's painting offered a radical social critique without the solace of formulaic revolutionary solutions.

Particularly in this aspect, Biggers's mural stands in striking contrast to most representations of the black soldier in the visual culture of contemporaneous publications like *The Crisis*. While short fiction, poetry, and editorials appearing in the publication between 1942 and 1945 frequently called into question the hypocrisies of a Jim Crow military and the extent to which military service actually promised to improve the collective situation of African Americans, the *photographs* and *illustrations* of African American troops on these same pages seem generally consistent with *The Crisis*'s long-standing tactic of foregrounding black exemplars of model citizenship as a refutation of racist ideology. Specifically, *The Crisis* featured photographs and illustrations of male and female African Americans actively engaged in tasks ranging from work in defense plants on the home front to the operation of tanks, airplanes, and heavy artillery. *Crisis* photo-essays of the World War II era thus served to broaden conceptions of American identity in a manner similar to the California history murals of Woodruff and Alston: namely, by depicting African American subjects within an iconographic vocabulary previously reserved almost exclusively for white individuals—in this case, the role of the heroic soldier.

To cite these and other instances of 1940s visual culture that positioned black soldiers as heroes and potential agents of democratic change with regard to the civil rights of African Americans is not to suggest that Biggers was alone in his ambivalence toward black participation in World War II. As early as the mid-1930s artists and writers were criticizing the hypocrisy of the U.S. federal government and of prominent Americans who offered statements of concern regarding the human rights abuses of fascist Europe while ignoring similar outrages perpetrated against blacks within America's own borders. For example, in a 1934 *Crisis* illustration a young Romare Bearden combined an actual quote from U.S. General Hugh S. Johnson stating, "A few days ago, in Germany, events occurred which . . . made me . . . physically sick" with a striking image of the general turning his back on a U.S. landscape filled with the tombstones of lynching victims in order to gaze across the Atlantic Ocean at the social ills of Nazi Germany. What distinguishes Biggers's *Dying Soldier* is the artist's willingness to articulate these sentiments of bitterness and frustration not in the usual domains of the political cartoon or graphic art media, but in the relatively enduring and large-scale public art medium of the mural.

With the possible exception of Charles White's *Contribution of the Negro to Democracy in America*, it was not until 1952 that another African American artist used the mural medium to express an openly militant sense of black anger and frustration in the same way as had Biggers's *Dying Soldier*. That artist was John Wilson, with his painting *Incident*. Although Wilson had executed a rudimentary mural for the Roxbury Boys Club as early as 1939 and later had assisted Karl Zerbe on murals during his training at the Boston Museum School in the early 1940s, his first sustained work in the mural medium occurred not in the United States, but in Mexico City. Like many other American artists—including White, Alston, Woodruff, and Biggers—Wilson was especially attracted by the public quality of Mexican art: "It was an art that was designed to relate to the masses of everyday people. And it did! People would stand in line, tourists as well as Mexican peasants. When they got to the city they would go to see Diego Rivera's murals with the stories of the Mexican revolution and Orozco with his huge murals of war and conflict and social change. . . . It was that aspect of it that excited me."[67] Fired by this sense of enthusiasm, Wilson acquired a John Hay Whitney Fellowship to study in Mexico in 1950 and, once there, sought out leading Mexican muralists such as David Alfaro Siqueiros and Diego Rivera. In an early 1990s interview with Robert Brown for the Archives of American Art, Wilson recounted joining Siqueiros on his scaffolding for a discussion of the mural that the Mexican master painter was currently executing at the new Institute Politechnico. Similarly, through his contact with expatriate American artist Pablo O'Higgins, Wilson visited Diego Rivera at the latter's Zocolo mural site. In fact, O'Higgins and Rivera wrote fellowship recommendations that enabled Wilson to extend his residency in Mexico.

As his direct engagement with artists like Siqueiros, Rivera, and O'Higgins suggests, Wilson's foremost objective in traveling to Mexico was "to do large, public murals with the kind of imagery that would reflect those concerns I had through the experience of being a black person" (Fax, "John Wilson" 94). Toward this end, Wilson also became affiliated with the famed Esmeralda School of Painting and Sculpture, where he studied fresco techniques with Ignacio Aguirre, an artist who himself contributed graphic art on several occasions to U.S.-based leftist publications such as *New Masses* and *Masses and Mainstream* during the 1940s and early 1950s (see also LeFalle-Collins and Goldman 61). Because of the limited available wall space, Esmeralda students typically executed apprentice murals in the school's courtyard, took photographs, and then the next group of students would tear down this work and begin plastering the section of wall for a new mural. However, at least one of the frescoes that Wilson executed in this context—his *Incident* mural—had another fate. Wilson recalls that when Siqueiros, then a government minister for the Preservation of National Art, visited the school and saw this work, he was so impressed that he decreed that *Incident* would remain in the courtyard on a permanent basis.[68]

The *Incident* mural depicts a stern-visaged black man with a gun standing protectively between his wife and child and an overseen "incident" in which hooded Klan members lynch another black man—a subject that demonstrates that Wilson's sojourn to Mexico did not constitute an attempt to escape the pressing concerns of racist oppression facing blacks in the United States.[69] To the contrary, Wilson explains, "Of course news of continuing racially motivated lynchings, legal and illegal, seeped down to me from the States in Mexico, which prompted me to express my feelings about these horrors directly in my work."[70] Wilson also retained vivid memories of American racism from growing up in the United States:

Above all, the kind of images that affected me as a young man were gotten from picking up a newspaper (mainly from the Black Press, the *Pittsburgh Courier* or the *Baltimore Afro-American*) and seeing pictures of black men, burnt, lynched, and tortured. Once every two or three months there would be a lynching. Emotionally, I felt that

every one of these victims was me because white racists were out to subdue, dehuman-
ize and kill black men, and ultimately, intimidate the entire black community. I didn't,
as a child, consciously intellectualize or rationalize this. I know that this became an
image and an experience that I had to cope with. One of the things, in retrospect, that
I know I was doing with my art was trying to create and shape images that would exorcise these kinds of experiences. I was trying to make sense out of them or concretize
them so that I could deal with them. (Fax, "John Wilson" 95)

In fact, as early as 1946 Wilson had developed the theme of white mob violence
against African Americans as an oil on paper work *and* as a series of lithographic
prints, both of which shared the *Incident* title. Yet, it was only in transferring this
theme to the mural medium in 1952 that he added the element of the black man
with a gun, prepared to defend his family against such acts of aggression. There
were, of course, precedents for Wilson's representation of this mode of overt antiracist radicalism in the visual culture of earlier decades. For instance, both the
socialist *Messenger*'s depiction of *The "New Crowd Negro" Making America Safe
for Himself* (September 1919) and *Crisis* illustrations such as Romare Bearden's
For the Children! (October 1934) present armed self-defense as an option that is
viable and also noble and politically necessary. Significantly, however, these earlier works appeared in the medium of the political cartoon, which historically had
permitted a much greater amount of explicit social commentary than had the
mural.

It seems telling, then, that when Wilson crafted his explicitly political and
contemporarily charged *Incident* mural as late as 1952—over a full decade after
what scholarly accounts have tended to mark as the end of both social realism and
American mural painting (at least until the latter's resurgence in the 1960s)—he
did so not on U.S. soil, but in Mexico. In this regard, one should note that in addition to enhancing their facility as muralists through direct engagement with
their Mexican contemporaries, several African American visual artists found
Mexico itself a liberating locale, a site conducive to an extension of social realism
well beyond the movement's ostensible early 1940s demise. Indeed, Mexico comprised one of the preeminent facilitators of African Americans' sustained engagement with social realism into the early 1950s.

In the United States, African American artists most often operated via the
mode of historical allegory when working in the mural medium. Through such
allegories, social realist painters realized at least three aims: (1) to document the
contributions of African Americans (and certain white radicals) to the history of
progressive politics in the United States; (2) to document the historical obstacles
faced by African Americans, with many works, notably, resonating with oppressive forces contemporary to the 1930s and 1940s (the World War I era scenes of

John Biggers's *Dying Soldier* being perhaps the most piercing case in point); and (3) to explicate, albeit allegorically, exemplary strategies appropriate to contemporary liberation struggles. (Charles White's *Technique to Serve the Struggle* and *The Contribution of the Negro to Democracy in America* murals undertake this latter task most directly.) Significantly, when African American muralists operating on U.S. soil did dispense with historical allegory in favor of unabashedly contemporary scenes of social crisis—as in Biggers's *Sharecropper Mural*—they typically did so within relative safe havens such as college and university campuses. Availing themselves of strategically located sites, pursuing a range of patronage sources (most notably the Rosenwald Foundation), and hewing primarily to the depression-tested mode of historical allegory thus comprised the three most crucial means by which African American muralists were able to extend their engagement with social realism into the 1940s and early 1950s.

Chapter Three

Chronicling the Contemporary Crisis: Graphic Art

> *Most young intellectuals in cultural fields during the 40s and early 50s,*
> *if they had any sense of being avant-garde, they were critical of capitalist*
> *culture, capitalist lifestyles. And most of them were Marxist in some form*
> *or another, or socialist in some form or another. . . . You had to criticize,*
> *you had to examine, you had to be analytical. . . . And I was a part of*
> *that whole milieu.*
>
> JOHN WILSON

As evidenced by the preceding chapter's survey of African American murals, the emergence of social realism in the visual arts entailed at least two pressing objectives: (1) an exploration of themes that cultural workers deemed relevant to the lives of poor and working-class people; and (2) a discovery of ways to make art qualitatively more appealing and accessible to a mass audience. Alex Stavenitz, Graphic Committee chairman of the American Artists' Congress, described this transition as "a deep–going change that has been taking place among artists for the last few years . . . a change which has taken many of them not only to their studio window to look outside, but right through the door and into the street, into the steel mills, coal mines, and factories." Consequently, observed Stavenitz, artists were increasingly "filling their pictures with their reactions to humanity about them, rather than with apples or flowers" (5). Hughie Lee-Smith, a black Cleveland artist not known primarily as a social realist, illustrates the way in which these imperatives might have influenced the average artist in a series of lithographs titled *Artist's Life #1–#3* (1939).[1] In *Artist's Life #1,* for example, a male art teacher assists a young female student at a table in the foreground, while an artist at work in the midground of the image faces a scene with two distinct components: a nude woman posing in a chair and a policeman with a nightstick poised to strike the head of a man at the forefront of a picket line (figure 9). As Lee-Smith once glossed this image, it comprises a type of self-portrait representative of the choices open to him as an artist in the late 1930s: "The artist with a canvas [is] choosing between the non-involvement of studio painting, symbolized by the nude model, and . . . the class struggle as portrayed by the confrontation between the policeman and the picket-line demonstrator" (Williams and Williams 33). Even if most of Lee-Smith's own subsequent work did not fall neatly into either the academic formalist or social re-alist camps that he presents in this print, the self-reflexive issues he raises in this series of lithographs epitomize the type of questions that almost all progressive-minded artists were confronting during the 1930s and 1940s.

Implicit in *Artist's Life #1*, of course, is a biting critique of artists who would continue to operate in a sphere apart from the most pressing contemporary social issues. Specifically, Lee-Smith aims to denaturalize what he perceives as the apo-litical position of the academic formalist by illustrating that the degree of a given artist's involvement with social crises is a matter of conscious choice—and, at least for Lee-Smith, a rather clear *moral* choice at that. Charles Alston described the nature of this choice as especially pressing for African American artists:

> That's why I think the Negro painter in this country has a slightly different problem from a white painter. . . . while you're concerned with these things that involved the aesthetics of art, you cannot but be concerned about what's going on around you and how it affects you, your people. . . . So you're torn—at least I know that I am—you continuously ask yourself this question . . . Should I commit my painting to visualiz-ing, as I see it, the struggle that's going on? Or should I close my eyes and keep myself apart from that, involve myself in other ways that relate to the struggle but keep the painting apart?[2]

Through much—although certainly not all—of their art from the 1930s, 1940s, and early 1950s, African American social realists clearly opted to engage the so-cial struggles they saw going on around them. Put simply, social realist artists struggled to redeem themselves from the seeming perils of ivory tower isolation and an exclusively upper-class system of patronage by forging work that was both *about* and *for* poor and working-class people.

Particularly in the latter regard, it seems quite suggestive that Lee-Smith ex-ecutes his meditation on the artist's social responsibility in a graphic art medium. In this same vein, John Kwait proposed that the John Reed Clubs of the early 1930s might most usefully orient their exhibits around graphics and other media not previously classed as "high art," such as "series of prints, with a connected

Figure 9. Hughie Lee-Smith (1915–99), *Artist's Life #1*, 1939. Lithograph, 11 × 8½ in. (All rights reserved, The Metropolitan Museum of Art, Gift of Reba and Dave Williams, 1999 [1999.529.112]; © Estate of Hughie Lee-Smith/Licensed by VAGA, New York, New York.)

content, for cheap circulation; cartoons for newspapers and magazines; posters; banners; signs; illustrations of slogans; historical pictures of the revolutionary tradition of America. Such pictures have a clear value in the fight for freedom. They actually reach their intended audience, whereas the majority of easel paintings are stuck away in studios" (Shapiro 68). Significantly, just as artist Jacob Burck rejected Kwait's implication that "the *only* art suitable for the working class is agitational" (Shapiro 71, emphasis in original), most social realists never sought to abandon oil painting altogether. However, many artists *did* share Kwait's interest in exploring the possibilities of nontraditional media—especially the graphic media of lithographs, linocuts, and woodblock prints—as a means of more effectively reaching poor and working-class audiences. After all, the type of technical skill involved in graphic art processes resonated with social realists' desire to identify themselves quite literally as "cultural workers," since they were well aware of the fact that graphic media like woodblock prints possessed roots in a working-class craft tradition (Whiting 29).

Foremost among the appealing qualities of these media to social realists was reproducibility. As WPA lithographer Elizabeth Olds observed, "By virtue of the fact that prints can be created as multiple originals in an edition numbering thousands rather than tens, their price is low enough so that they can be bought by the average citizen, not just the wealthy collector" (Olds 142). Hence, when the American Artists' Group formed in 1936, members described the graphic arts as "essentially democratic in purpose" and stated as one of their central aims, "the issuance and distribution of certain original etchings, lithographs and woodcuts in unlimited quantities at an exceedingly low price of about two dollars per print."[3] Clearly, then, for many social realists the shift to graphic media seemed consistent not only with their desire to reach a *larger* audience per se but also to extend their work to an audience qualitatively *different* from the leisure class citizens who typically patronized museums and art galleries. As African American poet and artist Margaret Burroughs echoed this sentiment, "I don't care whether the academies or the Art Institute or the Metropolitan Museum or whatever never show my work, because I have concluded that the main audience for my work, as far as I'm concerned, the important audience, are the little people, the street people."[4] As part of a like-minded outreach to a mass audience through a self-consciously "public art," exhibits of government-sponsored graphics during the 1930s and early 1940s were held less often in prestigious galleries than in public libraries, schools, hospitals, parks, settlement houses, and other community centers—that is, locales similar to those also being targeted for more enduring mural installations by the New Deal art programs.

In this spirit, one of the first collective activities undertaken by the American Artists' Congress was to organize the *America Today* exhibit, which displayed an identical set of one hundred prints simultaneously in thirty cities in conjunction with the meeting of the congress. Graphic Committee chairman Stavenitz explained that the rationale behind this format was "to help the artist reach a public comparable in size to that of the book and motion picture" (6). Indeed, artists were well aware that by the 1930s their work had to compete with Hollywood cinema, mass market paperback covers, posters, and billboards for the attention of their intended audience—hence, the widespread interest of artists in graphic art media, which, they hoped, could rival these better-financed (and often less politically progressive) forms of visual culture. Graphic art media, it seemed to many social realists, could effectively synthesize the aura of "art" with the accessibility of mass culture.

In addition to the reproducible quality of graphic media, artists also found prints to be particularly appropriate for dealing with topical political concerns of the day. Several artists drew a conscious distinction between the graphic arts and the medium of mural painting in this regard. For instance, graphic artist Karl Schrag wrote in response to an exhibit of the early 1940s, "The graphic arts can be like a magic mirror in which the essence of the time is reflected. . . . Mural or easel painting cannot express it. Photographs lack human feeling and concentrated expression" (Landau 3). That graphic art media were so often singled out for this particular brand of cultural work—that is, reflecting the pressing social issues of the contemporary moment—owed both to the example established by preceding generations of politically engaged artists and to pragmatic concerns related to the little magazine venues toward which so much social realist graphic artwork was directed. Not coincidentally, it was through leftist little magazines and art publications that many U.S. artists became aware of the fact that graphic media such as linocuts, lithographs, and woodblock prints possessed a long-standing association with radical cultural work (Gold, "Masses Tradition" 46–47). And with the emergence of social realism, artists began to defend the legitimacy of graphic media with renewed vigor by citing particular examples of the legacy of art forms such as (1) the nineteenth-century graphic arts of Daumier and Goya; (2) the German Expressionist prints of Käthe Kollwitz; and (3) U.S. artists associated with the radical little magazines of the 1910s and 1920s, such as *The Masses* (1911–17) and *The Liberator* (1918–24).

Nineteenth-century artists like Daumier and Goya proved particularly attractive models for social realists because of their interest in depicting the lives and labor of poor and working-class people, often in such a way as to level a biting critique against prevailing socioeconomic hierarchies. For example, in a manner that clearly would have resonated with the anticapitalist caricatures of depression-era political cartoons and social realist art, an 1848 Daumier lithograph captioned "Look how they've mucked up my chimney flues!" satirizes the self-interested fussiness of a well-to-do French gentleman as proletarian laborers work to rebuild Paris. And, like social realists, Daumier singled out corruption in the courts and the political sphere for especially intense scrutiny.[5] Moreover, both Daumier and Goya also executed graphics that depicted the horrors of war in extremely gruesome and uncompromising terms. Goya's *Disasters of War* series of 1863 proved especially influential in this regard; Jacob Lawrence recalls seeing copies at Charles Alston's "306" studio during the 1930s, to cite just one example (Landau 1; Wheat 36). Drawing loosely on incidents from the war between Spain and Napoleonic France, the *Disasters of War* series consists of approximately eighty etchings that unflinchingly depict the mutilation of soldiers' bodies, the murder and rape of innocent women and children, and brutal acts of torture. In short, Goya renders war as a nightmare of senseless violence.[6] Not surprisingly, these works gained renewed poignancy for social realists as a Second World War loomed on the horizon during the mid-1930s and, later, became a manifest reality. Particularly in the years preceding America's entry into World War II, when antiwar sentiment still prevailed among much of the American left, such works provided social realists with a model for the critique of escalating global militarism by both fascist and ostensibly democratic nations.

African American graphic artists such as John Wilson, Charles White, Elizabeth Catlett, and Hale Woodruff also drew special inspiration from the work of Käthe Kollwitz, a German Expressionist noted for her woodblock prints and etchings of poor and working-class subjects. She was a highly visible artist in leftist cultural circles of the 1930s and 1940s, with work in book and magazine reproductions, as well as exhibits sponsored by groups like the Chicago John Reed Club (Whiting 29–33). While Kollwitz did occasionally produce graphic works depicting revolutionary collective action by members of the working class, such as the etching *Weavers on the March* (1897), more often she turned her attention to the everyday life struggles of proletarians. For instance, her lithograph *Poverty,* from this same series of *The Weavers' Revolt*, depicts a somber domestic scene of a family wrought with grief over the fate of an ill, malnourished infant.[7]

In stylistic terms, Kollwitz's work also provided an affirmation that artists could employ the stark black and white chromatics of most graphic media in such a way as to attain dynamic aesthetic effects. As Charles White explained, "You can say if Kollwitz . . . did a painting, nobody has ever seen it, that I know of, yet she was a great artist. If Daumier or Goya had never painted, they still would have been great artists. So I always felt this way about black and white."[8] Moreover, Kollwitz explicitly connected her chosen aesthetic style to a radical brand of cultural politics. As she wrote in response to a Nazi art critic who found her sense of aesthetics vulgar and ugly, "But what had I to do with the laws of beauty, with those of the Greeks, for instance, which were not mine, and with which I had no sympathy? The proletariat was my idea of beauty" (Nagel 90). In much the same way, most American social realists did not simply apply the stylistic conventions of academic art to poor and working-class subjects. Rather, they formulated an aesthetic that self-consciously eschewed conventional notions of "beauty" for a style that aimed to capture a more dynamic sense of what they took to be the rough-edged quality of life among the masses of America's citizenry. In this regard, Elizabeth Catlett stated of Kollwitz's art, "I like her feeling for people. I would love to do for black people what she did for poor German people, working people if I could" (Beauchamp-Byrd and Coleman 18).

Of course, the most immediate reference point for American social realists who opted to work in graphics was the artwork featured in leftist little magazines of the preceding decades, particularly the work of artists affiliated with *The Masses* during the 1910s. Perhaps most significant in terms of the legacy of *The Masses* for social realist art, works by the likes of John Sloan, Robert Minor, and Boardman Robinson demonstrated that the stark lines and textures of graphic media might, in fact, prove *more* efficacious than easel or mural painting in conveying a politically charged scene of labor violence or everyday proletarian life. These artists were able to carve out a distinct space for engravings and crayon drawings that drew from both "high art" concerns of aesthetic craftsmanship and the didactic communicative aims of political cartooning. For their part, political cartoons of the sort that populated the pages of *The Masses* provided a visual language for depicting capitalists, workers, and the often discordant relationship between these factions that would prove influential to subsequent generations of political cartoonists and to social realist graphic artists. In this respect, it is hardly coincidental that social realists like Charles Alston and Hale Woodruff did substantial work in cartooning early in their respective careers.[9] To be sure, social realists generally did maintain a relatively clear sense of distinction between their graphic art and political cartooning—a distinction highlighted most notably in the omission of captions from the overwhelming majority of graphics.[10] Yet, if most social realist graphics were not quite as didactic or prone to outright caricature as the political cartoons of a William Gropper, such artists nonetheless shared a certain iconographic vocabulary and ideological framework with the era's radical cartoonists; and graphics were considerably more didactic, on the whole, than were murals. In this vein, Charles White, for one, revered Gropper as "a monumental figure in the annals of progressive art . . . [and] in the history of American art . . . an artist linked with the noblest principles of humanism as exemplified by Kollwitz, Daumier, Goya, and Rembrandt."[11] Whereas adherents of the conventional hierarchies of academic art would have scoffed at the notion of taking artwork from the genres of cartooning and graphic art as seriously as master works of easel painting, White—like his *Masses* forebears and like most social realists of his own day—drew his thematic and aesthetic influences from across the spectrum of available visual culture models.

More broadly, the graphics of *The Masses* were influential in that they placed a special emphasis on legibility and mass distribution of art, criteria that possessed special resonance with the generation of social realist artists who came of age during the 1930s and 1940s. In practical terms of making graphics at least potentially accessible to a wide readership inclusive of the working classes, it is worth noting that Minor and Robinson were able to considerably advance the technology for mass reproduction of such artwork (Zurier 132–39). It is in conjunction with this latter point that the artists associated with *The Masses* provided one further crucial precedent for social realist graphic artists: much as Rebecca Zurier has shown that the artists of *The Masses* used this magazine as a kind of alternative to conventional art galleries during the 1910s, social realists were able to undertake and *sustain* contemporarily focused and politically charged cultural work in the graphic arts in large part due to the consistent presence and support of radical little magazines during the period under study. The *Crisis, Common Ground,* and *New Masses,* among others, routinely published social realist graphics, including a substantial amount of work by African American artists. So too, graphic artwork reproductions were frequently sold in portfolio form at relatively accessible prices through advertisements in the pages of these same little magazines.

Given that social realists often aimed their graphic art projects for unconventional "exhibition" venues, as opposed to the relatively permanent, public wall installations typical for mural paintings, it can hardly prove surprising that one finds a general pattern of striking contrasts in the content of works in the two media—including cases in which artists like Charles White and Hale Woodruff worked in both murals and graphics. In other words, while graphic art media obviously did not offer the air of permanence or the impressively grandiose scale of a mural painting, graphics did seem to offer artists a viable avenue for reaching nontraditional, working-class viewers via little magazines and affiliated portfolio projects. Significantly, too, where mural projects often faced considerable scrutiny with regard to politicized content, leftist little magazines as an exhibition venue were not only tolerant of but even openly sympathetic to the radical politics of much social realist graphic art. Indeed, within the context of these leftist little magazines, engaging contemporary subject matter simply made good sense, helping to give tangible form to the labor strikes, courtroom battles, and antifascist campaigns chronicled in the editorials, reportage, short fiction, and poetry of such publications.[12] Nor did graphics serve merely to "illustrate" the "real" literary and journalistic content of these magazines; rather, graphics themselves comprised an active and, at least at times, extremely *effective* component of leftist print culture. The significance of graphics to the overall impact of many of the social realist era's little magazines is suggested by one reader's 1946 letter to *New Masses*, which stated, "I find a well illustrated issue of *NM* a quicker introduction to deeper contents of the magazine itself than any haranguing. . . . I hope the section of the staff responsible for this part of the layout will continue to recognize the importance of keeping the magazine attractive and up-to-date as further 'selling-value' for the contents within" (LaCour 21). And clearly the importance of graphics on this score was recognized by many of those who produced such leftist publications. It is telling, for example, that even a self-described shoestring operation such as Jack Conroy's *New Anvil* saw fit to undertake the expense of reproducing graphics as an essential component of the magazine's cultural work. A detailed examination of the career of John Wilson can serve to illustrate how a particular artist was shaped by and contributed to the visual culture of social realism, as well as the way in which international experiences served to enhance his cultural work. Significantly, too, this proves to be the case despite the fact that Wilson did not even enter the professional art world until after social realism's supposed demise.

The Graphic Art of John Wilson

At the age of twenty-one, the precocious Boston artist John Wilson won the 1943 Atlanta University annual exhibition's John Hope Purchase Award for his oil painting *Black Soldier*. This important early painting presages many of the thematic and aesthetic concerns that occupied Wilson's work during the 1940s and early 1950s in both easel painting and graphic art media. Overcast with what Wilson refers to as "a kind of blue period Picasso technique," this somber scene depicts a uniformed black soldier looking over his shoulder at his wife and child, while a Roxbury tenement house and an ethereal image of the Statue of Liberty loom in the background (figure 10).[13] Notably, the Statue of Liberty featured even more prominently in Wilson's preliminary sketches for *Black Soldier*. However, whereas Wilson's preparatory study foregrounded the soldier in monumental and heroic scale, the artist's completed painting rearranges the figures so as to elucidate the soldier's ambiguous feelings about his impending departure and to call more poignant notice to the impact of military service on the families of black soldiers. Particularly given its blue tonality and the mist enshrouding its upper registers, Wilson's rendering of this symbolically representative black soldier seems more bleak than heroic.

Although Wilson did not serve in the American armed forces himself, the theme of his painting emerged out of a deeply personal sense of social injustice.[14] Like many other African Americans at the time, Wilson experienced consider-

Figure 10. John Wilson (b. 1922), *Black Soldier*, 1942. Tempera, 26½ × 15½ in.
(© John Wilson/Licensed by VAGA, New York, New York.)

able frustration over the hypocrisy of America's calling on black soldiers to risk their lives overseas for democratic ideals that they seldom enjoyed themselves on the American home front. In this sense, the positioning of the soldier in midground of the painting plays a clear symbolic role, highlighting the subject's sense of being caught betwixt and between the promises of democratic inclusiveness connoted by the Statue of Liberty and the everyday reality of dilapidated urban housing in which segregationist practices force he and his family to live. Citing his own childhood in Boston neighborhoods of this sort during the depression, Wilson explains: "A sense of living in a tenement ghetto . . . always [involved] a sense of decay. . . . There were old wooden houses. . . . In a black neighborhood nothing is repaired. . . . There's a sense of living in a kind of neglected, down-trodden [community]." In glossing the details of his *Black Soldier* painting, Wilson notes the small plant growing up through cracks in a sidewalk as an emblem of this urban decay and points out that the child stands on "a blood red sidewalk of bricks, and I wanted it to be seen as blood somehow." Although he acknowledges that this imagery seems almost "corny" and "obvious" in retrospect, Wilson affirms that at the time, "I didn't care or mind. I was simply trying in the most direct way to express this sense of indignation and anger."

Significantly, Wilson first heard of the Atlanta University exhibition through fellow Bostonian Allan Rohan Crite, an established African American artist with whom Wilson met independently on occasion during his days as a student at Boston's Museum School in the early to mid-1940s. Explaining the significance of this artist's example, Wilson has remarked, "There were no black people who made paintings and drawings as serious careers that I had ever heard of . . . until someone told me of Allan Crite."[15] As Wilson's case suggests, not all African American social realists experienced the same tangible sense of interconnection with fellow black artists and intellectuals that I have described in the case of the Harlem Artists' Guild and Chicago's Arts and Crafts Guild. Even with the presence of Crite, Wilson lamented from Boston in 1946 that "there just aren't enough Negro artists around to justify calling a meeting of young artists an interracial group."[16]

Especially given that Wilson had relatively limited contact with fellow African American artists (other than Crite) during his early career in Boston, it seems telling that his *Black Soldier* arrived at a theme strikingly similar to that of John Biggers's *Dying Soldier* mural, painted at Hampton Institute the previous year. At the very least, this parallel suggests just how pervasive such ambivalence was among African Americans on the left during the war. Even more intriguing, both artists forged a brand of social realist aesthetics that conjoined naturalistic figural representation to a quasi-surrealist juxtaposition of iconic imagery—in Wilson's case, a counterpoising of the hovering presence of a mist-enshrouded Statue of

Liberty against a Roxbury tenement house. Clearly, even as they selectively appropriated techniques from movements such as surrealism, Biggers and Wilson—like many of their African American peers—continued to find in social realism a vital aesthetic framework during the 1940s.

One should note that Wilson also came of age as an artist in a milieu in which certain of his politically engaged Boston peers were concerned with representing America's distinctive ethnic communities. For example, Wilson once reflected on the importance of meeting Jack Levine during the period in which Wilson was at work on *Black Soldier:* "I was just beginning to try to put into paint some of the things I felt about the Negro and his life in the United States and I was groping around trying to conceive of symbols or some approach that would express what I had in mind. Around this time I was introduced to Jack Levine and on seeing his work I was struck with the fact that he was doing largely in relationship to the Jewish people what I was attempting to do with the Negro."[17] For Wilson, this sense of connection had a concrete basis, since many of the Roxbury Jewish immigrants depicted by Levine "shared the same sort of physical world of three-story wooden tenements" that Wilson knew from his own youth. More broadly, this encounter with Levine seems to have helped Wilson to recognize that African American artists were hardly alone in seeking to produce works of art that were simultaneously ethnically distinctive and pluralist, or in shuttling between ethnically based artist organizations and the broader American art world—as did prominent Jewish social realists such as William Gropper, Louis Lozowick, Raphael Soyer, and Levine (Hills, *Social* 13).

Further, notwithstanding Wilson's relative geographic isolation from the centers of African American art, he did come into at least passing contact with other black artists and their work through travel, exhibitions, and publications. In particular, much as the young Charles White was invigorated by an encounter with *The New Negro,* Wilson has cited the importance of Alain Locke's "anthology" of African American visual arts, *The Negro in Art* (1940): "[Locke's book] was a *very* important thing for me—to see all of this and to see that there was a history to this. . . . It was psychologically very important to know that . . . I wasn't alone." Through his participation in African American art exhibitions over the course of the 1940s, particularly the Atlanta University annuals, Wilson himself gained considerable national visibility on the black arts scene, drawing accolades from Locke and others.[18] In fact, such was the degree of Wilson's success on this front that fellow artist Vernon Winslow wrote to Wilson in 1955, "If memory serves me right, you have won so many prizes at the Atlanta Exhibitions, you should be called 'Mr. Atlanta University prize-winner.'"[19] So too, early in his career Wilson met and gained encouragement from fellow African American social realists on occasion, as when Charles White and Elizabeth Catlett visited Boston in 1943

(Fax, "John Wilson" 93). In all of these ways, Wilson emerged as an artist with a profound racial consciousness, despite having relatively limited face-to-face interactions with other African American cultural workers.

At the same time, Wilson also achieved a remarkable rise to the forefront of the "mainstream" American art world in spite of the racial barriers that still characterized many aspects of this milieu in the 1940s. Like Charles White, Wilson received some of his earliest formal art instruction through the auspices of a local settlement house. By these means, Wilson gained exposure to the media of mural painting and the linocut while still in high school, albeit that his work from these early years bears little resemblance to his mature art. More important, Wilson's settlement house art teachers encouraged him to submit his work to the Boston Museum School, where he received a scholarship and soon became one of the institution's "star" students.[20] By the years 1943–45, Wilson was participating in exhibitions at galleries in Baltimore, Chicago, Albany, Atlanta, Pittsburgh, and Washington, D.C., as well as college and university shows at Hampton Institute, Smith, and Wellesley. Further, by the close of 1945, reproductions of Wilson's work had appeared in prestigious venues such as *Art Digest* and *Time* magazine, and in 1946 he took a five-hundred-dollar portrait prize at the Pepsi-Cola annual *Paintings of the Year* exhibit. Put simply, Wilson's ascendance in the American art world was meteoric by any measure, all the more so given his humble socioeconomic background.

Wilson, whose parents were from Guyana, knew the depression's hardships firsthand. Despite his experience as a technician in a sugar-processing plant in his native country, Wilson's father faced recurring unemployment and the family had to endure dependence on government welfare programs for long stretches during the 1930s (Tarr n.p.). In terms of artistic work, this dimension of Wilson's familial experience emerges most clearly in his 1942 lithograph *Breadwinner*, one of his first efforts in this graphic art medium. This semiautobiographical print resonates with the iconography of much U.S. art and literature of the 1930s in the sense that depression-era unemployment seems to have caused particular distress among men, who typically had held the role of economic provider in times of relative prosperity.[21]

Of course, the way in which artists treated this highly charged figure of the displaced male breadwinner during the 1930s and 1940s varied considerably. For instance, whereas the Treasury Section murals studied by Barbara Melosh typically offered mass audiences a panacea of images of productively engaged male industrial labor, social realist prints such as Wilson's lithograph more directly confront the disheartening reality of the depression era's socioeconomic crises. In the latter case, in addition to marking a widespread impoverishment, works of graphic art that depicted idle men during the 1930s and 1940s typically encoded a considerable psychological strain—and Wilson's *Breadwinner* is no exception on this count. In Wilson's print, a male in working-class attire reclines on a park bench with sober expression, holding a newspaper with the bold headline of "WAR," while an empty lunch pail rests at his side and a small group of pigeons clusters at his feet. Even more poignantly, this man sits idle in spite of the fact that the newspaper headline and the billowing smokestacks in the upper right corner of the image both suggest the wartime resurgence of America's industrial economy during the early 1940s (figure 11). In this way, Wilson calls attention to the fact that the economic upswing that accompanied wartime defense production left many African American workers disenfranchised, even though President Roosevelt's Executive Order 8802 officially desegregated America's defense industries in June 1941.[22]

Distinguishing itself to some degree from the prevailing masculinist trend of depression-era social realism, Wilson's *Breadwinner* seeks to render something of the psychological impact that joblessness brought to bear *not only* on male breadwinners but also on entire African American families. Hence, as in *Black Soldier,* Wilson places a mother and child spatially removed from the figure of the husband-provider; in *Breadwinner,* a woman and child (presumably the wife and son of the central figure) stand together in the rear of the park, dwarfed in scale by the man on the bench in the print's foreground. Thus, Wilson captures the frustration of a man unable to find work by which to support his family in the expected manner (as indicated by the stern expression on the man's face and his despondent posture), as well as a sense of the psychic and relational strains that this type of forced idleness might create between a man and his family (as suggested by the spatial distance between the figures in the print). Further, in the upper left background, over the man's shoulder, Wilson depicts a series of narrow and tilted buildings, as if to evoke in visual shorthand the type of tenement housing where this sort of family might be forced to reside. Thus, at least in this image, family, home, and even a trip to the local park seem to offer African Americans very little in the way of solace regarding America's wartime confluence of economic and racial woes.

Adolescence (1943), another of Wilson's earliest lithographs, turns his quasi-journalistic artist's eye to the shaping influence of a similar Roxbury environment on a male youth. In this work, an African American boy stares out at the viewer from amidst a congested back alley in a tenement housing community that hosts a range of activities: young people play cards; mothers with small children gather to talk near a doorway; and relatively well-dressed pedestrians pass by on an adjoining street. Amidst this flurry of action, discarded newspapers and other debris lie scattered on the ground.[23] As Wilson describes this image, the boy is something of an autobiographical figure and the scene depicted draws on the

Figure 11. John Wilson (b. 1922), *Breadwinner,* 1942. Lithograph, 18¾ × 14 in. (© John Wilson/Licensed by VAGA, New York, New York.)

artist's own childhood neighborhood. Here, as with *Breadwinner,* Wilson sought to use aspects of his own life to form an image representative of what he felt to be a prevailing set of African American experiences. In a 1947 letter to patron Albert Reese, Wilson wrote of *Adolescence,* "In it I attempt to express the bewilderment and search for understanding of a Negro boy growing up in the middle of the inconsistencies, the squalor, and the cramped confusion of life in a typical Northern American Negro ghetto."[24] In particular, by framing his scene within a series of overlapping tall and narrow brick buildings in such a way that one barely even sees the sky, Wilson conveys the sense of confinement that he sometimes felt during his own youth in such communities. Standing faced away from the alley's activity, the boy seems a part of the street around him and yet not entirely at home in this environment. Relating this youth to memories of his own childhood, Wilson states that the books carried by the boy signal his desire to explore a larger world beyond the tenement housing community through education.

Yet, even granting Wilson's gesture toward creating representative images of social ills in this way, his portrayals of poor and working-class African American communities typically do *not* illustrate a milieu of unrelenting race and class oppression in the manner of Richard Wright's *Native Son* or Ann Petry's even more naturalistic novel *The Street.* As scholar David Peeler has argued of the depression era's social realist painters, "[Philip] Evergood and the others [i.e., fellow social realists] understood 'naturalism' to mean painting that aimed to give pure literal renditions of the objective order. This intention seemed wrong to them because they believed that one must not simply copy the objective order; any such exercise made the painter more of a passive transcriber than an active interpreter of his world" (200). Likewise, for Wilson, a work such as *Adolescence* is hardly a literal transcription of life or a didactic statement of social protest—at least not one directed at any clear causative agent. Rather, Wilson's early art reflects both his fascination with and ambivalence toward the decayed old houses and varied people of his own Boston neighborhood. As he explains, "I would feel the discomfort of living in this kind of neglected [neighborhood], but at the same time it was my turf, it was my home. . . . I belonged there." Even more, Wilson recognized a certain *vitality* in poor and working-class urban communities, the capacity of people "although poor . . . to have a sense of their collective identification and the ability to put aside their frustrations and struggles so that they could enjoy many aspects of their lives."[25] In his choice to grant dignity to impoverished and oppressed subjects, rather than simply render them as victims or proofs of a political thesis, Wilson almost surely was influenced by Allan Crite, who was one of the first prominent painters to attribute this type of vigor to poor and working-class black communities (Hills, *Social* 18). As Wilson once ruminated of Crite's paintings, "I was drawn to them because they came off as images of people with a sense of dignified humanity that was totally missing in the stereotyped description of my people. That was all we could find in the mass media of those times."[26] Not coincidentally, it was around the time that Wilson was executing graphic works like *Breadwinner* and *Adolescence* as a student in the Boston Museum School that he claims to have gained a sense of art as "images which somehow become important historical documents." Thus, even though Crite was not a politically engaged artist in the same sense as Wilson was, the elder Bostonian nevertheless offered Wilson a model of art centered in a sensitive documentary impulse and concern for the relatively unconventional artistic themes of everyday life in an urban African American community.

In formulating his own politically engaged mode of visual art, Wilson assimilated additional aesthetic and thematic influences during his training at the Boston Museum School. Although he became aware of "moderns" such as Picasso and Dali during the early 1940s through his classes at the school, Wilson was primarily fascinated in this period with the work of Mexican painters, which he encountered through books and exhibits such as the *One Hundred Twentieth Century Prints* show at the Boston Institute of Modern Art in 1944. This exhibit included graphic artwork by Siqueiros, Rivera, Orozco, and Rufino Tamayo, as well as several American artists—including the young prodigy Wilson himself, who was represented by his *Adolescence* lithograph.[27] As for so many African American social realists, the work of the Mexican muralists possessed special resonance for Wilson as an artist interested in depicting poor and working-class people of color. Early in the 1940s, Wilson developed a special admiration for what he describes as Orozco's "powerful kind of paintings about revolutionary events and people who were trying to change the world we live in." In the mid-1940s, this affinity even moved Wilson to journey to Dartmouth College for the express purpose of viewing Orozco's *The Epic of Civilization* murals in the Baker Library (Fax, *Seventeen* 41–44; Fax, "John Wilson" 93). Stylistically, as well as thematically, Orozco's work offered an important alternative to the murals that Wilson had previously seen. Wilson explains: "If you look at the murals by [John Singer] Sargent in the staircase of the Boston Museum, you see Greek myths, gold leaf. . . . There's a kind of pasty, pastel make believe world, whereas the world I lived in was blood and guts." In striking contrast to the work of Sargent and more in tune with his own lived experience, Wilson observes of Orozco's murals, "there's nothing refined about them." This is equally true of Orozco's graphic artwork, in which he adopted a deliberately coarse style to articulate politically charged themes, as in his antilynching lithograph *Hanging Negroes* (1930).[28] Such a consciously unrefined aesthetic sensibility seemed to Wilson to offer an innovative and appropriate mode for approaching poor and working-class lives. For Wilson, as for Mexican artists like Orozco, this new, politicized subject matter demanded a break with the conventional, polished styles of academic painting *and*, at least at times, a break with the medium of painting itself.

In addition to these diverse artistic influences, Wilson also took inspiration from cultural work in other fields entirely. Notably, in his response to the questionnaire circulated by Romare Bearden and Harry Henderson for their 1993 book *A History of African-American Artists*, Wilson cited "the feel, the stance and the style/philosophy of a Paul Robeson," and literary titans such as Richard Wright, Langston Hughes, and Ralph Ellison—all prominent figures on the African American left when Wilson entered the scene in the early 1940s—as key influences on his artistic work. Wright's social realist fiction played an especially important role in Wilson's developing consciousness with regard to issues of race and class. When one of the white socialist friends who frequented Wilson's studio across from the Museum School introduced him to Wright's fiction with a copy of *Uncle Tom's Children*, the book came as "a very powerful revelation, [although] I had known about oppression in the South through news articles in black newspapers, of course. [Wright's work] not only suggested in a very powerful poetic language the deep emotional feelings and the tragedy underlying the wasted lives and the horror and all the rest of it. . . . I got the feeling from that [book] of a kind of organized understanding of a liberation struggle."

In response to his encounter with Wright's dynamic fiction during the early 1940s, Wilson completed a lithograph titled *Native Son* in 1945. However, rather than attempting to render a literal scene from the action of Wright's widely read novel of the same title, Wilson's *Native Son* lithograph depicts a muscular young African American man seated at a table in a shirt and overalls. One might presume this to be an image of Bigger Thomas, the central character of Wright's *Native Son*. As with Wright's protagonist, Wilson seems to intend his "native son" to stand as a representative figure for young African American men. Yet, where Wright involves Bigger Thomas in a psychologically gripping drama of violence and racial injustice, Wilson depicts his subject in a more contemplative moment, seeking to capture the pathos besetting many young black men of the 1940s by portraying a "Bigger Thomas" figure with a posture and facial expression that convey a sense of exhaustion and despair.[29] In other words, whereas Wright more or less directly spells out the context of social forces that constrict his protagonist's life opportunities, Wilson—perhaps presuming his viewer's general knowledge of the socioeconomic factors described in Wright's novel—seems more concerned with conveying a sense of the alienation and hopelessness that can result from such forces.

This distinction becomes even more apparent when one considers fellow social realist Charles White's handling of the "native son" theme. Inspired by Wright's literature and his firsthand encounters with the young author in Chicago, White executed at least three *Native Son* works during the early 1940s (Horowitz 17). Whereas Wilson treats this theme in a relatively restrained manner, White portrays the protagonist of his *Native Son No. 2* (1942) with oversized hands and a massive, bulging musculature that seems virtually to burst through his torn shirt (figure 12). By illustrating his "native son" figure in this manner, White at once foregrounds the specifically proletarian quality of an archetypal Bigger Thomas and dramatizes the fugitive status of Wright's protagonist. In contrast, Wilson depicts his "native son" seemingly in the midst of a more existential crisis of faith regarding the prospects for his future. Arguably, Wilson's print is no less poignant for having adopted a subtler mode of social realist aesthetics in this way.

In any event, it is telling that Wilson encountered both the fiction of Richard Wright and the work of Mexican artists like Orozco as part of a still vital leftist milieu in Boston. As Wilson described his initial engagement with this radical political culture to Elton Fax: "Along with looking and listening I began to read. I read Marxist philosophy and I read *New Masses*. When I read Richard Wright's *Uncle Tom's Children*, man, I flipped! I realized that there had been a lot of pretending—pretending that America was a great and good and generous place where anybody could make it by pulling himself up by his bootstraps. Orozco's paintings told it like it was! So did the stories of Richard Wright!" (*Seventeen* 40–41). For Wilson, the appeal of leftist political culture—as embodied in Marxist theory, the tangible example of little magazines, and the cultural practice of social realists like Orozco and Wright—involved not only a straightforward quality of "telling it like it is" but also the way in which this culture's discourse seemed to offer a systematic analysis of the racism and class oppression of the existing American social order. Like Richard Wright, Wilson was particularly interested in establishing a conceptual framework through which to understand American inequalities of race and class, even if he generally avoided adopting a doctrinaire position in his cultural work. As Wilson elaborates, "I was certainly interested in some other social philosophy or direction because clearly capitalism or whatever I was living in wasn't working for me, it wasn't working for black people."

Not least of the specific factors contributing to the appeal of leftist politics for Wilson during the 1940s was the way in which socialists, communists, and like-minded progressives advocated interracialism while simultaneously respecting ethnic pluralism. In Wilson's words, the young socialists with whom he interacted in Boston in the 1940s offered a vision of diverse ethnic groups "living together and contributing whatever their strengths were—the attitude being that all ethnic groups have their particular special history and their special strengths. . . . What today is called cultural diversity, they were doing that way back . . . and I found it very attractive because it included me." So too, in terms

Figure 12. Charles White (1918–79), *Native Son No. 2*, 1942. Drawing. (Howard University Gallery of Art, Washington, D.C.)

of visible public practice, Wilson has explained in reference to the activity of communists on issues such as the defense of the Scottsboro Boys in the 1930s and 1940s that, quite simply, "There was no other official group doing this." To be sure, Wilson retrospectively claims never to have been a Communist or Socialist Party member himself, owing to the fact that he found the internal politics of socialist and communist organizations to be "disquieting." (In Wilson's estimation, CP officials often seemed willing to exploit well-intentioned and idealistic grassroots members.) Nonetheless, the Marxist theory and activist campaigns of these leftist political organizations clearly provided the young Wilson with a vitally important conceptual model for interpreting issues of social (in)justice. "What they gave me," Wilson states, "was a rational basis on which to understand the world around me better, cope with it better and also some sense of what was happening in terms of people attempting to make changes." In short, socialists and the CP offered Wilson a relatively malleable "blueprint" for social critique and social change, much as they had for the young Richard Wright during the 1930s.

A 1943 lithograph titled *Deliver Us from Evil* crystallizes Wilson's leftist political vision in a particularly dramatic fashion. Consciously executed with the compositional complexity of a mural, Wilson's print layers multiple components in order to draw an explicit parallel between the anti-Semitic violence of Nazi Germany and the racist violence committed against African Americans in the United States (figure 13). Toward this end, Wilson centers the right half of his lithograph around a young African American man, woman, and child—that is, a family group similar to those of his *Black Soldier* and *Breadwinner*, but here presented as huddled closely together in a single cohesive unit. Around this family, he groups several distinct scenes: an exterior rendering of two adjacent tenement buildings; an interior scene of a black family confined within a rundown apartment, presumably inside of a tenement building; a noose-brandishing man in a suit and a policeman with raised club preparing to lead a lynching party, at least ostensibly on behalf of the smugly smiling white woman who stands sheltered between them; and an actual lynching, with white men, women, and even a child gathered around the tree that bears the mob's black victim. In the lower right register of the print, Wilson offers a visual commentary on the economic roots of racial violence in the form of a corpulent, cigar-smoking capitalist tycoon who sits at an expensive dining table with his wife and laughs as representative black and white industrial laborers engage in violent struggle, their hands literally at one another's throats. The black man and child in the center of these striking vignettes look outward, as if directly interrogating the viewer's response to the social scene that surrounds this family.

As a counterpoint to this African American family, Wilson centers the left half of the lithograph on a Jewish man, woman, and child. Surrounding the Jewish

family are a saluting Adolf Hitler, flanked by two fellow fascist military leaders and a menacing array of cannons; a regiment of marching Nazi storm troopers; bomber planes flying over European cities; a Jewish lynching victim hanging from a gallows; and Jewish captives imprisoned within the barbed-wire fence of a concentration camp. Notably, the placement of the Jewish concentration camp prisoners is such that Wilson seems to be implying a certain parallel to the entrapment of the African American family within the tenement apartment in the upper right corner of the print (Williams and Williams 36). At the base of the left half of Wilson's print, the broken columns and pediments of classical Western architecture lie toppled over a pile of naked human bodies, suggesting the gruesome fall of civilization under fascist rule. Significantly, Wilson draws no distinct border between the German and American halves of his lithograph.

Deliver Us from Evil clearly reflects the antifascist impulses prevalent among American artists and writers during the late 1930s and early 1940s. Thus, it is not coincidental that when Wilson submitted this lithograph to *New Masses* for an art contest in 1944, the editorial staff of that magazine proposed the alternate title *The Evils of Fascism*.[30] The biblical source of Wilson's own title suggests that, indeed, he did see the antifascist struggle as an epochal clash against forces of evil. As Wilson later reflected, "The epitome of evil was Adolf Hitler and the whole Nazi Fascist philosophy. . . . For me, the ruthless, efficient, invincible German storm troopers became a symbol of all powerful forces of oppression in which individuals were molded into collective killing machines fueled by ideologies of hate and racial superiority."[31] However, given the way that Wilson *also* used this lithograph to explore the growing threat of fascism in terms of its particular implications for African Americans, *Deliver Us* refuses to grant white America the conceit of playing the virtuous hero to Nazi villainy. Wilson's thoughts in this regard bear quoting at length:

> I felt this evil going on in Europe, which was aimed at elevating the Aryan race as the dominant race. And of course the low men on the totem pole—the niggers of Europe—were the Jews, who were being physically eliminated. On the other hand, during that time I was being asked to join in this fight against Hitler to create a free, democratic world, to free these poor victims in Europe. When I would then pick up a newspaper and see someone lynched in Alabama or [that] the Scottsboro Boys' trials were still going on, or I would go to get a job and they would laugh in my face if it was anything other than shining shoes. . . . this whole business of my going to liberate dehumanized people in Europe when the same thing was happening here. . . . I had this sense of indignation that this world that I was living in could be perpetuating these things and calling themselves a land of freedom and justice. . . . And so I essentially wanted to unmask this.

Wilson's choice of the term "unmask" supports art historian Richard Powell's contention that the artist composed this print to act somewhat in the fashion of "a speech or political tract" (10). Like a speech or tract, Wilson's lithograph serves to transform or intensify the race and class consciousness of his audience—in this case, by providing a systematic decoding of ethnic exploitation by the forces of reactionary bigotry and capital on a global scale.

In this act of unmasking the parallels between German and American manifestations of ethnic genocide, Wilson rearticulates a sentiment that had been prevalent within the Popular Front milieu of the mid- to late 1930s. To be sure, vigilance with respect to the domestic half of this equation had become somewhat muted in leftist cultural discourse by the time Wilson executed this lithograph in 1943, but African American cultural workers helped to sustain this line of cultural critique—as evidenced, for example, in John Biggers's *Dying Soldier* mural. Wilson himself insists that virtually all African Americans at the time understood on some level that "what was going on in Europe in essence was happening here. Maybe the 'final solution' wasn't being carried out because they needed black bodies for cheap labor. . . . The point is they weren't killing us *physically* as they would be in Europe, but it was a kind of slow death." In a similar vein, essays published in journals like the *Crisis* almost routinely offered comparative observations of Jewish and African American persecution. As early as 1934, in a *Crisis* essay whose title posed the rhetorical question, "Can America Go Fascist?" prominent white socialist Norman Thomas wrote: "There is no nation where there is greater and more violent race and class prejudice. Hitler has not yet been able to teach the German people to practice toward Jews or any other group such instinctively diabolical, sadistic cruelties as Americans practice in their lynching, particularly when, as is usually the case, the victims are Negroes" (11). Similarly, *New Masses* editor Lloyd Brown remarked of a postwar lynching case in 1946, "These lynchers were no maddened mob, killing in a momentary craze. No, they were an organized detachment of bilbos and rankins, executing their victims with the cold-blooded efficiency of the Gestapo exterminating Jews" ("Death" 3).

So too, in the leftist visual culture of the depression era, analogues abounded for Wilson's juxtaposition of Nazi and U.S. brands of white supremacy. For instance, Hyman Warsager's illustration *The Law*, which was reproduced in the January 9, 1934, issue of *New Masses,* depicts a lynching victim hanging from a tree that has its roots in a stately building labeled "U.S. Courts." Significantly, Warsager illustrates a swastika inscribed on the facade of this building, thus framing a pointed critique of the institutional dimension of American racism through an explicit parallel to Nazi anti-Semitism. Likewise, in February 1935, the *Crisis* ran a political cartoon that paralleled the racist atrocities for which Hitler and a bloody-handed Uncle Sam stood accountable. With regard to this confluence of issues, at least, *New Masses* and the *Crisis* thus bore a rather striking similarity to one another. In the 1940s, African American artists again played the primary role in articulating this analogy. A 1942 *People's Voice* illustration by radical cartoonist Ollie Harrington made this indictment in a particularly graphic manner, placing a bullet-riddled victim of Nazi murder side by side with the African American victim of a particularly notorious wartime lynching in Sikeston, Missouri.[32]

Given Wilson's immersion in leftist print and visual culture, the aesthetic and conceptual parallels between *Deliver Us* and political cartoons by the likes of Warsager and Harrington are hardly coincidental. This resonance with the spirit of radical little magazines holds particularly true in the case of Wilson's tableau of the capitalist tycoon and struggling black and white workers in the lower right corner of his print. Much as Charles White's murals integrated iconography and aesthetics derived from political cartooning in deliberate disregard for the widely presumed sanctity of painting vis-à-vis such a "low art" graphic medium, Wilson here engages in a similar act of strategic appropriation—and with good reason. As Cécile Whiting documents in *Antifascism in American Art* (1989), radical illustrators were among the earliest and most persistent social critics of fascism during the 1930s and early 1940s; in forging their critiques, these illustrators frequently drew connections between American capitalists and the fascist dictators of Europe and Japan. Political cartoonist William Gropper, in particular, evidenced a penchant for depicting American capitalists in complicit alliance with fascist leaders like Hitler, Mussolini, and Tojo during the 1930s. For example, in *Rot Front*, which appeared in the February 1933 issue of *New Masses*, Gropper portrays Hitler, a crowned European head of state, and a portly, stick-wielding capitalist advancing together toward a violent confrontation with a crowd of anonymous workers.

Perhaps even more specific in its influence on the jolly capitalist and struggling workers scene of Wilson's *Deliver Us from Evil* is Orozco's mural *The Rich Banquet While the Workers Fight* (1923) from the National Preparatory School in Mexico City, which Wilson may have seen in reproduced form by the early 1940s.[33] As James Oles explains, the ideologically charged iconography employed by artists such as Orozco—that is, "obese and often distorted figures of men wearing evening clothes and clutching at moneybags"—remained, well into the 1940s, an important emblem of capitalist abuse of power with reference to both the United States and the corrupt regimes of postrevolutionary Mexico (195).[34] In fact, Orozco's use of such iconography itself owes to leftist political cartoons of the sort I referenced in discussion of *The Masses* earlier in the chapter. Being an avid reader of the black press and interracial leftist publications, as well as an admirer of the Mexican muralists, Wilson was well aware of this representational convention and its ideological underpinnings. It is hardly coincidental, then, that

Chapter Three

Wilson's *Deliver Us* print itself gained its greatest visibility when it was published by *New Masses* in July 1945 as the second place winner in its Art Young Memorial Cartoon Award contest. Later, *New Masses* also made arrangements with Wilson for the mass distribution of reproductions of this print on "a 50/50 basis."[35]

Thus, *Deliver Us from Evil* signals not only the importance of leftist politics to Wilson's interpretation of the root causes of American racism but also his allegiance to leftist strategies for the mass distribution of art. Owing to his engagement with socialism, Wilson became increasingly convinced "that the root was the fact that this was being perpetuated by institutions and powerful people who profited from the fact that they could get cheap labor." Consequently, Wilson observes, "Unions were being broken because businesses would hire blacks during a strike break and, of course, racism made it impossible for black and white workers to collectively get together so that they could fight for their own common best interests." Significantly, then, Wilson attributes American racism (and Nazi anti-Semitism) to a combination of factors of race and class, within what is essentially a Marxist framework. At times, Wilson's retrospective reflections even seem to privilege issues of class over race: "It wasn't a question of race, it was a question of the fact that race was another expedient gimmick to exploit people. What was happening to blacks was happening to millions of other Americans . . . as long as they were not in the upper classes . . . that is, if they were punching a time clock and working for a boss who controlled the nature of their work program." In this regard, Wilson's statements seem akin to leftist articulations by groups like the American Artists' Congress and publications like *New Masses* during the previous decade.

Yet, whereas the work of William Gropper and his leftist peers generally became relatively optimistic regarding the capacity of the U.S. and Soviet working classes to defeat the Axis powers by the early 1940s, Wilson's print seems to share with the early Gropper illustration *Rot Front* a pronounced uncertainty regarding the outcome of the struggle between fascist and antifascist factions—both at home and abroad (see also Whiting 17–19). Notably, the forces of fascism are everywhere abundant in Wilson's lithograph; by contrast, the efforts of antifascists remain to be enacted. In fact, Wilson seems to have been relatively critical of artists he felt had adopted a naive leftist idealism. For instance, he remarks of Diego Rivera, "Rivera, I'm sure, felt an identification with the frustrated lives of the average person, but Diego Rivera had a formula for how it could be resolved—the Marxist, Communist formula of socialism and the enemy was big business and capitalism, and socialism and the Soviet Union and Stalin would create a whole new world, which would throw out these enemies of the people and build this . . . wonderful world of equality." In counterpoint to what Wilson perceived as the contrived and formulaic solutions of certain Rivera murals from the

1930s, he found Orozco to be more broadly against "power being used arbitrarily to truncate the lives of the average person" and argued that Orozco "was not as much of an ideologue as Diego Rivera. He had this sincere involvement with and compassion for the everyday lives of the ordinary Mexican people, which were lives of conflict and frustration and poverty. . . . He identified with all this in the same way that Käthe Kollwitz identified with the serfs and the peasants in Germany." Arguably, Wilson draws an overly sharp distinction between Orozco (and Kollwitz) and Rivera on these matters. Still, his description of Orozco tells us a good deal about Wilson's own political sensibilities and also captures a sense of the motivation that Wilson felt for extending his artistic development in Mexico. That ambition, however, would have to wait until 1950.

A top graduate of the Boston Museum School in 1947, Wilson received a James Wilson Paige Traveling Fellowship to fund his further study.[36] Although Wilson expressed his desire to use this fellowship to study with Orozco and other muralists in Mexico, the fellowship committee was insistent that its funds would be better spent, and Wilson's career better served, by study in Europe. Museum School administrator Russell T. Smith advised, "I suspect from your letter that what is happening is that you are trying to find influences from the future for your painting rather than influences from the past. Having been in Mexico myself, I know very well that you would get very little out of it as far as art is concerned."[37] As I shall suggest momentarily, when Wilson eventually traveled to Mexico in 1950 he found the experience considerably more enriching than Smith's rather smug prognostication would have indicated. However, Wilson used the Paige Fellowship to travel to France and did, in fact, find his time there to be extremely productive—albeit not entirely for reasons that academic art officials like Smith might have foreseen.

To be sure, among its other benefits, residence in Paris granted Wilson firsthand exposure to the work of wide-ranging Western master artists such as Picasso, Monet, and Seurat. However, while studying in France, Wilson also spent considerable time at Paris's Musée de l'Homme, which provided him with his first substantial exposure to works of African art and culture, as well as the arts of the Far East and other non-Western cultures. Interestingly, whereas modernists like Picasso and Braque had engaged African art primarily on the level of form, Wilson found in these non-Western art traditions a vital model for the integration of artists with their respective communities—a motive that had been at the heart of much cultural work by Americans during the depression era (see also Peeler 269–71). In his words, "[African artists] created art that served their collective communal needs. By contrast, contemporary European Art seemed increasingly 'affected.'"[38] Significantly, one could hardly confuse Wilson's reflections with Alain Locke's Harlem Renaissance–era meditations on African art. Whereas Locke's influential *New Negro* essay "The Legacy of the Ancestral Arts" posited African art foremost as a mine of classical design motifs from which African American artists might draw inspiration, Wilson found in African art an example that affirmed his own ambitions to fashion a politically engaged art for a mass audience. Notably, too, this position stood in direct contrast to the notion of artist as heroic individualist that was by then permeating much of cold war–era high modernism in the U.S. art world.

Equally important, the Paige Fellowship enabled Wilson to spend almost two years of study with Fernand Léger. In selecting Léger, one of the most noted European muralists of the day, Wilson's foremost goal remained learning the techniques of fresco painting so that he could undertake murals in the fashion of his primary role model, Orozco. Wilson recalls that his Paris mentor was an adamant leftist who occasionally offered lectures on Marxism, both to students and to a more general public. In keeping with these political sympathies, Léger frequently sought out proletarian subjects; Wilson accurately recollects many of Léger's works as illustrating an idealistic socialist future in which man and man-made artifacts of architecture and machinery are harmoniously integrated. At the same time, however, Léger's work remained unabashedly modernist in terms of his aesthetic technique of reducing objects to elemental geometric forms. For Léger, not only was such a modernist style potentially accessible to a mass audience, but also such formal innovation was *essential* if the politically engaged artist was to compete with "the daily allurements of the movies, the radio, large-scale photography and advertising." In a 1937 speech that was reprinted in *Art Front*, Léger defended his brand of "new realism" by asserting, "An art popular in character but inferior in quality—based upon the excuse that [the masses] will never understand anything about art, anyway—would be unworthy of them" (7–8).

The influence of Léger on Wilson's graphic artwork in the late 1940s and early 1950s is striking. For example, Wilson's treatment of the human figure in the lithograph *Blvd. de Strasbourg* (c. 1950), in which he attempts to capture the bustle of life on a Paris street corner, is considerably less naturalistic than in an early 1940s street scene like *Adolescence*. Influenced by Léger's brand of cubism, Wilson's *Blvd.* treats facial features in angular, succinctly drawn terms and renders the overall human figure in something much closer to basic geometric forms than what one finds in his earlier prints. In this regard, one can see why Wilson states that Léger's "robust use of color, form and space" was of particular interest to him.[39] Still, in explicating this work, Wilson emphasizes his intention that viewers be able to recognize that this print includes distinct figures such as a white-collar worker and blue-collar skilled laborer. Hence, although Wilson here moves away from the more photographic likenesses of his early prints and selects a

French rather than an African American subject, what remains constant is the artist's abiding interest in working-class themes. Wilson himself insists on the thematic continuity between this lithograph and his previous work: "I'm not painting upper middle class ladies in their boudoir with white silk dresses like Sargent; I'm using people, ordinary people in the street." In other words, Wilson emphatically does *not* want viewers to conceive of works like *Blvd. de Strasbourg* as "abstract art." Rather, he aims to capture the essence of a working-class subject in such a way that "the viewer can go out in the street and recognize [its] connection to reality. . . . The other aspect about using shapes is it forces you to recognize [it] at a glance and see the thing as a symbol, so that it's a boy, it's a worker, [but] not a particular worker."

When Wilson returned from France, the Henry Wallace campaign of 1948 was already over, but he soon joined activists from Boston's Progressive Party circle in undertakings such as picketing a Woolworth's in Roxbury for its failure to hire African American employees. (It was also through the Progressive Party that Wilson met his wife, Julie Kowitch.[40]) With certain of these same leftist friends, Wilson relocated to New York City, where he soon became personally acquainted with fellow African American artists such as Robert Blackburn, Elton Fax, Romare Bearden, and Ernest Crichlow. Through Crichlow, Wilson learned of an interracial Workers' Children's Camp in New Jersey known as Camp Wo-Chi-Ca and sponsored by the International Workers Order. As with many of the cultural programs backed by the IWO during the 1930s and 1940s, this camp stressed the values of ethnic pluralism—in this case, by teaching songs, dances, and other activities from a range of cultural traditions and in a range of languages, such as Yiddish, Spanish, and Chinese. Guest performers and lecturers at the camp while Wilson served as its art instructor included Paul Robeson, Charles White, and leftist folk singers of various ethnic backgrounds and nationalities. In fact, White, Elizabeth Catlett, and Crichlow all had formerly taught art at this same camp.

In spite of having found a personal connection with fellow African American artists in New York deeper than he had ever known in Boston, Wilson remained eager to study with Mexican master artists like Orozco. Toward this end, he applied for and received a John Hay Whitney Fellowship for study in Mexico for 1950–51. Although Wilson's prime motivation for going to Mexico was to learn techniques and an aesthetic vocabulary appropriate to mural painting, in point of fact he did much more substantial work in graphic art media than in murals during his years "south of the border." As Wilson has described the nature of his work in graphics during this period, "The reason I turned to printmaking was again this business of producing an art form that would reach a wide audience, the sense of doing things that could have a direct kind of influence on as many people as possible. I was excited about the Mexicans because they did art that was designed to reach a large public." In the absence of mural commissions, Wilson found that "[d]oing lithography was the next best thing" (Fax, "John Wilson" 94). In keeping with these objectives, Wilson sought out Mexico's Taller de Gráfica Popular, in large part because this collective specialized in producing prints, posters, and broadsides for the Mexican labor movement and other progressive political causes.

At this stage in his career, Wilson began to apply the insights of his recent European experiences with Léger to "the socially conscious direction of the Mexican artists."[41] From Wilson's perspective, the Mexican artists, Léger, and his own art all shared an overarching ambition to fuse modernist aesthetic innovation with politically engaged content. Not surprisingly, then, a Mexican period work such as Wilson's 1951 lithograph *Trabajador* encompasses both the modernist economy of form that one finds in *Blvd. de Strasbourg* and the special concern with working-class citizenry that characterized the artwork of the Taller de Gráfica Popular. Specifically, *Trabajador* portrays a bricklayer at work at a construction site. In this lithograph, Wilson takes special care to articulate the skill and precision with which the craftsman executes his task by granting prominent size and detail to the figure's hands.[42] Comparing Wilson's *Trabajador* with the disenfranchised laborer of his 1942 print *Breadwinner* offers further evidence of the definite stylistic shift in Wilson's work over the course of his early career. Whereas Wilson renders the countenance of the man in *Breadwinner* quite naturalistically, the artist's *Trabajador* seems of ambiguous African American or Mexican ethnicity and possesses smooth geometrized features in the manner of an African mask. This aesthetic transition reflects both the influence of Léger's modernist aesthetics and Wilson's informal study of African artifacts in the Musée de l'Homme while in Paris. In sum, *Trabajador* suggests that Wilson's Mexican period graphics continue to reflect the artist's concern with working-class themes, even if his aesthetic sensibility by the early 1950s bears only a loose resemblance to the predominant proletarian modes of depression-era social realism.

Wilson also maintained an avid interest in specifically African American issues of social justice throughout his stay in Mexico. A 1951 lithograph titled *The Trial* bears out this point. In this print, Wilson positions an African American man looking up at three justices who stare down remorselessly from a towering bench. To the left of and below these justices, but still elevated above the man on trial, sits a white woman in a witness chair (figure 14). With this female figure, Wilson symbolically evokes the long-standing tradition of U.S. courts' citing "protection of white womanhood" as a justification for the incarceration of numerous black men; simultaneously, he seems to indict the complicity of certain

Figure 14. John Wilson (b. 1922), *The Trial,* 1951. Lithograph, 13½ × 10 in. (© John Wilson/Licensed by VAGA, New York, New York.)

white women in this dubious pattern of rationalization. (Recall that the artist critiques this same historical pattern in *Deliver Us from Evil*.) As Wilson well knew, use of this rationale extended from the Reconstruction era through the Scottsboro case of the early 1930s and into the early 1950s; it manifest itself not only in the courts but also in extralegal brutalization and murder of African American men by white lynch mobs—as witnessed most infamously by the tragic case of Emmett Till in Mississippi four years after Wilson's 1951 lithograph. Wilson attributed the origins of *The Trial*, then, to his feelings of "monumental rage" as he received news in Mexico regarding "lynchings illegal and legal" in the United States.

Significantly, all four of the print's white figures wear theatrical masks. Here, one might profitably compare Wilson's *Trial* lithograph with an oil painting from the same period by Robert Gwathmey titled *Masks* (1946).[43] In Gwathmey's work, a corpulent, well-dressed white man stands next to a black man whose hands are bound together with rope; the white man holds up a minimally detailed white mask in front of his own face and a broadly smiling black mask in front of the African American man's face. Significantly, whereas the white mask is rather expressionless, the black mask is an exaggerated racist caricature akin to the "comic" tradition of blackface minstrelsy. Further, in Gwathmey's rendering the wealthy white man controls the public face of both himself and his symbolically representative black peer. As in Gwathmey's painting, Wilson's placement of theatrical masks on the white agents of the justice system in *The Trial* suggests that white racial identity is itself a type of performance, one that serves to legitimize the oppression of African Americans: "These people are wearing masks to suggest that not only are they indulging in deceptive fantasies but that they are hiding and disguising their own true humanity," Wilson explained. While revealing racial identity as a type of performance, Wilson recognized that such performances held concrete and oppressive consequences—both for African Americans and for whites, inasmuch as it prevents the latter from expressing anything like what Wilson terms "true humanity." The function of the work, then, was to serve as both explication and catharsis: "I felt as if I had to shape something which might exorcise the terror and sense of intimidation that these incidents grafted on to my psyche as I was growing [up] in 'freedom loving' America."[44]

Although he never personally had to confront a racially charged courtroom trial, Wilson has described his own encounters with racism as numerous and intensely felt. For instance, in the early 1990s he could recall with still palpable bitterness the harassment that he and his Jewish wife experienced on those occasions when they periodically had to travel from Mexico City to Texas border towns to renew their visas and related documents. And later, based on the advice of fellow artist and Dillard University instructor Vernon Winslow, Wilson decided to forgo the prospect of teaching art at a southern college or university because of his interracial marriage.[45] By contrast, in Mexico Wilson not only found instances of racism much less prevalent, but he also encountered an empathetic community of "progressive" artists and other intellectuals. While living there Wilson met artists like Siqueiros, Ignacio Aguirre, and American expatriate Pablo O'Higgins and established a sense of camaraderie with fellow African American artist Elizabeth Catlett, who had relocated to Mexico in 1947. In addition, Wilson fondly recalls Margaret Burroughs staying in the same apartment building as he and his wife when she made an extended visit to Mexico City in 1952–53 (Fax, "John Wilson" 97). Yet, in spite of the many appeals of life in Mexico, Wilson chose to return to the United States in 1956, in part owing to the difficulty of supporting his family as a freelance artist in Mexico City and in part due to a compulsion to participate more immediately in the emerging African American Civil Rights movement (96–97). At least in his own retrospective account, Wilson has explained that "wanting to make some statement about what was happening to black people in the United States was something that . . . I felt I had to be there. In other words, I couldn't be a Richard Wright, who created his powerful novels and felt the horror of living in Jim Crow America and went to Paris."

Wilson's art and political activism in Boston, Paris, New York, Mexico City, and ultimately back in the United States provide a prime illustration of the extent to which many cultural workers continued to pursue the type of issues most often associated with the Popular Front political culture of the late 1930s well into the cold war era. Like Charles White, for instance, Wilson maintained involvement with the Joint Anti-Fascist Refugee Committee—in his case, by contributing design work to the Boston branch of this organization in early 1950. In addition, Wilson was a member of the Independent Citizens Committee of the Arts, Sciences, and Professions, which proposed goals of full employment, limiting expansion and use of the atomic bomb, international cultural cooperation, and combating discrimination as a manifestation of native fascism. Notably, a partial list of Wilson's fellow sponsors of this organization suggests that the cultural milieu of the American left in the mid- to late 1940s remained a genuinely interracial one: members included Jo Davidson, Louis Adamic, Mary McCleod Bethune, Philip Evergood, Howard Fast, Langston Hughes, Canada Lee, Orson Welles, Raphael Soyer, Van Wyck Brooks, Lillian Hellman, and Paul Robeson— Popular Front veterans, one and all.[46] And lest one conclude that participation in such groups consisted merely of signing various petitions and political position statements, one also might consider that when Wilson returned to the United States in 1956, he found employment in Chicago producing posters for trade union strikes and boycotts, as well as covers and illustrations for labor publications like *Packinghouse Worker* and the *Reporter*.

So too, while still in Mexico at midcentury, Wilson continued to publish re-productions of his graphic art in radical laborist journals of culture. For example, *The Straphanger,* an illustration that resonates with numerous depression-era images of fatigued workers aboard buses and subway cars, appeared in the May 1950 issue of *Masses and Mainstream.* Like much of Wilson's output, *The Straphanger* points to important broader trends in the field: namely, the contem-porary orientation of much social realist work in the graphic arts, and, again, the fact that social realism had hardly disappeared as the spirit of the cold war became a dominant ethos of American life. In fact, each of the themes that I examine in the final section of this chapter—including racial violence, inequities in the U.S. legal system, and both rural and urban scenes of working-class life—continued to receive treatment by artists like Wilson during the 1940s. Meanwhile, World War II itself generated *new* grist for the proverbial mill of social realist graphic art by African Americans. Moreover, Wilson's publication of prints such as *Deliver Us from Evil* in *New Masses* and *The Straphanger* in *Masses and Mainstream* should point us toward the centrality of little magazines and their affiliated cultural ven-ues in sustaining such radical cultural work through the 1940s and early 1950s.

Graphic Artists as Partisan Documentarians

Turning back to the ostensible depression-era heyday of American social realism, as one examines the membership rolls, political agendas, and actual cultural work produced under the auspices of the John Reed Clubs, the Artists' Union, the American Artists' Congress, and similar leftist artist organizations, it becomes clear that African American social realists were not alone in their use of graphic arts to explore African American–focused themes. To be sure, Aaron Douglas did critique the representation of African Americans in social realist art in his speech at the 1936 American Artists' Congress, stating: "It is when we come to revolu-tionary art that we find the Negro sincerely represented, but here the portrayal is too frequently automatic, perfunctory and arbitrary. He becomes a kind of prole-tarian prop, a symbol, vague and abstract" (Baigell and Williams 84). Yet, while nonblack social realists may at times have been better grounded in ideologies of interracialism than in concrete experiences of such realities, some such artists did at least attempt to explore contemporary, politically charged African American subject matter in graphics, much more so than with the medium of mural paint-ing. One of several notable artists in this regard was Prentiss Taylor, whose de-pression-era lithographs included works such as *Town of Scottsboro, Black Boys, Roxbury Foundry,* and *Christ in Alabama.* Significantly, Taylor's work appeared frequently in the *Crisis* in the early to mid-1930s and was exhibited at the Howard University Art Gallery in the spring of 1942.[47] Because of his extensive and relatively sophisticated handling of African American themes, Taylor also provided the illustrations for books such as *The Negro Mother* (1931) and *Scottsboro Limited* (1932) by the radical poet Langston Hughes. For their part, African American graphic artists spearheaded the chronicling of at least five important terrains of contemporary social struggle: (1) racial violence; (2) legal injustice; (3) antifascism and the Second World War; (4) working-class experience, with a special emphasis on African American defense workers; and (5) poverty and joblessness.

As in works like Taylor's *Christ in Alabama* (1932), racial violence—particularly lynching—received considerable attention from social realist artists of varied ethnic identities. Of course, the use of art to dramatize the root causes and horrors of such violence was not new to the 1930s. For example, in 1923 Ashcan School artist George Bellows fashioned a lithograph titled *The Law Is Too Slow*, a grisly lynching scene that subsequently appeared as the jacket cover to NAACP officer Walter White's *Rope and Faggot: A Biography of Judge Lynch* in 1929.[48] Moreover, politically engaged African American publications—most notably the *Crisis*—had long employed images of lynching victims as a way of attempting to mobilize political opposition to racist terrorism. Toward this end, the journal published documentary photographs and essays on specific lynching cases, editorials and advertisements regarding particular federal antilynching bill campaigns, and more general antilynching political cartoons. In all of these frameworks, the *Crisis* consistently trained a proverbial spotlight onto lynching as the most dramatic illustration of the persistent gap between American promises of democratic civil equality and the nation's frequent practices of racist oppression.

Even more directly pertinent to this study, Walter White and the *Crisis* helped to organize and sponsor an exhibit called *An Art Commentary on Lynching* at the Arthur Newton Galleries in 1935.[49] In keeping with the spirit of most social realist artists of the period, White's correspondence from this project indicates his desire to gather works of both aesthetic merit and sociopolitical efficacy. That is, while White wanted to produce a prestigious show of high artistic quality, he *also* intended the exhibit to perform the specific political function of mobilizing support for the passage of federal antilynching legislation in the form of the Costigan-Wagner Bill, a measure deemed particularly urgent in light of the resurgence of lynchings in the early 1930s. In a letter to Gloria Vanderbilt Whitney, White wrote, "Even a morbid subject can be made popular if a sufficiently distinguished list of patronesses will sponsor the exhibit and the right kind of publicity can be secured for it. . . . I fear I have put this somewhat crudely and inadequately but I trust that you will be able to understand how I am trying delicately to effect a union of art and propaganda" (Park 326). Indeed, the political angle of the exhibit was sufficiently clear that the Jacques Seligmann Galleries, originally scheduled to host the show, backed out at the last moment due to what Seligmann termed "political, social and economic pressure" and a desire to "keep the gallery free of political or racial manifestations" ("Art Exhibit" 106; Vendryes 154).

As staged at the Newton Galleries, the *Art Commentary on Lynching* exhibit included oils, watercolors, prints, and sculpture by artists with a wide range of aesthetic styles and political orientations: Regionalists Thomas Hart Benton and John Steuart Curry; Ashcan School artist George Bellows; social realists such as Harry Sternberg and José Clemente Orozco; and Japanese American modernist sculptor Isamu Noguchi. Not coincidentally, artists seem to have particularly favored graphic media for their contributions to this exhibit. For certain of the white artists included in the show, such as Reginald Marsh and Paul Cadmus, the choice of an openly political antiracist theme comprised something of an exception in their respective oeuvres. In fact, some artists crafted works specifically for the *Art Commentary on Lynching* exhibit at the behest of Walter White. White artists like Taylor and Julius Bloch, by contrast, actually were best known in the 1930s for their work on African American subjects.

In terms of drawing out something of a common theme from the works of white artists in this exhibit—and it is worth emphasizing that exceptions exist on this count—David Peeler suggests that "though they usually showed the victims with open sympathy, the [white] artists' chief concern was with the barbarity of the lynchers" (224). One certainly sees this quality in evidence in works like Paul Cadmus's *To the Lynching!* and Reginald Marsh's *This Is Her First Lynching.* Presenting lynchers as snarling, scarcely human monsters in the midst of committing ravenous violence against a black male figure, Cadmus inverts the rhetoric of white supremacist ideology by presenting lynchers—not their African American victim—as uncivilized beasts (see also Vendryes 164–66).[50] For his part, Marsh makes a similar point through a more ironic tack: by depicting a woman holding a small girl aloft over a crowd, presumably to provide her with a better view of the lynching act, Marsh critiques the way in which many white communities seemed to regard lynching as a type of celebratory public ritual. Similarly, in adding their voices to those urging the passage of federal antilynching legislation through introductory comments for the *Art Commentary* exhibition catalog, writers Sherwood Anderson and Erskine Caldwell concentrated their remarks on describing lynching as a sign of social backwardness, a "descent into the slough of barbarism" in Caldwell's terms. Thus, art historian Margaret Rose Vendryes notes that in both the art itself and associated editorial rhetoric, "the lynch mob . . . was in most cases addressed as existing somewhere beyond the civilized confines of the art gallery" (172).

As one would expect, Walter White also recruited the work of African American artists for this exhibit. The ten black artists among the exhibit's thirty-eight contributors included Henry Bannarn, Samuel Brown, E. Simms Campbell, Allan Freelon, Wilmer Jennings, Malvin Gray Johnson, and Hale Woodruff. Even though Vendryes is correct in arguing that these African American artists generally "preferred to focus on victimhood and those potential victims left behind" (168), it is nonetheless true that they also poignantly indicted the brutality and barbarism of lynching. For example, a reviewer for the *Amsterdam News* observed that Freelon's *Barbecue—American Style* (c. 1935) "shows the distorted figure of a Negro burning at the stake, while a crowd of whites, including children, are looking on" (Park 332). In much the same vein, Hale Woodruff's *Giddap* (1935) depicts a group of white lynchers, whose clothing seems to mark them as rural southerners, as they prepare to remove a wagon that precariously supports the feet of an African American man whose neck lies within a noose; raised fists, a tightly grasped rock, and a rifle bode still further violence to the victim's body following the hanging, as in many actual lynching cases.[51]

Like white peers Harry Sternberg and Philip Guston, Woodruff also issued a special critique of the religious hypocrisy of lynchers who professed Christianity. For example, *By Parties Unknown* (c. 1935), a woodblock print, depicts the bound body of a lynching victim on the steps of a decrepit, wood-frame church (figure 15). With such critiques, notes art historian Marlene Park, "Woodruff was literally laying the blame at the doorstep of the Southern poor whites who professed to be Christians" (338). The phrase from which Woodruff took the title for this piece was one that white communities frequently employed in disingenuously absconding from their responsibility to persecute lynchers; in fact, the use of this particular phrase as a point of contestation for antilynching activists was hardly new to Woodruff's linocut. For instance, the October 1930 issue of the *Crisis* included a photograph of a lynching in which an entire community oversees the barbarous ritual, with the bitterly ironic caption, "Civilization in the United States, 1930: The lynching of Tom Shipp and Abe Smith at Marion, Indiana, August 7, 'by parties unknown.'" Thus, although Woodruff does not depict the guilty parties in this particular woodcut, a contemporaneous audience would have understood that local white churchgoers and law enforcement officers typically were well aware of the parties responsible for a lynching—if, indeed, those same local constituencies were not themselves participants in the lynching.

A somewhat younger generation of African American artists, including Elizabeth Catlett and Charles White, continued to explore the lynching theme in graphic art during the 1940s. Significantly, this generation came of age during the pinnacle of antilynching activity by groups like the NAACP and artists such as Woodruff in the mid-1930s, and themselves became involved in such leftist political causes even in their youth. Samella Lewis explains that Catlett "would, for example, stand in front of the Supreme Court building with a hangman's noose

Figure 15. Hale Aspacio Woodruff (1900–1980), *By Parties Unknown,* c. 1935. Linocut on paper. (Gibbes Museum of Art/Carolina Art Association [2001.22.05].)

around her neck as part of an organized protest against the existing practice of lynching," while a student at Howard University in the mid-1930s (11). So too, Lewis has recalled from firsthand experience as a student that Catlett's vigorous political activism engaged a range of progressive causes during her tenure at Dillard University in New Orleans between 1940 and 1942: "She stood up to everybody, and involved herself in affairs that were unpopular at that time for both Blacks and women. Her immersion into civil rights movements, labor movements, and human rights in general was a threat to the status quo and an embarrassment to the conservative officials of the university. . . . She confronted police on brutality, bus drivers on segregated seating, and college administrators on curriculum" (15). Following the lead of those depression-era artists who participated in the *Art Commentary* exhibit, Catlett also directed her cultural work as a visual artist toward political campaigns that aimed to curtail racist violence and secure full civil rights for African Americans. For example, as with Woodruff's *By Parties Unknown*, Catlett's 1946–47 linocut *And a special fear for my loved ones* presents the lynched body of a black man as the central image of her composition.[52] Also like Woodruff's print, Catlett's indictment of those responsible for the lynching is no less powerful for eschewing a direct portrayal of the murder itself and opting, instead, for a snapshot of the immediate aftermath of such an event. Specifically, the dramatically posed lynching victim of Catlett's linocut lies at the feet of three pairs of shoes. Composing her print in this manner, Catlett preserves the anonymity of the murderers in such a way as to make for a more open-ended artistic statement. That is, she places this representative victim of racial violence virtually "at the feet" of (white) viewers of the print, much as Woodruff had lain the body of a lynching victim at the proverbial doorstep of American churchgoers in *By Parties Unknown*.

In both the 1930s and the 1940s, African American social realists also executed a number of works of graphic art specifically concerned with the family members of victims of lynching and related forms of racist terrorism. Typically, the artists addressed this subject matter in a much more subdued manner than when they portrayed lynchers themselves. For instance, the effectiveness of Elizabeth Catlett's 1946 lithograph *Mother and Child* seems to turn on the viewer's familiarity with the withered tree as an icon of lynching in leftist and African American visual culture of the day. In light of the prevalence of such imagery, the dying tree that Catlett places beyond the foregrounded mother and child might stand as a marker not only of poverty and loss but also of a particular set of racist perils that the distraught mother recognizes as a threat to the future of her infant child (figure 16). Similar in this regard is a lithograph titled *Hope for the Future* (c. 1947), by Catlett's husband at the time, Charles White. White's print employs a compositional scheme that is nearly identical to Catlett's *Mother and Child*, but

Figure 16. Elizabeth Catlett (b. 1919), *Mother and Child,* 1946. Lithograph, 7¾ × 5¾ in. (All rights reserved, Metropolitan Museum of Art, Gift of Reba and Dave Williams, 1999 [1999.529.34]; © Elizabeth Catlett/Licensed by VAGA, New York, New York.)

makes the antilynching element of his work even more explicit by adding the element of a noose looming from the limb of a withered tree, which is visible through a window just over the mother's shoulder. In addition, White renders the mother's hands in an oversized fashion, as if to dramatize the mother's desire to protect her child from the foreboding future indicated by the emblem of the noose.[53]

Art collectors Reba and Dave Williams suggest that the form of White's mother and child may derive from a Congo Madonna and child that the artist saw as part of a Harmon Foundation exhibit of African art organized by Alain Locke in the early 1930s (24–25). If so, it seems highly suggestive that whereas Charles Alston referenced African art from Locke's collection as an emblem of classical black heritage in his Harlem Hospital murals, White drew upon a similar reference point as a means to more powerfully chronicle contemporary African American anxieties in the graphic medium of the lithograph. Whether the specifics of the Williams's hypothesis are correct or not, both White's *Hope for the Future* and Catlett's *Mother and Child* clearly do combine a modeling of the human figure based on African sculpture with poses that consciously resemble the Madonna and child iconography of Christian art. On this front, one might contrast Catlett and White's respective uses of the Madonna motif in these antilynching prints with Winold Reiss's *The Brown Madonna* of 1925.[54] Whereas Reiss's pastel portrait served to signal the dawning of a new efflorescence of black culture when it appeared as the frontispiece to Alain Locke's *The New Negro* anthology, Catlett and White employ the black Madonna and child archetype as a way of eliciting an empathetic audience response to the unjust persecution endured by African Americans and the psychic strain that the ever-present threat of racial violence introduces into African American life. Thus, while the Catlett and White lithographs share with Reiss's *New Negro* frontispiece the revisionist gesture of positing a black Christ child, the strategic deployment of the Madonna and child motif by Catlett and White would seem to have much *more* in common with a piece such as Dorothea Lange's famous photograph *Migrant Mother* (1936)—that is, a social realist work that depicts the imperilment of the Madonna and child as a way to more dramatically call attention to the social struggles facing contemporary mothers and their children.[55]

Madonna and child iconography is only one of the motifs borrowed by social realists from the annals of Christian art. Equally striking is the abundance of imagery that parallels black victims of racial violence to the crucified Christ. During the 1930s and early 1940s, E. Simms Campbell, John Biggers, and Frederick Flemister each drew on the conventions of Christian iconography in such a fashion: Campbell's *I Passed along This Way* (1935) places an African American subject pulled by a rope around his neck alongside Christ in the pose of one of the

Chapter Three

stations of the cross; Biggers's *Crucifixion* (1942) portrays a gaunt black man hung with a rope from a crucifix; and Flemister's *The Mourners* (c. 1940) depicts the aftermath of a lynching in the mode of a pietà. In this same vein, one might consider Prentiss Taylor's *Christ in Alabama* and John Steuart Curry's *The Fugitive*, two lithographs from the 1935 *Art Commentary on Lynching* exhibit that overtly render the African American victims of racist terrorism as Christlike martyr figures.

Significantly, social realists also applied a similar iconography to other politicized subjects as a way of dramatizing contemporary human suffering. For instance, Benton Spruance's *Souvenir of Lidice*, a prizewinning lithograph in the 1943 *Artists for Victory* exhibit, used a crucifixion motif to comment on the Nazi massacre of a Czech civilian community.[56] More broadly still, social realist poets and novelists also deployed a comparable kind of Christ imagery to enhance the resonance of revolutionary white American martyr figures, perhaps most famously in the character of Jim Casey from John Steinbeck's *The Grapes of Wrath* (1939). Of course, the appropriation of such imagery to capture the travesty of racial and ethnic violence did not originate with social realism per se. For example, Robert Minor's *In Georgia: The Southern Gentleman Demonstrates His Superiority* illustrated a crucified Jew and black man amidst a southern landscape for the August 1915 cover of *The Masses* in the immediate aftermath of the Leo Frank murder earlier that same month.[57]

Such was the extent of artists' use of Christian imagery in representing the victims of ethnic and political violence during the 1930s and 1940s that Marxist cultural critics sometimes took artists to task on precisely this point. For instance, *New Masses* reviewer Stephen Alexander lamented of the *Art Commentary on Lynching* exhibit, "Many of the works are so permeated by religious spirit as to be little more than prayer in graphic and plastic form" (29). Yet, where critics like Alexander were inclined to view the choice of such motifs simply as a manifestation of misplaced sentimentality or religious fatalism, I would argue that it is important to recognize these works as attempts by artists to formulate a visual language that was both accessible and emotively charged for a mass audience. In this regard, it seems telling that the reviewer for the *Amsterdam News*, an African American paper, was considerably more sympathetic to the religious iconography in the exhibit, singling out E. Simms Campbell's *I Passed along This Way* for special praise (Park 332). Certainly, it is not coincidental that a similarly politicized brand of black Christ imagery also appears in the work of several social realist poets of the 1930s and 1940s.

Clearly, the images of racial violence against African Americans produced by social realist artists focused predominantly on male victims. One noteworthy exception is Ernest Crichlow's 1938 lithograph *Lovers*, a work produced while the artist was employed by the Federal Art Project in New York City. In this iron-ically titled print, Crichlow depicts a hooded Klansman in the midst of raping a young black woman, who struggles to free herself from his grasp. As art historian Marlene Park astutely notes, Crichlow dramatizes the violence and struggle of this scene through an overturned, broken chair and through the sense of com-pression engendered by the sharply receding space behind the two central figures (350).[58] Much as antilynching prints by artists like Cadmus, Marsh, and Woodruff inverted white supremacist rhetoric by rendering lynchers as the truly uncivilized members of American society, Crichlow's lithograph sets out to oblit-erate racist mythologies of black female sexual promiscuity by portraying a white male figure as sexual aggressor. In this regard, Crichlow's symbolically charged rape scene consciously evokes a long history of white male sexual violence toward black women, as well as the legacy of struggle by African American women to re-sist these acts of sexual and psychic domination.

A related set of themes frequently explored by social realists through graphic art media pertained to the racial injustice that continued to characterize America's court system through midcentury (and beyond). As in other genres of social realist cultural expression, the Scottsboro case was one of the earliest events to attract graphic artists' attention, inspiring prints such as Prentiss Taylor's afore-mentioned *The Scottsboro Limited* (1932). A striking articulation of the theme of racial injustice in the courts on a more general level is Elton Fax's illustration for Grace Tompkins's short story "Justice Wears Dark Glasses," which appeared in the July–August 1944 issue of *Negro Story*. In this story, an African American woman is wrongfully arrested and summarily convicted for shoplifting when the white staff of a department store does not want to allow her to try on their dresses. For his accompanying illustration, Fax portrays a fiercely scowling white judge seated behind his courtroom bench. Not only does Fax render the judge literally wearing dark glasses, but he also suggests that the justice system's blindness re-garding issues of race derives from a willful intent by placing a Nazi swastika on the end of the judge's raised gavel. For Fax, as for John Wilson, the parallel be-tween American racism and European fascism thus retained considerable reso-nance well beyond the mid-1930s cultural moment in which this concept first attained prominence in leftist political discourse.

Charles White joined Fax and Wilson by dramatizing the parallels between white supremacists of the United States and fascist Europe, as well as the collu-sion between American racists of the North and South, in graphics based on noted cases of the day such as the wrongful incarceration of the Trenton Six, the trials of Rosa Lee Ingram and her sons, and the slaying of African American servicemen in Freeport, Long Island, in 1946.[59] In the Freeport case, the four

Ferguson brothers (two of them active soldiers, one other a veteran) got into an argument after they were refused service at a restaurant in the Freeport bus terminal. Soon thereafter, a policeman reportedly stopped the brothers, lined them against a wall, and then began shooting. Two of the brothers died and one was seriously injured. Even more, the officer received no reprimand for his action. Notably, White did not limit circulation of his artwork on such cases to gallery exhibits. Rather, in keeping with the spirit of social realism, he placed reproductions of these graphics in publications that were both left leaning and laborist in orientation: *Congress Vue/ Congress View* (a publication of the National Negro Congress); *Fraternal Outlook* (a publication of the International Workers Order); the *Worker Magazine* (a publication of the Communist Party); *Sing Out!* (a radical music journal that enjoined musicians to pledge "ever greater efforts to end the barriers of racial hatred and to build a unity of Negro and white Americans whose songs will make the walls of hate and prejudice come tumbling down"); and Paul Robeson's *Freedom* (with its motto of "Where one is enslaved, all are in chains!"). Further, certain of White's topically themed illustrations and prints reputedly sold as many as one hundred thousand copies (at a penny per copy) in the form of pamphlets produced by the *Daily Worker* specifically for mass distribution.

One such pamphlet was *Dixie Comes to New York: The Story of the Freeport Slayings* (1946), with text by Harry Raymond.[60] In this rendering of the Freeport tragedy, White depicts a zealous, almost gleeful policeman looming with a raised pistol over three of the Ferguson brothers; one of the brothers lies dead, while the other two kneel in horror. A robed Ku Klux Klansman stands directly behind the policeman, with one hand seductively on the officer's shoulder and the other bearing a torch. Interestingly, White also crafted a second illustration of the Freeport case, this one for the March 1946 issue of the NNC's *Congress View*. In this work, a southern judge hands a policeman a document labeled "permit to kill Negro vets and civilians," while a robed Klansman looks on approvingly with lynch rope in hand. Behind these conspirators, White displays one of the fallen Ferguson brothers at Freeport and the victims of a recent large-scale white riot against the black community in Columbia, Tennessee. However, towering over this grim scene stands the ghost of a second of the murdered Ferguson brothers in a torn military uniform, bearing a torch to shed light on these injustices. Significantly, this figure also bears a torn noose and broken chains, emblematic of his struggle for freedom. Thus, in keeping with the mission of the National Negro Congress, White's second rendering of the Freeport tragedy introduced a prominent element of African American resistance to such outrages.

Given the nature of White's murals, it can hardly prove surprising that his corpus of graphic art also includes portraits of individuals such as Harriet Tubman,

Sojourner Truth, and Frederick Douglass. What *is* striking, however, is the openly politicized way in which the artist conjoins these historical freedom fighters to the racial justice martyrs of his own day in several of his graphic projects. For instance, White's *The Living Douglass,* which appeared on the front page of the February 12, 1950, issue of the *Worker Magazine,* portrayed a giant Douglass tearing down barbed-wire fencing to free the Trenton Six, a group of young men convicted and sentenced to death for the alleged robbery and murder of a white storekeeper by means of what many on the left felt to be fabrication of evidence, forced confessions, and the prosecution's pandering to base racial stereotypes.[61] Notably, by placing the Trenton Six behind barbed wire instead of typical prison bars, White intentionally evokes a parallel with documentary photographs and newsreel footage of Nazi concentration camps—images still fresh in the minds of many Americans circa 1950—even as he also links the cause of these defendants with the historic struggle of Douglass's generation for freedom from chattel slavery.[62]

For her part, Elizabeth Catlett received a Rosenwald Fellowship in 1946–47, which she used to develop a series of linocuts around the theme of *The Negro Woman.* Begun in New York City and completed in Mexico at the Taller de Gráfica Popular, this series merges the exemplary lives of historical heroines and the struggles faced by contemporary black women in a particularly provocative fashion. One of the more well known of the contemporary images from this series, *I have special reservations,* depicts four African American women seated directly behind a "Colored Only" sign at the back of a bus. Nearly a decade before Rosa Parks's courageous stand against segregated bus seating in Montgomery, Alabama, Catlett's image suggests the mounting frustration and determination of black working-class women through the somber expressions of her protagonists.[63] In compositional terms, the tightly cropped framing of this scene serves to accentuate the sense of spatial confinement characterizing life in a racially segregated society (Powell 13). Other Catlett prints from this series offer similar sentiments of protest against Jim Crow restrictions with respect to housing and employment opportunities.

By including figures like Harriet Tubman and Sojourner Truth in this series, Catlett stresses not only the historical rootedness of contemporary social problems pertaining to American racism but also the long history of African American struggles to *resist* race and gender oppression. Hence, Catlett's *In Harriet Tubman, I helped hundreds to freedom* presents Tubman as a lean, muscular leader whose strong gesture points the way to freedom for a group of fugitive slaves. In a similar fashion, by presenting Sojourner Truth in a fiery orator's pose, standing over an open Bible, Catlett dramatizes the importance of literacy and religion to African American empowerment much in the manner of John Biggers's treatment of Truth in his later *Contribution of the Negro Woman to American Life and Education* mural.[64] In forging images of revolutionary women from African American history for this series, Catlett undoubtedly was influenced by the work of artists at the Taller workshop, who had already undertaken similar work in a specifically Mexican context. In terms of aesthetics as well, Catlett clearly shares an affinity for the Taller style of crosshatched line and the penchant of Taller artists to frame a procession of radicalized people moving forcefully toward a goal that is implied rather than explicitly rendered (LeFalle-Collins and Goldman 58).

As with Biggers's treatment of similar historical heroines in his *Contribution* mural for the Houston YWCA, Catlett's Tubman and Truth appear as militant agents of African American self-empowerment, whose legacy bears a clear message to twentieth-century audiences. Particularly in the context of Catlett's larger Rosenwald series (i.e., works such as *I have special reservations*), one imagines that her Tubman could just as well be pointing the way to black liberation from Jim Crow segregation and related racist practices of the 1940s as from antebellum slavery. Indeed, this is precisely the type of cultural work that Catlett hoped for her Rosenwald series of linocuts to perform; she has even stated that the original conception for this series drew inspiration from and was intended *for* black working-class women like those she encountered while teaching at the leftist George Washington Carver School in New York City between 1944 and her departure for Mexico in 1946 (Herzog 36–40).[65] Notably, even in the midst of racist oppression, Catlett's working-class subjects seem to remain determined to persevere; hence, the title of the final print of the *Negro Woman* series boldly and hopefully asserts, *My right is a future of equality with other Americans.*

If it is the case that post–cold war scholarship has tended to underplay the interest of white social realists in topics such as racial violence and injustice, it seems equally apparent that scholars often have overlooked the extent to which the causes of the American left during the 1930s and 1940s were also causes championed by progressive-minded African American artists. To cite one example, among the many art exhibits organized as a means of generating funds and moral support for the peoples of Spain and China in the late 1930s was *An Exhibition in Defense of Peace and Democracy*, sponsored by the Chicago Artists' Group in February 1938. Among the participants in this interracial show were local black artists of varied styles such as Eldzier Cortor, Charles Davis, Bernard Goss, Archibald Motley Jr., Margaret Burroughs, and Charles White.[66] In a 1969 interview, White recalled his "*great* empathy with the Loyalists of Spain and the people of Spain," as well as his concrete work on their behalf through a chapter of the League against War and Fascism.[67] Thus, while Mussolini's invasion of

Ethiopia was one important referent in generating antifascist sentiment among African Americans, it was hardly their *only* point of concern on this front. Before and during the Second World War, African American cultural workers seem to have been attuned to the implications of the power struggle between Europe's fascist and antifascist factions for the fate of democracy in their own country.

By the same token, Charles Alston's lithograph *Who Likes War?* or *Justice at Wartime* (c. 1938) is thoroughly consistent with the antiwar sentiment that pervaded the American left during the late 1930s. In this woodblock print, Alston portrays Justice as a malevolent skeletal figure who holds a cannonball in her hands, while her scales are loaded with bullets, knives, and other implements of war. Significantly, too, Alston positions his *Justice at Wartime* within a graveyard landscape that is littered with both tombstones and stacks of rifles (figure 17). Mirroring the sentiment of Alston's lithograph, Arthur Emptage flatly declared in an American Artists' Congress statement as late as 1940, "The Congress believes that war destroys culture and therefore that peace is an absolute necessity if artists are to produce their work and the public to enjoy it."[68]

However, while in 1940 Emptage criticized fascist governments for enlisting artists to "make posters or camouflage war machines," many leftist artists enthusiastically offered to perform exactly these same kinds of services for the Allied Forces following America's entry into the war. Noted radical artist William Gropper wrote to Treasury Section administrator Olin Dows in 1942, "I can't understand it, we have thousands of good artists who are eager to draw and paint vivid pictures to awaken and lift the morale of the country, many of these artists are willing to do this for nothing. Just think of it, war murals on trains and trucks, pictorial incidents of Nazi terror, cartoons in shops and office buildings, posters and sketches of every possible phase that concerns the people at home and the boys in camp" (Contreras 228). Toward this end, many artists, including Gropper, formed a group called Artists for Victory and devoted their collective talents to serving the government's cause at home and on the military front. In addition to decorating military buildings and staging weekly radio shows in New York, this group organized a handful of important art shows—including an exhibit of one hundred prints titled *America in the War*. As with certain of the American Artists' Congress graphic art shows of the 1930s, this exhibit took advantage of the reproducibility of print media in order to open simultaneously in twenty-six museums across the country (Landau 1–3). And, while it is telling that the *America in the War* exhibit included *no* works by African American artists, black artists did create a certain amount of work supporting African American participation in the Allied war effort. For example, James Lesesne Wells executed a lithograph called *Muscles Mans the Guns, Voyage 13* (1946) in tribute to the heroism of Dorie Miller. Much celebrated in the black press of the day, Miller's heroism was espe-

Figure 17. Charles Alston (1907–77), *Who Likes War?* or *Justice at Wartime,* c. 1938. Blockprint, 7¼ × 6⅜ in. (Art and Artifacts Division, Schomburg Center for Research in Black Culture, the New York Public Library, Astor, Lenox, and Tilden Foundations.)

cially poignant because his racial identity had relegated him to the role of mess man aboard the naval battleship the uss Arizona. Yet, during the Japanese attack on Pearl Harbor, Miller rushed above deck, saved the life of at least one white superior officer, and manned a large mounted machine gun skillfully enough to bring down four Japanese planes. For these heroics, Miller received a Presidential Citation and the Navy Cross (Williams 36–38). As the title indicates, Wells's print portrays Miller operating the aforementioned machine gun, surrounded on deck by the bodies of his fallen white comrades. In short, Wells presents Miller in a fairly conventional heroic battle pose, leaving any critique of the racial segregation of the U.S. military forces implicit rather than overtly rendered.

Yet, most African Americans did not possess the striking ideological clarity evidenced in Wells's Dorie Miller print regarding participation in the war effort, especially given that leftist visions of interracial working-class cooperation had yet to consistently manifest themselves in concrete terms on the home front. I have shown, for instance, that artists like John Biggers (*Dying Soldier*) and John Wilson (*Deliver Us from Evil*) looked to the collective social condition of African Americans as a critical signpost for the relative success of radical democratic projects of social reform and found the United States wanting. Specifically, these artists felt that the special dilemmas and hypocrisies that confronted African American soldiers during the Second World War crystallized the persisting gap between America's rhetoric of democratic inclusion and practices of racial discrimination. The concern of African American social realists with this nexus of issues should hardly prove surprising given the number of black artists who themselves were either drafted or enlisted for military service: this group included Charles White, John Biggers, Raymond Steth, Hughie Lee-Smith, Romare Bearden, and Charles Alston. In terms of graphic-art engagements with these issues, Charles White again provides an interesting case. White initially followed up his *The Contribution of the Negro to Democracy in America* mural with a renewal of his Rosenwald Fellowship for 1943–44 based on a project in which he planned a series of oil paintings examining African American participation in World War II. In actual fact, he wound up completing more work in graphic art during this period, and the tone of these works captures an artist torn between conflicting impulses of hope and anxiety. Representative in this regard is an untitled 1943 graphic for the National Negro Congress publication *Congress Vue* that depicts Hitler whispering a proposal for "Jim Crow in the Armed Forces" into the receptive ear of a representative of the Reactionary South, with each of these figures sporting a swastika. However, at the same time, an interracial group of men shred this Jim Crow proposal with bayonets. On the one hand, the Hitler and Reactionary South figures tower in size over this oppositional faction of "Negro and White United." On the other hand, White does seem to suggest that the progressive interracial collective has at least a fighting chance of success.

If anything, such strains of optimism for meaningful reform—at least via African American contributions to World War II—seem to diminish in White's graphic art in the war's aftermath. For instance, his 1947 lithograph *Our War* pictures an African American man with a military helmet and jacket gesturing with one hand for a crowd of black bystanders on a city street to redirect their attention from some unseen danger in the sky and follow him. Here, it seems notable that the soldier's helmet bears the insignia of a Civil Defense uniform rather than that of a member of the U.S. Army. For while, on one level, the viewer can see the foregrounded figure as pointing civilians toward shelter from an aerial siege, in the context of the then recent "Double V" campaign, White's suggestive title might also point one toward an additional level of meaning: the way in which the soldier of *Our War* shines a flashlight almost directly out of the print toward the viewer seems to suggest that the African American masses would do well to turn their attention to domestic struggles at the level of everyday city life before being concerned with entering any further international conflicts on behalf of the American military.[69] In effect, the print might well imply a war unfinished on the U.S. home front—all the more so given that the spirit of cold war retrenchment against progressive politics was beginning to exert itself by 1947. Equally significant, White produced this work as a contribution to a Taller de Gráfica Popular portfolio titled *Negro, USA*—marking it as part of a broader project intended primarily for the same sort of everyday people depicted in the lithograph.

Still other uses of graphic arts were less radically oppositional in tone but equally vigilant in sustaining the Double V campaign's insistence on equating domestic racism with the fascism of the Axis powers. In this vein, organizations like George Schuyler's interracial Association for Tolerance in America focused on the domestic half of the Double V campaign through a program of mass education of white citizens. Schuyler explained of the organization, "Its purpose is to present the facts about colored people in word and picture in order to counter vicious propaganda by circulating truth. . . . It wastes no time in conferences and debate over the obvious but concentrates on such mass education projects as it can afford."[70] Toward this end, Schuyler's organization sought to position graphic art not in the pages of leftist periodicals, but rather within the mechanisms of American mass culture by placing an Elton Fax graphic portrait of an African American soldier alongside a caption reading "500,000 of these lads are fighting for You! Let Them and Theirs Share in Our Democracy" on 120 streetcars in the industrial city of Gary, Indiana, in June 1944 ("Miscellany" 108–9). An even more aggressive permutation of the Double V campaign's aims appeared in a regular advertisement for the *Chicago Defender*, which positioned the widely read black paper itself as an armed soldier, "always on guard to prevent any and all attempts to violate our civil rights."[71] Like the murals, poetry, and novels described elsewhere in this study, art interventions such as White's and Fax's shared in drawing a clear parallel between the fascist oppression of Axis nations and American racism, suggesting that the African American masses would profit from training their collective focus on the U.S. half of this equation and related domestic struggles.

Owing to the canonical periodization of social realism as a phenomenon of the 1930s, most accounts of the movement have included little or no consideration of works pertaining specifically to World War II or the early cold war era. In addition to writing out of the picture many of the works discussed above, this historical blind spot also has served to downplay how certain of the more prominent themes of depression-era art—such as the class struggle of industrial workers and the presumed heroic virtues of proletarian laborers more broadly—received artistic treatment both during *and after* the 1930s, particularly in graphic arts. Such was the appeal of this quintessential social realist topic that even the conservative Regionalist artist Thomas Hart Benton flirted at least briefly with radical laborist art during the strife of the early depression years. And, not coincidentally, when he did so it was primarily through graphic art media. For example, in his 1933 lithograph *Strike*, policemen fire guns against unarmed pickets in front of the shadowy backdrop of an industrial infrastructure.[72]

Among African American graphic artists, James Lesesne Wells produced one of the most substantial bodies of work regarding black working-class laborers during the social realist era. In fact, Wells was one of the earliest U.S. artists to articulate a social realist aesthetic, since he began producing works in a class-conscious mode even before the onset of the depression. For instance, Wells's *The Farmer*, a naturalistically rendered portrait of an elderly rural woman, served as the cover illustration for Carter G. Woodson's *The Rural Negro* (1930) but originally appeared in the October 1928 issue of *New Masses*. As art historian Richard Powell observes, this early Wells print seems to anticipate the proletarian manner of depicting the rural working classes in graphics by Mexican artists such as Rufino Tamayo and, subsequently, the members of the Taller de Gráfica Popular (Powell and Reynolds 12–13). Also representative of Wells's numerous contributions to leftist, class-centered publications between the late 1920s and midcentury is the lithograph *Negro Worker* (c. 1938), which appeared on the cover of the September 10, 1946, issue of *New Masses*. This sort of individuated portrait, framed by the backdrop of an industrial landscape, stands in decided contrast to the serialization and hypermuscularity typical of an artist such as Hugo Gellert. Deriving in large part from exposure to Soviet proletcult art, Gellert's depression-era graphics often subsume the identity of their chosen working-class subjects into a utopian CP narrative of labor radicalism and what scholar Walter Kalaidjian describes as "a universal allegory of primordial, masculine prowess" (143). Wells, by contrast, seems more concerned with conveying the simple human dignity of his subject than with inscribing this worker within a narrative of proletarian revolution.[73]

Not least of the problems confronting members of the American proletariat like Wells's *Negro Worker* was the fact that, especially preceding the rise to prominence of CIO interracial labor organizing, the practices of established labor unions themselves were often decidedly segregationist during the depression era. Particularly in the case of the relatively entrenched AFL, African American laborers struggled, often in vain, for the right to full union participation. Indeed, Horace Cayton and St. Clair Drake noted in their 1945 study *Black Metropolis* that African American workers remained justifiably wary of the white-dominated labor unions of the AFL since such organizations frequently seemed to do almost as much as corporate policy to inhibit black job advancement in the industrial workplace (304–8). This unsavory reality is captured by an unsigned *Crisis* cartoon from March 1934 with the caption "Boys—Remember Our Constitution!" in which white trade union members literally thumb their collective nose at "Negro labor." Even in northern states and even on the federally sponsored work projects of the New Deal agencies, interracialism was relatively limited in actual practice during the pre–World War II era. In this light, it is perhaps not coincidental that African American artists executed relatively few epic strike scenes of the sort often remarked in social realist art.

Yet, when the campaigns of the CIO and IWO gained momentum in the late 1930s and 1940s, artists comprised an important part of this movement. In this regard, one might note the insistent quality of Catlett's title *My role has been important in the struggle to organize the unorganized* (figure 18). This 1947 linocut from the artist's *Negro Woman* series portrays three African American labor organizers, including one woman who seems to act as spokesperson for the group, as they attempt to share union literature with two white fellow workers. Notably, the female organizer dramatizes her oration with a raised fist gesture that hearkens back to Big Bill Haywood's plea for labor solidarity as part of the International Workers of the World (IWW) organizing campaigns of the 1910s. (Looking forward, of course, this same gesture prefigures the Black Power iconography of the 1960s.) In short, Catlett not only depicts African Americans participating in an activist brand of organized labor but also actually shows them taking a lead role in sustaining such activist politics among their white fellow workers. Certainly, as I have been laboring to suggest, Catlett and her fellow African American cultural workers themselves made precisely such a contribution in the arena of visual art during the 1940s and early 1950s.

Figure 18. Elizabeth Catlett (b. 1919), *My role has been important in the struggle to organize the unorganized,* 1947. Linocut, 6⅛ × 9 in. (© Elizabeth Catlett/Licensed by VAGA, New York, New York.)

Given the fact that work of African American artists shares many of the thematic concerns and representational conventions of the broader social realist movement regarding working-class subjects, so too do certain of their works fall subject to critiques that recent scholars have directed toward the art of this era. Arguably, the most important of such critiques involves the predominant focus on male subjects in labor-centered works of social realism, a trend that served to render women's work in clerical, domestic, nursing, teaching, and other nonindustrial fields nearly invisible (Melosh 83–93). The vast majority of working-class subjects depicted by Wells in his social realist graphics are male laborers, to cite one example. However, at least some politically engaged critics and cultural workers, such as Elizabeth Gurley Flynn, recognized the homologous links that bound together issues of gender with issues of race and class (6). Among artists operating on the American left between 1930 and the early 1950s, African American artists often were at the forefront in recognizing these sorts of connections. I have already detailed the prominent role of militant, activist women in murals such as Hale Woodruff's *Settlement and Development* and John Biggers's *Contribution of the Negro Woman to American Life and Education.* To be sure, the male figures of Charles White's murals and graphics of this period often display a hyperreal musculature (kindred to Soviet proletcult aesthetics) that seems suggestive of underlying anxieties regarding a relative absence of black male empowerment. Nonetheless, White, too, deserves recognition for consistently including female figures among his catalog of heroes, both historic and contemporary. Still, it was Elizabeth Catlett who produced the most significant body of work on this front in her aforementioned graphic art project on the theme of *The Negro Woman*. Through this series of linocuts, Catlett self-consciously labored to correct the long-standing pattern of artists' neglect of black and female working-class subjects. As she explains in reference to her larger oeuvre: "Many artists are always doing men. I think that somebody ought to do women. Artists do work with women, with the beauty of their bodies and the refinement of middle-class women, but I think there is a need to express something about the working-class Black woman and that's what I do" (Samella Lewis 102).

Nor was the achievement of African American social realists in this regard merely a matter of recognizing figures such as Sojourner Truth as champions of both African American and women's rights, for turning to the portrayal of black women at this stage in U.S. history posed special challenges to the artist. "How are Negro women usually represented in artistic work today?" asked John Pittman in the *Daily Worker* in 1951. In the case of working-class black women, he suggests, "They are portrayed as Beulah, the quaint and amiable, but bowing-and-scraping servant" (n.p.). Consequently, the project of artists such as Catlett was at least twofold. First, Catlett worked to undo patterns of historical erasure when she included a dignified (and politicized) African American woman at the head of the group of labor recruiters in the aforementioned *My role has been important in the struggle to organize the unorganized* linocut. Even more, artists like Catlett endeavored to reconfigure popular culture caricatures of the sort referenced by Pittman—particularly the image of the black female domestic as ever-pleasant nurturer—into working-class laborers of the sort common to social realist expression.[74] Much like her former husband, Charles White, Catlett had grown up observing her mother employed in work such as washing the floors of public schools and thus knew from experience that this sort of intensive labor seldom left a person feeling "quaint and amiable." Hence, as Melanie Herzog observes, Catlett's *I have always worked hard in America* portrays the same woman engaged in multiple tasks of cleaning laundry and floors as a way of suggesting "the repetitive, harsh, physical drudgery of domestic work" (60). Stylistically, Catlett's use of incised lines on her figures enhances the visual impact of the print, as this domestic's "countenance [is] literally etched and weathered by excessive labor coupled with the ravages of time" (Beauchamp-Byrd and Coleman 9).[75] By the same token, in *I have special reservations*, the most prominent figure is an African American woman whose head wrap seems intended to suggest her status as a domestic. Yet, as I have noted, this domestic is no amiable and nurturing

Mammy figure, but rather appears fully conscious of and angered by the Jim Crow conventions that relegate her to second-class citizenship, even during her transportation to and from a day of intensive labor.

African American artists synthesized their interests in black labor and black contributions to World War II in works centered on African American participation in the U.S. defense industries. Much as photo spreads like "The Negro in the United States Army" from the February 1942 *Crisis* and "Ground Crewmen: Their Work Is Important Too" in the July–August 1944 issue of *Negro Story* visualized African Americans as part of a heroic corps of American defense workers, graphic artist Raymond Steth fashioned a celebratory composite representation of such laborers in his 1944 lithograph *Beacons of Defense*. Through his use of a mural-like compositional scheme that features an overlapping series of thematically related scenes, Steth manages to include wide-ranging work tasks such as men loading crates and armaments aboard trains and ships; engineers laboring at drafting tables; women at work in a factory; a man tightening the bolts on an airplane tire; farming; coal mining; and two construction workers making repairs to a girder. Framing and subdividing this image are two large spotlights in the lower corners of the print, which project beams that cross at a diagonal angle in the center of the composition and serve, quite literally, to highlight certain of Steth's miniature scenes of defense industry jobs (figure 19). Thus, as did the above-cited examples of photojournalistic coverage of African American participation in the war effort, Steth's ambitious print includes workers from a fairly representative range of jobs and regional locales, with a significant nod to women's active participation in America's defense industries. Further, Steth's defense industry work crews are emphatically interracial—in fact, more so than was often the case in reality, as if to model a vision of working-class cooperation that the artist deemed worthy of emulation both during and subsequent to the wartime crisis.

On an even more pragmatic level, Steth elsewhere sought to turn graphic arts into a tool of education for American soldiers. Dismayed by the lack of familiarity or concern with safety guidelines that they witnessed at the ammunition depot where they were stationed, Steth and a white sergeant named W. Ralph Perry drafted a lengthy memo to their commanding officer requesting the creation of a new Department of Graphic Information. In their minds, the graphic art produced by such a department could adopt the techniques and motifs of mass market advertising toward the goals of improving workplace safety and boosting the morale of American soldiers. Hence, their memo reads, in part, "We propose to wage psychological warfare against the forces attacking morale on this Base; to use the Silk Screen as a weapon. We think the Silk Screen admirably suited to this task because it is a method of reproducing in volume and in color directives and factual material which often goes unheeded in the quiet black and white mimeographing of the Work Sheet."[76] Steth later recalled that he took a chance on being court-martialed for this seemingly innocuous proposal because, by highlighting the need for enhanced workplace safety, this memo implicitly addressed a controversial subject: namely, the disproportionate number of African American soldiers assigned to high-risk military tasks, such as the handling of ammunition supplies. As Steth explained, "There were several Naval bases that supplied ammunition for the South Pacific at that particular period and they were having many accidents and many people—many sailors—were being injured and killed in the explosions as a result and it became a very grave kind of situation, especially with the black soldiers, because that's where they had most of them—in that very, very dangerous work handling the ammunition. . . . Most of the casualties were among black seamen."[77] Indeed, the NAACP organized a protest campaign around this very issue. And artist John Biggers experienced just these sorts of dangerous tasks firsthand while stationed at a naval base in Norfolk, Virginia, in 1945. In fact, the stress of this work seems to have contributed substantially to the mental duress that shortly led to Biggers's discharge from the navy (Wardlaw, *Art* 33). Hence, in fashioning an image like *Beacons of Defense*, Steth was not blind to instances of racial discrimination within America's armed forces and defense industries, even though he joined artists like James Lesesne Wells (*Muscles Mans the Guns*) in hoping that African Americans' participation alongside their white peers in the war effort might bring about certain positive social transformations.

However, other politically engaged artists adopted a considerably more confrontational approach than did Steth with regard to the nation's "beacons of defense," observing that the social position of African Americans vis-à-vis the defense industries helped to bring the hypocrisies of American racism into particularly sharp focus. Most notably, of course, it took the passage of the controversial Executive Order 8802 by President Roosevelt simply to desegregate employment in these industries in the early 1940s. Naturally, artists recognized this as a positive development, albeit one long overdue. Still, even with the government having taken this important step, episodes of racist violence and discrimination continued to flourish. In one particularly bloody incident, a white mob of two thousand in Detroit rioted to prevent five hundred African American defense workers and their families from occupying the government-funded Sojourner Truth Homes (Ottley 51–56). The reality of everyday life in the workplace, as well, for black defense workers was more problematic than a print like Steth's *Beacons of Defense* might suggest. For instance, it is not coincidental that all three of the African American women interviewed for Connie Field's important documentary film *The Life and Times of Rosie the Riveter* (1980) describe de-

Figure 19. Raymond Steth (1917–97), *Beacons of Defense,* c. 1944. Lithograph, 14⅞ × 21¾ in. (All rights reserved, The Metropolitan Museum of Art, Gift of Reba and Dave Williams, 1999 [1999.529.152].)

tailed incidents in which supervisors and/or fellow workers challenged their very presence in the industrial workplace on both gender and racial grounds during World War II. Reflecting this type of conflicted experience, Elizabeth Catlett's 1944 lithograph *War Worker* joins proletarian dignity with an expression that seems to mingle fatigue and concern. The socially critical aspect of Catlett's print attains even greater clarity when one compares Catlett's *War Worker* with Julius Bloch's lithograph *Sheet Metal Worker* (c. 1943), as the gentle eyes and soft features of Bloch's subject seem to owe only in part to his more youthful age. By way of contrast, one might reasonably speculate that the furrowed brow and focused, downcast gaze of Catlett's *War Worker* suggest frustration with the continuing second-class citizenship endured by such workers in spite of their heroic contributions to safeguard democracy, both at home and abroad.[78]

In a similar vein, John Wilson's 1945 lithograph *The Passing Scene* (alternately titled *Street Car Scene*) offers a decidedly ambiguous representation of the social position of African American defense workers. In this print, a black man travels to work on a Boston streetcar, his status as an employee in a naval defense yard indicated by a badge that he wears pinned to his jacket. On the one hand, this shipyard worker's participation in the newly desegregated American defense industries seems emblematic of a significant advance for the African American working class during the 1940s. As Wilson has described this shift in socioeconomic opportunities, "After the soldiers went off to war, women were recruited to work in factories, and eventually, the defense industries began recruiting black people, who were unemployable before. On my street, everybody was on welfare in the 1930s. Suddenly, blacks became welders" (Grimes c16). On the other hand, *The Passing Scene* also conveys a sense of this worker's isolation. He is the only visible African American (and the only male) on the streetcar, and his fellow passengers seem indifferent, at best, to his presence (Williams and Williams 33–34). Moreover, when interviewer Amy Tarr asked Wilson whether one should interpret *The Passing Scene* as being about this worker's pride in having a chance to serve his country, the artist replied: "That was the last thing on my mind. I wanted to see Hitler defeated like everyone else, but I resented the fact that almost everyone on my block was on welfare until they needed us in the shipyards and factories. And I resented the idea of blacks going off to fight for other people's freedoms while ours were being neglected here at home." This is, after all, the same John Wilson who had fashioned the caustic *Deliver Us from Evil* lithograph two years earlier.

If many people today tend to think of social realist art in terms of images with clearly demarcated battle lines between the revolutionary working class and their perceived enemies (i.e., capitalists, the police, judges), it bears emphasizing that in actual practice most social realist artists fashioned images of frustrated and exhausted working-class individuals at least as frequently as they depicted a revolutionary proletariat engaged in collective political activism or heroic labor. The graphic art of William E. Smith is a case in point, as many of his prints focus on urban figures burdened by chronic unemployment, or else work that brings little relief from perpetual poverty. Although not widely known today, Smith drew praise during the 1930s and 1940s from the likes of Howard University artist and art historian James Porter, who lauded Smith as "one of the dominant personalities of Negro printmaking" in his 1943 publication, *Modern Negro Art* (152). A Cleveland artist affiliated with Karamu House, Smith published work in periodicals such as the *Crisis* and the progressive interracial journal *Common Ground*. Particularly in the latter context, a linocut like *Nobody Knows*—which depicts only the imploring gaze of an African American, devoid of the context that may have generated this figure's apparent sorrow—might have operated in a manner somewhat akin to Langston Hughes's blues poetry (something *Common Ground* also published); that is, by offering an Ellisonian "fingering of the jagged grain" of depression-era travails. So too, the title of this linocut pointedly evokes the lament of the famous spiritual: "Nobody knows the trouble I've seen." One of the central aims of artists like Smith was to ensure that this did not remain the case by bringing the suffering of the poor and racially oppressed to a broader public visibility.

In the 1940 linocut *Poverty and Fatigue,* Smith explores the material and psychic toll of depression-era socioeconomic hardships in more explicit terms through a male figure who sits on a city stoop with his hands folded idly between his legs and his head bowed, as if asleep or disconsolate (figure 20). In a similar fashion, Smith's 1938 linocut *Skinny Depressed* communicates as much through body language—the young man's slouched posture, tilted head, and grim facial expression—as through the subject's patchy clothing.[79] Both of these prints clearly resonate with the tendency of Smith's social realist peers to depict the depression's impact on poor and working-class individuals in terms of a tangible ethos of despair and exhaustion. For example, one might compare Smith's *Poverty and Fatigue* with white artist Eli Jacobi's *The New Deal—Pro and Con,* in which destitute men huddle together in an alleyway. As Marlene Park and Gerald Markowitz have observed, Jacobi's linocut clearly seems to suggest "that the inhabitants of the Bowery were *not* getting a New Deal, and that the Bowery was an apt metaphor for the Great Depression" (90, my emphasis).[80]

Significantly, in depicting frustrated and exhausted subjects, social realists such as Smith and Jacobi only occasionally offered viewers anything in the way of an "explanation" (Marxist or otherwise) of the reasons behind their subjects' despondency. In both Smith's and Jacobi's prints, the very inactivity of the people

Figure 20. William E. Smith (1913–97), *Poverty and Fatigue,* 1940. Linocut on joined Japanese papers, 9 × 8 in. (All rights reserved, The Metropolitan Museum of Art, Gift of Reba and Dave Williams, 1999 [1999.529.149].)

depicted comprises the most compelling indictment of the broader socioeconomic ills of the depression. Even more, in many cases, social realists depicted a similar state of physical and psychological fatigue as characteristic of the lives of those members of the working class who retained employment as well. In this vein, a veritable genre of subway scenes depicting exhausted workers on their way to or from their respective jobs emerged in social realist art of the 1930s and 1940s. For instance, John Wilson's aforementioned lithograph *The Straphanger* (1947) depicts a blue-collar African American man standing aboard a streetcar. Although Wilson does not render the fatigue and frustration of his "straphanger" in an overtly manifest manner, as with William Smith's urban denizens, his central figure does stand slightly stooped in the shoulders and seems to stare somewhat vacantly over the top of the folded newspaper that he holds in his right hand. Moreover, by rendering the compression of bodies aboard the streetcar—hence, the need for the central African American figure to stand holding a strap for support—Wilson suggests that a sense of spatial confinement and social alienation characterizes the concrete details of everyday lived experience for the urban working class. In this case, one might speculate that the worker's sense of alienation from his surroundings is amplified by the fact that he seems to be the only African American passenger on the streetcar, much as in the artist's *The Passing Scene* from 1945.

The interest of social realists in the stresses of poor and working-class life also extended to rural subjects. Much as John Biggers's social realist murals of sharecropping families served as a rebuke to the optimism of Regionalist art, so too did progressive artists (including Biggers) use graphic arts media to dramatize the material poverty and anxiety of life in rural America. For example, in his 1952 lithograph *Despair*, Biggers portrays a gaunt black man, overwrought with emotion, who holds his head in his hands. Similarly, Robert Blackburn's *Toil* pictures a male laborer straining with his back bent under the weight of a large sack as he traverses a sparsely vegetated landscape. It bears noting that while Biggers's and Blackburn's prints certainly invite sociopolitical interpretation regarding issues that confronted many rural African Americans during the depression, such as the overtaxing nature of rural labor and the oppression of the sharecropping system, neither work directs an explicit social critique at a specific causative agent. Much less do they offer resolution of the scenarios depicted via a vision of working-class revolution.[81] In this regard, they resonate quite strikingly with William Smith's urban scenes.

Other artists did not even rely exclusively on the human figure in conveying their general sense of rural impoverishment. In particular, I have noted that Hale Woodruff and several of the students who came of age as graphic artists under his tutelage at Atlanta University during the 1930s gained a collective notoriety of sorts as the "Outhouse School" (Catlett 5). Woodruff explained, "On those days when weather permitted, a group of the students and I would go on sketching and painting trips into the areas in and around Atlanta. In the countryside, we noted the prevalence of 'outhouses.' Somehow, we always seemed to include one in our paintings. Later, a magazine, when learning of this, called it (us) the 'outhouse' school of art" (Stoelting 73). Yet, contrary to the quaint folkishness that this nickname would seem to suggest, Woodruff and his protégés executed works of graphic art that are striking in the gravity of their social content.

Even early in the 1930s, Woodruff used funding from a Rosenwald Fellowship to paint a series of landscapes designed specifically to illustrate the consequences of soil erosion (LeFalle-Collins and Goldman 51–52). Moreover, desolate landscapes soon acquired a broader social meaning for Woodruff and his students, as both a semiliteral transcription of material poverty and a metaphor for the larger social and spiritual impoverishment endured by African Americans due to a lack of equal opportunities in education, housing, and employment. Although they rendered several such works in oil, Woodruff and his understudies also fashioned even more examples of this type of landscape in graphic art media. A typical example of such a work is Wilmer Jennings's 1939 wood engraving *Hill Top House*, which depicts a cluster of four wooden buildings amidst an uneven, hilly landscape of intermittent grass and dead or barren trees (figure 21). Notably, as in many such landscapes by the Atlanta artists, Jennings depicts buildings without illustrating any inhabitants, perhaps in an effort to enhance the print's sense of emptiness and loss.

African American artists did not always locate such landscapes specifically in the South. For instance, Alston's student, Robert Blackburn, executed a lithograph titled *Upper New York* in 1938. While a trail of smoke from a chimney suggests that farmers still inhabit this homestead, the windswept look of the land, the dilapidated condition of the barn and other buildings, and the broken power lines all serve to evoke an ethos of unalleviated depression-era hard times. In a lithograph called *Desolation* (1938), Cleveland's Hughie Lee-Smith depicts a similar topography in a more surrealistic aesthetic mode. In this print, vultures fly over a scene that seems to contain little more than rubble, dead trees, bones, and dust.[82] As was the case with John Biggers's social realist murals, the fact that these works seem more akin to the documentary photography of peers like Dorothea Lange and Arthur Rothstein than to the work of fellow artists such as Thomas Hart Benton and Grant Wood is no accident. Eschewing what they perceived as the naive optimism of Regionalist painting, African American graphic artists ranging from Woodruff to Lee-Smith all linked their work to a well-established social realist convention: the use of a desolate landscape as an emblem of the larger failures of America's promises of limitless abundance. That African American graphic artists

Figure 21. Wilmer Jennings (1910–90), *Hill Top House,* 1939. Wood engraving. (Howard University Gallery of Art, Washington, D.C.)

located this theme in southern locales more often than midwestern dust bowl settings does not diminish the important, but too often overlooked, connection between their artistic concerns and those of their more renowned depression-era peers in photography, folk song, visual art, and literature.

Stepping back to assess the strategies employed by African American social realists in the graphic arts in a broad sense, in fact, one might draw an important analogy with the work of depression-era photographers. While the period's photographers displayed an impressive range of aesthetic strategies, one can posit a kind of continuum between those who unabashedly employed the medium as a "weapon" of race and class struggle and those who constructed their images in such a manner as to present the impression of a more strictly "documentary" brand of cultural work. Within this loose framework, certain social realists used graphics in a similar fashion to muckraking photojournalist John Spivak and his contemporaries, seeking to bring striking, confrontational images of depression-era southern poverty and cases of racial injustice to a mass audience as broad as possible with the aim of effecting progressive social change. Much as Spivak used photography to indict particular social practices, such as the types of labor and torture inflicted on southern chain gangs, like-minded work in social realist graphics did not hesitate to direct its critique at specific causative agents. John Wilson's *Deliver Us from Evil*, Elton Fax's *Justice Wears Dark Glasses*, and Ernest Crichlow's *Lovers* all operate very much in this openly politicized vein, for instance.

Other photographers of the depression era, of course, sought to employ documentation itself as a brand of social commentary. While we know that, in fact, photographers like Lange and Rothstein often labored meticulously over the construction of their "documentary" photographs, their work does seem distinct from that of a Spivak in the sense that they trusted the snapshots of reality presented in their finished products to "speak for themselves," in essence. At least in the absence of accompanying text, works such as Lange's *Migrant Mother* and Rothstein's *Farmer and Sons Walking in the Face of a Dust Storm* (1936) seem more immediately focused on the travails of the poor and working class than the task of exposing the underlying social forces that have shaped these circumstances—although, by extension, certainly these photographs might lead politically conscious viewers to ask such questions.[83] In this regard, William Smith's linocuts of urban joblessness and Elizabeth Catlett's *War Worker* are among the comparable examples from the body of African American graphics.

As with the period's photographers, it bears emphasizing that particular artists seldom pigeonholed themselves exclusively within either of these niches. Hale Woodruff, for example, produced graphics that ranged from prints that pointedly indicted the hypocrisy of lynchers who professed Christianity (*By Parties Unknown*) to a print such as *View of Atlanta* (1935), which depicts a row of rather dilapidated houses without a specifically directed social critique.[84] Most African American social realists experimented with a similar range of strategies in their graphics, all the while keeping their eyes trained consistently on the contemporary scene. Perhaps more important, whether issuing open political commentary or operating in a more strictly documentary mode, African American graphic artists sought to direct the attention of a mass public to the most pressing social concerns of their present day, with a view toward transforming the conditions thus chronicled. As I will detail in the following chapter, the poets of social realism show a similarly diverse range of strategies but on the whole gravitate markedly toward the explicit use of their chosen medium as a weapon, one possessing instrumental value in campaigns for greater class equality and racial justice.

Chapter Four

Forging a Language of Radical Exhortation: Poetry

Since I take pride in being considered a social realist, my work will be looked upon as blatant propaganda by some not in sympathy with my goals and as fine poetry by others of equal discernment who agree with me.
FRANK MARSHALL DAVIS

Viewed retrospectively, the confluence of poetry and African American social realism appears so fertile and abundant as to suggest that their union was virtually predestined. In poetry, African American social realists found a medium that they deemed particularly well suited to addressing a wide range of politically charged issues, including matters of race and class, of domestic and international concern, and of pertinence to better understanding both history and the contemporary moment. Yet, such a productive output was not a foregone conclusion; rather, it resulted from considerable work by African American poets, who consciously reshaped their medium into a distinctly social realist vehicle for cultural activism. Even more so than graphic artists, poets chose to examine their selected subject material with an emphasis on *explication*—explications inflected by black nationalism, Marxist politics, or, quite often, an idiosyncratic melding of these two ideological frameworks. Further, poets typically pursued such explications with a directness found in relatively few murals by U.S. social realists.

Indeed, it was in the medium of poetry that social realists most intensely sounded the clarion calls for revolutionary change and for a radically new brand of cultural work during the early 1930s. And few poets announced this new direction more emphatically than Langston Hughes, who signaled the shift with both the tone and publication venue of poems such as "Call to Creation," which first appeared in the February 1931 issue of *New Masses*. In this poem, Hughes issues an explicit call to action that urges cultural workers to abandon their ivory tower isolation and, instead, "Look at hungry babies crying, / Listen to the rich men lying, / Look at starving China dying" (Rampersad 135).[1] Like Hughie Lee-Smith's *Artist's Life #1* lithograph, Hughes's poem offers the artist a stark choice between two clearly defined options: the poet can continue to pursue ostensibly timeless notions of "beauty," which bodes increasing obsolescence, or the poet can turn his or her attention to present-day social crises, which offers the cultural worker a chance to play a significant role in transforming far-reaching cultural and political events, an opportunity to be among the "new world-makers" of what promises to be a revolutionary chapter in American history.

The enthusiasm of African American social realist poets regarding the potential of their chosen medium to serve progressive political ends did not wane appreciably in the 1940s. For instance, Margaret Walker's poem "Today," from her celebrated 1942 volume *For My People*, opens with a declaration of the poet's intent to engage the present crises of fascist militarism, racism, and economic hardship:

> I sing of slum scabs on city faces,
> scrawny children scarred by bombs and dying of hunger,
> wretched human scarecrows strung against lynching stakes,
> those dying of pellagra and silicosis, rotten houses falling on
> slowly decaying humanity. (28)

In this way, poets coming of age in the 1940s, like Walker, announced their commitment to a brand of radical writing similar to that which had been encouraged by fellow writers such as Hughes a decade earlier. Notably, too, both Hughes's and Walker's poems pose rhetorical challenges to their readers, who are imagined as being as yet uncommitted to the poet's own sense of radical politics—a framework that suggests the special role poetry was to play as a kind of radical exhortation to a mass readership.

Poets had several reasons to feel confident that their medium offered a capable means of pursuing this brand of cultural work. First, much as graphic artists could essay a glance backward to the likes of Daumier, Goya, and Kollwitz, social realist poets looked to forebears who had sought to use poetry as a means of working radical changes on the consciousness of their readers. Walt Whitman, for one, came to be something of a patron saint for leftist poets during the depression decade for the democratic mindedness of his turn to "everyday Americans" as a fit subject for poetry (see C. Nelson 134). In addition, the style of Whitman's prosaic free verse offered poets of the 1930s and 1940s a *form* whose straightforwardness coincided with their own objectives of producing a broadly accessible "people's poetry" in plainspoken language. Along these same lines, books like Louis Untermeyer's *Modern American Poetry* (1921) championed a group of "vigorous new poets" of the early twentieth century precisely for the accessibility of their poetic form and language. Among those poets lauded by Untermeyer for having "ushered in a respect for the use of everyday speech, freedom of choice in subject matter, and an unembarrassed celebration of American culture" were figures such as Carl Sandburg, Edward Arlington Robinson, and Robert Frost (Gabbin 24–31)—not coincidentally, all writers who appealed greatly to African American social realists like Hughes, Walker, Frank Marshall Davis, and Sterling Brown during the 1930s and 1940s.

So too, although numerous commentators have censured the Harlem Renaissance as lacking a sufficient element of political critique, several African American poets were writing verse that addressed matters pertaining to poor and working-class Americans in the 1920s, especially—but not exclusively—issues of racial disfranchisement. Hence, when Nancy Cunard compiled her radical *Negro* anthology for publication in 1934, she included poems from the 1920s, such as Countee Cullen's "Incident," alongside the early 1930s proletarian verse of poets like Langston Hughes and Alfred Kreymborg.[2] While Claude McKay's verse was not included in *Negro,* a poem such as his oft-cited sonnet "If We Must Die" (1919)—with its fiery closing lines, "Like men we'll face the murderous, cowardly pack, / Pressed to the wall, dying, but fighting back" (*Harlem Shadows* 53)—seems very much in step with the spirit of the revolutionary poetry of the 1930s. As William Maxwell has detailed in his recent study, *New Negro, Old Left,* this poem first appeared in the radical journal the *Liberator* (for which McKay served as a coeditor) and was part and parcel of a lengthy and mutually influential engagement between McKay and the left in both the United States and the Soviet Union (44–46). Likewise, Langston Hughes was occasionally publishing anticapitalist poems such as "God to Hungry Child" in leftist publications like *Workers' Monthly* (a later incarnation of the *Liberator*) as early as the mid-1920s. And Sterling Brown's "Cabaret" caustically juxtaposed voyeuristic cabaret scenes against grim images of the contemporaneous tragedies being endured by black sharecroppers during the 1927 floods along the Mississippi River. In an important sense, these currents in Harlem Renaissance poetry prefigure the revolutionary temperament of the subsequent decade's cultural politics, as well as the concern of social realists with the suffering and injustice endured by America's poor and working-class masses.

As Alain Locke recognized, the existence of this political strand within African American poetry of the 1920s should not prove surprising given that the journals most important to the promotion of the Harlem Renaissance's cultural growth—*Crisis* and *Opportunity*—were sponsored by explicitly political organizations such as the NAACP and the Urban League, respectively (Stewart 27). Even more dramatically, A. Philip Randolph and Chandler Owen's *Messenger* articulated a black proletarian politics that encompassed the cultural spheres of literature, visual art, and drama during the 1910s and 1920s (see Kalaidjian 75–79). Likewise, in terms of the broader American literary scene, one should note that publications like *New Masses* printed proletarian modes of verse, such as mass recitations by Michael Gold, from the early stages of the magazine's inception in 1926.[3] Indeed, African American and leftist little magazines made a wide range of politically engaged poetry available as models to aspiring young writers from at least the World War I era onward.

Significantly, social realists also drew inspiration from Soviet proletcult forms of poetry. One example was the mass chant, a type of poem fashioned with the dramaturgical context of public performance in mind. As U.S. communist writer and literary critic Michael Gold explained his concept of the "mass recitation" in the July 1926 issue of *New Masses*, "Mass recitations are meant to be acted, not read. . . . No tinsel stage or stage settings are necessary; the rough bare platform of any ordinary union hall or meeting hall is enough, is the most fitting stage, in fact." Envisioning such poetry as a means of generating audience participation, Gold further suggested, "The lines must be chanted, not spoken; in clear full sculptured tones, each word as sharply defined as a rifle shot" ("Foreword" 19). In this vein, it is hardly coincidental that poet and journalist Frank Marshall Davis would later recall Richard Wright's poetry from the depression era as being "almost like oratory" (Randall, "Mystery" 44). Consider, for example, a passage from Wright's "Rise and Live" (1935):

> Is this living?
> Is this living here idle living?
> Is this living here holding our empty hands
> Feeling with our senses the slow sweep of time
> Rising, eating, talking and sleeping,
> And every so often crawling to plead for a handout of crumbs?[4]

As the poet repeats the basic question "Is this living?" with increasingly complex rhetorical flourishes, one can virtually imagine the text of this poem being recited from the stepladder of a political organizer in an attempt to bring a crowd to an increasingly fervent pitch of revolutionary enthusiasm. Even more pointedly, Robert Hayden structures his early poem "Speech" (c. 1940) along the lines of an oratory directly addressed to a specific target audience of black and white workers. After opening with the plea, "Hear me, white brothers, / Black brothers, hear me," Hayden proceeds to attribute racial violence and antilabor violence to "the same hand" (27). Significantly, both Wright and Hayden construct their poems as they do not merely to *mirror* the political discourse of interracial coalition building and CIO labor organizing. The poets offer their cultural work as itself *a part of* this discourse. If the poems are not precisely identical to soapbox speeches—in that they exist on the page, rather than as an actual dramaturgical performance—the intent behind the poems is in many respects kindred to that of "real" labor oratory.

Social realists articulated this form not only to the ends of labor organizing but also to mobilize support for antiracist causes. For instance, Langston Hughes's "August 19th . . . A Poem for Clarence Norris" (one of the Scottsboro defendants) contains an unrelenting boldface refrain of "August 19th is the date" to remind his audience of the dire straits of Norris's case:

> *August 19th is the date.*
> Thunder in the sky.
> *August 19th is the date.*
> Scottsboro Boy must die. (Rampersad 205)

Like other authors of mass chants, Hughes here pursues a topical cause with a genuine sense of urgency. He forges a poetry that demands concrete reader engagement in the here and now, insistently pressing the point that the fate of his subject is quite literally "dated" through the poem's use of parallel syntactic structures. Even more, when this poem originally appeared in the *Daily Worker* in June 1938, Hughes attached a telling note:

> Read this poem aloud, and think of young Clarence Norris pacing his lonely cell in the death house of Alabama, doomed to die on August 18. When used for public performances, on the last two verses punctuate the poem with a single drumbeat after each line. AUGUST 18TH IS THE DATE. During the final stanza, let the beat go faster, and faster following the line, until at the end the drum goes on alone, unceasing, like the beating of a heart. (Rampersad 647)

Clearly, Hughes crafted this poem specifically for the context of dramaturgical performance and intends it to exert a visceral, emotive impact upon his audience. Thus, even when confined to the written page, Hughes prompts the individual reader to *imagine* such a performance context for the poem.

While the appeal of a proletcult form such as the mass chant to American social realists is readily apparent, it bears emphasizing that African American poets of the 1930s and 1940s drew at least as profoundly from works of American modernism—a point that, at least until recently, was all too often obscured by a caricatured notion of social realist verse as didactic doggerel. Certain statements from black poets themselves seem to reinforce this distancing of modernism and African American literary production. For instance, Frank Marshall Davis claimed that he could not relate to poets like Ezra Pound and T. S. Eliot due to "their preoccupation with myth and ritual," and because these poets seemed to Davis to lack a spirit of rebellion (Tidwell, "Interview" 106). However, Pound and Eliot hardly comprised the whole of modernist poetry. Put simply, social realist poets drew on a wide array of the aesthetic resources available to them, and not least among these resources were formal techniques typically ascribed to modernism. Particularly as social realist poetry came into its own in the early 1930s, African American poets were both aware of and participating in the interplay between modernist aesthetics and political concerns in verse. For example, in "Elderly Leaders" (1936) Hughes employs a type of modernist typography, the full effect of which is specific to the poem as it appears on the page. After critiquing the accommodation and opportunism of establishment figureheads, Hughes's poem concludes:

> They clutch at the egg
> Their master's
> Goose laid:
> $$$$$
> $$$$
> $$$
> $$
> $
> . (Rampersad 193–94)

Here, one finds a poem very much in the spirit of social realism, but with aesthetic effects expressly intended for print media, rather than public expression in the manner of the period's mass chants. (Indeed, one is led to wonder how the poet might read the ending of this work aloud.) In a decidedly modernist fashion, Hughes's dollar signs disrupt reader expectations regarding narration, but with a significant departure from canonical modernist verse in that Hughes intends this disruption to encourage socially critical reflection and engagement regarding existing (black) leadership. Aesthetically, one would have to consider this Hughes poem as related to the typographical experimentation of a poet like e. e. cummings, albeit that, in ideological terms, these two poets could scarcely have been more dissimilar.

One can point to similar cases of substantial engagement with the formal experimentation of modernism in the work of several of Hughes's African American peers, including the multiple voicings of Sterling Brown's masterful "Cabaret." To cite a less well-known example from a writer whose poetry has often been taken to exemplify the excessive dogmatism of proletarian verse, Richard Wright's "Hearst Headline Blues" (1936) gives the appearance of a collage composed of headlines from the conservative mainstream press of the day. Specifically, the poet arranges twenty seemingly disconnected headlines into five rhyming quatrains. For instance, the fourth stanza reads:

"Woman Dynamites Jail to Free Her Lover"
"Starvation Claims Mother and Tot"
"Roosevelt Says the Worst Is Over"
"Longshoreman Picket; Two Are Shot"[5]

Within a given stanza, one thus encounters an unresolved mix of tabloid sensationalism with news of disturbing political developments on the domestic front. Significantly, the "meaning" of the poem is *not* didactically given. Rather, much like the newsreels of John Dos Passos's *U.S.A.* trilogy (1930–36) in the novel medium, Wright's juxtaposition of these "found" texts within a conventional poetic form encourages readers to fashion their own conclusions about the relationship between, say, Roosevelt's optimism regarding America's economic recovery and the continuing starvation of America's poor. In this manner, Wright joins poets like Hughes and Kenneth Fearing in attempting to turn the language of America's capitalist mass media against itself.[6] Here, too, one might note that even in their modernist aesthetic experimentation, Hughes and Wright continue to adopt a consciously accessible diction and style in an attempt to target a mass working-class audience. In other words, even those social realist poets engaging with modernist aesthetics were concerned that their poetry remained "legible" to a broad body of readers.

In addition to the "usable past" that social realists found in the field of poetry, a second reason that African American writers might have consistently turned to poetry as a vehicle for the explication of social crises has to do with the qualities of narration inherent to the medium itself. To begin with, by its very literariness and orality, poetry arguably possesses a capacity for narrative that even a relatively complex mural painting would be hard pressed to match. And certainly African American social realists cast much of their poetry in this vein, either using poetry as a storytelling medium or adopting a rather different brand of oratory: radical prophecy. Yet, the practical appeal of poetry was not only a matter of its capacity for narration per se. More specifically, a number of social realist poets used the medium to experiment with the use of Sandbergian "plain speech" or more specific regional and ethnic vernaculars. Not coincidentally, this brand of social realist experimentation in African American poetry took shape during a 1930s decade in which leftist little magazines featured numerous forms of workers' testimony, ranging from documentary interviews to transcribed affidavits from the victims of southern racist brutality to Michael Gold's presentation of "worker correspondence" in verse. A work such as Gold's generically titled "Examples of Worker Correspondence" (c. 1935), for example, takes the form of two letters addressed from proletarians in middle America, with line breaks introduced to give the words a poetic aura. In this same vein, Tillie Olsen based her famous poem "I Want You Women Up North to Know" (1934) on an actual letter to *New Masses* from a garment worker named Felipe Ibarro.[7]

Like Gold and Olsen, poets ranging from Margaret Walker to Frank Marshall Davis to Langston Hughes sought to forge artistic work that would speak *about* and *for* poor and working-class people while being cast in a language that at least approximated poets' notions of the voice *of* poor and working-class people themselves. For African American social realists, such a literary project proved particularly appealing in at least two regards. First, it offered a means of recasting the identities of America's anonymous black masses away from the prevailing imagery of exoticism, romantic folkishness, and minstrel show buffoonery and toward a greater semblance of living, breathing, and proletarian human beings. Second, and more specifically, it offered a means to demonstrate the capacity of the vernacular to convey a full range of human experiences, thus redeeming African American folk voices from what James Weldon Johnson had rather famously declared in the early 1920s to be the limitations of dialect writing to the registers of "humor" and "pathos" (41). These agendas coalesce, among several other places, in the corpus of Sterling Brown's depression-era verse, in which the poet renders some poems entirely in a first-person black vernacular voice or else, as in the case of works like "Old Lem," gives the poem over to such vernacular voices after the most cursory of prologues by a first-person narrator in "standard" diction. As Brown was well aware, such a gesture of ceding narrative control in this manner served to grant his poem a sense of "insider" authenticity and the rhetorical power of documentary witness, qualities that a more elevated brand of poetic diction would have been hard pressed to offer.

Even more, social realist poets like Brown explored not only vernacular *language* but also vernacular verse *forms*, including blues and ballads. Again, this decision owed in part to poets' desire to forge a poetry that would resonate aesthetically with a mass readership. Not coincidentally, many white poets and critics were arriving at similar conclusions with respect to vernacular labor music traditions in this same period. For example, Henry George Weiss, writing in *New Masses* in 1929, urged fellow poets to follow the model of labor songwriter Joe Hill, who grafted topical lyrics onto the tune of familiar ballads and hymns as a way of waging the battle for the attention of America's masses in terms already familiar to that audience. As Weiss put the question, "Can art be of the masses, loved and taken up by them, nourish its roots in the soil of the working class, if it is not understandable in form?" (9). Over the course of the depression era, many poets and singers seem to have answered such calls. Woody Guthrie, Josh White, and other folk singers associated with the Popular Front reshaped the melodies of familiar hymns and popular tunes with new lyrics that articulated the plights of dust bowl farmers and refugees, the dangers of Hitler and fascism, the importance of labor unions, and the need to combat racial discrimination. In this era, as well, in the strike-torn hills of eastern Kentucky, Florence Reese was adapting the melody of the Baptist hymn "Lay the Lily Low" to forge the now classic union anthem "Which Side Are You On?" while Sarah Ogan Gunning reworked the hymn "Precious Memories" into a song of miners' travails titled "Dreadful Memories."[8] With good reason, then, leftist cultural critics of the 1930s and 1940s often referred to folk singers like Guthrie, Joe Hill, and the Almanac Singers in cataloging poets of consequence. As suggested by the fact that Aunt Molly Jackson performed selections of her labor verse at the 1939 American Writers' Congress and saw her lyrics featured alongside the verse of more literary-minded poets in the 1935 *Proletarian Literature in the United States* anthology, the generic boundaries between poetry and song were remarkably permeable in this cultural moment. Moreover, for both social realist poets and laborist folk singers, the turn to vernacular aural forms such as blues, ballads, and work songs comprised an attempt to transform the political consciousness of a mass audience by operating from *inside* the existing terrain of working-class culture, rather than by assaulting this mass audience from the position of a cultural outsider (see C. Nelson 58–61).

Yet, it is not the case that African American poets simply followed the lead of their white peers or folk music colleagues in this regard. Rather, their fashioning of black folk voices and forms helped to *shape* (even lead) the broader social realist movement's interest in vernacular-inflected verse forms. And in the poetry of Sterling Brown, Langston Hughes, and Margaret Walker, one finds some of the era's most well crafted adaptations of vernacular forms toward political ends. As a representative example in this regard, one might consider Sterling Brown's "Southern Road" (1930), which conjoins formal elements of the blues and work song traditions into what Joanne Gabbin aptly describes as "an innovative hybrid—the blues work song" (122). Published in an era during which leftist reportage was mounting an increasingly vigilant campaign for reform of southern prisons and the chain gang labor system, this first-person tale of a black convict reads, in part:

> Double-shackled—hunh—
> Guard behin';

Double-shackled—hunh—
Guard behin';
Ball an' chain, bebby,
On my min'.

. . . . .

Chain gang nevah—hunh—
Let me go;
Chain gang nevah—hunh—
Let me go;
Po' los' boy, bebby,
Evahmo'. . . . (Harper 52–53)

Employing the AAB structure of a twelve-bar blues, Brown drives home the pathos
of his speaker's tragic tale through spare language and repetition. Notably, too, the
repeated exclamation "hunh" mirrors the groan of prison laborers as they might
swing a hammer or ax to the timing of such a work song. As a poetic device, this
technique serves both to remind readers of the context of the speaker's tale and to
literally punctuate each phrase of the stark reality being described. Brown works
active changes on his chosen vernacular models by blending the blues and work
song conventions in these ways and by eschewing the improvisational flow of
verses one finds in most documented work songs in favor of stanzas that work together to form a coherent and individually specific narrative. "As a result," Mark
Sanders has ably argued, "he effects the same visceral immediacy of the folk form
while portraying a set of events and circumstances creating the need for the song."
In this way, as well, Brown manages to articulate the speaker's plaint to the broader
physical and metaphysical factors shackling the lives of many poor and working-
class African Americans during the depression era—even as the poem's ritual enactment of song marks a means of grappling with, perhaps even resisting, the
tragic circumstances thus described (Sanders, *Afro-Modernist Aesthetics* 56–58).

In the context of the proletarian literature of the early 1930s, the fact that
Brown turned specifically to the work song as one of his formal models should not
prove surprising. Concurrent with the emergence of social realism, black and
white intellectuals on the left began to look less to the spirituals, which had enjoyed considerable acclaim during the Harlem Renaissance, and instead turned
with increasing frequency to secular music genres that were associated more
specifically with black proletarians—namely, work songs and blues. As Philip
Schatz wrote in the pages of *New Masses* in 1930:

> Negro culture is perhaps the most genuine workers' culture in America despite the
> fact that it is being corrupted by bourgeois influences. However, spirituals are not the
> most genuine expression of the Negro culture.

The black worker finds little place in his workaday songs for a "heavenly father." . . .
He sings not of any "sweet chariot comin' for to carry him home," but of the freight train
which will take him to the next construction job or turpentine camp. (6)

For Brown, as for Schatz, the folk cultural forms of the work songs and blues
offered a stoic outlook on the harsh realities of everyday life for African American
laborers, in which factors of race and class were always already intimately com-
mingled. After all, Brown recognized (as did poets like Hughes and Margaret
Walker) that if many folk blues, ballads, and work songs pertained to intraracial
conflicts and relationships, these genres of vernacular expression themselves also
contained numerous examples of sociopolitical commentary in verse form. In Ma
Rainey's performances of "Backwater Blues," for instance, these poets recognized not simply a source of inspiration, but the work of a *peer* of sorts. Blues, ballad, and work song forms thus offered social realist poets a model for verse that
seemingly would be both *about* and *of* the culture of its intended poor and working-class audience, providing writers such as Brown a chance to craft African
American folk voices that were at once articulate, politically engaged, and au-
thentically rooted in vernacular culture.

As James Smethurst explains in compelling fashion in *The New Red Negro*
(1999), the fact that African American poetry of the 1930s and 1940s so often took
such forms also owes in no small measure to the willingness of poets to draw selectively from the CPUSA's "Black Belt" political program in such a way as to
affirm the distinctiveness and value of African American vernacular expression
(21–32). As in the theoretical writings of Richard Wright and Alain Locke,
African American social realist poets put into cultural practice the conviction
that pursuing distinctively black cultural idioms *and* a Popular Front mode of
interracial coalition building need not prove contradictory objectives. Indeed,
poets like Brown and Hughes often used African American vernacular voices
specifically to articulate the need for an integrationist and laborist brand of
politics.

At the same time, poetry proved appealing to social realists not only because
it offered ways of explicating social crises in narrative and vernacular terms but
also because it provided a means of voicing such explications within a relatively
compressed format. Thus, social realists concerned with strategizing means to
reach a nontraditional readership inclusive of the nation's working classes—as
most of the African American poets discussed in this chapter quite clearly
were—deemed the spatial concision of poetry and consequent immediacy of its
impact to be key virtues.[9] These qualities were especially significant in light of depression-era debates among the American left regarding the most appropriate
form(s) for proletarian literature. In such discussions, for instance, the viability

of the novel was repeatedly called into question as an allegedly unwieldy and inaccessible "bourgeois" form. By contrast, the relative brevity of most social realist poetry enabled writers in this medium to site their work conveniently within the pages of leftist little magazines, pamphlets, and the like, even when the publication of poetry in the form of full-length volumes proved an obstacle in the depression years. Much as in the case of graphic arts, little magazines offered a place for the social realist poets of the 1930s and 1940s to discuss and publish their work, providing what scholar Walter Kalaidjian describes as "a populist forum for showcasing unknown talent and otherwise marginalized feminist, minority, ethnic, and proletarian constituencies" (46). Jack Conroy's *Anvil* and *New Anvil*, for instance, brought together work by seemingly diverse writers such as Meridel Le Sueur and Langston Hughes, William Carlos Williams and Margaret Walker; *Left Front*, an organ of the Chicago John Reed Club, published early poetry by Richard Wright; and the August 1932 issue of the *Rebel Poet* alone included a page one "Call to Negro Poets and Writers," poems in black vernacular by Langston Hughes ("A Negro Mother to Her Son") and white CP cultural critic Victor Jerome ("A Negro Mother to Her Child" and "Communis' Blues"), two Scottsboro poems by white writers, a Scottsboro-themed graphic by Dan Rico depicting a muscular black man bursting the chain that shackles his wrists, and a review of Sterling Brown's first volume of poetry, *Southern Road* (1932). Thus, the material record of African American poets' publication history—which, significantly, also includes magazines targeted more specifically toward black readers, such as *Crisis, Opportunity*, and *Challenge/New Challenge*—suggests just how deeply and concretely the work of African American writers was enmeshed within the larger field of U.S. social realist literature.

Moreover, as Cary Nelson's *Repression and Recovery* has convincingly demonstrated, it was precisely in little magazines that social realist poetry performed some of its most vital cultural work, intersecting in such publications with editorials, reportage, and graphic arts. Nelson notes, for instance, the way a poem such as Jerome's "A Negro Mother to Her Child" and a somber, black and white woodblock print of a lynched black man by Olga Monus (titled *Southern Silhouette*) mutually enhance one another in their appearance on the cover page of the aforementioned August 1932 issue of the *Rebel Poet* (119–22). Indeed, with a verse such as "Daddy is a Bolshevik / Locked up in the pen / Didn' rob nor didn' steal / Led de workin' men," it is as if Jerome's poem offers a potential explanatory note to Monus's graphic, pointing viewer interpretation of her heavily muscled figure away from mere victimhood and toward something much more like the heroic martyrdom of a Marxist "race rebel." In a similar vein, little-known African American poet Esther Popel crafted a work called "Blasphemy—American Style," based on a news article about a Kentucky mob that ridiculed a black man's attempt to pray before his brutal execution. When the poem appeared in the December 1934 issue of *Opportunity*, it was accompanied by two illustrations from Howard University artist and art historian James Porter: the first depicting the man's capture, and the second his lynching (burning) by an enraged mob. Perhaps most notably, Porter highlights the religious hypocrisy dramatized in Popel's poem by placing a church spire in the background of the lynching scene. (One might recall Woodruff's *By Parties Unknown* from the preceding chapter in this respect.) Significantly, too, by situating their work in the pages of *Opportunity*, Popel and Porter sought readerships that were at least in some measure qualitatively different from the high brow, academic, and predominantly white imagined readers that social realists (rightly or wrongly) tended to associate with the poetry of 1920s modernism.

At times, social realist poets sought to capitalize on the relative malleability of their medium by inserting their verse into even more unconventional kinds of public spaces. Often these ventures were not only sympathetic to Popular Front politics, but also entailed the active support of organized labor. For example, the International Workers Order sponsored the publication of Hughes's 1938 poetry volume *A New Song* and also lent aid to Hughes's pet drama project, the Harlem Suitcase Theatre, by offering the IWO Community Center as the initial performance space for the group. As reviewers of the day noted, the Suitcase Theatre was very much in keeping with the larger effort of leftist American cultural workers to build a "people's theatre," centering its work around accessible, formally spare agitprop performances (Larsen 360; Berry 274–75). One such Suitcase Theatre production was Hughes's *Don't You Want to Be Free?* (1937), a work driven by adaptations of the playwright's own poetry and culminating in the unification of black and white workers on stage (with an invitation to audience members to do likewise).[10]

Other poets sought to expand the reach of their work in verse through interdisciplinary ventures with like-minded musicians. In this vein, poet Waring Cuney and musician Josh White collaborated on *Southern Exposure: An Album of Jim Crow Blues*, a collection of six songs released by the radical Keynote Records label in 1941 with liner notes by Richard Wright (F. M. Davis, *Livin' the Blues* 271–72; Denning 357–59). Tracks included the title song, a scathing attack on southern racial discrimination and class exploitation, as well as "Defense Factory Blues," which critiqued the same hypocrisies that so vexed visual artists like Charles White, John Wilson, and John Biggers—that is, a young African American man laments being shut out of defense work despite his own father having sacrificed his life in the First World War. Together with the Almanac Singers, White later performed Hughes's "Freedom Road" on the album *Songs of Citizen CIO* (1944) as part of the Popular Front effort to simultaneously support the Allied cause in World War II and bring an end to class- and race-based oppression on the home front. During this same period, Paul Robeson recorded "King Joe," a tribute to the boxing champion Joe Louis with words by Richard Wright and music by Count Basie for the Okeh record label. (The record was advertised in *New Masses,* among other places.) Simply put, social realist poets like Cuney, Hughes, and Wright made a conscious effort to issue their verse through conventional poetry volumes, leftist little magazines, the stage, and the mechanisms of popular culture—all of which, I would argue, speaks volumes regarding the importance poets placed on reaching a genuinely mass audience with their work, as well as their degree of confidence that their cultural work was up to the task of engaging working-class readers. Frank Marshall Davis certainly was drawn to the medium by similar imperatives as a fledgling writer in the midst of the depression, and he continued to employ his proverbial pen as a means of cultural activism into the late 1940s.

The Poetry of Frank Marshall Davis

Social realist poet and journalist Frank Marshall Davis delighted in contradicting reader expectations, particularly by adding complexity to America's conventional wisdom regarding African American identity. It seems fitting, then, that this self-described "black maverick" came of age in neither the established urban centers of Afro-America nor the southern Black Belt. Rather, like Langston Hughes and Aaron Douglas, Davis hailed from the Midwest, where he was one of only four African Americans in his high school's graduating class. Yet, if the early stages of Davis's life did not offer him a particularly strong sense of identification with a broader African American culture, the predominantly working-class character of his Arkansas City, Kansas, upbringing did help to set the tone for much of his later social realist poetry. Davis's own father was a railroad laborer who participated actively in the unionization of his field. And Davis himself engaged in a certain amount of proletarian labor as a youth, carrying bricks and pouring tar as part of a street-paving gang at the age of thirteen. Finding the work physically punishing, Davis was left with little inclination to wax rhapsodic about the nature of working-class life in his later verse or work as a journalist. Upon graduation from high school with, as he put it, a "magna cum laude in bitterness" (4), Davis enrolled at Kansas State, where he later recalled being the only African American student in the school's journalism department.[11]

Arriving in Chicago in 1927, after two years at Kansas State, Davis found a city with an established black music scene, but only nascent developments in African American art and literature. As he later explained to scholar John Edgar Tidwell, "At this time Harlem had plenty of Black writers. But except for Fenton

Johnson and possibly two or three more, when I reached Chicago in 1927, it was as barren of Black writers as the Sahara." Nonetheless, Davis quickly developed a partisan allegiance to the rough-and-tumble character of his new home city. Although Davis readily acknowledged his awareness of Harlem Renaissance writers such as Carl Van Vechten, Rudolph Fisher, Jean Toomer, Langston Hughes, Countee Cullen, and Claude McKay, he found himself most captivated by a set of midwestern writers who explored proletarian themes and the vernacular language of America's poor and working classes. Specifically, he notes in his memoirs the influence of Carl Sandburg, Edgar Lee Masters, and Vachel Lindsay, although taking exception to the latter's racial chauvinism (130). Sandburg seems to have been particularly influential in fostering Davis's interest in geographic specificity, most notably his desire to "paint [Chicago] in verse" (Tidwell, "Interview" 106). Sterling Brown, himself also indebted to Sandburg, noted this influence in a review of Davis's first volume of poetry in 1935. As with Sandburg, Brown observed, Davis's vocabulary is "American speech, not dialect" ("Two" 220). Davis himself once described Sandburg as "far and away my greatest single influence. Sandburg became my idol because of his hard, muscular poetry, which turned me on" (Tidwell, "Interview" 105). Yet, if Davis's poetry and subsequent reflections represent the urban Midwest in terms of spare language and unabashedly masculine, proletarian personifications that owe a debt to Sandburg, Davis also paints a Chicago that is more profoundly multiethnic than that of his literary forebears. For example, "Chicago's Congo" (1933), a response to Sandburg's "Chicago," presents a vision of the city as a microcosm of sorts for the broader American nation: "Chicago's blood is kaleidoscopic / Chicago's heart has a hundred auricles / . . . the artist who paints this town must / use a checkered canvas" (*Black Man's Verse* 17).

Another appealing quality of Sandburg's poetry for Davis was the former's extensive use of free verse. In this vein, Davis also admired the work of poets like Maxwell Bodenheim, who had articulated free verse forms to leftist political ends as early as the 1910s (*Livin' the Blues* 247; see also Tidwell, "Interview" 105). Significantly, Davis's free verse explorations drew equally upon politically engaged poets such as Sandburg and Bodenheim and the aesthetics of the "new poetry" of modernism. In fact, when Davis first became interested in writing poetry through a class assignment at Kansas State, his excitement was triggered by the discovery of a magazine of what he aptly described as "experimental poems": "*Others Magazine* walloped me almost as hard as hearing my first jazz and blues some years earlier. I felt immediate kinship with this new poetry and felt I could write something in a similar vein" (Tidwell, "Interview" 105). Davis's affinity for free verse thus derived at least in part from its relatively open and improvisatory quality, which he took to be consistent with an African American vernacular music aesthetic. Equally important, like many of his social realist contemporaries (and predecessors such as Sandburg), Davis also used free verse as a way of making his poetry accessible to a mass audience. "I believe that my verse had Sandburgian directness," he once pointed out to Tidwell. "I aimed to make my verse easily understood by the average person. I wanted to be easily read and understood" ("Interview" 106).

Given this agenda, as well as Davis's sense of regional allegiance to the midwestern literary scene, it is not entirely surprising that the African American writer he most often cited as a formative influence on his own work was the poet Fenton Johnson. Davis met Johnson shortly after arriving in Chicago and both participated in "a small, short-lived writers' group" during the late 1920s (Tidwell, "Interview" 106). As early as 1914 Johnson had been forging radical free verse about poor and working-class African American subjects, and these were the poems of Johnson that most appealed to Davis.[12] For example, in "Tired" Johnson writes:

> I am tired of work; I am tired of building up somebody else's civilization
>
> . . . .
>
> Throw the children into the river; civilization has given us too many. It is better to
> die than it is to grow up and find out that you are colored. (Stewart 56)

Not all of Chicago's ruggedness and brutality was of a positive nature, of course, particularly following the onset of the depression. And like most of his social realist peers, Davis was profoundly impacted by the widespread poverty and deprivation that he saw around him during the early 1930s. As he recalled in his memoirs, "All over the Windy City it was a common sight to see the ragged and hungry that winter fighting with numb fingers over garbage thrown away by restaurants and markets; the dailies carried many stories of men and women and children frozen to death sleeping in the doorways and vestibules of apartment houses in sub-zero weather" (*Livin' the Blues* 177). Consequently, while Davis's portraits of midwestern urban centers like Chicago and Gary, Indiana, are boldly inflected with leftist politics, they seldom present a falsely optimistic or overly idealized rendering of poor and working-class life. Rather, Davis's poetry features both the redeeming and less savory aspects of his chosen milieu. Hence, in "47th Street" (c. 1948) Davis's panoramic vision of city life encompasses both the collective activism of successful "Don't Spend Your Money Where You Can't Work" boycott campaigns *and* the quotidian urban realities of prostitution, both the good times of the "garrulous gin gobblers" at Mojo Mike's Beer Garden *and* the "concentration camp of the pawnbroker's window," full of broken dreams (*47th Street* 16–19).

Yet, while the depression contributed significantly to Davis's political radicalization, he personally weathered these hard times far better than most of his peers through a series of journalism jobs, including stints with the *Atlanta World* and the Associated Negro Press in Chicago. In this way, Davis again challenges the conventional portrait of the American social realist writer in terms of his relative independence from the patronage of both the Communist Party and the Federal Writers' Project. The publication history of Davis's first two books of verse also is somewhat novel, in that they were not tied to either a leftist or mainstream publishing house. Instead, through his relationship with a white woman named Frances Norton Manning, Davis arranged for Norman W. Forgue's independent Black Cat Press to publish his first volume of poetry, *Black Man's Verse,* in 1935. Independent of direct leftist patronage as this volume might have been, the poetry nonetheless was shaped by a radical political sensibility, and Davis shared many of the objectives of his social realist peers regarding the kind of cultural work he wanted to see his poetry perform. Consequently, it was particularly disappointing when, by Davis's own account, his debut volume of poetry sold "poorly" and he was forced to realize that this volume had little chance of reaching a mass audience of poor and working-class Americans: "Beautifully bound and printed, the price tag of three dollars was a lot of money during the Depression. I knew few novels sold well and poetry had an even smaller market" (Randall, "Mystery" 39; *Livin' the Blues* 226).

Not completely discouraged, however, Davis turned to the same source of funding that had proven so critical to sustaining the social realist projects of visual artists like Charles White and Elizabeth Catlett: the Rosenwald Foundation. And from this fund, Davis received a fellowship in 1937 to continue his work in verse. The $125 per month stipend that Davis received from the Rosenwald fund was, as he recalled in his memoirs, "big money for that period" (252). Even more, whereas work on the WPA Writers' Projects occupied a considerable amount of a writer's time with local history and quasi-sociological research, Rosenwald money went directly to the support of cultural work. Completed in part with the aid of the Rosenwald funding, Davis's second volume of poetry, *I Am the American Negro,* was published by Black Cat Press in 1937. Together with *Through Sepia Eyes* (1938), a limited edition volume from Black Cat Press composed of previously published work, and his later volume *47th Street* (1948), these books made Davis one of the most well-published African American poets of the social realist era, second only to the prolific Langston Hughes.

During this same period, Davis also was placing his verse in publications such as *Quill,* the *Parnassian,* the *Crisis,* and a Chicago-based magazine, *Abbott's Monthly.* By the 1940s, Davis would expand his voice to openly leftist venues like *New Masses* and his own labor newspaper, the *Chicago Star,* as well. Further, peers and critics of the day recognized the themes and aesthetics of Davis's work as being very much a part of social realism. As early as 1936 Alain Locke noted Davis's "etcher's touch and an acid bite to his vignettes of life that any 'proletarian poet' or Marxian critic might well envy and emulate." In particular, Locke praised Davis's "unanswerable realism," "devastating irony," and conceptual sophistication (Stewart 58–59).[13] Davis also garnered praise from the likes of Harriet Monroe, the editor of *Poetry: A Magazine of Verse*, and William Rose Benét, who later proved an influential champion of the young Margaret Walker's poetry (*Livin' the Blues* 226).

Accolades aside, one of the most important practical outcomes of the publication of Davis's first two volumes of poetry was to bring him into more extensive contact with other writers. While African Americans including Davis, Fenton Johnson, and Lucia Pitts had joined briefly in an attempt to found a writers' group in Chicago as early as 1927, it was not until the mid-1930s that such a collective enterprise actually took hold in the form of the South Side Writers' Group. Although Davis and Richard Wright were aware of one another's poetry in the early 1930s, the two promising young Chicago poets did not become personally acquainted until shortly after the 1936 National Negro Congress, the event that directly catalyzed the birth of the South Side Writers' Group. If relatively short lived (c. 1936–38), this group performed important cultural work at the pinnacle of its vitality. In particular, this collective workshop setting offered Davis a chance to share his own work, including a draft of the long title poem for his book *I Am the American Negro*, with like-minded social realists who were equally committed to the leftist, labor-oriented politics of the NNC, such as poet Margaret Walker and playwright Theodore Ward.[14] Just as important, this institutional framework established ties between Davis and his peers that lasted beyond the life span of the South Side Writers' Group per se. Thus, for example, Davis and Wright continued to meet on Wright's occasional visits to Chicago from New York in the late 1930s and early 1940s. On one of these occasions, Davis shared with Wright and Walker selections from the poetry that subsequently appeared in *47th Street* (1948).

Following the dissolution of the South Side Writers' Group in 1938, Davis continued to interact regularly not only with the mainstays of the South Side Writers' Group but also with fellow writers such as novelist William Attaway and Fern Gayden, a coeditor of *Negro Story*. Like the artist Charles White, Davis also passed through the Allied Arts Guild (c. 1938–39), which included "writers, dancers, singers, pianists, and painters" (241). And through the same 1940 American Negro Exposition that marked White's emergence as an artist of first rank, Davis met poet and artist Margaret Burroughs, who became a lifelong friend and supporter of Davis's work. Out of his participation in the exposition and acquaintance with Burroughs, Davis became involved with the South Side Community Art Center, where he participated in activities such as a panel called "The Writer's Role in Wartime" with Theodore Ward and Jack Conroy in 1943. Echoing peers like Burroughs and White, Davis later recalled the SSCAC as being "a focal point for all the arts," noting that it hosted diverse creative artists such as Gordon Parks, Eldzier Cortor, and Hughie Lee-Smith (278, 303; see also Mullen 81–105). As part of this milieu, Davis also met "often, socially and informally" with fellow writers at the apartment of Gwendolyn Brooks and her husband, Henry Blakely, beginning in 1943. Thus, the poems that comprised Davis's 1948 volume *47th Street* had their roots in both the South Side Writers' Group of the 1930s *and* the networks of African American cultural workers that continued to flourish in Chicago during the 1940s.[15] Moreover, Davis remarked that these diverse fellow writers and artists were far from being ossified relics of the depression-era left. To the contrary, both he and they were very much attuned to issues specific to the 1940s, "quite conscious of the special problems of creative persons during the war and after victory" (*Livin' the Blues* 303–4).

In addition, partly through his connection with Richard Wright, Davis became acquainted with many white leftist writers, several of whom worked on the Federal Writers' Project. Among these new acquaintances, Davis singled out Jack Conroy as "one of the few white writers who could be depended upon to participate in South Side activities"; and, by the same token, Davis served as an associate editor and helped to raise funds for Conroy's *New Anvil* (*Livin' the Blues* 303; Wixson 440–41). By the late 1930s, Davis was deeply entrenched in the interracial political culture of the Popular Front. As an active member of the Chicago chapter of the League of American Writers, Davis met regularly with writers such as Jack Conroy, Nelson Algren, and fellow South Side Writers' Group member Theodore Ward for discussion and to raise funds for causes like the Spanish Civil War, Chinese anti-imperialism, and the defense of Ethiopia from Italian military aggression, as well as domestic issues. Occasionally, Davis even hosted meetings of the group in his apartment on Chicago's South Side, recollecting that "even when mine was the only dark face in the group, which often happened unless Ted Ward was present, I found nothing identifiably chauvinistic" (*Livin' the Blues* 245–49; Tidwell, "Interview" 107). As I will illustrate momentarily, Davis's immersion in the cultural politics of the Popular Front—through his participation in the activities of *both* the League of American Writers and the South Side Community Arts Center—profoundly informed his work as a poet.

Participating in such wide-ranging networks of fellow cultural workers, Davis necessarily negotiated between the sometimes compatible, sometimes conflicted agendas of leftist class-centered politics and black nationalism in both his political activism and his literary work. As Davis explained his sense of simultaneously operating within and outside of the mainstream of social realism in this regard,

"I am not a ghetto poet. I was not brought up in a ghetto. . . . But I am a Black poet, definitely a Black poet. . . . At the same time," insisted Davis, "some of my work could undoubtedly be considered not too different from that of a number of white poets because of the subject matter" (Randall, "Mystery" 43). As this quotation suggests, Davis was by no means a black separatist. More so than many of his peers, Davis was dissatisfied with the nationalist framework of the Communist Party's early 1930s "Black Belt" thesis of African American self-determination. Although his remarks may be shaped in part by historical hindsight, Davis claims in his memoirs that "my frankly expressed reaction was that Stalin's criteria in the Soviet Union had no practical relevancy among us souls who couldn't care less about Stalin's views, and that at the time the prevailing goal was complete integration, not separation into a black nation" (*Livin' the Blues* 282). Indeed, at least by the mid-1940s, Davis was thoroughly committed to the abolition of race as a social and political category, albeit that he retained a sense of distinctive African American cultural traditions. After referencing scientific evidence to support his case, he explained in the foreword to *47th Street:*

> Neither facts nor logic support the popular conceptions of race. This concept is basically political, the false barriers of race being utilized to justify the domination of an "inferior" by a "superior" group and discouraging an alliance between the exploited members of both. So long as the white mill worker can be led to believe in a racial superiority over the black sharecropper, or the Welsh coal miner over the Hindu, just so long will the imperialists and monopolists wallow in wealth while the millions of common people fight for pennies. (11–12)

In this instance, at least, Davis offers a Marxist analysis in which race merely serves to disguise the essentially similar experiences of the world's working-class laborers. And it bears emphasizing that Davis issued this statement in *1948,* reflecting his ongoing participation in the political circles of Chicago's radical left.

Yet, Davis was also an ardent advocate of black cultural pride from the late 1920s until his death in 1987. Critiquing what he perceived as an impulse to homogenize the nation's varied ethnic groups in the name of "Americanizing" them, Davis wrote: "I oppose this attempt to turn everybody under the Stars and Stripes into a copy of whitey—especially when whitey shows little inclination to banish his pet prejudices based on color. I firmly believe each group must cherish, reinstate, and reinforce its cultural patterns which deepen and enrich the entire kaleidoscope of America. There is no sound reason why other peoples ought to renounce worthwhile customs only because they did not originate in Western Europe" (*Livin' the Blues* 319). Moreover, Davis recognized that in practical terms race still often assumed primacy over one's class status in American society. For instance, the poem "Adam Smothers" (c. 1948) describes an automobile accident in which a white secondhand-store clerk hits and kills a wealthy black businessman, yet receives only a fine for driving while intoxicated as punishment. By way of summation, Davis quips with his typical gallows humor, "'All coons look alike to me' / Runs a Southern song / And if there is a moral / This is it" (*47th Street* 93). In this way, Davis continued to advocate against racial injustice even when the broader American left's attentiveness to such issues waned somewhat following the onset of World War II. Uncomfortable with what he perceived as the Communist Party's attempt to "soft-pedal" issues of racial justice during the war, Davis later claimed that he found himself being pejoratively labeled a "black nationalist" by certain leftist peers. At least in terms of racial justice concerns, Davis ironically found "Roy Wilkens and his associates at *Crisis* far more belligerent than the avowed Reds of that era" (*Livin' the Blues* 279–82).

Ultimately, however, Davis was more supportive than critical with respect to the efforts of the Communist Party. On the one hand, Davis was somewhat sympathetic to Richard Wright's decision to break with the Communist Party, particularly with respect to what both of these writers perceived as the CP's lack of respect for the importance of cultural work. However, Davis was quite critical of Wright's subsequent essays assailing the Communist Party: "I was not surprised when Wright quit the Communist Party. I thoroughly understood his antagonism. But I thought his resultant series of articles in widely read publications was an act of treason in the fight for our rights and aided only the racists who were constantly seeking any means to destroy cooperation between Reds and blacks" (243). Thus, whatever its inconsistencies and shortcomings, Davis clearly considered the CP an ally in the struggle for social justice in the United States. Developing an increasingly militant and collectivist stance toward the issue of racial justice and civil rights in the 1940s, Davis explained, "From now on I knew I would be described as a Communist, but frankly I had reached the stage where I didn't give a damn. Too many people I respected as Freedom Fighters were listed as Red for me to fear name calling. . . . My sole criterion was this: Are you with me in my determination to wipe out white supremacy?" (277). One might speculate that Davis's retrospective account underplays the extent of his own involvement with the CP—after all, scholar John Edgar Tidwell has documented the fact that Davis was almost surely an active party member during the early 1940s ("Introduction" xxxv). Yet, whether Davis was a member or "fellow traveler" of the CP, the more important point remains that he engaged CP-affiliated institutions and cultural networks throughout the late 1930s and into at least the late 1940s via work with groups like the League of American Writers and American Youth for Democracy.[16] Further, it was in no small measure due to such engagements that Davis's politics actually became more radical during the 1940s—again, *after* the supposed end of social realism (see Mullen 42).

In his efforts on behalf of causes of racial and economic justice, Davis considered himself a fellow traveler not only of the CP but also of organized labor. Specifically, Davis praised the CIO's support for early civil rights and racial justice struggles during the late 1930s and early 1940s. In fact, owing to CIO-led campaigns to integrate the American labor movement, Davis found that African American workers in Chicago became "a solid, militant force in organized labor" during World War II: "Unlike at the end of World War I, the strikes in the giant meat-packing industry in Chicago now found even the black middle class supporting strikers by providing funds and food. Some picket lines were so predominantly black that union leaders rushed white strikers into them to avoid any possibility of the demonstration being turned into a racial confrontation" (*Livin' the Blues* 298). During his long career as a journalist, Davis himself worked for several labor newspapers, including the *Gary American* and the *Chicago Star*, the latter of which he served as executive editor and a regular columnist beginning in 1946. In this capacity, Davis joined fellow cultural workers like Charles White and Willard Motley in supporting Henry Wallace's presidential campaign on the Progressive Party ticket in 1948 (287, 298–99). By the same token, in poems directly addressed to black and white workers—such as "Peace Quiz for America" (c. 1948), in which the poet describes "the marching sweating fighting people" as "the breathing facts of democracy"—one can see that Davis's engagement with interracial leftist cultural politics increasingly shaped his literary work of the 1940s as well.

The overlap between Davis's concern with labor politics and racial justice in *both* his journalism and his poetry during the 1930s and 1940s is not coincidental, as Davis intended that each type of writing perform a transformative brand of cultural work on its respective readers. Equally bold as a columnist, editor, and reporter as he was in his verse, Davis drew death threats for his forthright commentary regarding the Scottsboro trials and other politically charged cases as editor of the *Atlanta World* during the early 1930s. Then, in 1935, Davis joined the staff of the Associated Negro Press in Chicago as an executive editor, a position he held until 1947. This latter position served to expose him to a wide range of news stories affecting African American life around the country. As Davis later recounted of his work as ANP editor, "Each week I read virtually every black newspaper in the nation, from thirty-five to forty key dailies from every section of America. . . . It was essential that I know what was happening to black people everywhere as well as remember names and past events; I needed to be an ambling encyclopedia as well as a writer" (227). It seems natural, then, that Davis drew extensively upon these journalistic news items in selecting subject material for his poetry. In his own words, "My poetry was often triggered by my experiences as a journalist. . . . As a social realist, I had to be influenced by my experiences as a newsman" (Tidwell, "Interview" 108). Put simply, Davis's journalism and poetry shared a documentary impulse: a desire to bring to wider public attention often-neglected events that seemed representative of the everyday life struggles of poor and working-class peoples. However, as proved the case with social realist work in the graphic arts, Davis's documentary impulse manifested itself in a chronicling of the events of the day that was anything but impartial. Rather, Davis's journalism and poetry routinely dispensed with all pretense of presenting apolitical documentation, choosing instead to explicate what he perceived as the root causes of the social crises of the 1930s and 1940s.

Frank Marshall Davis's wide-ranging body of poetry includes satiric biographical portraits and panoramic sketches of Chicago street life, as well as meditations on time-honored poetic motifs such as black music, love, and death. Here, however, I focus on three recurring themes of Davis's social realist verse: (1) critical revision of rhetorics of "Americanism"; (2) antifascism; and (3) struggles for African American liberation. Although Davis wrote numerous poems focused on Chicago, he also proved quite capable of extending his field of vision to forge commentary on American society writ large. In this regard, much of Davis's poetry finds common cause with works of visual art like Charles White's *The Contribution of the Negro to Democracy in America* and John Wilson's *Deliver Us from Evil* by dramatizing the persistent failure of the nation to enact its own democratic rhetoric with respect to African Americans. Yet, Davis approached this crucial nexus of issues through strategies of satire that bore only a loose similarity to the works of White and Wilson—even though the ideological thrust of Davis's message is strikingly similar to that of his peers in the visual arts. An excerpt from his poem "What Do You Want America?" (from the 1935 volume *Black Man's Verse*) is representative of the ways in which Davis used the medium of poetry to reproach American society:

> Your Constitution gone blah-blah, shattered into a
> thousand pieces like a broken mirror
> Lincoln a hoary myth
> (How many black men vote in Georgia?)
> Mobs, chaingangs down South
> Tuberculosis up North
> —so now I am civilized. (21–22)

Where artists like White and Wilson voice their sense of disfranchisement from U.S. society with unmistakable gravity, Davis joins Fenton Johnson's poetry in seeking to work rhetorical changes on the concept of American "civilization," attacking the nation's hypocrisies in a jaded, even flippant tone. In effect, Davis uses ridicule in an attempt to expose and, hence, undermine the self-flattering lies that (white) America tells itself, a tactic that places this poem in closer company with the political cartooning of a William Gropper than with the dignified murals of a Charles White or the equally grave and earnest graphic art of a John Wilson. (To cite one example, Gropper's July 8, 1947, illustration for *New Masses* portrays a pair of capitalist tycoons in the process of revising the Declaration of Independence to exclude "Reds, Negroes, Jews, liberals, foreign-born, trade unionists, artists, New Dealers, government employes [sic], [and] women.")

The broader corpus of Davis's poetry takes the failure of America to enact the idealism of its founding documents—here, "your Constitution gone blah-blah, shattered into a / thousand pieces like a broken mirror"—and opens it to an interrogation that reaches beyond the parameters of racial injustice per se. For example, Davis's "Self Portrait," from the 1948 volume *47th Street*, extends the poet's indictment of the disparity between American rhetoric and reality to matters of socioeconomic class:

> Of course
> You understand this democracy;
> One man as good as another,
> From log cabin to White House,
> Poor boy to corporation president,
> Hoover and Browder with one vote each,
> A free country,
> Complete equality—
> Yeah—
> And the rich get tax refunds,
> The poor get relief checks. (101)

As in "What Do You Want America?" Davis seeks to dismantle sacred cows of American self-imaging, in this instance by casting light on the fundamental inequalities that "one man, one vote" rhetorics and the perennially serviceable Abraham Lincoln biomythography serve to obfuscate. And again, what arguably seems most striking is the way in which Davis does this: through humor, a trait markedly absent from social realist murals and only infrequently seen in the movement's graphics (save, of course, political cartoons). Indeed, "tongue-in-cheek Marxist" would seem an apt descriptor for the narrative voice of this poem. Yet, if poems such as "What Do You Want America?" and "Self Portrait" are decidedly sarcastic in tone, they nonetheless aim to illustrate the quite serious consequences of the nation's willingness to accept the hypocrisies and half-truths of prevailing notions of "Americanism."

Somewhat more sober in tone, albeit equally irreverent, Davis's "To Those Who Sing America" (1948) directly addresses itself to "You flag wavers / You rabble rousers / You who ask that I sing America." In this poem, Davis issues a stinging critique of America's racial and class disparities by literally supplying a radical subtext to the lines of a key patriotic text, "The Star Spangled Banner." An excerpt from Davis's poem reads:

> "Sweet land of liberty . . ."
> (Do you remember Sacco and Vanzetti in Boston, Tom Mooney in California, nine Scottsboro boys in Alabama?)
> . . . .
> "Land where my fathers died! . . ."
> (While strongarming Indian owners . . . starving to fill money sacks of Mister-morgan, Misterdupont, Mistermellon . . . human guinea pigs testing crazy social systems) (*47th Street* 51–52)

Very directly, then, Davis signals that he is setting out to craft an ambitious revision of American history. Much as Diego Rivera's *The New Freedom* (from his 1934 *Portrait of America* mural series) juxtaposed the Statue of Liberty against a scene of police brutality and images of Sacco and Vanzetti, Tom Mooney, and the Scottsboro Boys, Davis's poem puts seemingly disparate victims of race- and class-based injustice into dialogue with one another via a leftist political frame of reference. Note, for example, Davis's positioning of the U.S. government's eradication of Native Americans alongside the very same iconic political prisoners who appear in Rivera's mural. Further, the wordplay through which Davis conjoins the names of capitalist tycoons (e.g., "Mistermorgan") aligns his poem with a brand of radical midwestern verse epitomized by H. H. Lewis, who coined words such as "flagrags" to suggest a spirit of nationalist war mongering and playfully referred to American communists as "evolved Jeffersonians" in his poem "American Etiquette."[17]

The intersection of Davis's "To Those Who Sing America" with the larger currents of American social realism becomes even more apparent as the poem continues:

> "Land of the Pilgrims' pride! . . ."
> (The Pilgrims, gentlemen, had not seen my country as a land of peons down South, wage-slaves up North . . . her wooded hills stripped to stony nakedness by lumber corporations . . . signboards selling beer and bunion cures blocking her native scenery . . . lynched black bodies swaying from trees in a morning breeze)
> "From ev'ry mountain side . . ."
> (Including airy skyscraper and penthouse for the few, disease cradling tenement for the many) (52)

As the following chapter will make evident, Davis here finds company with novelists like William Attaway and Richard Wright in depicting an American landscape characterized by divergent, but equally destructive forms of racism and labor exploitation that confront working-class African Americans in both the urban North and rural South. So too, like John Wilson's *Deliver Us from Evil,* which also incorporates vignettes of southern lynching parties and crowded northern tenements, Davis's poem offers no easy solution to the problems of African American disfranchisement through the process of northward migration. Rather, Davis succinctly interweaves markers of rapacious industrialism, commercialism, and racial violence as the unsavory consequences of the "triumph" of American capitalism on a national scale. The poem continues on a note that seems similarly shaped by a Marxist orientation:

> "Let freedom ring!"
> (Although the rich are counting dividends and dodging income taxes while the
> poor are scrambling for crumbs dropped from the Table of Capitalism, let us
> hush . . . the Politicians and Professional Americans wish to lift their voices
> in song) (52)

Davis's poem thus tweaks the "Politicians and Professional Americans" who exploit jingoistic idioms to serve their own ends, as well as the general populace's compliance with such received rhetorics of Americanism. Davis's injunction to acquiescence—"let us hush"—obviously is ironic in tone, as the very poem itself constitutes tangible evidence of the poet's unwillingness to be cowed into silence. To the contrary, Davis again seeks to unmask the hypocrisies of nationalist discourse via parody, thus seeming to hold out some measure of hope that his readers might themselves become more astute interpreters of such rhetorical manipulation through an engagement with his own caustically comic poem. In effect, Davis urges his imagined mass audience to "read between the lines" of American political jargon—in this case, quite literally—in order to recognize the disjuncture between the bombastic imagery of a "Star Spangled Banner" and the injustice characteristic of many dimensions of contemporary American life. And it is in this light that the marked absence of lyricism and meter from Davis's parenthetical proclamations begins to make a certain kind of strategic sense: Davis means to contrast the prosaic voice of his explicative free verse subtexts (read: free thinking and well reasoned) against the sing-song rhythm and end-rhyme scheme of "The Star Spangled Banner" (read: conformist and simple minded).

Much as Earl Browder's Popular Front proclamation asserted that "Communism Is Twentieth-Century Americanism," and in much the same way that H. H. Lewis reworked conventional framings of American history to position individuals like Thomas Jefferson and Thomas Paine as prefigurations of his own depression-era radicalism, Davis also labored to critically revise received notions of Americanism through his explorations of black history themes in verse. For example, in "What Do You Want, America?" the poet repeatedly poses the rhetorical query of his title and then proceeds to catalog a wide range of black martyrs (Crispus Attucks, Peter Salem), artists (Phyllis Wheatley, Paul Laurence Dunbar, James Weldon Johnson, Countee Cullen, Langston Hughes, Claude McKay, Henry Ossawa Tanner, Roland Hayes, Paul Robeson), entertainers (Bert Williams, W. C. Handy), intellectuals (George Washington Carver, Booker T. Washington, W. E. B. Du Bois, Benjamin Banneker), athletes (Jack Johnson, Eddie Tolan), and even a pilot (Bessie Coleman)—notably, several of the very individuals that Davis's contemporaries in the visual arts singled out for memorialization in their history murals.[18] In so doing, the poet ably demonstrates that African Americans have fulfilled every ostensible American ideal and yet remain widely disfranchised.

Similar in theme is Davis's "War Quiz for America," which first appeared in the April 1944 issue of *Crisis*. Retitled "Peace Quiz for America" when it appeared in *47th Street*, this poem attempts to weave numerous black figures into the larger historical narrative of the United States, including black military heroes ranging from Revolutionary War notables Crispus Attucks and Peter Salem to World War II's Dorie Miller; cultural workers such as Roland Hayes and Marian Anderson; and martyrs of racial violence and legal injustice in sites such as Detroit and Scottsboro. Significantly, this revisioning of American identity also includes "Paul Robeson singing 'Ballad for Americans' through loudspeakers of radios all over the nation" (55). Like Robeson's performances of this Popular Front anthem, Davis's poem offers a populist but socially critical reconfiguration of America's past, as well as a more optimistic possible trajectory for its present and future. Moreover, Davis structures this poem "to be read aloud by eight voices" in the manner of a song or dramatic performance, composing parts for the various voices that sometimes operate solo and other times in chorus. Although I have found no instances of Davis's poems actually being recited in such multiperformer formats, this sort of *design* nonetheless seems quite suggestive. In numerous instances, in fact, Davis offers similar "stage directions" and/or notes for musical accompaniment for his poems, which bespeaks his awareness of similar work in this vein, such as Langston Hughes's aforementioned historical verse pageant *Don't You Want to Be Free?*[19] In this way, poems like "Peace Quiz" seem to invite not only placement in the pages of progressive little magazines but also staging in public venues. At the very least, Davis enjoins his readers to engage his poetry in an imaginative social space modeled on the widely familiar format of public rallies—precisely the kind of setting that contemporaries like Robeson used to such rhetorically powerful ends during the 1930s and 1940s.

A second set of themes central to Davis's wide-ranging body of poetry pertained to war and the politics of antifascism, a fact that can hardly prove surprising in light of Davis's involvement with organizations like the League of American Writers during the mid- to late 1930s. After all, support of the antifascist struggles of nations such as Ethiopia and Spain comprised some of the principal projects of the league. And this is precisely the context that gave rise to Davis's most explicitly antifascist poem, "Modern Man—the Superman," from his 1937 volume *I Am the American Negro*. Subtitled "A Song of Praise for Hearst, Hitler, Mussolini and the Munitions Makers," this poem opens with a caustic call for a "pedigreed, civilized war." In the second stanza, Davis writes:

> In a day of big business
> Mass production
> Sanitary methods
> And "untouched by human hands"
> With millions of acres
> To seed the dead
> Tons of lead and steel
> For guns and bullets
>
> . . . .
>
> Politicians and moneyed men
> For masterly direction—
> In such a day
> War takes on
> A respectable dignity. (51–52)

As these lines suggest, Davis's antipathy for fascism and its "master race" ideologies was amplified by a deeply felt mistrust of "mass production" and industrial "progress," or at least the misuses to which he felt industrial technology was being put under both fascism and capitalism during the depression decade. This point becomes even more clear as the poem unfolds:

> Let us revere the machine which gives to us our life, our joy, our well-being, our progress
>
> . . . .
>
> Up and down in streets outside machines run . . . they carry men and women to work at different machines for food and clothing more machines have made . . . they use their rubber legs and metal backs hauling men to murder with other

machines called guns . . . they crush blood and life in scornful vengeance from those not moving by steel and oil. (52–53)

Here, Davis clearly parts company with that vein of New Deal–era cultural work that celebrated developments in industrial technology as the sign of a reinvigorated proletarian workplace. For instance, one might contrast the way in which many of the decade's government-sponsored murals depicted a relatively seamless integration of man and machine with the pungent sarcasm of Davis urging, "Come let us sing mechanical hallelujahs / to a pile of levers and pulleys / high as the Chrysler Tower" (53).[20] For Davis, the technologies of mass industry simply remained too complicit in the destructiveness of modern warfare to merit idealistic rhapsodies.

In terms of form, even though I have noted that Davis sought to distance himself rhetorically from poets like Eliot and Pound, "Modern Man—the Superman" is yet another work in which he employs fantastic, modernist musical annotations. Again, even if not intended for literal performance, Davis's marginal notes are partially constitutive of the poem's meaning. Consider these two annotations:

> Eight airplane motors, each keyed to a different pitch, are turned on and off to furnish musical accompaniment within the range of an octave . . .

> Music of an organ supplants the airplane motors only to be drowned out after a few bars by the whir of a dynamo, an occasional shriek from a factory whistle, and the approaching and receding gong of an ambulance. (51–52)

These background sound effects of an airplane, an industrial factory, and an ambulance all bespeak the extent to which a spirit of militarism seemed to pervade the fabric of everyday life during the late 1930s, particularly in the context of an ongoing Spanish Civil War and a planet seemingly poised on the precipice of a cataclysmic Second World War. Indeed, this fascistic militarism is precisely what the main body of Davis's poem sets out to critique in the most uncompromising terms. Further, the fact that Davis presents this militaristic soundscape as a "song" evokes the special threat that fascism posed to culture. This was, after all, not only the era of social realism but also the era of Italian Futurists like F. T. Marinetti, who gleefully celebrated the appropriation of cultural media to serve the ends of nationalistic state fascisms, as in his infamous statement, "War is beautiful because it establishes man's dominion over the subjugated machinery by means of gas masks, terrifying megaphones, flame throwers, and small tanks. . . . War is beautiful because it enriches a flowering meadow with the fiery orchids of machine guns" (Benjamin 241). Davis drives home this implication in a subsequent marginal annotation: "The accompaniment again changes. A uniformed marksman fires a loaded pistol at eight differently pitched bells, each giving a strong metallic sound when hit. They are labeled 'Jews,' 'Negroes,' 'Socialism,' 'Communism,' 'Tolerance,' 'Independence,' 'Free Speech,' and 'Individuality'" (53–54). Especially in this context, the figure of the armed marksman embodies the danger that fascism, both foreign and domestic, poses to American minorities, civil liberties, and culture itself. Notably, Davis's final margin annotation indicates, somewhat pessimistically, that the bells representing Jews, Negroes, socialism, free speech, and so forth "break and fall to the ground as the song ends" (54).

In light of the rampant militarism to which Davis's margin notations are so keenly attuned in "Modern Man—the Superman," I should reemphasize that opposition to America's entry into the Second World War was quite widespread on the American left during the late 1930s, when Davis wrote this poem. However, whereas many social realist poets and artists (including Langston Hughes and Charles Alston) threw themselves behind the American war effort in the early 1940s, Davis continued to write and publish emphatically antiwar and antifascist verse throughout the 1940s decade—much of it tinged with anticapitalist sentiments, asserting a pointed indictment of war as primarily a venture of self-interest for corporate "munitions makers" and the like. For instance, the poem "For All Common People" (1944) poses the rhetorical questions:

> Do common people beg for war?
> Left alone would the people fight?
> Who whams the drums of battle?
> The people? Or the grafting global gangsters?[21] (*47th Street* 66)

By "grafting global gangsters" Davis had in mind munitions makers and other war-mongering capitalist tycoons of precisely the same sort that he lambasted in his earlier poem "Modern Man—the Superman." I have indicated, of course, that this configuration of the capitalist as a caricatured, money-grubbing "gangster" pervaded not only social realist poetry but political cartooning and graphic art as well—appearing, among many other places, in Wilson's *Deliver Us from Evil* lithograph.

In this vein, the fact that Davis includes William Randolph Hearst among his catalog of "grafting global gangsters" in the subtitle to "Modern Man—the Superman" is extremely significant. With this sort of rhetorical move—that is, linking the American mogul Hearst with dictators such as Hitler and Mussolini as would-be Nietzschean "supermen" run amok—Davis joined numerous social realist peers in drawing an explicit parallel between the exploitative agents of American capitalism and Axis fascism. Moreover, for Davis, as for peers ranging from Richard Wright and Orson Welles to artists like John Wilson and Elton Fax, racism comprised one of the principal forms of domestic fascism against which progressive-minded Americans needed to actively defend their country. As Davis put the matter in his memoirs, "We would be called upon to help preserve 'the American way of life'—but if this American way of life would continue to consist of lynching, segregation, disfranchisement, and the master race theory of Hitler, it was not worth fighting for. . . . It made no sense to go abroad to fight the same kind of ideology millions faced daily in Dixie unless white supremacy were concurrently attacked on the home front" (*Livin' the Blues* 263). Notably, this statement could virtually serve as a caption to a work such as Wilson's *Deliver Us from Evil* lithograph or John Biggers's 1942 mural *Dying Soldier*. In verse, however, Davis captures the widespread ambivalence of African Americans toward the war effort on this count somewhat differently than either Wilson or Biggers. Approaching his task more obliquely than his visual art contemporaries, Davis presents the reader with a collage of several fragments of black vernacular conversation in his long poem "47th Street." One such passage, set in 1942, reads:

> Remember a barrage of talk on corner, in barbershop,
> > saloon
> "I ain't mad at nobody I ain't seen. If I gotta shoot
> > somebody,
> > make it Ol' Man Cunningham down in Mississippi an'
> > I's ready. Wuhked on his plantation ten long yeahs
> > with no payday an' when I left I finds I owes him
> > money"
> "Hitler? I knows a dozen white men's worser'n Hitler
> > just in Oglethorpe County, Georgia. . . ."
> (*47th Street* 24)

Davis thus presents this type of sentiment as operative not only in the discourse of leftist political culture per se but in the everyday, vernacular conversations of America's black masses. To those who attributed African American ambivalence toward the American war effort to communists and other miscellaneous "outside agitators," Davis wrote in a *New Masses* symposium, "The Negro needs no Communist to tell him when he is being discriminated against, to point out to him that he is sacrificing and dying abroad for Four Freedoms and democracy he hasn't received in his native land" ("Communists" 16).

As a means of counteracting these fascistic elements within American society, several of Davis's poems—especially those from the 1940s—exhort members of America's poor and working classes to seize control of their country with an unabashed revolutionary optimism. For instance, in the aforementioned "For All Common People" Davis issues a broadly inclusive call to enact a politics congruent with Henry Wallace's Progressive Party vision of "the century of the common man." After enjoining "the people" to "Chase the munitions makers to the poor house, / Spade soft soil over the warlords, / Sterilize the minds of all Hitlers from Berlin to Birmingham," Davis then urges the world's masses to "mold a bombproof peace" out of a "common dream" of working-class brotherhood (*47th Street* 67). If retrospectively this poem seems somewhat fanciful in its idealism, it is worth bearing in mind that Davis's aim in such a work obviously is not to picture America as it is, but rather to envision the nation he would like for America to become: a country that lives up to its own democratic rhetoric. Certainly, social realist works like Raymond Steth's *Beacons of Defense* lithograph (1944) and Elizabeth Catlett's *My right is a future of equality with other Americans* (the concluding linocut of her 1946–47 *Negro Woman* series) had done no less in the visual arts. And, as with Steth and Catlett's artistic images, such moments of apparent optimism in Davis's poetry by no means constitute a case of naïveté regarding America's present state of affairs. Rather, they involve Davis urging his readers to take concrete steps toward making a progressive societal transformation a reality. This, clearly, is poetry intended to *do* something—namely, to sharpen the political consciousness of working-class Americans of various races. As Davis explained in the foreword to *47th Street*, "Since I am also one of the common people, and realize that this specialized treatment is a way of keeping us [i.e., black and white workers] divided for continued domination by the economic rulers of the world, I write of all the common people, even though I know that many of another color and culture in their confusion consider me foe instead of friend" (12–13). In this regard, one also might note that "For All Common People" is—à la the Henry Wallace campaign—a *populist* imaging of the American masses rather than a strictly Communist Party formulation of an industrial proletariat. Nonetheless, in the context of 1940s America, the antifascist and antimilitarist activism to which Davis beckoned his readership were radical tasks indeed.

Finding common cause with a range of social realist peers, Davis explored the nature of black liberation struggles through the comparative framework of international fascism and through poetry keyed to conditions specific to African American experiences in the United States. One of Davis's most ambitious treatments of racial justice themes is the long title poem to his 1937 volume *I Am the American Negro*, a work that he subtitles "A sequence to be imagined." In the manner of a theatrical script, Davis's poem opens with italicized stage directions and a monologue for "a very small, dark lad dressed in a linen robe of dazzling whiteness [who] stands speaking on a busy corner." Through this figure, Davis offers a direct address to (white) readers, requesting that they "listen awhile" to the voice of "your already forgotten / twelve million brown stepchildren" (13). This scene gives way to the interior of a temple structure—symbolic of "America's Social System," as Davis later reveals—in which a representative black male giant, with arms and legs shackled, kneels before an altar, lamenting his plight to an unseen God. Through the self-effacing tone of this giant's prayer, Davis inscribes a pointed critique of what he perceives as the hesitancy of the black working-class masses to struggle assertively for their own emancipation from second-class citizenship:

> But most of all, dear Lord, I have no guts and I refuse to heed the law of self-preservation.
> I cry . . . yet, I will not heal those ills bringing tears to my eyes.
> I will not support men and movements battling for my betterment.
> I will not pool my dollars to fight in the courts atrocities committed against me or illegal laws denying rights guaranteed by the Constitution of my country.
>
> . . . .
>
> If I am lynched or shot or my women raped I will complain in low whispers to my black brothers and sisters . . . more I dare not do.
> I am afraid to protect myself against anything white. (15–16)

Davis augments his readily apparent disdain for such sentiments through italicized notations that describe a group of white faces that "peer through the dark windows [of the temple] showing increased satisfaction at every word" (14). Further, Davis implies that African Americans' self-perceived powerlessness is at least somewhat illusory, as the unwillingness to engage in struggle expressed in this prayer contrasts strikingly with Davis's figuration of Afro-America in the form of a muscular proletarian male giant—a giant who, unfortunately, fails to recognize his own latent strength.

Significantly, however, as the giant American Negro begins to formulate a more assertive critique of American racial injustice—citing lynching, the enforced peonage of sharecropping, and the Scottsboro trials as cases in point—Davis's dramaturgical "stage directions" indicate that the white listeners who had been discreetly observing this giant's soliloquy from outside of the temple structure "cease their smiles and, one by one, leave the windows" (16).[22] The radicalization of the giant's consciousness is further accelerated when an asexual, racially indeterminate figure—later revealed to be a personification of "experience"—appears in the latter stages of the poem. This "Voice" of experience urges the black giant:

> Arm your Christ with a shotgun . . . hire six
> attorneys to work with Jehovah . . . teach your
> priests how to uppercut . . . if David had slung
> a prayer and a hymn Goliath would have chalked
> up another win.
> Sure, we all know there's one of you to nine of
> them so try to win sitting down . . . but if that
> won't work let 'em have it, buddy . . . you can't
> live forever anyhow! (20)

Following this revelation of experience, the poem concludes with Davis's newly radicalized American Negro, like a modern Samson, pulling himself free of his chains, which in turn causes "the temple of America's Social System" to collapse (16–22). Hence, this experimental long poem comprises a warning to conservative and white readers that to continue to neglect issues of racial justice is to place the entire project of American democracy in very real jeopardy, as well as a dramaturgical injunction to African American readers to mobilize themselves for much-needed collective activism.

While Davis certainly was critical of depression-era racial and socioeconomic oppression, John Edgar Tidwell aptly remarks that he was not, in either his memoirs or his poetry, always at pains to explain how one might best combat such potentially debilitating forces ("Reliving" xx). At times, in fact, Davis seems an utter cynic with regard to the ostensible "progress" of life in an increasingly industrial America and to the prospect of altering the status quo of American race relations. Certainly, the prophetic imagery of "I Am the American Negro" seems to portend destruction as being at least as likely a fate for African American radicals as the attainment of utopian revolutionary social change—even as the poem aims to forestall such a tragic outcome. Perhaps not surprisingly to readers of this poem, then, Davis later wrote that the most depressing quality of life in the American South during the early 1930s was what he perceived as "the mass acceptance of racism" and failure of African Americans to engage in collective challenges to the Jim Crow status quo. "As a group in 1931, we were black defeatists. When you stuck your neck out, you did it alone," lamented Davis in his memoirs (*Livin' the Blues* 192–94).[23]

Davis's tone in the poem "'Mancipation Day" (c. 1937) is even more sardonic, offering mock adoration of Lincoln and wondering, in short, just what African Americans (in either the North or South) have to celebrate in terms of their alleged emancipation:

> In Birmingham they ride jim-crow cars to a nigger park guarded by white cops
> ready to shoot to kill if the black bastards annex the idea they're human and Citi-

zens of Alabama . . . listening brown folk balloon with pride as sweet speeched speakers canonize Lincoln—the air reeks with the stench of burned brothers lynched in courthouse yards. (*I Am* 41)

In a similar snapshot from Gary, Indiana, Davis adds a further irony of steel-mill workers carrying out an homage to their freedom when these same celebrants stand to lose their jobs overnight to white immigrant laborers. Meanwhile, all of these workers—black and white, immigrant and native born—"sweat gold for the gods of / the steel corporation in whose shrines none may walk" (*I Am* 41). Further, through parenthetical stanzas inserted among his account of the hypocrisies of Emancipation Day celebrations, Davis draws a parallel between the social location of African Americans within U.S. society and the situation confronting recently released convicts, who find themselves "free" to join the depression generation's vast masses of hobos and migrant laborers. "In the hobo jungles let there be barbecues and long winded programs," writes Davis in the final stanzas of the poem: "Praise ye Warden Laws of Sing Sing / And the New York Board of Pardons and Paroles: / They gave us our freedom!" (42). Here, Davis seems to suggest—again, via sarcasm—that for both recently released convicts and African Americans, "emancipation," in and of itself, means little without full citizenship. In this way, Davis seems to anticipate the polemic of Malcolm X and other radical black orators of the 1960s that life in America constituted little more than a virtual prison for the masses of African Americans. Indeed, Davis seems to desire that this poem will jar his readership into recognizing this prison and its proverbial steel bars of unequal access to socioeconomic opportunity and political empowerment.

Characteristically, however, the pronounced cynicism of Davis's poem seems to cast doubt on the potential efficacy of his own cultural work (or similar leftist projects) to effect such a radical reorientation in the mindset of a mass readership. And Davis did not wholly shed this jaded outlook with his own increasing radicalization during the 1940s. Hence, although the black masses of Davis's "47th Street" do voice their anger over U.S. hypocrisies regarding African American participation in World War II, the poet depicts the same working-class men who voice such frustrations as being more likely to discuss the "newest styles from Esquire / Reigning kings of the baseball field / And whether it really pays / To trust a woman" than to pursue the rights of labor or a project of political activism (27–28). Like many social realist cultural workers, that is to say, Davis retained throughout the 1930s and 1940s a characteristic ambivalence toward the very working-class masses with whom he most urgently sought to communicate in his poetry. On the whole, however, revolutionary optimism surged as strongly in poetry as in any other medium of African American social realist expression.

Poets as Revolutionary Exhorters

As the somewhat idiosyncratic trajectory of Frank Marshall Davis's literary career might suggest, individual African American poets did not arrive at participation in the social realist movement by identical trajectories, nor did they engage its principal themes and aesthetics in precisely the same manner. For the Williams College and Harvard University educated Sterling Brown, social realism offered "the best way" among a handful of literary models capable of addressing the pressing concerns of America's rural and urban black folk communities ("Problems" n.p.). Langston Hughes, who was arguably the most visible of all American social realist poets for a considerable time during the 1930s and 1940s, wrote poetry ranging from blues verse to Soviet proletcult-styled mass chants and forged ties with numerous radical fellow writers through his travels across the Soviet Union, China, Mexico, Spain, the Caribbean, and the United States. For Margaret Walker, to aspire to serve as a voice for America's black masses was, of necessity, to engage with both fellow African American writers in Chicago workshops and the broader traditions of social protest poetry in U.S. literature. And Richard Wright, who began his rise to fame among the American literary left as a promising young poet in the Chicago John Reed Club during the early 1930s, published Marxist-inflected free verse in little magazines such as *New Masses*, *Anvil*, and *Left Front*.

Moreover, as Walker astutely noted at midcentury, certain prominent African American poets not conventionally regarded as social realists issued first volumes during the 1940s that "reflect either a note of social protest or a growing concern with the terrible reality of war" ("New Poets" 348). Among the poetry cited by Walker in this regard, arguably the most important volumes are Robert Hayden's *Heart-Shape in the Dust* (1940), Melvin Tolson's *Rendezvous with America* (1944), and Gwendolyn Brooks's *A Street in Bronzeville* (1945). If scholars subsequently (and justifiably) have introduced the larger bodies of work by these three poets into the canon(s) of American literature primarily through other frames of reference, critics and fellow poets of the day generally recognized these respective first publications as largely consistent with the project of social realism (Stewart 308; Hughes, "Fine" 222). Poet and scholar Dudley Randall has noted specifically of Hayden, Tolson, and Brooks, "They were conscious of their Negro race, but they regarded it in the wider context of a world-wide depression and a world-wide war against fascism" ("Black" 231). As Randall observes, in their early work these poets joined social realists such as Davis, Brown, Hughes, Walker, and Wright in broaching both race-specific themes and leftist cultural politics in the broadest sense.

While these individual poets brought diverse experiences to bear on their respective bodies of work in verse between 1930 and the early 1950s, their poetry does seem united in at least two identifiable ways: first, by an interest in the particular kinds of aesthetic forms and issues discussed in the opening section of this chapter, and second, by a widely shared set of themes. In the latter respect, one finds that these poets explore several of the same issues of concern to African American visual artists of the day, particularly those who worked in graphic arts media. The primary thematic terrains that I examine here are: (1) urban and rural working-class labor; (2) migration; (3) racial violence and legal injustice; and (4) the black soldier and antifascism. In addition, I want to argue that, as a general rule, African American poets distinguish themselves by undertaking an additional issue seldom broached by the work of their social realist peers in the visual arts: the prospects for revolutionary mass action. In all of its thematic registers, social realist work in the medium of poetry exhibits a particular bent toward explication and strikingly direct forms of exhortation. By surveying these points of thematic common ground and shared qualities pertaining to aesthetics, one can arrive at a more thorough understanding of *how* African American social realists sought to use their poetry as a kind of radical exhortation and the specific social issues toward which they directed such calls to action.

I have noted that one of the figures of central concern to social realists was the industrial worker, and African American poets proved no exception in this regard. In fact, under the influence of Carl Sandburg's poetry, Langston Hughes was producing verse on the subject of black industrial labor as early as 1916–17, writing not so optimistically of "The mills / That grind and grind, / That grind out steel / And grind away the lives / Of men" (Berry 13).[24] Like Frank Marshall Davis, Hughes himself had engaged in a certain amount of proletarian labor while still a young man. As biographer Faith Berry surmises of Hughes's work loading trucks on a Staten Island farm during the early 1920s: "Working at this common occupation made him feel spiritually close to Walt Whitman, whose *Leaves of Grass* he was reading and whose influence he was beginning to feel. . . . Like Whitman, Hughes wanted to share the common man's experiences, for he wanted to be a spokesman for the common man" (32). By December 1930, Hughes had published an open letter in *New Masses* titled "Greetings to Soviet Workers" (Berry 108), in effect signaling his shift from a Whitmanesque populism to a more specifically Marxist orientation regarding class politics. Over the course of the ensuing decade, Hughes went on to explicitly direct numerous poems to American workers, black and white, issuing an increasing number of these poems in CP-affiliated publications like *New Masses* and the *Daily Worker.*

Nor was Hughes averse to publishing a given work in multiple venues as a means of reaching a diverse readership. To cite one example, Hughes placed a poem titled "Red Flag over Tuskegee" in the *Baltimore Afro-American* in June 1932, in the radical *Negro Worker* in July, and (with the alternate title "An Open Letter to the South") in *New Masses* that same year (Rampersad 641). Structured as a direct address from an anonymous African American worker to "white workers of the South," the poem urges, "Let us forget what Booker T. said, / 'Separate as the fingers,'" and, instead, calls for a socialistic collectivization of American industries through assertive action by a racially integrated union movement. (Notably, Hughes's call for such a movement precedes the birth of the CIO by some three years.) Hughes even concludes the poem with an optimistic gesture of masculine camaraderie across racial lines: "White worker, / Here is my hand. / Today, / We're Man to Man" (160–61). Yet, despite numerous such exhortations to action directed specifically to (male) working-class readers, Hughes crafted relatively few poems in which he sought to describe or otherwise narrate the contours of working-class labor itself—a fact that is all the more striking given Hughes's openly leftist political sympathies and the sheer quantity of his poetic output during the period under study.

Other poets, however, did take up such a task. For instance, the landscape of Melvin Tolson's long poem "Rendezvous with America" (1942) is decidedly proletarian in shading. Putting his ear to "the common ground of America," the persona of this poem hears a type of national music:

> Swells the *Victory March* of the Republic,
> In the masculine allegro of the factories
> And the blues rhapsody of express trains
> In the bass crescendo of power dams
> And the nocturne adagio of river boats,
> In the sound and fury of threshing machines
> And the clarineting needles of textile mills. (*Rendezvous* 11–12)

Like both Irving Berlin's "God Bless America" and folk singer Woody Guthrie's populist response to Berlin's self-congratulatory nationalism, "This Land Is Your Land," Tolson's poem presents an America that is panoramic in its geographic scope. (The poem also encompasses regionally diverse reference points such as shipyards, coal mines, cotton gins, salmon traps, lumber camps, and oil fields.) Yet, where *both* Berlin and Guthrie dwell upon features of the nation's natural landscape, Tolson sites his representative tropes in particular proletarian work sites. For Tolson, it seems, America is the sum of its productive labor. Even more, like a latter-day Whitman, Tolson finds a certain *music* in the sounds of factories, textile mills, coal mines, and the like. If the vigorous activity of these industries so shortly after the depression decade seems overly optimistic—and somewhat out of step with the anticapitalist critique by which scholars typically

define social realism—it is worth noting that this passage comprises the penulti-
mate section of a long poem that elsewhere encompasses both a catalog of America's masculine folk heroes and unsavory elements such as "the termites of
anti-Semitism," the Ku Klux Klan, robber barons, and "con men [who] try to
jimmy the Constitution" (9). In short, Tolson's "Rendezvous" alludes to both the
best and worst of what America has been en route to envisioning a possible multiethnic, workerist future for the nation. This vision, not coincidentally, was fully
consistent with the progressive pluralist politics of *Common Ground*, the magazine where Tolson first published this poem in the summer of 1942.

In less celebratory and sweeping terms, other poets attempted to capture a
sense of the physically taxing nature of the work tasks performed by America's
proletariat on an everyday basis. For instance, Sterling Brown's "Street Car
Gang" (c. 1937) describes "The trembling jerks in the arms, / The shattering,
persistent, in the nerves, / The metallic tattoo upon the eardrums" that characterize such labor (Harper 216). A little-known African American poet, David
Cannon Jr., suggests bitter ironies more distinctive to the African American
working class in his poem "Black Labor Chant" (c. 1937):

> Grow cotton!
> Burst cotton!
> I pick you!
> Send you to a great black mill!
> To make white sheets,
> For Ku Klux Klan
> To hang me with! . . .
>
> Burn light!
> Cut drill!
> To make coal dust for white men's trains!
> I taste it, in his "jim crow" car. (11–12)

Particularly in the production of materials used by white Americans to further
racial hegemony—that is, the white sheets donned by the Ku Klux Klan—Cannon amplifies the Marxist principle of workers' alienation from the products of
their labor by granting the concept a specifically racial inflection. Thus, for Cannon, members of the black working class find themselves exploited *both* economically and racially, gaining little in return for their labor save racist oppression and
violence at the hands of white Americans.

Notably, too, the short exclamations and action verbs that drive this poem help
to suggest the intense physical strain involved in the types of jobs being described.
Toward this end, Cannon even casts a later passage of this poem in the form of an

actual labor chant of the sort that African American laborers of the day used to time and pace collective work tasks.

> *(leader)* Swing!
> *(gang)* I mash rock into white men's roads!
> *(leader)* Heave!
> *(gang)* I mould guns which shoot me down!
> *(leader)* Bend!
> *(gang)* I make sheets to snap my neck! (12)

Much like Brown's "Southern Road," Cannon's "Black Labor Chant" thus seeks at least some semblance of the musical verse forms articulated by African American laborers themselves. Indeed, Cannon originally composed the poem especially for use by a verse-speaking choir at Virginia State College (*Black* 7). Yet, where "real life" labor chants might more likely incorporate boasts regarding rambling adventures and womanizing exploits, Cannon inscribes the form with a radical content that—like Davis's "47th Street"—attributes a nuanced political consciousness to the African American working classes through a representation of first-person proletarian voices. Eschewing the ambivalence that I have described as characterizing Davis's "47th Street," however, Cannon celebrates the manly labor of African American workers and their stoic endurance of the profound ironies inherent to their having to craft the very products used to secure the nation's racial hierarchies.

Although, on the whole, African Americans shared with the majority of their social realist peers a masculinist emphasis in poetry pertaining to labor, poets like Gwendolyn Brooks and Langston Hughes accorded considerable attention to female members of the African American working class. As in the graphic arts, much of this work focused on the figure of the black domestic worker. Exemplary among such work is Brooks's series of Hattie Scott poems from *A Street in Bronzeville,* which delineate the everyday hopes and frustrations of an otherwise anonymous domestic worker in an approximation of this character's own voice. In "the date" (c. 1945), for instance, Brooks writes:

> If she don't hurry up and let me out of here.
> Keeps pilin' up stuff for me to do.
> I ain't goin' to finish that ironin'.
> She got another think comin'. Hey, you.
> Whatcha mean talkin' about cleanin' silver?
> It's eight o'clock now, you fool.
> I'm leavin'. Got somethin' interestin' on my mind.
> Don't mean night school. (34)

Significantly, what Brooks narrates here is an interior discourse, capturing what scholar James Scott would term a "hidden transcript."[25] That is, Brooks expresses the necessarily internalized complaint of Hattie Scott regarding her employer's insensitivity to her life beyond the job—a sentiment that her protagonist presumably is not at liberty to vocalize. It seems telling, too, that while Brooks's Hattie Scott (both here and in the other poems from the series) is intimately aware of the socioeconomic and power disparities between her and her employer, she does not seem fully "class conscious" in the Marxist sense of the term. Perhaps seeking to differentiate her poetry from the more dogmatic strands of social realist verse, Brooks seems concerned with articulating the consciousness of a black female worker in all of its complexity, in such a way that her character sometimes seems politicized, but at other times considerably less so. After all, while "the date" certainly gives voice to a rebellious consciousness, it doesn't seem to be a union meeting that Scott is so determined to dash off to at the end of this poem.

This latter point stands in subtle contrast to what might otherwise seem a very similar poetry project: Hughes's "Madam Alberta K. Johnson" poems. Featured prominently during the mid-1940s in leftist little magazines like *Negro Story* and *Common Ground* (both places where Brooks also was publishing her work at this time), Hughes's poems resemble Brooks's Hattie Scott series in trying to give voice to a female domestic worker. What most distinguishes these two characters, arguably, is the assertiveness that Hughes grants to Madam Johnson. Not only does she insist on being referred to as "Madam," but when overburdened by an employer she does not hesitate to voice her complaint, as in the poem "Madam and her Madam" (1943):

> I said, Madam,
> Can it be
> You trying to make a
> Pack-horse out of me?
>
> She opened her mouth.
> She cried, Oh, no!
> You know, Alberta,
> I love you so!
>
> I said, Madam,
> That may be true—
> But I'll be dogged
> If I love you![26]

So too, Hughes's Alberta K. Johnson is an astute reader of the *Chicago Defender,* as illustrated in the poem "Madam and the Newsboy."[27] These differences noted, however, it is perhaps more important to observe how both Brooks and Hughes choose to work through a *series* of poems, capturing female domestic workers in their lives on and off the job, and in something like their own respective voices. Further, like Brooks's Hattie Scott poems, Hughes's "Madam" poems range impressively from tones of humor to pathos to anger. All of which suggests the commitment of both poets to fleshing out a fuller complexity for this often-caricatured segment of the African American working class, as if no *single* poem could serve to work the needed changes on such a pervasive stereotype as the "Mammy" or "Beulah" figure of American popular culture. (Elizabeth Catlett, one might recall, tackled a comparable task through her *series* of linocuts, *The Negro Woman*, in 1946–47.)

I have noted that African American poets also departed from the most often remarked forms and themes of proletarian verse by using the rubric of folklore more so than their social realist peers. Among other appealing qualities, folklore seemed to offer a set of narrative archetypes that was more familiar to most workers of the day than a Marxist discourse of class revolution. It is hardly coincidental, for example, that John Henry received such extensive treatment by poets, dramatists, and politically engaged folk singers during the 1930s and early 1940s. Social realist poets like Margaret Walker and Sterling Brown recognized that while John Henry ballads were rooted in long-standing traditions of African American folklore, such vernacular narratives also resonated with specifically proletarian notions of the heroic worker. Similarly, Philip Schatz described John Henry as "the hero of the greatest proletarian epic ever created" in a 1930 article for *New Masses* (7).[28]

Working from such a frame of reference, Walker's "Big John Henry" catalogs feats as a cotton picker, muleskinner, stevedore, and mill worker along with the more familiar railroad labor exploits of this "sho-nuff man" (49). In fact, this is only one of a series of poems from her 1942 volume *For My People* in which Walker adopts a dialect voice and ballad form to narrate the tales of larger than life folkloric characters. Others include "Molly Means," "Badman Stagolee," and "Kissie Lee." Granted, "Big John Henry" is the only strictly proletarian figure among Walker's literary pantheon of "bad men" and outlaw women. However, it is worth keeping in mind that while a Stagolee or Kissie Lee might not provide a direct model for revolutionary collective action—that is, Kissie Lee shoots a man who has "done her dirt long time ago" (39), for example—such figures do "express the profound anger festering and smoldering among the oppressed" and *a will to act* in their outbursts of violent retribution and defiance (Levine 418).[29] In this respect, such folk characters seem at least loosely akin to the more openly politicized brand of race rebels that social realists like Walker forged more explicitly in other poems.

Writing in a mode that he termed "critical realism," Brown takes up a similar strategy in "Odyssey of Big Boy," which first appeared in Countee Cullen's *Caroling Dusk* anthology in 1927 ("Son's Return" 17). The protagonist of this poem, who longs to join the company of African American folk heroes such as John Henry, Casey Jones, and Jazzbo, offers a lengthy résumé of the jobs he has performed over the course of his life: mule skinning and driving steel in Kentucky; stripping tobacco in Virginia; mining coal in West Virginia; shucking corn in Maryland; cutting cane in Georgia; planting rice in South Carolina; roustabouting in Memphis; stevedoring in Baltimore and Norfolk; slinging hash on a northern railroad line; and "busting suds" in New York (Harper 20). In short, Big Boy's decidedly masculine odyssey has encompassed both urban industrial and rural types of manual labor. While Brown does not frame Big Boy's experiences with these jobs in specifically Marxist terms, they are undeniably proletarian in character. Notably, the one job that might not fall into this category—dishwashing in New York (i.e., "busting suds")—elicits the emphatic disavowal from Big Boy, "Ain't no work of mine." Big Boy also swears off returning to work as a coal miner or rice farmer, but on the whole he evidences considerable pride in his life of labor. Indeed, he seems to structure his list of jobs as a series of conquests not wholly dissimilar from the range of female lovers that he goes on to claim in the second half of the poem. Moreover, Big Boy maps his life in insistently idiosyncratic—rather than collective—terms. At least in this work, Brown's protagonist identifies his life and legacy less in class specific terms than through the dynamic example of uncowed, rough-and-tumble folk heroes like John Henry and Jazzbo—in short, the "na'chul man" icon that so fascinated Brown throughout his literary career. One of Brown's signal achievements as a poet was to recognize how such seemingly individualistic figures could speak to the life experiences and desires of the African American masses.

The emergent social realist poetry of the early 1930s evidenced concern not just for America's industrial proletariat but also equally for the masses of America's rural workers, including chain gang labor, as in Brown's "Southern Road." Such cultural work focused most substantially on the embattled black and white sharecroppers of the southern United States. In a February 1933 *Opportunity* column, Brown remarked the emergence of "a different type of Negro" within American literature: "In contrast to the fabulous eater of hog-jowl and greens, the happy-go-lucky come day, go day buffoon, there appears the tenant farmer, hardworking, but doomed to poverty—bewildered and forgotten" ("New Trend" 56). Poems such as Brown's own "Old King Cotton" (1931) certainly helped to shape the contours of this new brand of protagonist by illustrating the oppressive economic system that so severely constrained the life opportunities of sharecroppers during the depression era:

Buy one rusty mule
To git ahead—
We stays in debt
Until we'se dead;

Ef flood don't git us
It's de damn bo' weevil
Crap grass in de drought,
Or somp'n else evil. (Harper 64)

Despite the obvious point of common concern that this poem shares with a work of visual art such as John Biggers's *Sharecropper Mural* (1946), the contrasts between the two pieces are equally significant. Whereas Biggers's mural ably captures a quasi-documentary sense of the material hardships of sharecropping (i.e., too many mouths to feed, meager housing and clothing), Brown's poem concisely explicates the root causes that produce these hardships—the corrupt form of debt peonage that virtually imprisoned many sharecropping families on particular parcels of land, as well as natural disasters ranging from the boll weevil to cycles of flood and drought. So too, while Biggers's deliberately coarse mode of naturalistic figurative depiction might aim for a sensibility in step with vernacular aesthetics, there is little gainsaying the fact that few (if any) sharecroppers produced anything quite like a mural painting. By contrast, while sharecroppers seldom published poetry in little magazines or in book form—collections such as Lawrence Gellert's *"Me and My Captain" (Chain Gang Songs): Negro Songs of Protest* (1939) notwithstanding—they *did*, at times, lament their hardships in the verses of ballads and blues. And writers with an awareness of such vernacular traditions, like Brown and Walker, availed themselves of these resources as a model for their own social realist poetry.

Along similar lines, through a narrator based on an individual Brown met during his days in the South, the poem "Old Lem" (1937) laments the special oppression of African Americans under the sharecropping system, suggesting that it imposes not only economic entrapment but also racialized emasculation: "Whippersnapper clerks / Call us out of our name / We got to say mister / To spindling boys" (Harper 180). As this poem goes on to illustrate, the maintenance of such conditions owes not to the lack of courage on the part of African American sharecroppers, but rather to the fact that the concrete power structure of southern life resides almost exclusively in white male hands:

They got the judges
They got the lawyers
They got the jury-rolls

They got the law
    They don't come by ones
They got the sheriffs
They got the deputies
    They don't come by twos
They got the shotguns
They got the rope
    We git the justice
    In the end
    And they come by tens. (Harper 180)

In terms of both content and cadence, this poem seems strikingly similar to Maxwell Bodenheim's "Gray Rivers" (1937), which declares, "They had the guns, they owned the ground, / The sheriff, judge, the lynching rope."[30] Yet, Bodenheim's poem ends with the success of an African American labor organizer, who wins an alliance with certain of his white fellow workers only after enduring three separate beatings from their hands for his efforts. By contrast, Brown's "Old Lem" ends with the tragic demise of an African American sharecropper at the hands of a white mob as the price for insisting on his manhood by "[speaking] out of turn / At the commissary" and refusing to heed the subsequent threats, "To git out the county." In this and similar poems, Brown thus consciously distanced himself from what he took to be the neoconfederate pastoralism of literary contemporaries such as the Southern Agrarians *and* from the overly tidy revolutionary idealism that characterized certain poems by leftist peers like Bodenheim.[31]

Equally important, Brown sought to articulate the perspective of Afro-America's otherwise anonymous working-class masses through an aesthetically crafted presentation of vernacular voices, much as Margaret Walker would later attempt to craft poetry not only *for* her people, but also from the perspective *of* her people in her 1942 debut volume, *For My People*. Certainly, this sort of narrative technique was most often built on a somewhat illusory polyvocality—after all, Brown himself seems to author both the vernacular and "standard" diction voices in his poetry. Yet, Brown, Walker, and their like-minded peers recognized that such an approach nonetheless seemed a potentially viable (and consequential) means of "democratizing" American poetry. For to change the perspective from which poetry of American life was articulated, even if by a kind of ventriloquizing of vernacular voices, was necessarily to alter the American story in significant ways.

One of the ways in which poor and working-class African Americans sought to escape the type of hardships referenced in poems like Sterling Brown's "Old

King Cotton" and "Old Lem" was through the ongoing waves of the Great Migration, dating from at least World War I forward into the era of social realism. In the previous chapter, I suggested that the mass migration of rural southern blacks to northern urban centers in certain respects loosely resembled the life experiences of their "dust bowl refugee" peers of the American Midwest, inasmuch as both of these groups of poor and working-class Americans forsook deeply rooted community ties in no small part due to depression-era socioeconomic constraints. As Farah Jasmine Griffin documents in her important study *Who Set You Flowin'?* (1995), the interwar Great Migration experience of African Americans played out in a number of cultural registers, including the blues of Muddy Waters, the stunning visual imagery of Jacob Lawrence's *Migration of the Negro* series, and, later, Ralph Ellison's landmark novel *Invisible Man*. From the centrality of the road as an overarching metaphor of Sterling Brown's *Southern Road* (1932) to the rural-to-urban continuum of Margaret Walker's "For My People" (c. 1942) to the migration theme of Langston Hughes's *One-Way Ticket* (1949), this collective experience proved a frequent and enduring reference point for social realist poetry as well.

In verse, one specific motif that united social realists' treatment of African American and dust bowl migrants was the sense of rootlessness that departure from native communities frequently entailed. Hughes's "Six-Bits Blues," first published in *Opportunity* in 1939, captures this sensibility in its broadest form:

> O, there ain't no place in
> This world to rest a-tall.
> Ain't no place for
> A man to rest a-tall.
> That's why I got to be a-sayin'
> Goodbye to you all.[32]

While Hughes clearly taps into the motif of mobility pervasive in blues lyrics of the day, the spirit of this poem also resonates with the cultural expression of certain of Hughes's white contemporaries. Particularly in light of Hughes's documented interaction with the Popular Front folk music scene, it seems appropriate to consider this stanza as related to the insistent refrain of a song like Woody Guthrie's "I Ain't Got No Home" (1939), with its narrative of a "wandering worker" who "go[es] from town to town." (Guthrie himself, of course, was a performer whose music bore the imprint of both Carter Family–style gospel and African American vernacular music [Garman 118–20, 179–80].) The narrator of "Six-Bits Blues" exclaims earlier in the poem, "Gimme six-bits' worth o' ticket / On a train that runs somewhere . . ." with a yearning for the promise held out by the prospect of mobility, much as African American migrants typically did hope for real change in their lives via the Great Migration—at least initially. And one simply does not find this note of hope for substantial progress through mobility in Guthrie's "I Ain't Got No Home." Still, in both Hughes's poem and Guthrie's song, masculine personas from America's underclass posit a sense of rootlessness and the absence of a stable sense of community as quintessential qualities of life during the depression and its immediate aftermath.

In a similar vein, Joanne Gabbin has described Sterling Brown's encounter with a man known as Revelations, "the placard covered halfwit whom Brown met on the dust roads of a Missouri village." This experience later found its way into a Brown poem titled "Revelations," in which the eponymous "halfwit" voices a Protestant hymn seemingly keyed to depression-era displacements (91–92): "*You gotta walk that lonesome valley, / You gotta walk it by yo'self, / Nobody heah can a-walk it for you / You gotta walk it by yo'self*" (98). (Significantly, Guthrie later adapted this same hymn to capture a sense of the dust bowl's wrenching material and psychic impact.) Later, in the concluding lines of the poem, the narrator paraphrases "the halfwit's text":

"If man's life goes
Beyond the bone
Man must go lonely
And alone.
Unhelped, unhindered
On his own. . . ." (99)

In the restless voice of Hughes's blues singer, in Guthrie's folk ballads of the depression era's dispossessed, and in the uncanny wisdom of Brown's Revelations are entire realms of cultural discourse that contemporary scholars seldom discuss in the same frame of reference with the canonical works of high modernist poetry. Yet one could well make a case that these politicized examples of vernacular verse offer an engagement with the theme of what Gabbin terms "the fundamental alienation and spiritual isolation of man" (92) every bit as gripping as the work of a poet like T. S. Eliot.

If to a certain extent materially and spiritually rootless and alienated, most African American migrants did, of course, retain some sense of hope and purpose in their journey to the urban North. Hughes's poem "One-Way Ticket" serves to crystallize the motivations and aspirations that united many of these migrants, as the speaker declares that he is "fed up / With Jim Crow laws" and with those who perpetuate a climate of fear and racial violence in the South. In short, the speaker longs for the promise of "any place that is . . . not Dixie" (Rampersad 361). Notably, in the 1949 volume of the same title, Hughes's "One-Way Ticket" appears alongside the reproduction of a black and white gouache by Jacob Lawrence that depicts a group of black migrants huddled together, awaiting departure in a train station. As Hughes's poetry and Lawrence's artwork serve to remind readers, both a commonly shared set of antipathies for the racism of the abandoned South and ambitions for the new economic opportunities of the North united literally thousands of African American migrants in something of a collective experience.

To point to the prevalence of racial violence as a motivating factor for migration is not to deny that many African American migrants experienced a conflicted sense of nostalgia for their native South, what literary critic Ulysses Lee described as "the strange contradiction of beauty in the low cotton country" in reference to the poetry of Margaret Walker (380). Indeed, Walker's northern protagonists frequently long for at least certain aspects of their remembered southern lifeways. In "Sorrow Home" (c. 1942), for instance, the poet yearns for a pastoral landscape of cotton, tobacco, cane, and "fallow ground." Yet, she must lament:

> O Southland, sorrow home, melody beating in my bone and blood! How long will the Klan of hate, the hounds and the chain gangs keep me from my own? (*For My People* 19)

Walker expresses a similar sentiment in "Southern Song" (1937). After voicing her anxiety at the prospect of mob violence creating "a nightmare full of oil and flame," the poet concludes:

> I want my careless song to strike no minor key; no fiend to stand between my body's southern song—the fusion of the South, my body's song and me.[33] (*For My People* 18)

In both of these poems, Walker eloquently expresses a sense of forced displacement from her rightful heritage. Much as the Joads of John Steinbeck's *Grapes of Wrath* find themselves driven from their midwestern farm by a confluence of drought, the machinery of industrial agriculture, and ruthless capitalists, Walker's African American migrants are separated from their "southern song" by the perennial threats of imprisonment, conscripted labor on a chain gang, and racist mob violence.

Don West, a now largely forgotten white southern poet who published regularly in journals like *New Masses* during the 1930s, voiced a similar set of conflicted sentiments regarding life in his native South. For West, as for Walker, these mixed feelings center around the poet's repulsion at prevailing southern patterns of racial oppression. In "My South" (1934) West confronts "my cold-blooded South" with its own brutality in the visceral image of "*a Negro's blood / Smeared over your mouth.*" Notably, this indictment wrenches the poet from a nostalgic longing for brotherhood with both black workers and "my own bleeched [*sic*] brothers," expressed in a desire to join the latter's sorrow songs.[34] That the South's need for redemption turns so clearly on issues of racial justice for both Walker and West suggests just how central such concerns were to the larger project of social realism, even as these poets seem to caution their leftist peers against simply dismissing the region with caricatures of irredeemable barbarity and political backwardness. Both poets, after all, express considerable nostalgia for redemptive forms of labor and song framed as distinctive to the South. Further, both Walker and West structure their poems as heartfelt appeals to their native region to right its course, albeit that each poet seems to harbor serious skepticism about the transformative impact that such exhortations will yield.

At the same time, Walker's poetry seems to counsel readers that the North is no promised land for poor and working-class African Americans. For instance, the speaker of Walker's "Sorrow Home" attempts to turn nostalgically to the South after voicing her dissatisfaction with the compressed space and noise of life in the "steam-heated flats" of the urban North.[35] In this vein, one also might consider Langston Hughes and Richard Wright's collaborative poem "Red Clay Blues," first published in the August 1, 1939, issue of *New Masses*. Lamenting, "Pavement's hard on my feet, I'm / Tired o' this concrete street," the speaker of the poem expresses his or her desire to return to a small farm in Georgia despite the remembered oppression of white landlords. In fact, in this poem Hughes and Wright go further, forecasting the demise of southern economic exploitation:

> I want to be in Georgia when the
> Big storm starts to blow.
> Yes, I wants to be in Georgia when that
> Big storm starts to blow.
> I want to see the landlords runnin' cause I
> Wonder where they gonna go! (Rampersad 212–13)

Here, as elsewhere in their respective bodies of poetry, Hughes and Wright employ the African American blues vernacular to articulate a revolutionary political vision that is Marxist in orientation. The ruling class of landlords is vanquished by a mass uprising of oppressed southern sharecroppers, the latter here rendered prophetically as an irresistible force of nature, a "big storm." In this light, the poem's reference to *red* clay adds both an element of southern geographic specificity and a not too subtly encoded reference to a specifically communist brand of proletarian revolution.

A third set of thematic concerns central to African American poetry during the 1930s and 1940s pertained to issues of racial injustice, with a special focus on the makeshift mob "justice" of lynchings and the often equally dubious "justice" accorded to African Americans within the nation's formal legal system. What may prove surprising, at least to readers not already immersed in the poetry of the period, is the extent to which African American poets succeeded in helping to bring this thematic register to the center of the broader social realist movement in American poetry. Hence, like the work of African American poets ranging from Frank Marshall Davis to Langston Hughes and the early Robert Hayden, "Americanism" (1935) by the white poet Henry George Weiss links icons of fervent nationalism (including "God Flag Constitution") with certain of the United States's more unsavory aspects regarding racial oppression, all to powerful rhetorical effect. Typical in this regard is Weiss's configuration of "ku klux klan / with declarations of independence / in one hand / and tar and rope in the other." Even more, Weiss closes his poem with an image of "Americanism / on a tree limb / swinging swinging / Georgia Alabama."[36] As exemplified by Weiss's rhetorical gambits, acts of racial violence comprised one of the most frequent themes used by both black and white poets to dramatize the disparity between America's rhetoric of democratic inclusion and practices of racist exclusion.

Richard Wright's "Between the World and Me" (1935) offers one of the most chilling accounts in verse of lynching from the perspective of a victim. Wright's poem begins with the speaker's discovery of the remains of a previous night's lynching on a morning walk through the woods. In effect, this horrific scene disrupts the type of communion with nature that one might expect from a more conventional poem. In concrete, vivid terms the narrator relates that, "the sooty details of the scene rose, thrusting themselves between / the world and me . . ." (Freeman 202). Further, as the speaker stands transfixed before the charred remains of the victim's body and personal effects, he undergoes a transfiguration in which these bones and ashes merge with his own flesh and he finds *himself* in the midst of the lynching ritual: "And then they had me, stripped me, battering my teeth into my throat / till I swallowed my own blood . . . / And my skin clung to the bubbling hot tar, falling from me in limp / patches. / And the down and quills of the white feathers sank into my raw flesh, / and I moaned in agony" (202–3).[37] While Wright's adoption of a strictly first-person perspective in this context is relatively unusual among poets, it is not without parallel. Like Wright's "Between the World and Me," "Georgia Nightmare" (1936) by the white poet Edwin Rolfe begins with the discovery of sixteen lynching victims in a forest and concludes with a reenactment of the lynching in which, the poet explains:

A heavy rope is flung into the skies,
a heavy rope hangs tautly from a tree,
a black man strangles above a sea of eyes.
The black man looks like me.[38]

Chapter Four

Significantly, neither Wright nor Rolfe clearly indicates whether these first-person experiences of lynching constitute real or imagined events. In this manner, both poets attempt to capture the full brutality of lynching and to force readers—whether black or white—to confront their own status as potential victims of such violence.

Whereas Wright's poem placed the reader metaphorically in the shoes of a victim of racial violence, Sterling Brown's "Call for Barnum" (c. 1937) sutures (white) readers to the identity of a perpetrator of such brutality. Much like graphics by artists such as Hale Woodruff (*Giddap*) and Reginald Marsh (*This Is Her First Lynching*), "Call for Barnum" conveys a sense of lynching as an all too frequent, grotesque, and even carnivalesque affair—an effect that Brown achieves by adopting the voice of one of the lynch mob's participants. In this white vernacular voice, the poet describes lynching's ritualistic racial violence as being "as good as a movie" and even extends the commercial entertainment analogy further:

All a crowd could want. Steel, hemp, lead, gasoline.
Plenty for your money, with some drinks thrown in,
And a scramble for souvenirs, to a pretty chorus,
"Give us all something to remember you by." (Harper 206)

In comparative terms, the textual medium of poetry seems to have afforded poets like Brown the license to delve into the most harrowing details of such terroristic violence (i.e., the "scramble for souvenirs")—details that, significantly, most social realists seem to have deemed too gruesome (or, perhaps, too disempowering) for visual display, even in the politicized media of graphic arts. So too, poetry allows Brown to convey a relatively detailed sequence of events of the sort that graphic artists typically sought to evoke through the "snapshot" of a single representative moment. Which approach might have proven more transformative to a working-class audience is, of course, an ultimately irresolvable matter. What is clear is that by revisiting the lynching theme in several poems and from a range of perspectives, Brown captures a sense of the ways in which lynching effectively dehumanizes all Americans: lynchers, victims, and those who stand idly by and take no action to halt the perpetuation of this widespread practice.

In dramatizing acts of racist violence, social realist poets also joined their peers in the graphic arts in that they frequently drew a direct or implied parallel between African American victims of lynching and the crucified Christ. Robert Hayden's "Brown Girl's Sacrament" (c. 1940), for example, pointedly pairs "the bruised body / Of Jesus . . . / Lynched on the hill of Calvary" to the "charred April body" of a young woman's lover, "Swinging from a tree in Dixie!" (39). Frank Marshall Davis offered a similar analogy in his poem "Christ Is a Dixie

Nigger" (1937). Adopting a mode of irreverent direct address that was in keeping with a prevalent leftist antagonism toward organized religion during the 1930s, Davis insists, "I've got a better Christ and a bigger Christ . . . one you can put your hands on today or tomorrow." Davis's Christ is "a black bastard" child of an African American mother and plantation-owning white father. Escaping north to Chicago, Davis's protagonist becomes a physician and then returns to the South to serve his native community. There, because "he talked / of the brotherhood and equality of man and of a / Constitution giving everybody a right to vote" and "healed a white woman other doctors / gave up for lost," this doctor is labeled a communist and lynched by the white community. Yet, rather than positioning his contemporary black Christ as merely a victim, Davis writes of a resurrected black Christ who continues to struggle for racial justice (*I Am* 28–29).

Clearly, like many leftist cultural workers of the depression era, Davis was frustrated with the general passivity and conservatism of organized religion, at least in so far as it had been used to sustain the societal status quo regarding issues of racial justice. Resonating with works such as Langston Hughes's more widely known "Goodbye Christ" and "Christ in Alabama," Davis's poem concludes:

> Remember this, you wise guys
> Your tales about Jesus of Nazareth are no-go with me
> I've got a dozen Christs in Dixie all bloody and black . . . (29)

As with graphic artists' treatment of this motif, Hayden and Davis's poems attempt to formulate a politics of racial justice in terms that are both accessible and emotively charged for a mass audience. Yet, where visual artists like John Biggers (*Dying Soldier*) seem to use crucifixion imagery *primarily* as a way of forging a sense of identification between (Christian) viewers and victims of racial violence, poets more often deploy such analogies as part of a pointed critique of the hypocrisies that they perceive as plaguing organized religion and (white) Christianity in particular. Directly addressing himself to the leaders of the contemporary church earlier in "Christ Is a Dixie Nigger," Davis writes:

> Your pink priests who whine about Pilate and Judas and Gethsemane I'd like to hogtie and dump into the stinking cells to write a New Testament around the Scottsboro Boys (*I Am* 29)

With his characteristically brash mode of exhortation, Davis thus insists on the necessity of religion being articulated to contemporary political issues if it is to play a meaningful role in the lives of America's poor and working-class masses. Especially in light of the frequent complicity of white churches with the project of white supremacy in the Dixie South, the use of such black Christ iconography constitutes a radical act of social and theological revision.[39]

Chapter Four

As hinted at by Davis's referencing of Scottsboro in the preceding lynching poem, social realist poets also framed cases of injustice within the U.S. legal system as a type of racial violence. With the CP's International Labor Defense frequently referring to the Scottsboro trials, in particular, as a "legal lynching" (Berry 130), this case provided a central point of reference for cultural workers operating in numerous genres of social realist expression. And notwithstanding the doubts expressed in Countee Cullen's "Scottsboro, Too, Is Worth Its Song" (1933), both black *and* white social realists produced a sizable volume of poetry dedicated to the Scottsboro case during the depression decade and extending into the early 1940s.[40] For these poets, Scottsboro served as a preeminent example of the racial injustice and violence to which all African Americans were potentially subject. Hence, in his long mass chant "These Are My People" (c. 1940), Hayden posits the Scottsboro Boys as a signpost of the larger failings of the U.S. justice system with imagery of "truth" as "an eagle / shot down from the sky; / a ravished woman / left to die / in the barren fields, / the flowerless fields / of Scottsboro" (62). Other poets, such as Langston Hughes, were moved to write multiple poems centered around the Scottsboro episode. For example, Hughes's aforementioned mass chant "August 19th . . . A Poem for Clarence Norris" pleads the case of one of the Scottsboro defendants scheduled to die in 1938, directly challenging the reader, "For if you let the 'law' kill me, Are you free?" (Rampersad 204).[41] Hughes had even personified American Justice's blindness by suggesting, "Her bandage hides two festering sores / That once perhaps were eyes" (Berry 135). In essence, Hughes's "Justice" (1923) seems to anticipate the motif of later graphics like Elton Fax's *Justice Wears Dark Glasses*—which, one might recall, even went so far as to equate the willing blindness of the U.S. legal system to Nazi fascism. Significantly, too, Hughes's "Justice" appeared, along with a handful of other poems and a play, in an illustrated booklet titled *Scottsboro Limited,* proceeds from which went to the Scottsboro Defense Fund (Berry 146). In fact, Hughes personally visited the Scottsboro defendants in jail and maintained involvement with their defense throughout the protracted trials and appeals process over the course of the ensuing decade (Berry 209).

Because Scottsboro served as a central reference point for leftist American cultural politics throughout the depression decade, social realist poets also frequently connected this case with other historic and contemporary struggles for racial and economic justice. In this vein, Hughes's "Scottsboro" (1931) links the looming martyrdom of the Scottsboro Boys with a radical legacy that includes personages such as Christ, John Brown, the French revolutionists, Moses, Joan of Arc, Nat Turner, Lenin, and Gandhi (Rampersad 142–43).[42] In a similar fashion, "The Trial" (1934), by Hughes's white contemporary Muriel Rukeyser, ties the fate of the Scottsboro Boys not only to prominent historical figures associated with the cause of black liberation—including John Brown, Nat Turner, Toussaint L'Ouverture, and Dred Scott—but also to more contemporary political prisoners associated with issues of class struggle, such as Sacco and Vanzetti, Tom Mooney, and Angelo Herndon.[43] These broader parallels were not lost on poets like Hughes. In "August 19th," for instance, Hughes connects the Scottsboro trials with the contemporaneous leftist cause of antifascism in China and Spain (see Berry 145). Further, Hughes's oeuvre of legal justice–themed verse included works such as "Chant for Tom Mooney" in addition to his numerous Scottsboro poems.[44]

It seems notable, too, that the invocation of historical legacies in poems like Hughes's "Scottsboro" and Rukeyser's "The Trial" seem to hold more in common with Charles White's graphic *The Living Douglass* than with the artist's *Contribution of the Negro to Democracy in America* mural. For while White's mural includes Nat Turner and similar nineteenth-century race rebels, its contemporary figures include heroes rather than political martyrs such as the Scottsboro Boys.[45] In graphics, by contrast, White seems to have felt considerably more at liberty to tie a *"living"* Frederick Douglass to the contemporary legal battles of the Trenton Six. Graphics, that is to say, tended to be much closer than murals to the contemporary focus and explicit exhortation to action that one finds in the poetry of writers like Hughes and Rukeyser.

If Scottsboro seemed to comprise a symbolic crucible of America's failings with regard to race for social realist poets of the 1930s, the participation of African Americans in World War II occupied an equally charged rhetorical space in the work of African American poets during the ensuing decade. Of course, ambivalent sentiments regarding war had constituted a well-established theme in modern American verse from the World War I era onward. For African Americans, in particular, lingering racism after the First World War only served to amplify this conviction. Hence, it should not prove surprising that Langston Hughes crafted a work such as "Poem to a Dead Soldier" as early as 1925. During the early 1930s, Hughes continued to reflect on the national betrayal of those African Americans who had "closed ranks" to aid their country during World War I—as evidenced in "The Colored Soldier" (1931), a poem in which a young black man dreams bitterly of his brother's death in France. Likewise, Hughes's address to the 1935 American Writers' Congress charged his fellow writers to "expose war . . . and the old My-Country-'Tis-of-Thee lie" while interrogating "the colored American Legion posts strutting around talking about the privilege of dying for the noble Red, White and Blue, when they aren't even permitted the privilege of living for it" ("To Negro Writers" 140). In short, Hughes saw in white America's ill treatment of World War I black veterans a preeminent sign of the nation's larger breach of good faith with African Americans writ large, much as did John Biggers in his 1942 *Dying Soldier* mural.

Despite expressing considerable reservations in the period preceding Hitler's invasion of the Soviet Union in 1941, poets such as Hughes, Richard Wright, and Robert Hayden eventually joined the majority of their leftist peers in offering their support to the U.S. war effort. So too, magazines such as *Crisis* and *Opportunity* published a certain amount of verse dedicated to the outright praise of African American war heroics. Just as often, however, the figure of the black soldier evoked the same sorts of conflicted loyalties for poets as for visual artists like Biggers and John Wilson. Gwendolyn Brooks's "Negro Hero (to Suggest Dorie Miller)," which appeared in the summer 1945 issue of *Common Ground,* perhaps best captures these mixed emotions of pride and frustration regarding African American participation in the war effort. Whereas artist James Lesesne Wells crafted a relatively straightforward celebration of Miller's heroism at Pearl Harbor in his 1946 lithograph *Muscles Mans the Guns,* Brooks's poem issues a pointed critique of those black and white mass media institutions that chose to focus on Miller's heroism without fully addressing questions about why Miller had been relegated to the role of mess man before his Pearl Harbor heroics. Adopting the voice of Miller, she writes:

> But let us speak only of my success and the pictures in the Caucasian dailies
> As well as the Negro weeklies. For I am a gem.
> (They are not concerned that it was hardly The Enemy my fight was against
> But them.) (30)

In other words, Brooks not only tweaks the facile nature of the accolades accorded to Miller as a kind of "exceptional Negro" in the press (both black and white) but also suggests how such glossy news features serve to obfuscate the domestic half of the "Double V" campaign's battle against fascism. Even more poignantly, the poet muses with respect to Miller's white fellow soldiers:

> Still—am I good enough to die for them, is my blood bright enough to be spilled,
> Was my constant back-question—are they clear
> On this? Or do I intrude even now?
> Am I clean enough to kill for them, do they wish me to kill
> For them or is my place while death licks his lips and strides to them
> In the galley still? (31)

It is in the context of these doubts and frustrations that the poet crafts her memorable lines, "Naturally, the important things is, I helped to save them, / them and a part of their democracy. / Even if I had to kick their law into their teeth in order / to do that for them" (30). As has so often been the case, African American freedom fighters must turn to the nation's stated principles of democratic inclusiveness ("their law") as a weapon of liberation when the actual social practices of white America so egregiously depart from its own ostensible ideals. Significantly, when Brooks's Miller uses "the law" as a weapon in this manner, it is through his own assertive action (on a literal field of battle, no less) and *not* in the context of a U.S. courtroom—which, of course, the Scottsboro trials, among many others, had shown to be so notoriously unreliable as a resource for African American liberation.

Brooks explores similar thematic terrain through "Gay Chaps at the Bar," a sonnet sequence crafted around the collective situation of African American servicemen during and immediately after the Second World War. She concludes "the progress," the final poem of this sequence and of her *Street in Bronzeville* debut volume, on a deeply conflicted note. On the one hand, speaking in the collective voice of these soldiers, Brooks observes:

> Still we applaud the President's voice and face.
> Still we remark on patriotism, sing,
> Salute the flag, thrill heavily, rejoice
> For death of men who too saluted, sang.

"But inward grows a soberness, an awe, / A fear, a deepening hollow through the cold," writes Brooks. And with good reason it would seem:

> For even if we come out standing up
> How shall we smile, congratulate: and how
> Settle in chairs? Listen, listen. The step
> Of iron feet again. And again   wild. (57)

As would also prove to be the case in her friend Willard Motley's later novel *We Fished All Night* (1951), the returning World War II veterans of "the progress" are unsettled, restless, and—for better or worse—possess a new sensitivity to the hollowness of uncritical patriotism. With her trademark attentiveness to the nuance of human feeling, however, Brooks observes that this dawning awareness does not entirely displace the pride (even patriotism) of African American veterans. Rather, the collective "we" encompassed in the poem seems poised awkwardly in a purgatory of conflicted sentiments, caught somewhere between joy and disillusionment with respect to their wartime achievement and, seemingly, equally uncertain regarding the prospects for postwar progress. For, as in Brooks's "Negro Hero," much remains unresolved in America's domestic sphere, despite the apparent victory in a war "to keep the world safe for democracy." Specifically, the poem's final imagery of "The step / Of iron feet again" and the typographically staggered word "wild" seem to portend a recurring threat of war and fascism. Whether this foreboding clamor sounds from abroad or from domestic soil, however, is a point that the poet seems to leave deliberately ambiguous.

Numerous other social realist poets portrayed the situation confronting World War II's returning African American servicemen in more emphatically negative terms. Robert Hayden's "Coleman" (c. 1940), for instance, describes the fate of a Negro veteran murdered by the Black Legion, a fascistic American organization operative during the 1930s and early 1940s (45). Equally skeptical, Hughes's "Will V-Day Be Me-Day Too?" adopts the form of a letter from a representative "Negro Fighting Man" or "GI Joe" to his (white) fellow Americans. The speaker inquires directly, "When I take off my uniform, / Will I be safe from harm— / Or will you do me / As the Germans did the Jews?" (Rampersad 303–4).[46] In a similar vein, fixing on an actual case of violence that had been visited upon a returning African American veteran, little known Raymond Marcus's "To Isaac Woodward on His Homecoming" links the blindness inflicted on Woodward by a racist South Carolina policeman with the "blind and heaving cities" of an American nation metaphorically blinded by race hatred.[47] For each of these poets, little seems to have changed since the World War I–era tragedies evoked in poems like Hughes's "The Colored Soldier."

Of course, to stress that many social realist poets employed the figure of the African American soldier in ways that sustained the Popular Front critique of racism as a domestic form of fascism should not overshadow the fact that African American poets *also* participated energetically in the cause of antifascism as it pertained to the international political sphere. Numerous poems in Melvin Tolson's first volume of poetry, *Rendezvous with America*, articulate such a globally minded politics. For example, Tolson's "The Idols of the Tribe" (c. 1944) is an explicitly antiracist and antifascist long poem that takes its epigraph from *Mein Kampf* and then proceeds to systematically deconstruct the manner in which "the myths of race / loot the people's will" (103). In the third and final section of the poem, Tolson situates racial mythologies in a Marxist framework, suggesting that they comprise a tool employed by social elites to divide the working classes. Specifically, the poet poses the question, "How many times / Does the ermine class / Throw scraps of hate / To the starved white mass?" (101). Further, Tolson insists that his readers consider how the false idols of racial tribalism have shaped human history on a global scale by cataloging (and mocking), in turn, divergent stereotypes constructed around African, Asian, and "Nordic" peoples. In effect, Tolson's poetry thus calls special attention to the antiracist impulse within the broader antifascist war effort, and does so in a manner fully informed by the sensibilities of the Double V campaign. Dismantling the white supremacist rhetoric of Hitler's regime, Tolson recognizes, is simultaneously a volley against similar rhetoric in the United States—hence, his linking of Hitler's Aryan race propaganda with the near genocide carried out against Native Americans and the memorialization of the "heroes" of the Confederacy's "Lost Cause" elsewhere in the poem. Nor are these links merely a rhetorical vehicle to better fa-cilitate the poet's assault on matters specific to African Americans alone; rather, waging a concrete assault on *both* fronts of this struggle seemed, quite literally, an urgent matter for the survival of human civilization during the years of the Sec-ond World War.

Hughes's "Song for Ourselves" (1938) also stressed the urgency of Americans combating fascism abroad, in this case even before the United States entered the World War II fray. Penned in the aftermath of the Nazi massacre of the Czech civilian community of Lidice, the poem opens with a chilling image of "Czecho-slovakia lynched on a swastika cross!" and concludes with the ominous questions, "Where will the long snake of greed strike / again? / Will it be here, brother?" (Rampersad 207).[48] Like their social realist peers, both Tolson and Hughes clearly seem to have been concerned that their poems serve a particular political end: the mobilization of American awareness of the growing threat of fascism to peoples around the globe. More specifically, one might note that in his attempt to achieve this effect, Hughes employs the same sort of crucifixion motif seen in the 1942 Ollie Harrington political cartoon that I referenced in discussion of John Wilson's *Deliver Us from Evil*. (This Harrington cartoon, one might recall, pairs a bullet-riddled victim of Nazi violence with the African American victim of a particularly notorious wartime lynching in Sikeston, Missouri, with both figures posed in a manner evocative of a crucifixion motif.)

In this same spirit, many African American poets lent their support to the Loyalist forces of the Spanish Civil War, participating alongside their fellow cul-tural workers in what came to be known in certain circles as "the Writer's War" (Folsom 14). Traveling to Spain as a correspondent for the *Baltimore Afro-American*, Hughes tried to put his writing skills in the service of the Loyalist cause through both poetry and reportage, as did white peers like Nancy Cunard and John Dos Passos.[49] For instance, Hughes wrote the long poem "Song of Spain" (1937) for a mass rally of the National Negro Congress and the American Com-mittee to Aid Democracy (Berry 254). Fashioned expressly for this laborist con-text, the poem included a special plea to workers to "make no bombs again!" and "lift no hand again / To build up profits for the rape of Spain! / Workers, see yourselves as Spain!" (Rampersad 196). Hughes addressed other Spanish Civil War poems specifically to African American readers. For example, in "Postcard from Spain (Addressed to Alabama)," Hughes writes optimistically in the voice of a black soldier in the Lincoln-Washington Battalion, "I done met up with folks / Who'll fight for me now / Like I'm fightin' now for Spain" (Rampersad 203). Yet, even in his enthusiasm for such democratic struggles—an enthusiasm fully consistent with his decade-long commitment to building international left-ist political and cultural alliances—Hughes poems like "Moonlight in Valencia:

Civil War" (c. 1944) seek to disabuse readers of any romantic notions they may hold regarding the glories of war:

> The planes meant death.
> And not heroic death.
> Like death on a poster:
> An officer in a pretty uniform
> Or a nurse in a clean white dress—
> But death with steel in your brain,
> Powder burns on your face,
> Blood spilling from your entrails. (Rampersad 306)

Explicitly rejecting the abstractions of propaganda, Hughes thus works to keep in view his principled opposition to war, even as he supports the Loyalist forces in this particular conflict. It is as if he wishes to caution readers against building too great a fervor for *any* militarist campaign, even one that a progressive reader (like Hughes himself) might deem just.

While Hughes was the African American poet most deeply involved in the Spanish Civil War, other African American artists and writers also extended their sympathies to the Spanish Loyalists, albeit in a somewhat more limited way. For example, Hughes, Countee Cullen, Richard Wright, and Frank Marshall Davis, along with luminaries such as Alain Locke and James Weldon Johnson, all contributed to *Writers Take Sides,* a 1938 League of American Writers publication that collected members' statements against fascism and in support of the Spanish Loyalist cause. In verse, multitalented Harlem Community Art Center director Gwendolyn Bennett joined a long list of poets who fashioned work around themes pertaining to the Spanish Civil War. In "Threnody for Spain," for instance, Bennett laments:

> The lovely names of Spain are hushed today—
> Their music, whispering with a muted tone,
> Caresses softly mounds of restless clay
> Where urgent seeds of liberty were sown. (Stewart 289)

From a less rhapsodic angle, Robert Hayden's "Words This Spring" (c. 1940) took its theme from the large number of youths dying in the Spanish Civil War (Randall, "Black" 227). In a tone similar to much of the antiwar poetry of the World War I era, Hayden focuses on the grotesque, dehumanizing, and seemingly senseless violence of Spain's militarized landscape:

> And when a-maying fair Corrina goes,
> She picks her way among the dead—

Finds instead

Of posies in the grass, a stark death's head. (17)

As with Frank Marshall Davis's "Modern Man—the Superman," the anxiety expressed in Hayden's poem gains particular moment in light of the fascistic aesthetics being articulated by contemporaries such as the Italian Futurist F. T. Marinetti, who jubilantly asserted the "beauty" of the technology of modern warfare. Especially in this context, for Hayden (as for many writers on the left), the looming specter of international war precluded a socially conscious poet's simply describing the pastoral subject of a beautiful woman gathering flowers in a lyrical and apolitical manner. Indeed, Hayden's "fair Corrina" sports a gas mask and "thinks of spring's first air-raid while / seeking spring's first rose." Likewise, Hayden's spring skies promise "No pastoral silences, no wreathing cries / Of birds—but steel and dum-dum agonies" (17).

To ignore this internationally minded body of African American poetry is to diminish both the full range of American antifascist poetry and the full complexity of African American cultural history. Indeed, one can scarcely stress enough that the social justice concerns of a poet such as Langston Hughes were remarkably international in scope. In numerous poems from the 1930s, in particular, Hughes linked the liberation struggles of peoples in prerevolutionary Russia, Haiti, the colonized nations of black Africa, China, Morocco, Central America, India, Spain, and the United States. As biographer Faith Berry eloquently writes of Hughes, "International poet, voice of the underdog, weary of oppression and corruption, he was as ready to support the fight of California's striking workers as he had been to urge China's masses to break their chains" (208). If the full range of Hughes's political concerns constitutes something of an exceptional case for any American poet, his example remains an instructive one. Moreover, as illustrated by poems like Frank Marshall Davis's "Modern Man—the Superman," Hughes's globally minded politics were hardly unique.

One of the most distinguishing features of social realist poetry in relation to the other media examined in this study is the willingness of poets to explicitly weigh the prospects for revolutionary mass action in the United States and, at times, to exhort their readership toward such ends. At their most optimistic, social realist poets embraced the idea that America's poor and working-class masses were on the verge of erupting in a collective social revolution of a specifically leftist and laborist sort. And it is worth noting that several poets on the political left—both CP members and so-called "fellow travelers"—did look to the Soviet Union as a model of worker-centered culture and, especially for African American poets, as an exemplar in its apparent support of ethnic minority cultures. For example,

Chapter Four

Hughes's "Good Morning Revolution," originally published in *New Masses* in September 1932, welcomes a personification of Revolution as "the very best friend I ever had" and offers a vision of workers seizing the means of production from corrupt capitalist bosses in nations around the world and then beaming radio broadcasts to the USSR. At least in this poem, Hughes prophesies that this worldwide proletarian revolution will mark a new era of idealistic global prosperity: "that day when no one will be hungry, cold, oppressed, / Anywhere in the world again" (Rampersad 162–63).[50] Hughes continued to celebrate the Soviet Union in his poetry of the early 1940s, particularly for its contributions to the Allied war effort. In a poem perhaps consciously titled to evoke his own "Good Morning Revolution" from the previous decade, Hughes's "Good Morning, Stalingrad" (1943) applauds the wartime achievement of the Soviets as a beacon for "simple working folks like me" and as an antidote, of sorts, for American "crooks and klansmen" (Rampersad 298).[51] Even more, Hughes contributed the latter poem to the 1944 collection *Seven Poets in Search of an Answer*, strongly suggesting that Hughes continued to see communism as a potential "answer" to global crises at least as late as this date. Thus, while many American cultural workers on the political left became disenchanted with the USSR by the early 1940s, Hughes numbered among those who sustained a certain admiration for the ideals, if not always the practices, of the Soviet Union.

However, as with social realist cultural workers in other media, African American poets' depictions of societal transformation turned to the politics of organized labor and a type of democratic populism more often than they adhered to a Soviet brand of communism. One finds one such populist, vernacular model in Margaret Walker poems like "For My People" and "We Have Been Believers," in which she intermingles the aesthetics of the African American sermon tradition with the spirit of radical political revolution. For example, in the final stanza of "For My People" Walker writes:

> Let a new earth rise. Let another world be born. Let a bloody peace be written in the sky. Let a second generation full of courage issue forth; let a people loving freedom come to growth. Let a beauty full of healing and a strength of final clenching be the pulsing in our spirits and our blood. Let the martial songs be written, let the dirges disappear. Let a race of men now rise and take control.
> (*For My People* 14)

Notably, Walker's parallel syntactic structures (i.e., "Let . . .") mirror the cadence of a preacher or political orator as she exhorts her readers to socially transformative action. In adopting this form for her poem, Walker not only accesses a widely familiar genre of vernacular culture but also appropriates for herself as poet something of the public leadership role often reserved for the (typically male) preacher or prophet. This becomes even more apparent in "We Have Been Believers" (c. 1942):

> Now we stand ready for the touch of one fiery iron, for the cleansing breath of many molten truths, that the eyes of the blind may see and the ears of the deaf may hear and the tongues of the people be filled with living fire . . .

Counseling readers that, "We have been believers believing in our burdens and our / demigods too long," Walker prophecies, "Now . . . the long-suffering arise, and our fists bleed / against the bars with a strange insistency" (*For My People* 16–17). Whereas many of her peers leveled biting attacks against the pacifying influence of Christianity in the lives of America's masses, Walker thus insisted on the vital importance of Christianity to the historical struggle for black liberation and articulated the language of the Bible to the contemporary needs of the black masses. Notably, Walker does urge her fellow African Americans to adopt a less passive mode of religiosity, one that involves not merely weeping and praying, but actively assaulting the proverbial bars of injustice. Yet, Walker typically inflected the revolutionary optimism of her poetry more with the language of biblical prophecy than with the language of Marxist revolution per se. In this way, Walker sought to reach her audience from the position of a cultural insider, formulating her critique *within*, rather than against, a biblical, vernacular frame of reference. The potent closing image of "our fists bleed[ing] / against the bars with a strange insistency" nonetheless bears a close resemblance to the notion of black masses poised for revolutionary assertiveness that one finds in more secularly oriented social realist poetry, such as Frank Marshall Davis's aforementioned "Christ Is a Dixie Nigger."

Interracial laborist politics proved an even more appealing rubric for African American poets in search of revolutionary social change. Such was certainly the case for Sterling Brown's "Side by Side," a poem from the suggestively titled "Road to the Left" section of his long-unpublished second volume, *No Hiding Place* (1937). This long poem reads at points almost as if it were a CP pamphlet or agitprop drama in its systematic articulation of a Marxist analysis of race and class issues. The narrator directly addresses two figures representative of white and black labor, John Cracker and Joe Nigg. Specifically, the poet sounds what had become a familiar note in CIO and CPUSA circles by 1937, warning these workers against allowing capitalists to divide them along racial lines to their mutual detriment. Acknowledging the very real and contentious divisions between black and white labor, the authoritative voice of the poem's speaker seems determined to address an array of white labor's anxieties regarding cooperation with black labor, yet neither does he hesitate to indict "John Cracker" for participating in the lynching of a black worker. Ultimately, the narrator pleads, albeit somewhat skeptically:

Listen John:
But you will probably never listen,
Your ears have been deafened by the roar so long,
You have told yourself there is nothing Joe can say
But "Yessuh" and "Nawsuh," and "Be right there, Mister John." (Harper 222)

Significantly, Brown portrays black labor as being somewhat more prepared than its white counterpart to conciliate and forge a broad workers' coalition, with Joe asserting tentatively, "Mr. John, Mr. John, / We cain't never make it dis way at all" (Harper 222). Brown thus repositions African American workers at the heart of the insurgent CIO labor movement, insisting with the subsequent graphic art of Elizabeth Catlett, *My role has been important in the struggle to organize the unorganized*. Further, one might note that "Side by Side" not only expresses points of working-class grievance with which Brown hopes readers will identify but also sketches the initial steps of workers attempting to forge their own routes to possible change. In this way, such a poem both *describes* and *models* a transformation of class consciousness for readers.

In a work characterized by a more pronounced messianic optimism, Brown's "Sharecroppers" (1936) tells the story of an African American member of the Share Croppers' Union who refuses to name his fellow members, "neither white nor black," remaining heroically defiant even though it means being beaten to death by a southern mob led by the local landlord and sheriff:

They lashed him, and they clubbed his head;
One time he parted his bloody lips
Out of great pain and greater pride,
One time, to laugh in his landlord's face;
Then his landlord shot him in the side.
He toppled, and the blood gushed out. (Harper 182)

In the moment of his dying, side pierced in manner loosely evocative of a crucifixion motif, this staunch union martyr prophetically forecasts the ultimate success of the interracial Share Croppers' Union: "We gonna clean out dis brushwood round here soon, / Plant de white-oak and de black-oak side by side" (Harper 182).[52] Not coincidentally, this poem appeared in *New Masses* (November 17, 1936) and later in Alan Calmer's radical labor anthology *Get Organized* (1939), which bespeaks the fact that Brown intended his poem to serve as a source of reflection—and perhaps even union recruitment—for an expressly working-class readership.

Notably, in both "Side by Side" and "Sharecroppers," Brown seems hesitant to depict hoped for developments in U.S. working-class interracialism that have not yet transpired in real life, much less the fundamental transformation of U.S. class relations that most social realists assumed would readily follow from such a progressive development, if attained. Indeed, most African American poets seem to have joined their peers in the visual arts in generally eschewing the utopian imagery of triumphant labor radicalization for which social realism has been subsequently lampooned, even though almost all of these poets at some point exhort their readers *toward* such radicalization. Not coincidentally, the two African American poets who *do* employ a substantial amount of such triumphalist imagery, Langston Hughes and Richard Wright, both were participants in CPUSA cultural circles during the so-called "Third Period" of the early 1930s, which was characterized by an unabashedly oppositional brand of leftist politics.

Following the lead of Third Period literary criticism, which he encountered as a member of the Chicago John Reed Club in the early years of the depression, the young Richard Wright forecast a proletarian revolution in the United States in idealized, even strident, terms. For example, Wright's "We of the Streets" (1937) concludes: "And there is something in the streets that made us feel immortality when we rushed / along ten thousand strong, hearing our chant fill the world, wanting to do what / none of us would do alone, aching to shout the forbidden word, knowing that we / of the streets are deathless . . ."[53] If such a poem seems excessively idealistic, it is worth bearing in mind that this quality has to do, at least in part, with the particular cultural work that those on the American left during the 1930s and 1940s thought that poetry could perform. One letter writer to *New Masses* argued with respect to the proper role of the "people's poet": "The poet today has to describe in heroic terms the great events of today, and stir the people in a different medium from that of the novelist, artist, teacher, musician, cinematic worker, etc., to move with the forces of progress. . . . His language should help stir those moods among the people that will cause them to do great deeds for progress behind the real leaders and organizers of the people's struggle for freedom" (Blair 19). In short, the perceived role of social realist poets was not simply to portray images of heroic workers, but to engage (and sometimes confront) particular audiences through modes of direct address, issuing personal and collective calls to political action.

Hence, social realist poets tended to conceive of their cultural work as a direct form of intervention into American social and political discourse. Perhaps more than any generation of American poets to date, their explicit aim, in many instances, was to reshape the consciousness of a mass audience toward progressive political ends. At times, then, the injunctions issued by social realist poets could be incredibly abrupt, as in the closing couplet of Lawrence Gellert's "Sharecropper": "Good crop, bad crop—no dif'ren' which one, / Til we start plowin' under with gattlin' gun."[54] Like the period's labor singers, social realist poets of revolutionary optimism aimed to build consensus in readers more so than they strove to exhibit qualities of self-conscious literariness in the manner of their high modernist literary peers. Much as the insistent refrain of Florence Reece's "Which Side Are You On?" sought to clarify the battle lines between union and nonunion in the coal fields of eastern Kentucky during the early 1930s, the pleas of poets such as Brown, Davis, Hayden, Hughes, Tolson, Walker, and Wright for black and white workers to "join hands" urged readers to choose sides in what seemed—especially in the context of the depression's drastic differentials in wealth—a morally rooted struggle between capital and labor, between fascism and democracy, between race hatred and human dignity.

Nonetheless, with the advantage of historical hindsight, Wright's romantic notion of an "immortal" proletariat and the persistently expressed faith in an impending CP-style revolution that characterizes early poems like "We of the Streets" may strike a contemporary reader as somewhat naive. Indeed, at times such revolutionary optimism even seems to cut against the grain of evidence presented in Wright's own poems themselves. For example, in what is probably Wright's most well-known poem, "I Have Seen Black Hands" (1934), the poet describes the vulnerability of African American industrial workers' hands "caught in the fast-moving belts of machines and snagged and smashed and crushed" and, later, "weak and bony from unemployment and starvation." As if such challenges alone were not enough, Wright goes on to describe in grisly detail the terror of white mobs lynching black working-class victims: "And the black hands fought and scratched and held back but / a thousand white hands took them and tied them, / And the black hands lifted palms in mute and futile / supplication to the sodden faces of mobs wild in the / revelries of sadism." Yet, Wright's poem moves directly from this image of "tall flames that cooked and charred black flesh" to a brief final section that conjures a Marxist vision of interracial working-class unity:

I am black and I have seen black hands
Raised in fists of revolt, side by side with the white fists of white workers,
And some day—and it is only this which sustains me—
Some day there shall be millions and millions of them,
On some red day in a burst of fists on a new horizon![55]

The contrast between the acknowledged reality of white racist violence against African Americans and Wright's prognostication of interracial working-class harmony is nothing less than jarring.

In this respect, the revolutionary optimism voiced by social realist poets like Wright again proves consistent with many labor songs of the day. Consider, for example, the closing verse of a Carolina cotton mill song that declares:

Just let them wear their watches fine
And golden chains and rings,
But when the Great Revolution comes
They'll have to shed those things.[56]

Much like Wright's "I Have Seen Black Hands," this closing optimistic note
rather abruptly shifts the tenor of a ballad that has outlined, through numerous
preceding verses, the despotic power of cotton mill owners and managers over
their employees. The proverbial ellipses that divide the grim documentation of
present realities and the optimistic visions of triumphant working-class revolution in both Wright's poem and this cotton mill song seem to speak volumes,
naming an absence that plagued numerous social realist cultural workers (and political activists of the period more broadly, for that matter): an answer to the question of *how* such transformations of American working-class consciousness
might be effected.

I have argued, of course, that social realists sought to address precisely this
challenge of transforming America's mass consciousness with respect to issues of
race and class through their cultural work. Yet, even in poetry—the medium
where social realists proved most inclined to radical exhortation—few writers
consistently expressed faith that such projects would prove entirely successful.
Simply put, poems of revolutionary optimism comprised but one strain of social
realist verse of the 1930s and 1940s. And even those same poets who, at times,
fashioned verse of seemingly unabashed revolutionary optimism also crafted biting portraits of the American masses, both white and black, in other poems.
For example, Langston Hughes, Sterling Brown, and Frank Marshall Davis all
proved quite capable of formulating *both* romantic idealizations *and* cynical critiques regarding the prospects for interracial working-class alliance building.
Moreover, all three fashioned poems in both veins without evidencing a sense of
contradiction. Hughes's poem "A New Song" provides an interesting case in
point. When this poem appeared in the January 1933 issue of *Opportunity* and two
months later in *Crisis*, its closing lines cautioned African American readers:

Take care!

Black World
Against the wall,
Open your eyes—

The long white snake of greed has struck to kill!

Be wary and
Be wise!

Chapter Four

Before
The darker world
The future lies.

Yet, when Hughes reprinted this work as the title poem of the booklet *A New Song* in 1938, under the sponsorship of the International Workers Order, he markedly revised these lines to read:

Revolt! Arise!

The Black
And White World
Shall be one!
The Workers World

The past is done!

A new dream flames
Against the
Sun! (Rampersad 171–72)

While one could attribute this apparent discrepancy simply to a change of heart or a whim of the poet, I would suggest, instead, that Hughes was highly cognizant of the cultural work he hoped for his poetry to perform in particular contexts. Without wanting to oversimplify, it seems quite probable that whereas Hughes had issued a note of caution to African American workers when publishing in little magazines with a predominantly black readership *(Opportunity* and *Crisis),* such a message hardly seemed compatible with the IWO objectives of building interracial working-class coalitions through sponsorship of a book of poetry— objectives that Hughes shared, of course. Just as significant, the disparity between these two versions of "A New Song" reflects the fact that Hughes remained equally capable of pragmatic skepticism and idealism throughout the social realist era.

As I have suggested in the case of Frank Marshall Davis, perhaps this willingness to alternately idealize and criticize America's working-class masses may have been a symptom of African American poets' deep-rooted ambivalence toward their targeted audience. If so, it is an ambivalence that they shared with many of their white peers. For example, one might consider the case of Joseph Kalar, a proletarian poet who had personally worked in the lumber and paper mill industries. While Kalar certainly forged numerous expressions of revolutionary optimism, a poem such as "Flagwaver" (1928) instead adopts the voice of what Walter Kalaidjian aptly terms "the reactionary vernacular of the American midwest":

When I get patriotic, I go on the big drunk.
I cut Wesley Everest, I hang that black Injun
Frank Little from a bridge, I put Joe Hill
Against a wall and fill the lousy bastard
With hot jets of lead,
I break the foreign heads of strikers,
Them yella slackers, them chickenlivered
Bastards.[57] (157)

Like Kalar, African American poets challenged members of America's working classes—whites in particular—to acknowledge and amend their own complicity in forms of ethnic and racial oppression against their fellow workers. In this light, African American poets' oscillation between idealization and critique of the masses, and between expressions of caution and encouragement to black workers regarding interracialism, might comprise less a case of ambivalence than an instance of poets adopting alternate modes of challenging their imagined working-class audience to enact its full socially transformative potential. That is, poets like Davis, Hughes, and Brown seem to have consciously used rhetorics of encouragement *and* chastisement as means of exhorting working-class readers toward a more radicalized consciousness. As I will detail in the ensuing chapter, African American novelists gravitated pronouncedly toward the latter of these strategies, illustrating a profound fracturing of the "American Dream" and casting serious doubt on the capacity of leftist, laborist political programs to fully heal these fractures.

Chapter Five

Fractured American Dreams and Revolutionary Skepticism: Novels

> Warning!---Dangerous Man at Work!
> *This is an honest book, brutal in its frankness, lewd almost in its delinea-*
> *tion. It is not meant for people who hold their hands up to their eyes. . . .*
> *This book is full of hard words, stony statements. What people say will*
> *be recorded here. What they do will be stated. . . . Those who don't like to*
> *know what some people in a big city are like had better find other reading.*
> *Chicago is no Pollyanna and this is no Pollyanna story. . . . You will find*
> *the dirt and filth of the big city scattered over these pages; all its hard-*
> *ness and harshness, glitter and tinsel. But also its beauty, intellect, culture.*
> *However, again, Warning!---Dangerous man at work! I am not going to*
> *pull any punches. I have warned you. Proceed at your own risk!*
> WILLARD MOTLEY, "A CHICAGOAN DISCOVERS CHICAGO"

In a brief but revealing moment in Richard Wright's *Lawd Today!* protagonist Jake Jackson reflects idly on an abstract desire to visit a local public library while on his way to meet workmates from the Chicago post office, "Then I can tell old Bob and Al and Slim all about the big books I seen and they'll be jealous as hell. . . ." (69). However, as he continues past the library, his thinking with respect to the value of books seems to shift decidedly for the worse:

> He walked toward 47th Street again, and near the end of the block he
> saw a black boy sitting in a window reading a book. He shook his head.
> *Too much reading's bad.* It was all right to read the newspapers, and
> things like that; but reading a lot of books with fine print in them and
> no pictures would drive you crazy. (69, emphasis in original)

239

Thus, although books possess a certain vague value as a status symbol in Jake's mind, the novel elsewhere makes abundantly clear that he regards even the pronouncements of a sidewalk medicine show (95–101), garish movie posters (52–54), and mass advertising circulars (38–42) far more seriously than any knowledge he might derive from a book obtained from the library. Indeed, when the reader does witness Jake reading it certainly is not a novel, but rather sensationalistic newspaper headlines from the conservative Hearst press—headlines that he consumes none too critically, as I will explain momentarily (28–34).

These suggestive passages from *Lawd Today!* seem to reflect Wright's awareness of the considerable scrutiny to which the novel medium was subjected in social realist circles during the 1930s. Kyle Crichton's 1935 *New Masses* opinion piece "Down with the Novel!" is representative in this regard: "[The novelist's] life will be incomplete until he has wasted six months manufacturing a set of fictional robots and producing a book which will be read by seven hundred people and have all the artistic significance of a subway poster. . . . What is the sense of bothering with the novel when a novel may not be what we want to write at all?" Instead, Crichton urged writers to turn to nonfictional genres, such as journalistic reportage and autobiography (29–30).[1] Such anxiety was particularly widespread during the early years of the Great Depression, given unavoidable facts such as those presented by Henry Hart at the first meeting of the American Writers' Congress in 1935: namely, that even a relatively successful proletarian novel like Robert Cantwell's *Land of Plenty* (1934) sold approximately only three thousand copies (Hart 161). Accounting for public libraries and secondhand reading of novels, such numbers still seemed woefully insufficient to catalyze a widespread transformation of American political consciousness, even if one assumed that proletarian novels exerted such an impact on those people who did read them.

Yet, the ways in which both established and aspiring writers responded to these charges regarding the novel's alleged lack of sociopolitical efficacy reveal an enduring faith in the importance of the form. The novels that I examine in this chapter include William Attaway's *Let Me Breathe Thunder* (1939) and *Blood on the Forge* (1941); Lloyd Brown's *Iron City* (1951); Willard Motley's *Knock on Any Door* (1947) and *We Fished All Night* (1951); Ann Petry's *The Street* (1946); and Richard Wright's *Lawd Today!* (c. 1935) and *Uncle Tom's Children* (1940). And these comprise only a partial sampling of African American social realist output in this medium.[2] Novelists like Brown, Motley, Petry, and Wright *did*, as Crichton had suggested, turn to various forms of nonfiction writing to comment on issues of social injustice such as racial discrimination, overcrowded and inadequate housing, and the plights faced by migrant laborers and vagrants. However, such endeavors did not spell the end of their respective attempts to explore these same sets of issues in novels as well. Thus, in addition to his poignant exploration of issues of race and class justice in autobiographical essays, the photo-essay volume *Twelve Million Black Voices* (1941), and *Daily Worker* reportage, Wright adamantly maintained that *creative* writers should play a distinct revolutionary role: "Writers and politicians move in a different tempo, on a different plane. Let the politician organize what the writer has set in motion. When a writer starts dabbling in politics, he gets sucked into an organization that amounts to leaving his work. He should put all of his passion into his work" (Kinnamon and Fabre 67).[3] Through organizations like the League of American Writers, politically engaged authors took concrete steps toward sustaining such a role for literature by attempting to increase available publication opportunities and visibility for social realist novels. For instance, persons associated with the league fashioned a leftist book club called the Book Union after the model of the commercially successful Book-of-the-Month Club. Such ventures, although often short lived, did help to promote publications like the anthology *Proletarian Literature in the United States* (1935) and the novels of social realist authors like Fielding Burke and Clara Weatherwax ("Book Union" 56; Rideout 235).

Put simply, most writers and cultural critics continued to hold out faith in the novel's potential to serve as an agent of societal education and political reform. And, in fact, there are anecdotal but significant indications that at least certain African American social realist novels *did* have an appreciable impact. For instance, visual artist John Wilson recollects that the publication of Wright's early works, particularly *Native Son*, was "a very dynamic experience in the black community, because here was a man who was speaking very directly about the oppression of blacks and doing it with such powerful writing that the white world couldn't ignore him. His book was a best seller because he had exposed this underbelly of America at some level."[4] In this same vein, Willard Motley spoke of having personally encountered many readers of *Knock on Any Door* among the underclass Chicago communities described in his novel: "They had all read the book and liked it. All West Madison Street seems to be reading it."[5] If Motley overstates the extent of the novel's poor and working-class readership here, it does bear mentioning that letters among Motley's correspondence tend to corroborate the relative breadth of his readership: a Long Beach, California, police officer wrote in praise of the novel's honest assessment of the corruption of some members of her profession; an aspiring high school writer from Detroit raved of Motley's mastery of the literary craft; and a chaplain at Riker's Island penitentiary thoughtfully explained what he perceived as the novel's potential relevance for the inmates under his charge, "I wish I could get a paper-covered edition; and give it out like a tract for them to read. I shall preach from it one of these Sundays; a sort of review in sermon form."[6] In this same vein, a review by former first lady Eleanor Roosevelt remarked on how affected she was by *Knock on Any Door*, explaining that it made her look on the Washington, D.C., cityscape around her "with a more curious eye."[7]

Even in terms of sheer numbers of books sold, Jack Conroy's reflection that Steinbeck's *The Grapes of Wrath* (1939) was the only proletarian "big seller" simply is not true, unless one holds a very narrow conception of what constitutes a "proletarian" novel (Salzman and Ray 163). In this regard, it is particularly misleading that scholars routinely refer to the social realist novel as a product exclusively of the 1930s, since the most commercially and critically successful works in this genre, at least for African American authors, were published during the 1940s and early 1950s. The most well known example, of course, is the publication of Wright's *Native Son* as a Book-of-the-Month Club selection in 1940. Not only was Wright's work the first black-authored novel to receive this distinction, but it was also the first *proletarian* novel so selected (Hapke 204). So too, *Native Son*'s best-seller status and sale of more than 250,000 copies in its first six weeks of publication is a far cry from Henry Hart's lament regarding sales figures of approximately 3,000 copies for popular proletarian novels of the early 1930s (Walker, *Richard Wright* 151; Hart 161). Similarly, Appleton-Century lavishly promoted Motley's *Knock on Any Door* in radio and print media as its lead book of 1947, helping it to sell 300,000 hardbound copies in its first year of publication.[8] Several social realist novels appeared as mass-market paperbacks shortly after their respective first publications; this quickly pushed sales of Ann Petry's *The Street*, for example, to more than 1.5 million copies (Holladay 13). Clearly, such numbers should give one pause before taking early depression-era laments regarding the novel as the definitive word on the medium's (lack of) vitality within the social realist movement. In fact, novels by Wright, Motley, and Petry reached a far *greater* audience than did work in other social realist media that were more often touted on precisely this count (that is, murals, graphic arts, poetry), vastly outstripping the sales of even the more popular of the leftist little magazines. Further, in practical terms, Wright pointed out in a 1946 interview that book publishers generally evidenced a greater openness to radical expression than did, say, censorship-bound mass media industries such as Hollywood cinema: "Every protest, every criticism, every denunciation of a social injustice gets to express itself through the medium of the novel. This is the way that my books have been able to appear" (Kinnamon and Fabre 112–13). As I have suggested, one could hardly have made the same claim for most work in the mural medium. It is perhaps all the more ironic, then, that as the cultural workers with access to the largest audiences and with a relatively free range of expression open to them, novelists—on the whole—proved the social realist movement's most pronounced skeptics regarding the possibility of radical social change.

Both the enduring faith that social realists held out for the novel and the marked tone of revolutionary skepticism that pervaded the majority of their efforts in this medium seem to owe a significant debt to the example offered by preceding generations of politically engaged novelists, especially the work of early twentieth-century American naturalist writers. First, with respect to social realists' faith in the novel's capacity to perform genuinely meaningful cultural work, it was evident to authors of the 1930s and 1940s that novels such as Frank Norris's *The Octopus* (1901) and Upton Sinclair's *The Jungle* (1906) had managed to use the medium to articulate powerful social critiques of American industrial capitalism run amok and its detrimental impact on the everyday lives of the nation's poor and working classes. Even more, Sinclair's novel helped to sound an important rallying cry for concrete social and political reforms, most notably the passage of the 1906 Food and Drug Act. Thus, social realists could look to the not too remote past for ready examples of novels being used to sway public sentiment and even public policy to some degree. Second, work by Sinclair and novels such as Jack London's *The Iron Heel* (1908) explored at least the possibilities of revolutionary socialist activism. Third, African American authors of the 1930s and 1940s also could look to the example of like-minded novels published closer to their own generation that used the rich detail of naturalist aesthetics to craft compelling portraits of distinctive ethnic communities within the broader U.S. urban landscape, including works like James T. Farrell's Studs Lonigan trilogy (1932–35) and Michael Gold's *Jews without Money* (1930). By the 1930s and 1940s, a generation of young black social realists had dedicated themselves to performing comparable work, principally (but not exclusively) with respect to the African American milieu.

In terms of the pessimistic tone that characterized so many African American-authored social realist novels, there was, to be sure, a tradition of utopian socialist literature in Britain and the United States dating back at least to ventures such as Edward Bellamy's futuristic *Looking Backward: 2000–1887* (1887). However, the more immediate examples for social realists of the 1930s and 1940s—that is, the authors with whom they were more widely familiar—included the likes of French novelist Émile Zola and, again, early twentieth-century U.S. writers such as Norris, Sinclair, and Theodore Dreiser. These latter authors painted the contemporary scene in remarkably grim tones, calling attention to the deprivations of poor and working-class protagonists buffeted by social and economic forces largely beyond their own control. With good reason, two of the most often cited hallmarks of American naturalist novels are violence and a sense of entrapment; these same motifs resurfaced with a vengeance in the social realist novels of the 1930s and 1940s.[9]

Focusing on matters of literary craft, one might note at least two further reasons that early twentieth-century naturalist writings proved such appealing forebears to the novelists of social realism. First, naturalist prose offered a model for exploring the interiority of poor and working-class peoples in greater detail than that offered by perhaps any other literary or visual art medium. Ironically, however, what novelists expressed through such portraiture, more so than peers in any other media, was a crisis of faith. With Lloyd Brown's *Iron City* constituting a notable exception, African American–authored social realist novels tended to depict two interlocking types of tragedy. On the one hand, their fiction remarked social crises pertaining to poverty, race and class oppression, nascent fascism, and the constrictive nature of prevailing gender ideologies. On the other hand, Attaway, Motley, Petry, and Wright all tended to portray poor and working-class characters who lacked either the political consciousness or tangible resources necessary to successfully contest these social forces. Indeed, quite often these social realists' protagonists are themselves either actively or passively complicit in furthering the above-named social ills. And this tragic view grew no less bleak with the arrival of the 1940s, as Ann Petry's *The Street* and the early novels of Willard Motley attest.[10]

A second formal trait of naturalist fiction that African American social realists sought to emulate in crafting their own novels involved the strategic use of documentary detail—displaying what their contemporary Jack Conroy described as a Whitmanesque desire to "vivify the contemporary social fact" (Salzman and Ray 133). In other words, these novelists aimed to fashion dynamic representations of the most pressing social issues of their day in a manner distinct from, but integrally related to, politically engaged photography, journalistic reportage, and sociology. At least three extraliterary resources enhanced the social realist penchant for documentation: the Federal Writers' Project, journalistic experiences, and an engagement with sociologists and sociological literature. Arguably no other institutional structure did more to concretize the prevailing documentary impulse of the social realist era among writers than the New Deal's Works Progress Administration. In a practical sense, the various state offices of the Federal Writers' Project provided a critical lifeline to numerous aspiring authors during the depression-era crises in the publishing industry. Among African American novelists, Wright, Attaway, and Motley all worked at least periodically on the Illinois Writers' Project in Chicago, for instance.

While it did not directly sponsor fiction writing, the Writers' Project did provide employees with the financial solvency necessary to undertake literary projects in their free hours.[11] Also, at least some policies and activities undertaken by the Writers' Project reflected motivations that resembled those of social realist writers themselves: that is, to make available to a larger reading audience information about the cultural lifeways and socioeconomic struggles of America's poor and working-class peoples. To be sure, some of the state offices of the Writers' Project pursued an antiquarian agenda of collecting what they took to be the quaint customs and lore of rapidly disappearing folk and ethnic communities; yet, key Federal Writers' Project administrators like National Folklore Editor Benjamin Botkin and Editor of Negro Affairs Sterling Brown urged state project employees to assemble representative documentation of vital dimensions of contemporary working-class culture as part of the FWP series of state guidebooks. Hence, although remarkably diverse in content, these state guidebooks typically blend local histories with what Botkin termed "living people lore." Immersed in this documentary-minded milieu, several social realists drew directly on Writers' Project research in fashioning their own literary and reportorial publications. Motley, for instance, drew substantially upon Illinois Writers' Project research that he had conducted among Chicago's Italian American communities in writing *Knock on Any Door.*

In addition to these Writers' Project experiences, Lloyd Brown, Wright, and Petry all worked as journalists during the late 1930s and 1940s: Brown as an editor of *New Masses* and *Masses and Mainstream;* Wright as director of the Harlem Bureau for the *Daily Worker;* and Petry as a reporter and columnist for the progressive *Amsterdam News* and *People's Voice* (Fabre 147–51; Holladay 22–23). As with certain of the Writers' Project assignments, this type of work enabled Brown, Wright, and Petry to explore topics such as the campaigns of organized labor, race and American popular culture, and the substandard, overcrowded housing conditions of Harlem—much of which mirrored the central themes of their novels. In other words, the journalistic and literary work of these authors enjoyed a constructive symbiosis much in the same manner that Frank Marshall Davis's work for the Associated Negro Press, *Atlanta World,* and the *Chicago Star* served to focus the thematic content of his poetry.

Not coincidentally, then, many social realist novels grew directly out of real stories, based on either an author's firsthand experience or documented news articles. As Petry recalled in a 1971 interview with John O'Brien, "*The Street* was built around a story in a newspaper—a small item occupying perhaps an inch of space. It concerned the superintendent of an apartment house in Harlem who taught an eight-year-old boy to steal letters from mail boxes" (Ervin 75). Such is the case, as well, with Brown's *Iron City,* a novel that details the efforts of African American communists to free a fellow inmate named Lonnie James, who has been framed for the murder of a white drugstore owner. As Jibari Simama has noted, Brown based the novel on his experiences with the case of William Jones, stemming from a time when the author was imprisoned in the Allegheny County Jail in Pittsburgh in 1941. Significantly, whereas Jones was executed despite the efforts of Brown and his peers, in *Iron City* Brown is able to craft a more hopeful outcome for the character Lonnie James (273–74; see also Wald, "Foreword" vii). Such revisions notwithstanding, the thematic emphasis on leftist collective activism that lies at the heart of Brown's novel derives directly from the author's own lived experiences. Moreover, the repeated references to real headline events of the day (whether news of Hitler's invasion of the Soviet Union or the radio broadcast of a Joe Louis bout) and Brown's detailed portrait of prison life (Brown even excerpts lists of prison regulations directly into his text, for example) both work to convince the reader of the novel's relevance and *authenticity*.

In addition to the diverse working-class social histories produced as part of the Writers' Project and firsthand experience with the techniques of journalistic reportage, emerging scholarship in the sociology of race and class—particularly the work of scholars affiliated with the University of Chicago—served as a third nonliterary reference point for African American novelists. In fact, African American literature was both shaped by and shaping of this sociological discourse, a fertile cross-pollination of ideas stemming in no small part from Horace Cayton's friendship with Richard Wright and many of the creative artists associated with the South Side Community Art Center scene in the early 1940s, including Willard Motley. As Cayton observed of Chicago in the course of a review of Motley's *Knock on Any Door*, "In no other place have social scientists studied a locality more intensively, and in no other city has there been such an outpouring of literary endeavor to explain an urban community. Science and literature have helped each other to understand America's most raw and brutal metropolis" ("Known City" 30). As Cayton recognized, both of these groups of intellectuals were interested in documenting and explaining the social crises confronting poor and working-class African Americans. So too, the objective of producing *representative* characters was just as essential to novelists like Motley, Attaway, Brown, Petry, and Wright in their own way, as were the tables, graphs, and maps employed by sociologists to chart representative trends in the socioeconomic circumstances of African American communities. Petry explicitly stated to James Ivy in an interview for the *Crisis* in 1946, "I try to show why the Negro has a high crime rate, a high death rate, and little or no chance of keeping his family unit intact in large northern cities. There are no statistics in the book though they are present in the background, not as columns of figures but in terms of what life is like for people who live in over-crowded tenements" (48–49). Hence, although Petry was not personally acquainted with sociologists like Cayton in the same way as many of her Chicago-based contemporaries, she clearly shared with these midwestern social realists a common sense of purpose that linked her fiction and the documentary impulse of progressive, reform-minded social science.

In Chicago, Wright already was consulting sociology texts in the early 1930s in an effort to systematically grasp the socioeconomic conditions of African

Americans and to ensure the documentary accuracy of his literary craft (Fabre 86). Unsatisfied with much of what he read, Wright insisted on the need for African American writers to conduct their own research, because so much of the existing work was simply unreliable and shot through with racial stereotypes (Kinnamon and Fabre 47). For Wright, however, one reliable source of information was the data collected by University of Chicago sociologists like Cayton and Louis Wirth. In 1941, Wright even drew on statistical data and other materials in the possession of Cayton for his *own* quasi-sociological photo-essay volume, *Twelve Million Black Voices* (Fabre 232–33; Walker, *Richard Wright* 167). More to the point, such was the importance of "Chicago School" sociology to Wright that, in introducing Cayton and Drake's *Black Metropolis* (1945), Wright cited the work of University of Chicago sociologists as both an inspiration for and proof of his fiction: "*Black Metropolis*, Drake's and Cayton's scientific statement about the urban Negro, pictures the environment out of which the Bigger Thomases of our nation come. . . . If, in reading my novel, *Native Son*, you doubted the reality of Bigger Thomas, then examine the delinquency rates cited in this book" (xviii, xx). Clearly, Wright seems to suggest here that his early fiction and the sociology of Cayton and Drake comprise alternative routes to a shared objective of understanding "the environment out of which the Bigger Thomases of our nation come."[12]

The research experiences of African American authors on the Writers' Project and in journalistic reportage, as well as the interpersonal networks that intimately connected many of them to the work of intellectual peers in the field of sociology, all left an indelible imprint on the social realist novels written between 1930 and the early 1950s—embodying what Michael Denning terms "a dialectic between fictional invention, autobiographical reflection, and urban fieldwork" (228). Further, the fact that many novelists explored a range of documentary modes of expression—including photo-essays, journalism, and autobiographical essays—should not prove surprising given the way in which these diverse media intermixed freely in contemporaneous little magazines ranging from *New Masses* to the *Crisis*.[13] Consider, for example, the range of material appearing in Dorothy West's *Challenge/New Challenge* during its brief and intermittent publication between 1934 and 1937:

- fiction by Langston Hughes, Arna Bontemps, Zora Neale Hurston, and William Attaway
- essays and reviews by Arna Bontemps, Carl Van Vechten, Roy de Coverly, Marian Minus, Bruce Nugent, Richard Wright, Eugene Holmes, Alain Locke, and Ralph Ellison
- poetry by Hughes, Countee Cullen, Lucia Mae Pitts, Helene Johnson,

Pauli Murray, Claude McKay, Frank Yerby, Waring Cuney, Robert Davis, Owen Dodson, Frank Marshall Davis, Sterling Brown, and Margaret Walker

- a Louisiana sharecropper's letter, presented as "an authentic word-picture" in the mode of Michael Gold's publication of worker correspondence in *New Masses* during the late 1920s and early 1930s

Particularly in the editorial statement of the lone issue of *New Challenge* (probably authored by Wright), this journal stressed the importance of *realism* to writers operating in all genres: "We want *New Challenge* to be a medium of literary expression for all writers who realize the present need for the realistic depiction of life through the sharp focus of social consciousness. Negro writers themselves and the audience which they reach must be reminded, and in many instances taught, that writing should not be *in vacuo* but placed within a definite social context" (3). As in Wright's "Blueprint for Negro Writing" (also published in *New Challenge*), the social realist writer is thus positioned as both documentarian and teacher, both artist and activist.

While borrowing most deeply from the example of American naturalist novels, social realists seem to have felt a considerable degree of leeway in decisions regarding the aesthetics of their respective novels. This point bears emphasizing if only because so much literary criticism, at least until quite recently, has tended to dismiss the quality of social realist fiction out of hand with presumptions regarding its unimaginative formal traits. To the contrary, if CP-affiliated critics and publications ever were fully wedded to the concept of "worker-writing" in the vein of Conroy's *Anvil,* with its motto "We prefer crude vigor to polished banality," or Michael Gold's experiments with the publication of worker correspondence in *New Masses,* such commitment waned by the mid-1930s.[14] Even more, I would join scholars like Barbara Foley, James Murphy, and Cary Nelson in stressing that this type of writing was only one among several models advocated in leftist literary criticism of the depression era. Hence, in formulating the aesthetics of social realism, African American novelists availed themselves of precedents in African American literature, fiction by naturalist peers, *and* the work of less politically engaged modernist contemporaries. As with the former two bodies of fiction, African American novelists engaged modernist aesthetics in a selective manner, seeking to articulate its innovative formal techniques to politically engaged content. In particular, scholars have noted the utility of modernists like James Joyce and Gertrude Stein to African American authors in terms of: (1) providing models of vernacular language that avoided the pitfalls of "dialect" conventions; and (2) freeing novelists from the conventional plot strictures of the "bourgeois novel" (Denning 242–43; Fabre 112, 285–86).

In attending to the ideological content of social realist novels, it is perhaps easy to overlook the fact that many of the African American authors considered here perceived their working-class protagonists as a type of vernacular or "folk" community. Yet, as Michel Fabre notes in the introduction to his biography of Richard Wright, "According to Wright, the experience of the black American crystallizes a more universal problem of Western culture created by the transition from a family-oriented, and still somewhat feudal, rural existence, to the anonymous mass civilization of the industrial centers" (xv). Given Wright's obsession with this issue of sociocultural assimilation, it should not prove surprising that he experiments with the use of vernacular speech in his first three substantial works of fiction. In the novellas that comprise *Uncle Tom's Children*, for example, much of Wright's narration oscillates fluidly between free indirect discourse in a black folk idiom and a limited third-person narration in "standard" diction. Indeed, in the novella *Big Boy Leaves Home*, Wright brackets the stream of consciousness flow between these two voices even less distinctly than a poet like Sterling Brown. So too, in Attaway's *Blood on the Forge*, the three African American Moss brothers and their Slavic coworkers in the Pennsylvania steel mills speak in dialects that differentiate the two groups from one another and from the novel's white authority figures. Much as it had for their peers in social realist poetry, the use of a modernist-inspired form of dialect offered novelists like Wright and Attaway a way to illustrate the distinctiveness of African American lifeways while simultaneously working to elide the essentialist caricatures of American dialect traditions (i.e., Reconstruction-era plantation literature, the minstrel conventions of U.S. popular theater, and the exoticized "folk speech" of certain literary works of the Harlem Renaissance period).

African American social realists also drew upon the formal techniques of modernism to escape conventional plot strictures associated with the "bourgeois novel" tradition in at least two important respects. One modernist formal innovation with which Wright, Brown, and Motley experimented in various ways involved the interjection of mass cultural "voices"—in the form of radio, newspapers, and popular music—into the novelistic narrative. Lloyd Brown uses newspaper fragments principally to advance the plot of *Iron City*. Both Motley and Wright seem to have been more directly influenced by the newsreels of John Dos Passos's *U.S.A.* trilogy (1930–36), which were composed of excerpts from news stories, speeches, popular songs, and headlines—all collated in such a way as to offer readers a glimpse of significant cultural and political developments that fall beyond the purview of many of the novels' characters. As Denning suggests, the Dos Passos newsreels "serve as a kind of historical chorus, answering the fictional events with a cacophony of wars, strikes, and revolutions" (170). To cite a related case from African American social realism, Wright's *Lawd Today!* employs three similar modernist appropriations of mass media discourse: a recurring radio commentary commemorating Lincoln's birthday; newspaper headlines; and mass mailing circulars. Each of these devices operates on multiple levels. In the case of the radio commentary, for instance, Arnold Rampersad remarks that the inflated rhetoric of this narrative "tells us that Wright is aware of the hollowness of the national myth of freedom and the master race's manipulation of the retelling of history to suit its own ends" ("Foreword" x). Much like Dos Passos's newsreels, however, Wright prompts the reader to recognize that the ironic gulf separating depression-era American realities from the promises of Lincoln's democratic rhetoric escapes Chicago postal worker Jake Jackson and his peers, suggesting that the radio's references to abolitionism, John Brown, and the Civil War float somewhere beyond the register of the protagonist's conscious thinking (e.g., 6, 65–67, 199). Indeed, this absence of historical and political consciousness seems completely consistent with Jake's willful insistence on ignoring the plight of black sharecroppers and lynching victims, particularly when it interferes with his belief in American meritocracy. Consider, for example, his assertion, "Nobody but lazy folks can starve in this country!" (33).

The modernist insertion of mass media discourse into the social realist novel thus has much more to do with the author's engagement with the reader than with catalyzing Jake Jackson's radicalization. Much as Barbara Foley observes in reference to Dos Passos's newsreels, the mass media discourse excerpts in Wright's *Lawd Today!* "requir[e] synthesis on the part of the reader . . . [and] challenge the reader to devise explanatory schemes that would draw apparently unrelated fragments together in a coherent totality" (429–30). Newsreels and similar prose collage devices also seem to have appealed to social realist authors as a way of resolving a crucial formal dilemma: namely, how to adhere to the often politically limited point of view of protagonists while simultaneously interjecting indications of the larger social forces that shape these characters' lives. As Motley wrote of his use of newsreels in preparatory notes for *We Fished All Night*, "Each headline will attempt also to set the tone of the chapter [and] illustrate how close each character was with the grasp of reality or how much at variance their lives were with the vital news of the day that was moving forward like a cloud of night to envelop each."[15] In fact, consideration of novelists' formally innovative use of radio, newspaper, and popular music fragments as a way of saturating fictive texts with points of direct connection to the real world of readers begins to lend credence to Denning's assertion that the documentary aesthetic of 1930s and 1940s cultural enterprises was itself "a central modernist innovation" (118; see also Stott 67–73).

A second key formal experiment undertaken by social realist writers consisted of a break with the novel's traditional single-protagonist framework. Albeit in quite different ways, Attaway, Brown, Motley, Petry, and Wright all explore the possibilities of multiprotagonist formats at some point in their social realist fiction. Foley has aptly noted that the use of multiprotagonist structures "enables the writer to explore relations among and between classes" in such a way that "typicality derives from the range of represented characters and actions rather than from the synecdochic status of any single character's political odyssey" (366–73). This description rings especially true of Petry's *The Street,* which not only explores the psyche of protagonist Lutie Johnson, as she struggles to eke out a living for herself and her son, Bub, but also details the interiority of many of the characters encountered by Lutie. Daring to humanize even the racist paranoia of a white schoolteacher, Miss Rinner, and the mad schemes of a would-be rapist, building superintendent William Jones enables Petry to deliver a multidimensional "thick description" of Lutie's Harlem community. In Jones and his timid wife, Min, for example, Petry offers further examples of how "the street" works to damage the lives of people caught in circumstances akin to Lutie's. Likewise, through passages rendered from the point of view of corrupt real estate kingpin Junto and his employees, Boots Smith and Mrs. Hedges, the reader learns some of the motives of those people who play an active role in perpetuating the oppressive social conditions that characterize Lutie's everyday life. In this way, the multiprotagonist format also enables Petry to avoid placing the burden of representation for an entire social group on a single character.[16] Whereas Wright consciously chooses to focus *Lawd Today!* on the consciousness of postal worker Jake Jackson as a representative of the black community, or at least a certain segment of the working-class black community, Lutie Johnson's experiences clearly comprise only one part of Harlem's larger, complex social fabric in *The Street.*

Attaway's use of brothers Melody, Chinatown, and Big Mat Moss as protagonists of *Blood on the Forge* works toward a similar end. Following the Moss brothers from a harsh life of sharecropping in rural Kentucky to an equally difficult way of life in a steel-mill town that closely resembles World War I–era Homestead, Pennsylvania, the novel explores how the cultural dislocation of such a migration impacts the brothers in distinct but equally destructive ways. By novel's end, Melody has injured his hand and can no longer play the blues music that sustained his spirit in Kentucky, Chinatown has been blinded physically and scarred psychically, and Big Mat has been killed in a fight with unionized Slavic fellow workers while serving as a strikebreaker. By crafting his novel in this way Attaway suggests that "[t]he full significance of the black migration to the North is embodied neither in Big Mat's ironic failure to shrug off his nationalism, nor even the fates of the three Moss brothers, but in the relations among *all* the workers— black and white, class-conscious and non-class-conscious—who have appeared in the novel. Meaning must be inferred from the represented totality" (Foley 372). Similarly, even in *Let Me Breathe Thunder*, which focuses on the journey of two white migrant laborers, Step and Ed, Attaway includes a memorable boxcar scene in which an assortment of vagrants and migrant workers reflect on their shared impulse for wandering and exchange half-wistful recollections regarding locales that range from Seattle to Alabama to Chicago to the Yakima Valley (53– 61). In this way, Attaway concisely establishes a sense of experiential bonds that connect the lives of members of America's depression-era underclass across diverse regions and ethnic identities.

Even more so than Attaway's *Blood on the Forge*, the protagonist of Lloyd Brown's *Iron City* resists easy classification. At many points, Brown's novel also seems to adhere to a tripartite protagonist framework, focusing on the experiences of Paul Harper, Henry Faulcon, and Isaac Zachary, three African American CP members who have been imprisoned in Pittsburgh in 1940 for having attempted to place communist candidates on election ballots. Brown gives each of these characters substantial development in his own right through extended monologues and flashbacks, such as Zachary's lengthy recollection of his (ultimately thwarted) youthful ambitions to become a railroad engineer. Yet, the structure of Brown's novel is somewhat more complex than this, for one could also build a case that Lonnie James is the protagonist of the novel. After all, the novel opens and closes with a view of James, and the central action of the novel turns on the CP campaign (orchestrated by Harper, Faulcon, Zachary, and their allies, both inside and outside the prison) to overturn James's wrongful conviction. Further, not only does Lonnie James comprise the subject of many scenes in which he himself is not present, but Brown also delivers several scenes that explore Lonnie's inner anxieties, memories, hopes, and evolving trust in his new-found communist allies. In this way, Brown achieves at least two important objectives: (1) he is able to portray a representative sampling of the range of life experiences that bring African Americans to an engagement with communism, refuting the notion that individuals give up their unique personas to become unthinking, unreflective drones upon joining the party; and (2) he is able to represent the impact of a mass organizing campaign on *both* that campaign's participants *and* the individual around whom the campaign is organized. Particularly in this latter regard, Brown arguably succeeds more fully than any work among the varied Scottsboro literature of the previous generation. In any event, the "meaning" of the Lonnie James campaign, for Brown, resides not in any one

Chapter Five

character's mode of explanation alone, but rather is left for the reader to synthe-size from a multitude of intersecting voices and life stories.

It is also worth stressing that Brown's novel introduces these levels of stylistic complexity in order to better facilitate his conscious break with the social deter-minism that had so profoundly shaped works of early twentieth-century natural-ism, as well as novels by Wright, Petry, Motley, and—to a lesser extent—William Attaway. In fact, while it may prove surprising to some readers, among African American social realists operating in this medium it is the Communist Party member Brown who most thoroughly calls into question naturalism's quasi-sociological perspective. Brown despised what he took to be the victimist por-trayal of African American life in novels such as Chester Himes's *If He Hollers Let Him Go* (1945) and Richard Wright's *Native Son* (Wald, "Foreword" viii, xvi). Significantly, Brown's dissatisfaction with these novels was *not* a matter of Himes and Wright focusing too much on racial oppression but rather what Brown took as the failure of these novelists to depict the full range of African American *re-sponses* to oppressive forces ("Which Way" 53–54). To make this point in his novel, Brown includes a newspaper clipping that tells of a lecture delivered by a "noted sociologist" to the Women's Civic League at a local country club, in which the speaker describes the "delinquency" of "fourteen million Bigger Thomases" as comparable to the behavior of laboratory rats (207–8). The sarcasm with which Brown's three black CP protagonists respond to this news item offers a clear indi-cation that the author intends *Iron City* as a critical revision of Wright's most widely acclaimed novel. Isaac Zachary, for instance, disingenuously laments, "I reckon . . . if I had as much school-learning as that Dr. Canfield, well maybe I would have known before just now what colored people are like without him hav-ing to tell me" (209).

This is not to say that Brown himself completely eschews the techniques of naturalism and related proletarian modes of writing, for his use of newspaper fragments, details of everyday prison life, and other elements of a "documentary" aesthetic clearly owe much to such sources. Yet, Brown also moves beyond such straightforward modes of representation at several points in the novel.[17] Most no-tably, Brown disrupts naturalistic conventions of narration by concluding the novel with a lengthy dream sequence centered around the character Henry Faulcon, which offers an allegory for radical coalition building. Significantly, Faulcon's dreamscape is populated by black folk heroes like John Henry, Railroad Bill, and Stackalee (figures who also feature in the poetry of Sterling Brown and Margaret Walker), as well as numerous local community members; and he insists on the importance of women's participation and interracial workers' brotherhood (247–53). Aptly, too, Brown renders this vision, which fuses black cultural na-tionalism and Marxist political analysis, as an as-yet-unrealized dream. Nonetheless, it is a dream toward which his central characters are striving as ably and sincerely as they know how.

In short, Brown skillfully and selectively employed the techniques of naturalism while simultaneously pushing beyond the limitations he perceived in this literary mode. For Brown, as for his peers, an effectively crafted social realist text constituted not merely a mimetic reproduction of "the real," but rather a hybrid product of documentary impulses and modernist literary influences. Thus, as with contemporaries operating in media of murals, graphics, and poetry, African American novelists fashioned a brand of cultural work that was united to the broader movement of U.S. social realism by both its politically engaged content, in which these authors took pains to convincingly document the experiences of poor and working-class Americans, *and* by its less frequently discussed formal innovations, in which these novelists engaged influences ranging from naturalism to modernism to forms of American mass media and popular culture. This certainly would prove the case with Willard Motley, who moved from an emphatically naturalist, single-protagonist first novel in *Knock on Any Door* to a more aesthetically complex, multiprotagonist format with his second major work, *We Fished All Night*.

The Novels of Willard Motley

As evidenced by his 1940 *Opportunity* article, "Negro Art in Chicago," Willard Motley was yet another social realist with strong ties to the city's well-developed networks of leftist cultural workers. Specifically, Motley was a part of the interdisciplinary milieu centered in the South Side Community Art Center during the first half of the 1940s. Still, it is worth remarking that although Motley was a native Chicagoan, the Chicago in which he came of age was in many ways quite distinct from the Chicago that artist Charles White knew as a youth. Perhaps most notably, Motley was raised in a firmly middle-class home in an area of Chicago's South Side where his was the only African American family on the block. Motley would later recall the prevalence of ethnic slurs and attempts to establish "restrictive covenants" (i.e., what Motley's grandfather termed "un-gentlemanly agreements not to rent or sell to Negroes or Jews") as a familiar part of his early life in this predominantly German and Irish neighborhood. On subsequent occasions, however, Motley also recollected that several of the family's neighbors came to their defense during the 1919 Chicago race riots; and, on the whole, Motley seems to have felt supported in both his academic and athletic endeavors at the multiracial Englewood High School, where he was something of a "teacher's pet" by his own recollection ("Let No Man" 1–2). Moreover, his "brother" (actually uncle), Archibald Motley Jr., was already a painter of considerable note by the time Willard Motley completed high school in 1929.[18]

Inspired in part by the example of Archibald's success, Willard Motley was determined to become a writer from an early age. Yet, notwithstanding his work as early as age thirteen with the children's pages of the *Chicago Evening Post* and *Chicago Defender* newspapers, Motley's rise to literary fame was far from meteoric. By the mid-1930s he had collected rejection slips for his short stories from the likes of *Esquire, Colliers,* the *New York Times,* and *American Magazine* (Fleming 20–21). Particularly as his failures on this front mounted, Motley grew frustrated with what he felt was his relative isolation from "real life." Thus motivated, in December 1936 he set out westward in search of adventure in a dilapidated Buick with a friend (identified in his diaries only as "John"), not returning to Chicago until August of the following year. Probably the most often recounted episode from these travels in scholarship on Motley involved a one-month stint in a Cheyenne, Wyoming, jail for vagrancy (Klinkowitz 106–15). Elsewhere, Motley and his travel companion periodically had to work odd jobs and the like simply to pay for a meal and to keep their car supplied with gasoline. Resonating with a widespread impulse among writers of the 1930s to "see America," this would prove to be the first of two such depression-era journeys into the western United States.

In terms of their impact on Motley's literary career, the significance of these rambles was twofold. First, albeit that the sojourns initially were motivated by wanderlust and a certain romanticizing of the American road, the life stories that Motley encountered in the Cheyenne prison and elsewhere on his travels genuinely helped to open his eyes to the harshness of poor and working-class existence, especially as amplified by the socioeconomic crises of the 1930s. Consequently, these experiences seem to have done much to efface the sentimentality of Motley's early writing. A series of travel stories that Motley culled out of these western odysseys for publication, for instance, operate in much more of a documentary mode relative to his earlier prose, with a considerably better ear for vernacular speech patterns.[19] Second, this period marks a shift toward what would prove a lifelong fascination with and sympathy for underclass characters. Interestingly, whereas Archibald turned to what is arguably an exoticized portrayal of the nightlife of Chicago's "Black Belt" in many of his paintings during the 1930s, Willard Motley became increasingly fascinated with a grittier, multiethnic panoply of underclass American life.[20] More specifically, at least a handful of the people Motley encountered on these trips into the West became the basis for fictional characters in his subsequent short stories and novels. For example, a Mexican American juvenile named Joe N——, who Motley first met in a Denver reform school in the fall of 1937, would become the initial prototype for Nick Romano, the protagonist of Motley's first novel, *Knock on Any Door* (Klinkowitz 146–48).

Before he would craft that novel, however, Motley returned to Chicago. Early in 1939, growing ever more weary of what he considered the staid nature of his family home, Motley decided to take up residence in a modest apartment in proximity to the Maxwell-Halsted–West Madison Street area of Chicago, a hardscrabble neighborhood full of bars, prostitution, and petty crime that soon became his stomping grounds of choice. This community was not a hotbed of progressive proletarian consciousness, much less a site of active labor organizing. Rather, this choice of locale enabled Motley to immerse himself in the same type of "underclass" life that had so engaged him during the course of his western travels. Motley saw in such marginal communities a kind of vitality and democratic tolerance that seemed lacking in more established middle-class communities—including, not least, a sense of ethnic tolerance. Writing for the *Chicago Sunday Sun-Times* in 1963, Motley recalled the Maxwell-Halsted–West Madison Street area: "This neighborhood was a small world, each nationality lapping over into the other, the whole picture held together by poverty; a few blocks of Mexicans, a few of Negroes, then several of Italians, followed by Jews, Poles, Greeks. And these people crossed easily and naturally, without passport, across the borders, sat in each other's homes, at each other's tables, in each other's bars" ("Let No Man" 3). Further, although this was much less often remarked in Motley's public statements, homosexuality proved considerably less taboo in this community than in neighborhoods of the sort where Motley had come of age—hence, the appeal to Motley's own sense of outsiderness on multiple levels.

Perhaps in part because of his extended absences from Chicago on his western travels and in part because he was by no means yet an established writer, Motley did not participate actively in groups such as the League of American Writers or the South Side Writers' Group during the latter half of the 1930s. However, at some point in 1939 he did find his way to Hull House (on South Halsted Street), which was an important nexus for leftist cultural workers of the day. (One might recall, for example, that this is where a young Charles White took mural-painting courses with Mitchell Siporin and Edward Millman.) Here, Motley met, among others, aspiring young writers Alexander Saxton and William P. Schenk. The son of a successful publishing house executive, Saxton, like Motley, had turned from the relative privilege of his own social class to seek out literary subject matter among the nation's poor and working classes. Notably, too, Saxton's first novel, *Grand Crossing* (1943), was enhanced by the informal research of actually working as a switchman in the railroad yards of Chicago—an approach that mirrored

Motley's own literary method of mingling firsthand with the subjects of his fiction. These writers shared their favorite works of literature with one another as well, with Saxton and Schenk helping to expose Motley to writers such as Jack London, Carl Sandburg, John Steinbeck, and John Dos Passos (Brennan 5).

Perhaps most significantly, Motley, Saxton, and Schenk in the fall of 1939 founded *Hull-House Magazine* (1939–40), a little magazine open to both fiction and nonfiction prose sketches, with a decidedly local emphasis (Fleming 27–28). Arguably the most intriguing of the pieces that Motley published in this venue is a prose sketch titled "Pavement Portraits," which represents life at the intersection of Maxwell and Newberry Streets as "the down-to-earth world, the bread and beans world, the tenement-bleak world of poverty and hunger. The world of skipped meals; of skimp[y] pocketbooks; of non-existent security—shadowed by the miserable little houses that Jane Addams knew" (2). By contrast, Motley's "Handfuls," which appeared in the very next issue of *Hull-House Magazine*, suggests a vital, democratic spirit as the defining feature of Maxwell Street through a scene in which Polish, Greek, Mexican, and African American residents join together and chip in money from their own scant resources in order to aid an Irish girl who has had her purse stolen (9–10). Read as a whole, then, Motley's contributions to *Hull-House Magazine* evidence both a systematic critique of poverty (and of the neglect and outright corruption that enable the perpetuation of such conditions) *and* a fascination with what he took as the vibrancy of life among America's underclasses—qualities that would coexist within Motley's subsequent work in the novel medium as well.

Although Motley's work with *Hull-House Magazine* was relatively short lived, he was able to find employment with the Illinois Writers' Project in April 1940 (Klinkowitz 165). Work on the FWP proved spotty, as Motley's diaries reveal that he bounced on and off the project somewhat sporadically over the next two years; so too, virtually all of the members of his FWP unit were transferred to a tedious map project for a time in 1942. Nonetheless, much of Motley's work for the Writers' Project did prove of personal interest and subsequent literary value. Specifically, Motley undertook case studies of life in particular ethnic communities that involved firsthand contact with community institutions, in-depth conversations with caseworkers and residents themselves, and opportunities for Motley to make use of his budding interest in documentary photography. The resultant projects, such as Motley's photojournalistic snapshot of life in "Little Sicily," thus resonated with his *Hull-House Magazine* sketches and, again, provided an important foundation for the exacting detail with which he rendered multiethnic Chicago cityscapes in his first two novels.[21] Further, while peers like Richard Wright and Margaret Walker had departed from the Illinois Writers' Project by the time

Motley arrived, it was through this work that Motley first met the white social realist author and little magazine editor Jack Conroy, who would prove a lifelong friend.[22] By the early 1940s, Motley's social circles included the predominantly African American South Side Community Art Center scene, the predominantly white Hull House crowd of aspiring writers and artists, and many underclass acquaintances and confidantes from the Maxwell-Halsted–West Madison Street neighborhood, several of whom would shortly appear in his fiction.

Motley's western travels, his prose sketches for *Hull-House Magazine*, and his work with the Illinois FWP all profoundly shaped his literary method as he turned in earnest to the writing of his first novel in the early 1940s. In particular, these experiences instilled in Motley a conviction that material for his literary work might be derived most effectively from his own firsthand immersion in the worlds inhabited by his protagonists (Klinkowitz 165). This point is fleshed out by Motley's first novel, *Knock on Any Door* (1947), which traces the path of Italian American protagonist Nick Romano from his early youth as an altar boy in a respectable Denver church through a detrimental sentence in a reform school to a life of petty crime in Chicago's West Madison Street milieu. Like his more famous literary counterpart, Bigger Thomas of Richard Wright's *Native Son* (1940), Nick eventually commits murder and must endure a melodramatic trial that leads to what, by then, seems an almost inevitable fate of death in the electric chair. As with the naturalist texts of predecessors such as Norris and Farrell, by the time the reader reaches the concluding scene of Nick's execution he or she most likely will be struck by nothing so much as the exacting detail with which Motley has delineated the environmental influences that have shaped the tragic course of his protagonist's life.

In contrast to novels such as Richard Wright's *Lawd Today!* and William Attaway's *Blood on the Forge*, which examine the interiority of protagonists who are already deeply flawed when readers first encounter them, Motley's *Knock on Any Door* is much more attentive to the developmental stages of Nick Romano's interior life. In other words, the key questions for Motley pertain to how and why Nick Romano passes from angelic altar boy and aspiring priest at the age of twelve to a motto of "live fast, die young and have a good-looking corpse" by the time of his sixteenth birthday (*Knock* 157). Motley's commentators generally have elided the details of this lengthy and involved trajectory by reference to the generalized trope of a "determinative environment" (Rideout 262). Yet, Motley's protagonist is not shaped by an abstracted "poverty" so much as the way in which poverty produces an absence and/or disruption of his foundational relational influences—namely, his family and the institutional role models offered by schools and the law (Ford 32; Fleming 36). What Motley's first novel ultimately offers is not a narrative of emerging class consciousness, but rather an in-depth portrait of how the environmental effects of poverty and urban life play themselves out in tragic fashion through Nick's failed interpersonal relationships.

Significantly, the origins of Nick Romano's descent into a callous life of crime begin with a fracturing of the classic "American Dream" narrative of an immigrant family's socioeconomic uplift through initiative and hard work. As the novel opens, Nick's father seems to be tangible proof of the soundness of the American Dream, operating a successful small business as an importer of Italian foods. Moreover, Nick's entire family dotes on him with considerable affection, and they live in a neighborhood where Nick is further affirmed at school and in the local Catholic Church. However, this sense of stability is rapidly undone by the onset of the Great Depression—the sudden arrival of which Motley evokes with the stark opening line to the novel's second chapter, "Then they were poor" (9). From this point, Motley works at length to illustrate how the depression-era collapse of the Romano family business impacts Nick not only through physical hunger and the other material pains attendant to poverty, but also in terms of his suddenly neglected needs for emotional, familial nurture. Once adoring of "Nicky," Nick's parents and siblings soon grow too borne down with concerns and stresses of their own to provide him with anything resembling their former level of care. Pa Romano, for instance, enters a state of depression that persists for the remainder of his life. When he is not effectively absent altogether behind a closed bedroom door, Nick's father now has only criticism and physical abuse to offer his son (9–11, 100–101).

The downturn of the Romano family's fortunes also results in the impoverishment of other potentially nurturing adults available to the young Nick Romano. In the church of his youth, Nick enjoyed serving as an altar boy under Father O'Neil, but after his family moves to a poorer neighborhood he encounters a much more malevolent authority figure in Father Scott at his new Catholic school. In this new community, the intimate experience of taking communion from Father O'Neil is displaced by the brutalizing hand of a priest uniformly despised by the youths of Nick's school: "Never before had Nick . . . thought that *priests* would ever whip anyone. That was what made him cry. And right then, with the beads rattling and the ruler coming down hard, something started feeling wrong inside of him" (15). Not surprisingly, these beatings at home and in school invariably drive Nick out of the house and back to precisely those "street" friends and locales that his parents and teachers so severely criticize him for embracing. And as he falls in with some of these juvenile youths, Nick winds up being sent to a reform school for a crime he did not even commit because he refuses to snitch on a fellow student.

The reform school, one of Motley's central targets in the novel, further solidifies Nick's experiences of relational rupture (Bayliss 20; Jarrett 520; Rayson

251). Motley foregrounds the sadistic treatment of children by reform school authorities almost immediately upon Nick's arrival, as he is awoken by the sting of a leather strap across his back on his first day at the "school." Soon thereafter, the gym instructor informs Nick and his fellow students: "The law says you'll stay here until you're reformed. Oh, yes. You'll be reformed when you get out of here. . . . If you refuse to work or are really the bad type we handcuff you to a cell in the basement and shoot the fire hose on you until the water knocks you out or you decide to behave. That's how we reform you" (29–30). School officials inflict this and other similarly sinister punishments gratuitously on Nick and his fellow students, resulting, in one case, in the death of Nick's Mexican American friend Jesse just days before the boy's scheduled release. Equally disquieting, reform school officials permit and even encourage the tougher, older boys to bully, terrorize, and otherwise prey on their younger peers. Hence, Nick himself begins to gain admiration and status among his reform school peers only through a savage brawl with a school bully named Bricktop (61–65). The impact of all of this violence on Nick's consciousness is crystallized when Principal Fuller lashes the bare buttocks of eleven-year-old Tommy in front of the entire school for organizing an escape attempt, leading Nick to reflect:

> He'd never be sorry for anything he ever did again. He'd never go crawling home to ask forgiveness again. He'd never try to reform now. He was on Tommy's side. All the way. For good. Forever.
>
> He knew how men treated boys. And he knew how they reformed them. He hated the law and everything that had anything to do with it. Men like Fuller were behind it. He was against them.
>
> For good. Forever. (60)

In this manner, Motley scathingly critiqued the ostensible efforts to "reform" wayward juveniles by suggesting that such methods actually served to further brutalize and alienate these youths from "mainstream" American society and its institutions. (Not coincidentally, Motley portrays these youths as being almost uniformly from impoverished backgrounds.) Hence, when Nick is assaulted by the novel's arch-villain, Officer Riley, and other policemen later in the novel (174, 194–98, 344–50), these acts only reinforce Nick's already established sentiments toward legal authority. Well before he encounters the likes of Riley, Nick reacts with hostility even to the friendly, paternal gestures of an Irish beat cop named O'Callahan soon after his release from reform school and arrival in Chicago (94–95, 99–100). Indeed, when Motley opens the thirty-fifth chapter of his novel with "Then he was sixteen" (155), the reader can hardly help but be startled as she or he realizes that the novel's hardened protagonist is still of such a tender age.

In detailing the tragic trajectory of Nick Romano's life, Motley follows the lead of radical social critics such as Clarence Darrow in situating the bulk of culpability for Nick's plight squarely on the shoulders of "society." That is, although Motley's first novel arrived rather late in the game by most accounts of social realism, he was even more of a deliberately hard-nosed naturalist than African American novelists such as Wright, William Attaway, and Ann Petry, whose respective first publications all preceded his own. And almost as revealing as the trajectory of the novel itself is the means by which Motley composed it. Part journalist at heart, Motley filled numerous notebooks with impressionistic prose sketches based on his observations of life around the same Maxwell, Halsted, and West Madison Street neighborhoods of Chicago frequented by his juvenile protagonist, Nick Romano. Suggestively, he referred to this informal research as "walking my beat." In addition, Motley assembled relevant press clippings and conducted extensive interviews with judges, lawyers, prison wardens, and juvenile criminals in an effort to ensure the absolute realistic precision of his novelistic representation. He even based lawyer Andrew Morton's lengthy courtroom defense of Romano on an actual closing argument by a Chicago assistant public defender named Morton Anderson (Kogan n.p.; Fleming 38). Correspondence between Motley and his editor indicates that his novel bore resemblances to the real world so striking as to require changes of names in order to circumvent the threat of libel lawsuits.[23] In short, Motley's craft was documentary to an almost obsessive degree.

Significantly, too, Motley wanted his fiction to perform a kind of cultural work similar to nonfiction exposés in many respects, as implied by his original title for the novel, *Leave without Illusions*. In this regard, Motley biographer Robert Fleming hardly overstates the point when he observes, "Viewed from one perspective, *Knock on Any Door* is not unlike a sociological case study" (47). Drawing on the aforementioned newspaper sources, experiential research, and interviews, Motley resembled the prominent sociologists of his era in marshaling "evidence" aimed at altering public perceptions and institutional practices (Fleming 43–44; Bone 456–57). Further, Motley was absolutely insistent about the representativeness of the "findings" that he presented in the story of Nick Romano, as the very title of the novel would suggest. Lest readers miss this point, Motley closes the novel with the line, "Nick? Knock on *any* door down this street" (512, my emphasis).[24] Within the novel, four brief interchapter prose passages establish a basic thesis regarding the shaping power of corrupt city streets on poor and working-class youths, of which the remainder of the novel offers "proof." One of these passages addresses Motley's central set of concerns in a manner that closely resembles the unrelenting determinism associated with naturalistic fiction:

Who is bigger than the city, or the city's streets, or the city's will? . . .
Who is broader than the city's walls? Who is muscled like these buildings? Who is
tougher than these rusted fire escapes? Who can stay awake in the leer of the neon light?
Who can sleep and dream beneath these roofs? . . .
Who can best the neighborhood? (252)

Even more, after his novel had been launched to considerable acclaim, Motley
worked with *Look* magazine to produce a feature story titled "Who Made This
Boy a Murderer?" which combined excerpts from *Knock on Any Door* with photographs of actual people from the Maxwell–Halsted–West Madison Street
area—further blurring the distinction between fact and his social realist fiction
(Fleming 61).[25]

A similar desire to reach a public as broad as possible with the issues raised by
his novel—that is, the imperilment of youth in poor urban neighborhoods, the
ethical bankruptcy of the juvenile justice system, and the public's general willingness to turn a blind eye to these social crises—was one of the motivating factors that led Motley to agree to a deal with MGM for a film adaptation of the novel.
Notably, Motley invited John Derek, the actor slated to play Nick Romano in the
film, to accompany him on an outing similar to the one on which he guided the
Look magazine writers and photographers: "I have written to [director] Nick Ray
today too and pleaded with him to come to Chicago if only just to see West Madison Street and the actual localities of the book. There's nothing like it on Main
Street I assure you. . . . We could wear old clothes and tramp West Madison day
and night until both of you got the feel and tempo of the street, the people down
there"[26] (Klinkowitz xix).

As I have suggested, Motley himself not only tramped these neighborhoods
but also personally got to know the vagrants, juveniles, and petty criminals
around whom he centered his first novel. In fact, Motley solicited feedback on
drafts of his work from fellow writers like Alexander Saxton and West Madison
Street friends like truck driver Matias Noriega ("Education" 13–20). More to the
point, Motley drew expressly on the experiences and testimony of three real life
juveniles to fashion the composite character of Nick Romano. For example, a
scene in which Nick shows the sympathetic sociologist Grant Holloway the welts
inflicted on the backside of Tommy by the reform school's sadistic director derives directly from Motley's own almost identical encounter during a visit with
the aforementioned Nick prototype, Joe N———, at the Denver Detention Home
in the summer of 1938 (Klinkowitz 162).

Like Holloway, who serves as a double of sorts for Motley in the novel, Motley
was a committed social reformer. That is, he not only wanted to generate public
awareness of and sympathy for the problems of poverty and juvenile delinquency

that are so extensively documented in *Knock on Any Door,* but was also very much concerned with the enactment of concrete political reform in relation to these issues. Hence, as the *Look* magazine feature story on his novel might suggest, Motley addressed these topics in a range of public forums in an effort to extend the cultural work undertaken by his novel. For instance, in a 1947 interview on a human rights radio program, Motley systematically indicted agents of "adult delinquency"—including corrupt policemen and politicians, racist and fervently nationalist educators, newspapers, movies, industrial interests, and unsympathetic churches—for many of the problems facing poor and working-class youths.[27] Likewise, Motley repeatedly expressed his concern that Nicholas Ray's film adaptation of his novel show as much as censorship would allow of Nick's execution because of his concern with abolishing the death penalty.[28]

Barbara Foley has explained of the proletarian literature of the depression era, "These writers may have assumed that, at least for a significant portion of their readership, the key issue to be addressed was not the knowledge or theory of class struggle, but practice: would the reader take sides and get out into the streets?" (396). Similarly, for Motley, if a writer were to be of use to society, he or she would naturally turn to issues of concern to poor and working-class people and write of these issues in such a way as to sway public sentiment and even public policy. Put another way, Motley perceived his cultural work as a novelist not as a tool for swaying readers to a precise political ideology but rather as an important means of encouraging a mass readership to enact radical reforms with regard to what he deemed key social issues. How readers would redress the problems of poverty, juvenile delinquency, ethnic bigotry, and so forth was seldom spelled out precisely in Motley's fiction; he seems to have been much more concerned simply that readers would be moved to *some* course of action. And, consistent with the social realist sentiments discussed in the preceding chapters of this study, Motley defended his choice of politicized subject matter without apology: "If this type of writing is propaganda then the modern writer is a propagandist; if this be 'inartistic' then art, 'pure art' has always been a parasitic growth scratching at the surface of life and reality and receiving board and keep from patrons whom it was desirable to please and flatter in exchange for the delight of being a fat and self-pleased parasite in an ivory tower" (Klinkowitz and Wood 129).

Piercing as Motley's indictments of American society were in his public statements from the late 1940s, and while similar critiques within the pages of *Knock on Any Door* lend Nick Romano's tragic path through life a certain air of inevitability, it bears emphasizing that Motley also casts a rather critical eye on his protagonist. Indeed, Motley seems to make a point of illustrating that it is not only some quality intrinsic to "city life" per se that leads to Nick's demise. Assuming such a simplistic environmentalist model is the mistake of well-meaning sociologist Grant Holloway, who naively hopes to help Nick by taking him away from the city on a camping trip to Wisconsin (190–93). By this point, however, Nick's problems are a matter of internalized values, dispositions, and expectations about the way the world works, rather than being strictly endemic to the city air he breathes or the "Skid Row" sidewalks that he strolls late into the night. In Blanche Gelfant's astute analysis, Nick's crisis lies in the fact that he is not merely frustrated by his environment but dissociated, not even knowing for certain what his goals are (22).

Motley also suggests that while the poverty and ethnicity of the Romano family are certainly key factors in shaping the trajectory of Nick's life, they are not wholly determinative of Nick's fate. Nick's friend Stash and his older brother Julian, for example, do emerge from a similar milieu to settle down into productive employment and family life; and Nick's reform schoolmate Tommy later works to mobilize people against the injustices of society as a union organizer (491–92). Yet, when Nick is presented with a proverbial "second chance" through marriage to the virtuous Emma, he fails miserably, remaining ultimately destructive of himself and those around him. Rather than positing a strictly deterministic set of economic constraints, Motley takes pains to show that Nick is able to secure several "respectable" jobs with relative ease during his attempt to settle into married life (275–79). Yet, he can hold none of these jobs because he cannot adjust to this unfamiliar, routinized lifestyle. Although still in his youth, Nick already has long been inured with the philosophy that "only suckers work" (155) and finds himself incapable of the self-sacrifice that sticking with these jobs would require. Nick seems incapable of requiting Emma's relatively selfless love, that is to say, because he simply does not know how to do so. Trying to be an ideal, conventional spouse only leaves Nick full of self-loathing; hence, his impotence with Emma even as he continues to pursue sexual liaisons with prostitutes and homosexual acquaintances on West Madison Street. This behavior leads, in time, to Emma's suicide, which fractures what remains of Nick's desire to reform his own life (see Fleming 57). The reckless criminal exploits that Nick pursues after Emma's death, the melodramatic confrontation with Officer Riley, Nick's flight from the police, and even the electric chair are all but postmortem violence perpetrated against Nick's "good-looking corpse." Despite the final resurgence of his will to live while on death row, Nick's psyche already has been virtually annihilated.

Examining Motley's novel in this way, one of the central metaphors that has attracted the attention of Motley scholars deserves particular attention. It is a story recounted by Ma Romano in Nick's youth and, subsequently, by Nick himself at key points throughout the novel (in the reform school and on death row): "One day by Rankin's grocery store a cat had a little bit of a mouse cornered and was playing with it—just pawing it and slapping it this way and that. A crowd of people were standing around watching. Do you know what Nick did? You couldn't guess! That child walked up, picked that mouse up and stuck it in his pocket and walked away as fast as he could! If Nick was to die he'd go straight to heaven" (5). At this early stage, Motley intends his readership to sympathize with the young Nick's entrapment as analogous to the victim status of the mouse. As John Bayliss observes, "Symbolically, the trapped mouse in the street is an object of tender pity; so very different from the rat in the opening pages of *Native Son*" (18). Yet, what discussions of *Knock on Any Door* generally have overlooked is Nick's complicity in the cycle of violence described by the novel. Put simply, at certain points in the novel Nick resembles the cat of this parable more than the mouse. Early on, Nick learns to use his good looks and innocent eyes to consciously manipulate others for his own self-interested purposes (128–29). Later, Nick not only learns to jackroll pedestrians and "play the phonies" (i.e., baiting and then extorting money from gay men) but also passes this knowledge on to other youths (e.g., 153). Clearly, then, Nick is not only exploited by society and its more unsavory characters but fully participates in exploitation of and violence against others—particularly women and gay men—as he becomes increasingly amoral over the course of the novel (see Fleming 58). So too, regardless of the fact that he remains a more sympathetic character to the reader than the aforementioned Officer Riley, Nick is subsumed into a seemingly endless chain of brutality in such a way as to almost fully become the monster that Riley was by the time he murders this nemesis. Nick goes to the electric chair not simply as a martyr or a sacrificial lamb to the proverbial slaughter, but as the prophetic signpost of a broader cycle of violence that hardly promises to be curtailed by his execution. Seeming to follow in the footsteps of naturalist novels like James T. Farrell's Studs Lonigan trilogy, Motley's *Knock on Any Door* thus takes substantial steps to illustrate the way in which cycles of poverty and violence eventually lead youths like Nick to become agents of their own disfranchisement.

Although to the extent that Motley remains known today it is largely for *Knock on Any Door*, his concern with leftist political causes finds its most fully developed literary articulation in his little-heralded second novel, *We Fished All Night* (1951), a book that Motley drafted, notably, with aid from the Rosenwald Foundation (and the Newberry Library Fund) "in the lean years of 1945 and 1946" (*We Fished* vii). Beginning around 1935 and extending into the late 1940s, Motley collected several files' worth of clippings from both the radical press and the Chicago daily papers that would help to shape this novel. Among these files, in addition to a sizable set of articles regarding the struggles of U.S. veterans following their return from World War II, were newspaper materials on varied topics such as Mussolini's invasion of Ethiopia; the Nazi siege against Communists,

Jews, and Catholics; the tarring and feathering of two California labor organizers; the arrest of African American communist Harry Haywood following an anti-Mussolini demonstration; the Spanish Civil War; Jesse Owens at the 1936 Olympics in Berlin; Father Coughlin's profascist rhetoric; the murder of four Republic Steel picketers by the Chicago police; Stalin's purges; and individuals who took public stands against policies of institutional racism in hospitals and the newspaper industry.[29] While certainly manifesting his naturalist penchant for exhaustive documentary detail, the far-reaching nature of this research also reflects Motley's attempt to move toward a more complex brand of social portraiture with his second venture in the novel medium. No longer would he train his attention relentlessly on the shaping of a single protagonist; rather, here he would shed light on a cross section of the Chicago scene, inclusive of a wide range of ethnic groups, ages, political ideologies, and degrees of empowerment.[30] Moreover, if Motley has struck some readers as being essentially "a decade behind" in artistic style and political ideology, in point of fact he drew upon his files of newspaper clippings in such a way as to articulate *We Fished All Night* to matters quite specific to the 1940s, including World War II, cold war nationalism, and the growing international atomic threat.

While *We Fished All Night* also incorporates the aforementioned research material to address diverse issues such as America's ethnic and racial intolerance, the corruption of "machine" politics, and the cold war–era struggles of organized labor, it is, first and foremost, an antiwar novel. In fact, Motley originally titled this novel *Of Night, Perchance of Death* after a Francis Thompson antiwar poem.[31] Although it was not completed and published until the height of the cold war era, Motley first sketched out the general contours of this novel as early as 1941—a moment in which widespread antiwar sentiment still existed among the American left—and he undertook intermittent work on it by 1943.[32] Describing the novel to editor and friend Ted Purdy, Motley explained, "This isn't a positive book. It is, I suppose, an anti-war book, with war the protagonist (villain)."[33] In this regard, brief but revealing scenes present minor characters named Milo and Dave in a positive light for being conscientious objectors to the war; Dave, an African American, even goes to prison for adopting this position on moral rather than strictly religious grounds (251). Like his social realist peers, then, Motley was well aware of the special hypocrisies pertaining to African American participation in the U.S. war effort. As he explained in response to the U.S. policy of segregated military training, "Why, then, is a thing so important to the welding together of all Americans in a single patriotic defense of America to start with undemocratic action? . . . I refuse to countenance a lie of 'equality . . . democracy' if this, *my country* does not choose to give me that democracy and equality we have all spoken about so loudly."[34] Yet, where many of Motley's African American contemporaries in the visual arts and poetry made this the preeminent focal point of their wartime social critiques, he ultimately scaled back his original plans to explore such sentiments by featuring Dave as one of the novel's major characters, in part to facilitate an even broader critique of the Second World War *as a war*.[35] Not coincidentally, Motley himself was a conscientious objector during World War II and continued to publicly voice his opposition to further military action as the cold war escalated during the mid- to late 1940s.

Motley also used his second novel to comment on the pervasive militarism in the years following the Allied victory, particularly the threat posed by the atomic bomb. Toward this end, Motley weaves newspaper fragments into the narrative of *We Fished All Night* that argue the feasibility of bomb shelters as a means of defense against potential atomic attacks by the Soviets and frame probomb sympathies in a manner suggestive of what Motley clearly perceives as the excessive nationalism of cold war rhetoric. After one such quasi-documentary newspaper excerpt, Motley seems compelled to interject editorial commentary as narrator: "And the newspapers began to suggest that any peace group or movement to outlaw the bomb was Communist or Russian inspired. It was un-American, undemocratic, inhumane to suggest that humanity should not be destroyed by atom bombs. It was un-American to say that humanity had no right to destroy itself" (260–61). Motley voiced a similar concern at a 1950 Chicago symposium titled "Humanity versus the H-Bomb," where he referred to the hydrogen bomb caustically as the "hell bomb" and asserted that the dropping of the atom bomb on Japan had constituted nothing less than "the most heinous crime in the history of the world."[36] In short, Motley feared the cold war threat of destructive technology being employed without any moral compass—an anxiety quite in step with a work such as poet Frank Marshall Davis's pre–World War II poem "Modern Man—the Superman."

Before introducing such grim musings on cold war militarism, however, Motley first establishes the antiwar theme of *We Fished All Night* in a prefatory prose passage that describes a parade of returning American soldiers in a fashion that is considerably more pessimistic than the patriotic imaging of these homecomings as portrayed in government-sponsored newsreels of the day. Focusing his literary camera lens beneath the surface pomp and ceremony of ritualized flag waving, Motley calls the reader's attention to veterans' battered psyches and disabled bodies. Motley's soldiers return not unambiguous conquerors, but rather "come in steady clump, in combat jacket, and staring straight ahead. Come in funeral effect." As in the biblical adaptation of Motley's title for the novel, these soldiers might well exclaim, "Lord, we fished all night and caught nothing." Most important, Motley recognizes that although "the boys are back," they are "not the same. They have seen things, been places. Done things of a night and of a day.

And now the killers come home." One veteran even replies to a well-meaning cheer of "Welcome home!" with a disillusioned reply, "This ain't home" (ix–xi). So too, in the midst of a climactic battle scene between corporate-sponsored police and striking workers, Motley closes his novel by returning to an image of "the coffins of the broken and defiled bodies" of American veterans, draped in "the solemn flag of the nation" (559). In both its opening and closing images, then, Motley's second novel presents the bodies and experiences of soldiers themselves as the primary form of evidence in his case against war. Even more, Motley posits the unsavory fates suffered by many veterans as a signpost of the abandonment of America's working-class masses by the same corporate and governmental powers that these workers recently have served, albeit somewhat unwittingly, as the foot soldiers of international military conflicts.

In the more than five hundred epic pages that bridge these framing images, Motley elaborates his thesis regarding the devastating impact of war on veterans and their families in physical, mental, and moral terms through three representative central characters. Emblematic of the physical debilitation caused by war, Don Lockwood returns to Chicago having lost a leg in North African combat. Drawing upon his prewar background in community theater, the ambitious Lockwood soon adopts a new role in Chicago machine politics. Recruited for his drawing power as a handsome and battle-scarred veteran by Ward Committeeman Thomas McCarren (a man Motley repeatedly refers to simply as THE POWER), Lockwood enters politics with a certain amount of liberal idealism. Indeed, he repeatedly insists to his leftist mistress and former theatrical mentor, Sue, that he is a "liberal" whose political platform as a candidate for the Democratic Party machine is essentially identical to that of Sue's genuinely interracial and class-conscious Progressive Party (328–29, 370–71).[37] However, as Sue chastises him:

> In my book . . . liberal is the most hated word in the language—liberal! . . . There are all kinds of liberals. Jews who are liberals only because they are Jewish and pro-Semitic—and think only of the suffering of their people. Negroes who are liberals only because they are race-conscious and their liberalism bleeds for their poor suffering people. White people, businessmen, rich people who are liberals simply because they are suffering from feelings of guilt. . . . You're not even a liberal. (387)

True to Sue's estimation, once Lockwood has learned the patronage, graft, and election-rigging techniques of the machine system—rendered by Motley in characteristically comprehensive detail—he openly abandons his pretensions of liberalism in all ways but superficial rhetoric. Eventually, Lockwood dons the almost cartoonish capitalist accouterments of a Homburg hat and gaudy diamond ring and successfully executes a Machiavellian scheme to unseat McCarren and assume the role of THE POWER in Chicago's Democratic political machine.

It bears noting that in a brief moment before formally embarking on his political career, Lockwood does walk out of his managerial office in the Haines Company to join a picket line of striking workers. As Motley narrates this episode: "Don laughed aloud. He felt freer than he had ever been. And with his laughter a bit of moisture stung the corner of his eyes. . . . He belonged to something. He belonged to the people. To something big. The people" (294). However, by the conclusion of the novel, Don Lockwood has so fully internalized his role as THE POWER that he openly sides with Haines Company chief executive Emerson Bradley in the next round of strikes by supplying Bradley with additional police and other political favors while accusing labor leader Jim Norris of being a communist when Norris comes to seek Lockwood's aid on behalf of the strikers (546). Even at this late stage, Lockwood insists to himself that he is "a good American." Yet, by this point he employs the latter phrase not in the Popular Front terms by which Norris and Sue's Progressive Party would define righteous citizenship, but rather as a cold war patriot: "[He] wasn't selling out to foreign isms, to labor, to the ignorance of people who didn't know what they really wanted and didn't know what was best for them" (554).

The way in which Motley uses this character as an indictment of the shallowness and ineffectuality of liberalism is especially apparent in Lockwood's ambivalence and shifting allegiances on issues of race and ethnicity. Even before entering the war, Don Lockwood, whose birth name is Chet Kosinski, struggles to free himself of what he perceives as the stigma of his Polish immigrant family's ethnic distinctiveness. As a way of dealing with this self-loathing, he adopts the name Don Lockwood (eventually making this change legal) and tells people that he is an orphan. After rising to power in Chicago's political machine, Lockwood continues to hide his identity and meets with his family only in secret—all while still discreetly and cynically exploiting his knowledge of the Polish language to win votes in this community. In short, Motley renders Lockwood's inability to resolve his sense of shame and guilt regarding the desertion of his ethnic background as part of this antihero's larger pattern of moral hypocrisy.

Further, to the embarrassment of those around him, Lockwood repeatedly greets the African American character Dave with awkward but seemingly well-intentioned comments such as, "I like your people. I want to help them" (251). However, in spite of such statements of interracial goodwill in his personal interactions with Dave and in his campaign rhetoric, Lockwood's underlying racist sentiments quickly surface in moments of personal crisis. For instance, whereas Lockwood begins his political career proud of girlfriend Rebecca Friedman's

Jewishness, he soon disguises her ethnic identity and then agrees to meet her only in secret. At one point, upset that he has lost his first campaign for state representative, he even belittles her with a crude impression of a Jewish accent and bitterly laments, "[I]t was the nigger vote that beat me" (445). Later, he concludes, "He had been in that Negro settlement during his campaign for office. He knew those people. . . . That's why people were anti-Negro and anti-Semitic. . . . They had a chance to help themselves but they never did." Then, much in the age-old tradition of exceptionalism that Zora Neale Hurston once termed "the 'Pet Negro' system," Lockwood immediately rationalizes that "Dave was different" (479). Sue's Progressive Party, by contrast, strives to address racial oppression not by means of rhetorical self-help bromides but through a program for concrete institutional reform centered in interracial laborist politics.

Much as Lockwood dreams of theatrical stardom in the early stages of the novel, Aaron Levin, too, begins the novel with creative ambitions. Specifically, he struggles to become a poet by adhering to a strictly "art-for-art's sake" philosophy. In this vein, Aaron begins to read the work of politically reactionary high modernists such as T. S. Eliot and Ezra Pound. As Motley describes Aaron's response to this work, tongue firmly in cheek, "He couldn't understand much of it but it excited him and it must be good poetry because it was so hard to understand" (36). Aaron also attends exhibits of abstract and surrealist visual art at Chicago's Art Institute in an attempt to absorb the "modern" aesthetic sensibilities that he seeks to emulate in his own work, with similar results: "It confused him, the lines and the colors, but he felt that he should understand it, if he had any real artistic feeling, or he should try to understand it in order to fully develop his sensitivity. Secretly he liked the Italian classics best" (36). Significantly, it is not the aspiring creative writer Aaron, but his father—a working-class laborer at the Haines Company, who has lost the tip of one of his fingers to a factory machine—who is the politically engaged member of the Levin household. Whereas Papa Levin is a reader of the *Communist Manifesto*, a devout union man, and a Progressive Party campaign volunteer, Aaron's investment in romantic notions of the artist's individualism and detachment immobilize him from undertaking a similar brand of direct political participation. Thus, during a discussion at the local diner regarding a prewar Haines Company strike, "Aaron averted his eyes. It seemed too vulgar. Walking in a picket line. Sure he was for it. But he couldn't take part. He'd be embarrassed. When he had arrived at work and seen the strikers he had taken the next streetcar home" (103). Highbrow aesthetic ideology thus impairs Aaron from availing himself of the strike as a potentially rich literary subject matter. All of this, even before a harrowing experience in military combat leaves him mentally crippled, seeming to suffer from something like what psychiatrists would later term posttraumatic stress disorder.

Clearly, Aaron's artistic philosophy constitutes a complete inversion of Motley's own objectives and ideals regarding the sociopolitical utility of literature. Aside from a brief stint with the Communist Party and a subsequent attempt "to speak for the millions of soldiers" in a novel, Aaron never produces any writing expressly concerned with what one might consider social realist themes. Not coincidentally, the progressive fellow writer Milo responds to Aaron's manuscript on war experiences with unprecedented enthusiasm. However, demoralized over the escalating global paranoia concerning the atomic bomb, Aaron destroys this manuscript before anyone else reads it and never again undertakes a sustained literary project (259–65). Rather, Aaron ends the novel virtually in complete isolation (even from his selflessly devoted, pregnant wife) as he wanders the Chicago cityscape, scribbling esoteric poetic fragments on scraps of paper and stuffing them, squirrel-like, into already overflowing pockets. In this fate, Motley seems to offer not only a portrait of the psychologically damaging effects of war but also a parable regarding the ultimately damning effects of art-for-art's sake philosophies. Again, for Motley, literature obviously possesses little relevance if it does not find an audience and produce real reforms of reader consciousness and, by extension, the concrete world of lived experience.

If Don Lockwood and Aaron Levin embody the physically and mentally crippling impact of war, respectively, then Jim Norris crystallizes the potential for war to engender moral breakdown. In Norris's case, he is haunted in particular by the memory of sleeping with a fourteen-year-old French prostitute, whose age he discovered only after having had intercourse with her. Although, like other soldiers, Norris tries to convince himself, "This was their lives over here. . . . It had nothing to do with what they were at home and would be again at home," he finds himself sexually disinterested in his adoring wife following the war. As Motley narrates Norris's first sexual encounter with his wife after returning home, "His hands were rough on her. His love-making was almost like a rape. Louise was shocked at his violence. And in the end he had been impotent" (146; see also 213). Further, whereas before his military service the handsome Jim Norris easily resisted the flirtations of numerous young women while helping to recruit union members among the Haines Company's office staff, he returns from war obsessed by a disturbing "sex hunger" for other women, especially minors (493). He goes so far as to stalk women on several occasions and even momentarily grabs one girl in a park before running away (515). In this context, several of the newspaper headlines read by Aaron Levin and, with anxiety, by Jim himself—such as, "GIRL SEVEN RAPED, KILLED BY EX-GI" (264)—document what Motley perceived to be a larger pattern of returning veterans struggling with similar issues.[38]

As part of his overarching critique of war, Motley also crafts an extended scene in an establishment known as Nick's Veteran Bar in which he expands the scope of his antiwar commentary beyond his three protagonists by intercutting the voices of numerous soldiers (most of whom remain anonymous) as they recount their war experiences. Presented as if overheard by a wandering bar patron, the scene's conversation fragments include one soldier's unapologetically racist boast of having killed "one of them goddamn little monkeys" (i.e., a Japanese soldier) and chilling tales of gang rapes committed against French and German women by U.S. soldiers (249–56). Even more unsettling, notes Robert Fleming, the recurring chorus of "You get your kiiicks / On Route Sixty-Six!" that cycles through the background of these conversations from the bar's jukebox suggests that these men have learned to "get their kicks" from such perverse acts of ruthless aggression (86). Among their other functions, then, these fragmented narratives illustrate the way in which Jim Norris's memories intersect with other types of violence and moral transgression committed by American soldiers. Through these war stories Motley indicts both the violence of war per se and the disturbingly callous mindset that war seems capable of engendering in soldiers. Indeed, as narrator, Motley explicitly describes war as a horrific enactment of masculinist ideology:

> With the change their guns had become phallic symbols, takers of life, proof of their manhood and masculinity and heroism. They shined their guns, took the greatest care of them and always had them near at hand. Their guns had become their best friends and bed companions. And now there was the same elation, the same high point in blasting death into the enemy as giving a child to a woman in peacetime. An exultation in killing, destroying, moving forward, forcing the enemy off the edge of the earth. . . .
> (214)

Ironically, of course, these seeming expressions of phallic power leave veterans like Jim Norris impotent following the war—and not only in terms of the disruption of healthy sexual relations with his wife. As the question occurs to Norris, "Once you had learned not to give a—his mind hesitated, then plunged forward—*shit* any more, how did you learn the way back to caring about people who you'd learned didn't care whether you did or not?" (209).

The sexual perversion and moral confusion of Jim Norris after the war stand in striking contrast to the workerist hero mode in which Motley casts Norris prior to his military service. The prewar Norris gives rousing platform speeches in which his handsome visage and forceful articulation of worker demands help to solidify a vision of the people's inevitable "forward march" (52–54). This vision finds tangible form in the aforementioned prewar strike of the Haines mail-order company employees, during which Norris and other enthusiastic strikers parade beneath an American flag, alternately offering satirical denunciations of Haines chief executive Emerson Bradley and rousing versions of labor songs on the theme of union solidarity (87–91). Motley further ennobles this strike by describing its success on a multicity scale and an unwillingness of delivery truck drivers and other workers to cross the ever-burgeoning picket lines of spirited Haines employees. If these scenes of the prewar Haines Company strike at times seem overly idealized in the manner of proletarian agitprop, Norris's death on the picket lines during the postwar Haines strike at the conclusion of the novel seems as if it could be narrating a social realist strike scene such as Philip Evergood's painting *American Tragedy* (1937):

> And Jim, seeing the man go down on the pavement under the impact of the club and the club turning in the night in search of Edna, leaped forward to defend her.
>
> The club caught Jim across the head. Other clubs beat his shoulders and head as Papa Levin, O'Keefe, Sue, Jane and Milo leaped forward toward Jim and the police with nothing to defend him with but their empty hands.
>
> Jim went down. And as he went down, the French girl, the old woman he had killed, the German soldier he hadn't saved, disappeared forever from his pangs of conscience and absolved him from any blame in this effort of his in the name of the people, the little people who seeded the entire world, who grew like grass across the world, who withered and died or who were cut down in youth. (558–59)

As in Evergood's painting, a heroic striker thus steps forward to accept a martyr's role in a clearly demarcated battle between corporate-sponsored police and underarmed but courageous strikers.[39] So too, in both Motley's novel and numerous examples of social realist artwork on this theme, the iconic central hero figure is a strikingly handsome, well-muscled young man.

Given the nature of Jim Norris's postwar trauma, his eleventh-hour burst of renewed vigor for the union and the martyr's death he suffers in the climactic battle between union pickets and police serves to redeem Norris morally and to recuperate his stymied sense of manhood:

> And Jim was the Jim of old. The fight! The people! The strike, the working for the people, the battle. This was his. His at his peak. The winning of a strike had always been a let-down for him. He liked the competition, the battle. He had been an athlete and the game, the struggle, was the thing. He was rugged. He was ready. If he, somehow, somewhere in his makeup doubted his masculinity this, the strike, the battle, was a way of proving to himself that he was a man. (538)

The connection between the strike and a military battle seems to be not only Norris's but also Motley's. As narrator, Motley repeatedly refers to the "angry groups" of hundreds, even thousands of Haines Company strikers in the novel's closing chapters as an "army" and to the strike itself as "a war" (545–48). In the clash of the opposing "armies" of strikers and corporate-sponsored police,

Motley even describes the police knocking down the flag bearer of the strikers and the American flag "being trampled underfoot" (558). For Motley, then, whereas the international military conflict of World War II had consisted of mutual atrocities that crippled the human pawns of government and industry, the class war waged by America's striking workers against these same corporate interests constitutes a "just war." Especially for Jim Norris, "this was another battle, another war. A good battle. A clean battle for high principles" (552).

However, in contrast to the success of the earlier Haines Company strike, the workers' prospects for a victorious campaign in this latter strike seem precarious, at best, which reflects Motley's increasing anxiety regarding the fate of organized labor during the cold war era. In fact, one could read *We Fished All Night* as a kind of postmortem for the revolutionary hopes that had first crystallized for Motley's generation during the depression era, albeit a postmortem that Motley renders only reluctantly. (Even while the book was still in its embryonic stages, Motley agonized over presenting a pessimistic view of organized labor, writing, "I don't want to do labor a disservice. Would such a novel be injurious?")[40] In the preceding chapters, I have suggested, on the one hand, that calls for a united American front served to moderate dissent among many white social realists during and especially after the war. Organized labor, on the other hand, remained quite active during this period—not least in the wave of general strikes that swept the nation in 1945–46, shortly after the war. As Motley was well aware, the tempering of U.S. labor radicalism owed more to the consensus politics that emerged in the cold war context of the late 1940s than to the Second World War itself.[41]

In this regard, an interchapter newsreel that opens the final section of Motley's novel concisely chronicles many of the concerns that seem to stem directly from the cold war, including the escalation of America's atomic weaponry and other military armaments; the rise to prominence of the House Un-American Activities Committee; and government attacks on organized labor. Meanwhile, this same newsreel calls attention to the fact that little has changed in the Jim Crow South, as African Americans continue to be denied voting rights in the postwar era (449–51). These points suggest that Motley is quite conscious of the way in which the fervent anticommunist rhetoric of the cold war served to stigmatize both labor dissent and leftist cultural work over the course of the 1940s. Thus, if he justifiably sees the CIO/IWO politics of racially integrated union struggle as having attained substantive advances during the late 1930s and early 1940s, Motley also seems to harbor real doubts regarding the potential efficacy of this movement in the post–World War II moment. Put another way, one might observe that Jim Norris's rather formulaic death on the picket lines near the end of the novel may afford him a measure of personal moral redemption, but, significantly, it by no means seems to guarantee collective advances for his fellow workers at the Haines Company, much less the broader progressive labor movement.

This rather defeatist note resonates, too, with Motley's own decision to relocate permanently to Mexico in 1951—a decision motivated, at least in part, by his sense of despair regarding life in the United States during the cold war era. Although this relocation would not bear a direct impact on his fiction until the posthumous publication of *Let Noon Be Fair* in 1966, the fact that Motley chose Mexico was far from incidental. True, he does not seem to have connected substantially with the social realist artists of the Taller de Gráfica Popular, but he did lead a writers' workshop in Mexico City in 1951. As did a number of U.S. radicals (including artists such as Elizabeth Catlett and John Wilson), Motley came to see Mexico as something of a safe haven during the most intense years of McCarthyite witch hunting. Further, like Wilson, Motley consistently lauded Mexico in his correspondence for its relative lack of ethnic bigotry, as well as the vitality and democratic spirit of its folk culture. In other words, Mexico seemed to Motley to provide virtues roughly comparable to those he attributed to the communities of Chicago's Maxwell-Halsted–West Madison Street underclass, without the political repression rampant in the U.S. cold war cultural milieu.[42] Broadening the scope somewhat, it seems telling that by the early 1950s so many African American novelists, in particular, had chosen exile beyond the United States entirely: Motley, Wright, Chester Himes, William Gardner Smith, William Demby, and James Baldwin, among others.[43] While it would be overly simplistic to generalize a direct correlation between these relocations and the shape of these writers' cultural work, this marked trend nonetheless makes it appear as if radical African American novelists were collectively in a type of retreat by midcentury—*not* from the idea of politically engaged literature, but from the social circumstances that most of them rendered in their fiction with such a tone of skepticism and despair.

Novelists as Castigating Prophets

The sense of rupture and loss that pervades Motley's novels is hardly anomalous among African American social realist work in this medium. Like graphic artists and poets, novelists trained the majority of their work on contemporary subjects, but they distinguished themselves from efforts in these other media rather markedly by the relative absence of revolutionary optimism from their work.[44] As with Motley's detailed treatment of Nick Romano's undoing in *Knock on Any Door*, this pessimistic tone perhaps owed to the way in which African American social realists chose to use the novel medium not simply to chronicle the qualitative experiences of contemporary social crises, but to offer remarkably meticulous examinations of *how* and *why* such conditions prevailed. In so doing, their work tends to leave relatively little room for ideological abstractions of a "romantic revolutionary" nature. This point of contrast falls into particularly sharp relief when one weighs novelists' respective treatments of some of the same motifs prevalent in other media. Among the themes I consider here are: (1) explorations of race and ethnic identity in relation to class identity; (2) parables of fascism; (3) narratives of migration; and (4) anxieties regarding masculinity that stem in large part from contemporary socioeconomic crises. Finally, I will examine the representation of working-class consciousness as it appears in African American social realist fiction, arguing that whereas exhortations to radical action outweigh critiques of the American masses in poetry, the balance of work in the novel medium falls decidedly toward disillusionment and portrayals of an irreparable fracturing of the American Dream.

James Young asserts of the generation of African American intellectuals who came of age in the depression era, "The 'problem' for these young radicals, unlike their elders, was essentially class, not race," arguing that most rejected the cultural nationalism of the CP thesis of "self-determination" for the Black Belt (4–5, 39). However, I have labored to suggest that most African American intellectuals, from the generation of Du Bois to the generation of Wright, seem to have been attuned to the impact of *both* race *and* class on the masses of poor and working-class African Americans during the 1930s and 1940s. As South Side Writers' Group member Marian Minus put the matter in an essay for the spring 1937 issue of *Challenge*, "The present Negro writer is facing the flood of two tides: The thought of the social realists which touches him as a creative person, and the attempt at the collection of the scattered remnants of what he can hold close to him as his exclusive cultural heritage as a member of a minority group" (11). Consequently, in attempting to negotiate the twin pulls of black cultural nationalism and class-centered ideologies, William Attaway's *Blood on the Forge*, Lloyd Brown's *Iron City*, Ann Petry's *The Street*, and Wright's *Uncle Tom's Children* all in some way raise the tension between what one loosely might term "race consciousness" and "class consciousness," only to leave the matter decidedly ambiguous—both in the minds of their respective protagonists and as the narrators frame these stories for the reader. In a sense, I would suggest that this seeming indeterminacy may constitute less an evasion on the part of the authors than a strategy for negotiating the complexities of a tension that was, perhaps, ultimately irresolvable.

The leftist cultural circles inhabited by African American social realists of the 1930s and 1940s did not demand that writers make such a choice, at least in their more progressive manifestations. From the mid-1930s until at least midcentury, prominent labor groups like the IWO committed themselves to the idea that ethnic autonomy and working-class universalism could coexist, forging a type of "pan-ethnic internationalism" that permitted American workers to sustain distinct linguistic and cultural traditions under a common banner of antifascism and labor-centered politics (Denning 76). In the case of the *cultural* activities sponsored by the IWO and the CIO, advocacy of a pluralist stance extended explicitly to African Americans, as well as white ethnic groups. Meanwhile, advice proffered by white CP critics to African American cultural workers over the course of the period under study oscillated, somewhat erratically at times, between demands for the subordination of racial concerns to class-minded politics and calls for an essentially black nationalist literature—mixed messages that, taken collectively, served to provide novelists a relatively free range of options on such matters.

In his 1937 "Blueprint for Negro Writing" essay, Richard Wright argued that African American writers "must accept the nationalist implications of their lives, not in order to encourage them, but in order to change and transcend them" (58). And he does seem in most respects to have followed this guideline with striking precision in crafting the *first* edition of *Uncle Tom's Children*, a collection of novellas originally published in 1938. Rooted in folk materials, as per the directive of his "Blueprint," these novellas trace an arc from dawning race consciousness in the traumatic experiences of *Big Boy Leaves Home* and *Down by the Riverside* through the militant black nationalism of Silas in *Long Black Song* to the triumphant interracial, class-based collectivism of *Fire and Cloud*. The latter novella, which Wright clearly seems to have intended as the culmination of an evolution in African American political consciousness, opens by scrutinizing the inner struggles of Reverend Daniel Taylor as he wrestles with what course of action to take in order to provide food for the starving black masses in his southern community. This dilemma is complicated by the fact that the town's white authorities will deem any action that involves the building of interracial alliances with the town's starving whites as communistic in nature. The mayor and the head of the local Industrial Squad (i.e., "Red Squad") even pointedly threaten Reverend Taylor on precisely this matter. In fact, two communists—one black, the other white—*are* among those urging Reverend Taylor to lend his support to a planned mass march on city hall to secure material relief for the town's impoverished citizens. Because Reverend Taylor refuses to take a stand against this march, as "requested" by the mayor, he is abducted by a group of white men, taken to a remote spot in the woods, and beaten to the point of unconsciousness with a whip. Yet, Christlike, Reverend Taylor passes through this symbolic death and rises from the whipping reborn. That is, after much agonizing, Reverend Taylor arrives at a new, transcendent vision for the salvation of his community through the forging of an interracial alliance, enjoining his son Jimmy: "Its the *people*! Theys the ones whut mus be real t us! Gawds wid the people! N the peoples gotta be real as Gawd t us!" (210). Instilled with this new vision, Reverend Taylor helps to catalyze the participation of the local black citizenry in a successful march alongside hundreds of white fellow demonstrators the following day, forcing concessions from the mayor in the form of relief for the town's needy, black and white alike. Significantly, the imagery of this climactic march scene mirrors almost exactly the revolutionary optimism of early Wright poems such as "We of the Streets" and "I Have Seen Black Hands":

> A baptism of clean joy swept over Taylor. He kept his eyes on the sea of black and white faces. The song swelled louder and vibrated through him. This is the way! he thought. Gawd ain no lie! He ain no lie! His eyes grew wet with tears, blurring his vision: the sky trembled; the buildings wavered as if about to topple; and the earth shook. . . . He mumbled out loud, exultingly:
> *"Freedom belongs t the strong!"* (220)

Thus far, then, Wright's collection seems to hew to a Marxist emphasis on class politics "transcending" black nationalism, as Wright himself had insisted it must do in his "Blueprint" essay.

However, with the addition of *Bright and Morning Star* as the final novella of the 1940 edition of *Uncle Tom's Children,* Wright revises the collection's "final word" on the race-class dialectic in such a way as to call into question a simple displacement of race consciousness with class consciousness.[45] This act of self-revision may reflect Wright's oft-remarked growing disaffection with the CP by the close of the 1930s, but given that Wright was still quite active in CP circles in 1940 (serving as an editor for the Harlem Bureau of the *Daily Worker,* for example), one could speculate that this revision of his collection also might simply reflect the general trends of African American social realist work in this medium. Specifically, *Bright and Morning Star* muddies the clear progression of consciousness implicit in the 1938 edition of the collection by highlighting tensions pertaining to the Communist Party's policy of interracialism. Set in the context of an organizing campaign among black and white Alabama sharecroppers in the depression era, the novella focuses on a mother and son named Sue and Johnny-Boy. Wright quickly makes apparent the high stakes of this campaign, as the reader learns that Sue's other son, Sug, is already in prison for his involvement with this same Share Croppers' Union. Ever subject to the threat of discovery by local authorities, Sue and Johnny-Boy both support the campaign's aims but are divided on the crucial issue of recruitment strategy. Whereas Johnny-Boy explains, "Ah cant see white n Ah cant see black. . . . Ah sees rich men n Ah sees po men," Sue remains more skeptical of the loyalty of whites to the well-being of

Chapter Five

blacks and thinks, "He [Johnny] believes so hard hes blind" (233–34). Subsequently, Sue's skepticism appears well founded when a white man (given the ironic name of Booker by Wright) turns out to be a spy for the local sheriff.

This is not to say that *Bright and Morning Star* dismisses the CP's advocacy of interracialism. For instance, in a scene rife with deliberate crucifixion imagery, Sue willingly sacrifices the lives of both her and her son partly to ensure that the names of their fellow union members (black and white) are not revealed to the authorities. In essence, then, Johnny-Boy and Sue both die in a manner strikingly resonant with the stoic martyrdom of Sterling Brown's poem "Sharecroppers." Wright also seems to point to the desirability of interracialism as an ideal through Sue's affection for white CP member Reva and by her approval of Reva and Johnny-Boy's love for one another. As Wright narrates Sue's feelings for Reva, "In Reva's trust and acceptance of her she had found her first feelings of humanity; Reva's love was her refuge from shame and degradation. If in the early days of her life the white mountain had driven her back from the earth, then in her last days Reva's love was drawing her toward it, like the beacon that swung through the night outside" (229). Thus, Wright seems to suggest here (as in *Native Son*) that race and class consciousness necessarily coexist—sometimes harmoniously, but more often in uneasy tension—in the lives of most African Americans.

Lloyd Brown depicts an equally intriguing interplay of impulses toward race and class allegiance in the three African American CP members who figure centrally in *Iron City*. As Alan Wald observes, the elderly Henry Faulcon comes closest to espousing a distinctly leftist brand of cultural nationalism. At one point, for example, he observes of the black wing of the segregated prison:

> I ain't joking this time and don't come accusing me of nationalism, but I'm telling you the *people* here are better. That's right. Look—we only been here a week but still you aint heard nobody Red-baiting us have you? No, the only ones we got to worry about is the guards. But up on the ranges it aint like that. All kinds of reactionary bastards up there—Coughlinites, Jew-haters, fascists and everything. . . . No sir, if there's going to be Jim Crow, please put me right in with my people. (65)

By contrast, Paul Harper seems to hew more closely to the primacy of class as a shaping social factor. Hence, before he realizes that Falcoun is "jiving" him with a line about wanting to live in the upper prison ranges designated for white inmates, Harper chastises the elder CP member: "Maybe you're getting so old you can't see so good any more . . . but those sure look like bars up there to me. Meaning we'd still be in jail just the same, just like the white workers in the mill are exploited even if they do get a better break than we do" (104). Still, even Harper clearly recognizes the central significance of race in the Lonnie James case—that is, the specific vulnerability of African Americans to scapegoating by the U.S.

legal system (a fact of life chronicled extensively by social realist graphic artists and poets as well). Hence, to the extent that Brown's novel suggests something like a positive resolution—a stay of execution and even an acquittal for Lonnie James seem a distinct possibility at novel's end—this note of cautious optimism derives from a campaign conducted with significant direction from a CP body politic that is well attuned to both the class- and race-based injustices of the American legal system. In other words, the campaign to free Lonnie James seems to stand a fighting chance of success precisely because it attends to *both* class and race concerns in a way that Wright's Johnny-Boy does not.

At the close of Attaway's tragic tale of the Moss brothers in *Blood on the Forge*, Melody Moss sits on a train bound for Pittsburgh with his brother Chinatown, who has been blinded in a steel mill explosion. In the seat across from the Moss brothers is an African American soldier in uniform, who has been blinded in the First World War. After a brief conversation, Chinatown and the soldier listen for the sound of guns, "sounds that didn't exist," in the rumble of the train; in the closing line of the novel, the narrator even explicitly describes these characters as "twins" (291–93). In effect, both men have been wounded—indeed, *blinded*—in the course of service to what later generations of leftists would term a military-industrial complex, the dimensions of whose exploitation these characters have been tragically unable to recognize. So too, both the African American industrial worker, Chinatown, and the African American soldier seem to have received precious little in the way of civic rights (or even fiscal remuneration) in compensation for their sacrifices on behalf of America's war effort. Although the plot of *Blood on the Forge* looks back to the World War I era, these issues also possessed clear and present relevance for the early 1940s moment in which Attaway crafted his novel.

As I have suggested in the preceding chapters, the participation of black soldiers in World War II constituted a point of deep ambivalence for many African Americans, comprising at once a hypocritical call to fight for a democracy abroad that most black soldiers did not enjoy themselves on the home front *and* a source of hope for smashing new barriers in the long struggle for racial justice in the United States. Ann Petry's *The Street* voices these conflicted responses in a brief but suggestive exchange between two anonymous men on the stoop of an apartment building:

> "I been in a war. I know what I'm talking about. There'll be trouble when them colored boys come back. They ain't going to put up with all this stuff"—he waved toward the street. His hand made a wide, all-inclusive gesture that took in the buildings, the garbage cans, the pools of water, even the people passing by. . . .

"Been like this all these years, ain't nothing a bunch of hungry soldiers can do about it."

"Don't tell me, man. I know. I was in the last war."

"What's that got to do with it? What did you change when you come back? They're going to come back with their bellies full of gas and starve just like they done before—" (338–39)

Aesthetically akin to Motley's use of anonymously voiced war stories in the Nick's Veteran Bar scene of *We Fished All Night* and the anonymously voiced ambivalence toward the war captured in Frank Marshall Davis's poem "47th Street," such a passage serves Petry's novel by allowing her to touch on issues that may not be of *direct* impact to protagonist Lutie Johnson, but nonetheless exert a significant shaping influence on the broader social world Lutie occupies. And, as with these contemporaneous works by Davis and Motley, Petry's use of such a technique allows her to express these sentiments in seemingly authentic vernacular voices, rather than by way of an imposed editorial commentary from the narrator.

Petry also introduces the war theme through the character of Boots Smith, a bandleader who for a time attempts to coerce Lutie into a sexual relationship in exchange for a singing job. Notably, Petry casts this generally unredeeming character in a somewhat more sympathetic light when discussing his adamant resistance to serving in the American military. As Boots explains to his white employer, Junto:

"They can wave flags. They can tell me the Germans cut off baby's behinds and rape women and turn black men into slaves. They can tell me any damn thing. None of it means nothing. . . . Because, no matter how scared they are of Germans, they're still more scared of me. I'm black, see? And they hate Germans, but they hate me worse. If that wasn't so they wouldn't have a separate army for black men. That's one for the book. Sending a black army to Europe to fight Germans. Mostly with brooms and shovels. . . . I've got a hate for white folks here"—he indicated his chest—"so bad and so deep that I wouldn't lift a finger to help 'em stop Germans or nobody else." (258–59)

As Smith points out, chief among the hypocrisies of "Uncle Sam's" recruitment of African American soldiers was the systematic racial segregation of troops within a military ostensibly fighting for democracy. Notably, too, this character's response closely mirrors the stance of Willard Motley's unpublished essay "I Discover I'm a Negro," where the young novelist even vows his personal willingness to go to jail rather than serve in a segregated unit.[46]

Petry's Boots Smith insists, as well, that Germans "are only doing the same thing in Europe that's been done in this country since the time it started" (260). Richard Wright voiced a strikingly similar sentiment in an antiwar speech that opened the Fourth American Writers' Congress in May 1941. In this speech, Wright terms the U.S. War Department's policy of racially segregating American troops "Fascist" and asks, "Who can deny that the Anglo-American hatred of Negroes is of the same breed of hate which the Nazis mete out to Jews in Germany?"[47] As I have noted in discussions of works such as John Wilson's lithograph *Deliver Us from Evil* and Melvin Tolson's poem "The Idols of the Tribe," the anxiety of cultural workers between the mid-1930s and mid-1940s regarding the potential for a white supremacist brand of fascism to surface within the United States was quite real, particularly for African Americans. In a 1937 essay titled "Problems Facing the Negro Writer Today," *New Challenge* contributor Eugene Holmes spoke to the special threat of domestic fascism to African American writers: "Langston Hughes, who was chased out of Carmel and forbidden to read his poems in Los Angeles, and Sterling Brown, who knows the terror of the lynch-ridden South, would not be sanguine about the exemption of the Negro writer under an American fascism. . . . That is why Negro writers do have obligations, along with white writers, not only for the protection of their craft, but also in defense of the culture fascism will seek to destroy" (69–70). Understandably, then, African American social realists were at particular pains to extend vigilance on this front during and beyond the Second World War.

In this same vein, situating Lloyd Brown's *Iron City* within the context of its publication in 1951, one scarcely can miss the author's implicit commentary on the way in which McCarthyism embodied—at least for many on the left—the *realization* of this threat of domestic fascism run amok in the post–World War II era. Described as a "civic temple" and a "Cathedral of Justice" in the city's boosterist promotional literature, in actual fact Brown's Monongahela County Courthouse and Jail disproportionately houses the poor, the black, and those who struggle for radical social reforms, like communists Paul Harper, Isaac Zachary, and Henry Faulcon. Brown further elaborates this line of commentary by describing the prison at one point as a type of "great ocean steamer" in which imprisoned men are "passengers lining the five long decks" (31)—decks literally separated by race, as is American society beyond the prison's walls to a large degree. The prison thus serves Brown as a metaphor for the larger Pittsburgh community and, by extension, U.S. society writ large—hence, the multivalence of the title of *Iron City*.[48] Significantly, Brown was not alone in crafting such a metaphor, as Frank Marshall Davis's "'Mancipation Day" and Richard Wright's "I Have Seen Black Hands" employ similar tropes. Compare, for example, Henry Faulcon's observation upon discovering the manufacturing imprint on his prison bars—"Half the guys in here, including me and Zach, have made McGregor steel. That's a fact, we made this jail for them to put us in" (103)—and the following stanza from Wright's poem:

And the black hands felt the cold steel bars of the prison they had made, in despair tested their strength and found that they could neither bend nor break them.[49]

In a strikingly similar manner, both Wright and Brown use the prison metaphor to stress the special vulnerability of America's working classes to social injustice. However, whereas Wright casts his "black hands" in the collective position of seemingly helpless prisoners, Brown's Henry Faulcon gains a certain measure of control over the bitter irony of his discovery through humor. This point of distinction reflects Brown's cautious optimism with regard to the prospects of revolutionary working-class agency—again, an attribute relatively unique among African American–authored novels of social realism. Further, it is clear that Brown's well-crafted metaphor speaks with equal poignancy to the early 1940s period in which *Iron City*'s events are set and to life during the oppressive cold war hysteria of the early 1950s, in the midst of which Brown published his novel.

Yet, the fear of African American social realists was not only that black citizens would almost certainly suffer disproportionate scapegoating under U.S. fascism, but also that the masses of poor and working-class African Americans were themselves susceptible to the appeal of fascist rhetoric. This anxiety is particularly apparent in Wright's *Lawd Today!* During the course of reading his morning paper, postal worker Jake Jackson expresses open admiration for capitalists like John D. Rockefeller and J. P. Morgan, gangsters, and Hitler's call for the world to "smash Jews," while loudly disparaging "Commoonists and Bolshehicks" (28–35). Notably, the individuals that Jackson singles out for praise here are precisely the figures targeted for satirical attacks by social realist poet Frank Marshall Davis in poems such as "Modern Man—the Superman" and "To Those Who Sing America." Yet, while Wright himself undoubtedly would have identified with Davis's biting, irreverent excoriation of these figures, he seems reluctant to grant anything approaching the same level of political consciousness to his representative working-class protagonist in this early novel. For Wright, it seems, the prevailing currents of poor and working-class consciousness may pose as intransigent a stumbling block to the revolutionary ambitions of American leftists (like himself) as do the more readily identifiable purveyors of fascist politics, such as U.S. robber barons and Axis dictators.

Similarly, whereas Jake finds much to admire in a parade of militarily outfitted Garveyites and a black precinct captain who he describes as "a race man," he helps to disparage an African American communist in a local barbershop as a "crackbrain" and later asserts that Booker T. Washington's policy of cooperation with "rich white folks" is the best route for African American advancement (57–64, 107–10). On the one hand, Wright himself found racial nationalism in the vein of Garveyites appealing in certain respects, remarking in his autobiography, "Theirs was a passionate rejection of America, for they sensed with that directness of which only the simple are capable that they had no chance to live a full human life in America. . . . I understood their emotions, for I partly shared them" (*American* 28). On the other hand, the Marxist in Wright perceived such movements as only one step removed from an incipient brand of intraracial fascist politics (see Kinnamon and Fabre 55). In this regard, one also might consider Wright's presentation of one of Jake Jackson's discussions with his African American coworkers at the Chicago post office:

> "Say, you remember that colored guy who use' t' preach over the radio?"
> "That guy who said everybody's got to come under one command?"
> "Yeah . . ."
> "But it'd take a strong guy to make all these folks come under one command."
> "You telling me?"
> "Like old Hitler . . ."
> ". . . and Mussellinni." (184)

Significantly, Wright renders these discussions in such a way that the reader can only occasionally attribute given statements to particular speakers, as if to suggest the author's sense of the pervasiveness of these sentiments among certain segments of the African American working class. It is in precisely this vein that Wright warned in his preface to Horace Cayton and St. Clair Drake's *Black Metropolis*, "Do not hold a light attitude toward the slums of Chicago's South Side. Remember that Hitler came out of such a slum" (xx).

Wright was hardly neglecting issues of racial oppression by pointing out what he took to be the shortcomings of black nationalism as a means of addressing the problems confronting working-class African Americans. In fact, whereas Jake Jackson's is only a *potential* for fascism, for Wright the various forms of racism embodied in lynching, segregation, and the systemic discrimination of America's legal system collectively comprise an *already active* and virulent strain of domestic fascism. Still, it is worth stressing that Wright perceived the antidemocratic impulses underlying white supremacy and black nationalism as historically distinct (and unequally empowered) manifestations of a single disturbing trend in international politics of the depression era: namely, the emergence of ethnically based fascisms. In this regard, Wright found company with contemporary African American intellectuals such as Alain Locke, who, in an essay for the November 1941 issue of *Fortune*, warned: "Even in the segregation and discrimination he endures, the Negro is finding strength. . . . He would be ready now to rally around a leader he could understand—a Negro Huey Long—and if he gets kicked around much longer he will probably find one" (Wheat 64).

A third often-overlooked element connecting the work of African American novelists with the broader social realist movement is the theme of migration. That migration should have figured prominently among the experiences documented by social realist novels of the 1930s and 1940s should not prove surprising given that novelists like William Attaway and Richard Wright (among others) had undergone some variant of this experience themselves. I have noted that the migration theme surfaced in white-authored material such as Dorothea Lange's photographs and Woody Guthrie's dust bowl balladry. In fiction, the sojourn of the Joad family from an impoverished Oklahoma family farm to the less than hospitable agricultural valleys of California constitutes the central motif of the period's most famous social realist novel, John Steinbeck's *The Grapes of Wrath.* Significantly, Steinbeck, Lange, and Guthrie present migration as emblematic of the larger social and economic dislocations experienced by working-class Americans during the depression era.

This is also the case with Attaway's tale of white migrants, *Let Me Breathe Thunder,* wherein protagonists Step and Ed seem either unable or unwilling to settle down, even with what seems to be the most idyllic of agricultural employment opportunities on Mr. Sampson's farm in the Yakima Valley. As Sampson remarks to these transient laborers, "There are hundreds of youngsters around your age who were jolted out of their patterns by the big depression . . . they became wanderers. And now that they don't have to drift any more, they can't hold down a steady job, they can't get back into the pattern" (158). To be sure, migrant life does seem to possess some appealing features. For instance, Attaway posits a certain level of interracial camaraderie among the novel's underclass of migrants, hobos, and outlaws, as suggested by Step's friendship with Mag, an African American ex-prostitute whose life he once saved. In a manner akin to the ethnic crossings that one finds among the West Madison Street denizens of Motley's *Knock on Any Door,* Attaway constructs a conversation between Step and several fellow travelers in a boxcar, in which an African American migrant remarks, "When I settles down it's gonna be where I can still mix with guys on the road. . . . Guys on the road ain't got prejudice like other folks" (57).[50] Further, Attaway counterpoises this brand of tolerance against a considerably less flattering portrait of established middle- and upper-class communities. Mag's husband, Cooper, remarks of "mainstream" American society, "It don't make no difference where you go . . . they always hating somebody somewhere. All along from Texas through New Mexico they hate Mexes worse'n a snake; down in lower California they get like mad dogs if you mention Japs; I ain't never been far east, but they say that out there everybody hates everybody else" (113–14).

Still, Attaway avoids overly idealizing the lives of his migrant protagonists by including references to harassment from railroad detectives, showing Step and

Ed's vulnerability to being run out of towns in which they have no established ties. As Ed observes, "[A] transient simply cannot afford to get into trouble" (17). Further, transients like Step and Ed lack the nurturing qualities that Attaway seems to take as stemming primarily from stable family environments. Hence, when the duo attempts to informally adopt a vagrant Mexican American youth, a lad they name "Hi Boy," the project seems ill fated from the start. While Step and Ed interact amiably enough with this youth at times, when Hi Boy encounters "trouble" (in the form of a self-inflicted injury to his hand) the two migrants seem equipped with neither the financial resources nor the wherewithal needed to provide the child with sustained medical care. Specifically, after Step mocks the boy for alleged cowardice and then for crying in response to these barbs, Hi Boy stabs his own hand with a fork in order to prove his toughness to these would-be father figures (67–72). Here, Attaway offers the novel's most poignant critique of the potentially damaging effects of the masculinist imperatives that prevail in the migrant culture of characters such as Step and Ed. Indeed, it is an infection stemming from this injury that eventually leads to Hi Boy's death during a perilous freight train passage through frigid mountains in the closing pages of the novel. During this vain attempt to reach a doctor in time to save Hi Boy's life, Step observes that, as stowaways on a train, he and Ed are ironically neither passengers nor freight: "We ain't even people. We ain't nothing" (245). Thus, Step and Ed ultimately appear bereft of family and community ties of any sort (beyond a tentative allegiance to one another) and seem destined to continue their restless wandering. True, Ed at one point remarks to Step, "Us traveling farmers should have a union—that's the trouble" (240); yet, as with Steinbeck's Joad family and Guthrie's "Dust Bowl Refugees," it is precisely the perpetual mobility of migrant laborers like Step and Ed that seems to prevent them from establishing substantial ties with any community of fellow workers.

For African Americans, particularly in the context of a transition from the oppressive sharecropping economy of the rural South to the new industrial employment opportunities of the urban North, migration acquired a quite different valence. Literary critic Houston Baker suggests that whereas the development of America's railroad infrastructure inspired anxiety in many well-to-do white American writers, as a disruptive machine in the garden of an ostensibly idyllic pastoral landscape, trains appeared to many African Americans as a symbol of new possibilities for geographic mobility and its correlatives of economic and social advancement (11). Hence, as Richard Yarborough puts it, "If the most symbolically charged geographical direction in the 'mainstream' (that is, white male) U.S. imagination is toward the west, then that in the Afro-American imagination is northward" (302).[51] The boosterism of African American newspapers like the *Chicago Defender* helped to generate this symbolic geography by employing the most glowing terms to describe the political liberties and economic opportunities ostensibly awaiting African American migrants in the urban North. How accurately these theoretical models and boosterist rhetorics capture something like the lived consciousness of African American migrants themselves remains open to debate, but Attaway's *Blood on the Forge* clearly suggests that whatever optimism of this sort did exist—and for his characters, at least, there is precious little—was profoundly misguided. In this sense, Attaway's novel obviously bears a closer resemblance to the bleak depression-era migrant narratives of Steinbeck, Lange, and Guthrie than to the rhetoric of the *Chicago Defender*—or even a more balanced but ultimately optimistic project such as artist Jacob Lawrence's 1940–41 *Migration of the Negro* series (Turner). Indeed, one would hardly overstate the case by observing that migration northward fails to solve anything for *Blood on the Forge*'s Moss brothers.

As with the narration of white migrant experiences in Guthrie's folk songs and Steinbeck's *The Grapes of Wrath*, Attaway's novel represents the Moss brothers' necessary decision to migrate as resulting from both a "push" and a "pull": the push comes mainly in the form of depleted Kentucky farmland and, more urgently, in the threat to Big Mat's life for having struck a white "riding boss," while the pull is manifest in a jackleg recruiter's promises of big wages offered by the steel mills of the urban North. However, Chinatown is presciently cynical toward the glowing images offered by the recruiter who arranges the Moss brothers' passage to the North: "There a snake under the door sill somewhere. . . . Man have to kill himself workin' to make the kind of money he was talkin' about" (54). True to Chinatown's estimation, in fact, Attaway's protagonists seem to join Richard Wright's *Twelve Million Black Voices* in perceiving little difference between southern "Lords of the Land" and northern "Bosses of the Buildings" following their arrival in the novel's western Pennsylvania steel town (35; see also Dickerson 33; Vaughan 425; Garren, "Playing" 13).

Nonetheless, African Americans did migrate in great numbers from places like Kentucky to clustered northern industrial sites like Homestead, Pennsylvania.[52] And, to Attaway's credit, *Blood on the Forge* attends more carefully than even most historical accounts to the material conditions of the migration journey itself. Attaway's account of the boxcar ride that serves as the migrants' mode of escape/transport from the Jim Crow South under cover of night offers a critical alternative to Houston Baker's optimistic interpretation of the train in African American culture:

Squatted on the straw-spread floor of a boxcar, bunched up like hogs headed for market, riding in the dark for what might have been years . . . there was no sun, they forgot even that they had eyes in their heads and crawled around in the boxcar, as though it were a solid thing of blackness. . . . Big Mat had ended in a corner. He crouched there, body shaking with the car. Now and then his head struck against the wall with a noise that was lost in greater noises. His big muscles cried out for movement. Warm urine began to flow into the corner where he sat. . . . The air, fetid with man smell and nervous sweat, the pounding of the wheels shaking the car and its prisoners like a gourd full of peas, the piercing scream of the wheels fighting the rails on a curve, the uniform dark—those things were common to all. The misery that stemmed from them was a mass experience. Big Mat could not defend his identity against the pack. (59–60)

In a manner evocative of the Middle Passage experience, Attaway's migrants are thus stripped of almost all of their material possessions, while the noises and buffeting of the metallic train car speak to a specifically industrial assault on both individuality and cultural identity (see Margolies 55). For the musically talented Melody Moss, this process manifests itself in "the rattle and jar of the wheels [that] kept [him] from singing although he was feeling bad and had his box with him. . . . Whatever came into his head was copied by the wheels" (60). Already then, mechanized, repetitive rhythms are reorienting the Moss brothers' sense of time and space in a concrete, bodily manner, forecasting their later experiences with the material apparatus of the Pennsylvania steel mills. Also in this scene, Attaway dramatizes a paucity of material links that might bind migrants to the families, communities, and lifeways of their former homes, a reality frequently demanded by the circumstances of the migration journey northward—a journey that, as for Attaway's Moss brothers, often necessarily commenced under cover of night. Attaway asserts that migrants' relative dearth of material links to their former lives did little to enhance the continuity of their cultural identity, kinship networks, and lifeways in their new locales. Examined in this light, Attaway's novel would seem to belong well within the mainstream of both U.S. social realist tales of migratory experience (including Steinbeck's *The Grapes of Wrath*, Tillie Olsen's *Yonnondio*, and Harriette Arnow's *The Dollmaker*) and the tradition of African American migration narratives (including Langston Hughes's *One-Way Ticket*, Ralph Ellison's *Invisible Man*, and the blues stylings of artists such as Bessie Smith and Muddy Waters).

If African American novelists share with the larger social realist culture of their peers themes such as race and class consciousness, antifascism, and migration, one also might ask to what extent their work reflects the less flattering characteristics of this ostensibly progressive cultural movement with regard to representations of gender. I have remarked that one of the hallmarks of U.S. social realism (especially during the 1930s) is that much cultural work in this vein seems driven by decidedly masculinist concerns, occasionally even displaying the anti–woman worker rhetoric prevalent in the depression decade writ large.[53] At times, otherwise radical African American novelists like Richard Wright resembled peers such as Sinclair Lewis, whose *It Can't Happen Here* (1935) framed the depression era's social and political crises as a dilemma of imperiled manhood (see Melosh 15–31). Yet, I would argue that while African American social realist novels are by no means devoid of subtle and not-so-subtle elements of sexism, these authors do attempt to frame masculinist ideologies in a more self-conscious and critical light than did many of their peers.

Wright's critique of African American men's blindness to their own gendered double standards emerges strikingly in *Lawd Today!* wherein Jake Jackson seems to express a remarkable amount of self-pity for his own circumstances while simultaneously voicing nothing but contempt for the everyday struggles of his wife, Lil, whom he terrorizes both physically and psychologically. Further, Jake and his peers display an especially vitriolic disposition toward African American female coworkers in the Chicago post office. In the midst of a discussion with male fellow employees, Jake remarks, "I'd like to horsewhip every black cunt who so much as looks at a white man" (140). Later, Jake's friend Al delights in recounting his supposed exploits with a former girlfriend, describing her to his admiring coworkers as a "woman who just craved for men to beat her" (156). In a similar vein, Silas, a relatively prosperous black farmer in Wright's novella *Long Black Song*, intends literally to whip his wife Sarah, "as she had seem him whip a horse," when he concludes that she has betrayed him by sleeping with a white man (143–45). (Notably, Silas does not pause to consider the possibility that this white man has taken advantage of his wife.) In each of these cases, the impulse toward acts of misogynist violence serves to further Wright's critique of his male protagonists in at least two respects: first, such incidents demonstrate the characters' proclivity for lashing out in a destructive and ultimately self-centered fashion at potential allies; and, second, to the extent that such characters feel that they possess little recourse save for acts of domestic violence, this serves to dramatize the absence of more constructive avenues for (collective) action in their respective mindsets. Thus, while statements such as Wright's frequently cited, hostile review of Zora Neale Hurston's *Their Eyes Were Watching God* (1937) clearly indicate his own weddedness to specifically masculinist notions of self-actualization, these passages from Wright's first two fiction projects nonetheless suggest that he was more self-critical of the masculine imperatives driving his protagonists than certain of his more vociferous detractors have been willing to acknowledge.

Like Wright's Jake Jackson, Big Mat Moss of Attaway's *Blood on the Forge* does not seem fully cognizant of the ways in which his class position results in the exploitation of his labor and delimits his socioeconomic opportunities. To the contrary, Big Mat initially thrives on the new opportunities for proving his merits as a worker alongside whites in the Pennsylvania steel mills by handling jobs himself that normally require two workers. Given the ways in which Big Mat's race and size have long imperiled his very safety and survival vis-à-vis white society in the South, he recognizes, "This was a good place for a big black man to be" (108; see also 113). Ultimately, however, Big Mat overestimates the mill's dependence on the masculine prowess of *his* labor, as in the reflection, "With his strength he could relight their fires or he could let them die cold. Without Black Irish they were dead" (286–87). So too, Big Mat misrecognizes the amount of authority and significance that he really possesses as a deputized strikebreaker, or "riding boss," for industrial interests. It seems Big Mat can recognize the limitations imposed by his social position only through dissatisfactions experienced in the domestic sphere. First, Mat and Hattie are unable to have a child in Kentucky, even after seven ill-fated pregnancies (a circumstance that Big Mat fatalistically attributes to a "curse"). Then, after leaving Hattie behind in Kentucky and taking up residence in the steel mill town with Anna, a fifteen-year-old Mexican prostitute, Big Mat grows outraged with this girl's apparent indifference to him following the first passionate days of their common-law marriage. While Attaway gives the reader to understand that Anna's frustration results from the inability of Big Mat to provide her a high-status life and a home in the hills among the town's social elite, Big Mat cannot seem to comprehend Anna's interiority to even the slightest degree and, consequently, he responds to their mutual frustration by beating her unmercifully (275–76). Much as in Wright's early fiction, this paucity of insight with respect to Anna is part and parcel of Attaway's broader critique of Big Mat's tragic lack of the vision necessary to improve his situation via collective identification with his family and other fellow members of the working classes.

For her part, possessing neither a revolutionary class nor race consciousness, Anna seems to accept conventional gender role expectations in her plans to improve her status through the agency of a hyper-masculine lover. As she spins a vision of her hoped-for lover relatively early in the novel to Melody Moss, "He will be a big man with muscles like a bear on the mountain. . . . He will have a pine tree on his belly, hard like rock all the night. He will get me high-heel shoes with bright stones in the heels" (103). Perceiving Big Mat to be such a man, she uses him in an attempt to fulfill her dreams of becoming "like the Americanos" in terms of class status and cultural distinction by purchasing glittering shoes and an elaborate beaded evening gown. However, the shoes soon fall apart and the dress grows filthy and wrinkled from dragging in the mud of the steel town streets, requiring Anna to wear it "pinned like a diaper between her legs" (154; see also 137, 143). Ironically, then, the icon intended as a symbol of womanly maturity and status comes to mark Anna's seeming childishness; particularly in light of her virtual entrapment before a crude oil stove within a spatially confined domestic sphere, such clothing comes to appear truly pathetic. Through the characters of Big Mat and Anna, Attaway thus suggests that prevailing class *and* gender ideologies constitute mutually reinforcing forms of oppression for both women and men in the American industrial milieu—with each of these ideological frameworks contributing significantly to an escalating sense of entrapment among the characters who embrace them.

Although differentiated from the work of her male peers by the fact that she centers her novel around a female protagonist, Petry's *The Street* also touches on the way in which masculinist ideologies could compound depression-era socioeconomic frustrations. For example, Petry reveals through flashbacks that Lutie Johnson's marriage dissolved precisely due to the tensions resulting from her husband's wounded manhood when he was unable to find steady employment: "He got used to facing the fact that he couldn't support his wife and child. It ate into him. Slowly, bit by bit, it undermined his belief in himself until he could no longer bear it" (168). Feeling emasculated as he is supported by his wife's work as a domestic for a wealthy white family in suburban Connecticut, Jim takes up with another woman in Lutie's absence, which leads to their eventual separation. More substantially than her male peers, however, Petry also directly illustrates the ways in which masculine anxieties of the depression era might impact the psyches of women. For example, Petry describes Lutie's recollection of a local grocer woman's prophetic warning about her plans to accept the ill-fated job in Connecticut:

> And again she remembered Mrs. Pizzini's words, 'Not good for the woman to work when she's young. Not good for the man'. Obviously she had been right, for here on this street the women trudged along overburdened, overworked, their own homes neglected while they looked after someone else's while the men on the street swung along empty-handed, well dressed, and carefree. Or they lounged against the sides of buildings, their hands in their pockets while they stared at the women who walked past, probably deciding which woman they should select to replace the wife who was out working all day.
>
> And yet, she thought, what else is a woman to do when her man can't get a job? What else had there been for her to do that time Jim couldn't get a job? (65)

So too, when Lutie searches for employment as a single mother, her options seem limited to the blue-collar labor of a steam laundry or a white-collar job as a filing clerk (55–56). The only lucrative alternative career path, becoming a professional singer, seems dependent on her willingness to be sexually exploited by agents and employers—a compromise Lutie is unwilling to make. Clearly, then, gender, as much as class and race, poses a constraint to Lutie's social mobility.

In an odd bit of symmetry, much as certain leftist cultural critics agonized over the alleged ineffectuality of the novel during the early 1930s, perhaps no medium of social realist expression has been dismissed as summarily by post–World War II scholars as the novel—albeit for quite different reasons in the latter case. For example, Walter Rideout's *The Radical Novel in the United States* (1956) catalogs what he takes to be "the deficiencies of the proletarian novel" as: "the infatuation with violence for its own sake, the melodramatic confrontations, the oversimplification, and therefore falsification, of characters, the recurrence of stereotyped motifs, the 'wish-fulfillment' endings, the tendency generally to tamper with the logic of the novel's own structure of relationships" (286). Given the manner in which critics like Rideout have so routinely dismissed social realist literature as being overly determined by Marxist formulas, it seems particularly important to illustrate the ways in which the works of fiction under discussion in this study depart from, and at times even subvert, the conventions typically attributed to proletarian fiction.

On this front, an anecdote from Willard Motley's fiction offers a useful reminder of the hesitancy of most American novelists to subsume their literary aesthetics to the protocol of any rigid political program. In *We Fished All Night*, Aaron Levin's encounter with the CP after his return from military service temporarily serves to rescue him from the ineffectual art-for-art's sake credos of his youth by endowing him with a sense of social purpose in his writing: "This was the companionship of struggle; he had found something to grab hold of. Some force to devote his life to. Something that gave purpose and meaning to his life. He wanted to sacrifice himself to something. He now had this sacrifice which offered nothing to him personally and demanded everything. The people. The abstraction of the people. Everything was for their good" (233). Yet, as Motley hints in the language of this passage (i.e., "the *abstraction* of the people"), the CP instructors of the Chicago Workers' School ultimately demand of Aaron a mechanical adherence to dogmatic rhetoric that precludes any space for individuality or leftist self-critique. Aaron notes the detrimental impact of these ideological directives on the novels of his friend and mentor Eric: "He had admired Eric so much because of his first book. The tremendous difference to him in the second book shocked him. It seemed only a recital of the Party line. The framework, the perfectly constructed novel, was there, and the clear, clean style. But to him it seemed as though it had lost all the poetry of the former book, all the penetrating and inspired observations" (236). In fact, Eric himself admits to Aaron, "When I write about capitalists I make them evil—I probably wouldn't have done that before. They become symbols, not people—although, of course, I know this isn't true" (238). As evidenced by the openly left-of-liberal stance of *We Fished All Night*, Motley does *not* intend this episode as a dismissal of radically politicized literature per se. Rather, like Aaron Levin in this moment of insight, Motley advocates a cultural space for the development of a radical literature that is free from the rhetorical rigidity of programmatic doctrines.

If recent revisionist scholarship by literary critics like Barbara Foley, James Murphy, and Cary Nelson is correct in suggesting that even CP-affiliated cultural critics actually tended to *critique* literary and theatrical works that presented flawless proletarian heroes and utopian revolutionary climaxes, the African American social realist novels published between 1930 and the early 1950s certainly should not have disappointed contemporaneous reviewers on this count. With the notable exceptions of the closing two novellas of Wright's 1940 edition of *Uncle Tom's Children* (*Fire and Cloud* and *Bright and Morning Star*), the Haines Company strike scenes in Motley's *We Fished All Night,* and Lloyd Brown's *Iron City,* African American social realist novels offer little in the way of the romantic praise of the common man that scholars like Richard Pells have described as typical of this era's radical fiction (200). While generally treating their protagonists with a certain amount of dignity, Wright, Motley, Attaway, and Petry do not tend to depict America's poor and working classes as inherently class conscious, let alone revolutionary.

Perhaps most significantly, in striking contrast to much depression-era visual art, poetry, and agitprop theater, African American social realist novels rarely portray harmonious interracial unity; and when they do portray such a quality, it is more often in the realm of America's underclasses than among a proletarian working class per se. Within the latter group, African American novelists tend to cast a less than savory reality of racial divisiveness as being closer to the norm. Hence, when these authors offer insights into the aspirations of their protagonists, such passages seldom reveal dreams of building coalitions with fellow members of the working class. To the contrary, the three Moss brothers of Attaway's *Blood on the Forge* (1941) seem to fall under the category of what Foley describes as the "antibildungsroman" of failed conversion (328). This point emerges most dramatically in the case of Big Mat, the eldest of the Moss brothers. Despite the fact that he initially thrives in the steel mills of western Pennsylvania and wins the admiration of a majority of his white fellow workers, Big Mat eventually accepts a position as a deputy in a band of strikebreakers. Only in the moment of his death, as he leads an assault on the union headquarters of Slavic fellow steelworkers, does Mat arrive at a point of class consciousness:

His vision faded. He was confused. It seemed to him that he had been through all of this once before. Only at that far time he had been the arm strong with hate. Yes, once he had beaten down a riding boss. A long time ago in the red hills he had done this thing and run away. Had that riding boss been as he was now? Big Mat went farther away and no longer could distinguish himself from these other figures. They were all one and all the same. In that confusion he sensed something true. Maybe somewhere in these mills a new Mr Johnston was creating riding bosses, making a difference where none existed. (288)

In this oft-quoted (and oft-criticized) passage, Attaway makes explicit what he has to this point revealed indirectly through the actions of his characters: the failure of the Moss brothers to fully grasp their place in the socioeconomic landscape of the Pennsylvania steel town in terms of *both* race *and* class. For while *Blood on the Forge* does offer some limited instances of interracial identification among workers—such as the Irish steelworkers nicknaming Big Mat "Black Irish" and the friendly mentorship that an elderly Slav named Zanski offers to Melody Moss—Attaway also suggests that these tentative identifications do not tend to bear up in moments of socioeconomic crisis. At such points race continues to divide American working-class communities. For example, the families of Slavic fellow workers assault the Moss brothers with rocks and insults on various occasions as a labor strike looms. By the same token, none of the Moss brothers joins the striking workers on the picket lines or in their union meetings.

In fact, it is precisely because of its failure to attract African American laborers that the steelworker's union of Attaway's *Blood on the Forge* seems doomed to failure. Attaway conveys as much in Big Mat and Melody Moss's response to the arrival of a new trainload of southern black migrants late in the novel:

Through the things under their vision they sensed the relationship of themselves to the trouble in the mills. They knew all of those men herded in the black cars. For a minute they were those men—bewildered and afraid in the dark, coming from hate into a new kind of hate. . . . And the Negroes were grouped sullenly around the leaders of the moment. They were here for four dollars a day and a chance to fight with white men. They did not care what the issue. (224–25)

Hence, the legacy of southern racism tends to generate mistrust of interracial coalition building among recent African American migrants to the industrial North. In the words of a white local sheriff, "Always be like that, I guess, as long as they come from the South . . . an' that there's one reason why the union ain't gonna win" (289). In addition, African American workers seem quite susceptible to the arguments of company-sponsored black spokesmen, who point out—with considerable validity (particularly in the World War I–era context of Attaway's novel)—the woeful record of American labor unions in looking out for the interests of African American workers (226–27). The repeated attacks experienced by the Moss brothers at the hands of the families of their Slavic coworkers hardly helps to reverse this pattern. Especially when coupled with the novel's closing imagery of the blinded African American soldier and a blinded Chinatown, the shortsightedness of Slavic union members and African American steelworkers like Big Mat with regard to the interlocking nature of race and class oppression suggests that a lack of vision is the leitmotiv of Attaway's collective portrait of America's working classes.

Likewise, I have already attested to the fact that even Communist Party member Richard Wright chose to accord a striking *lack* of political consciousness to the protagonist of his first full-length novel, *Lawd Today!* To be sure, the self-centered Jake Jackson and his fellow African American postal employees seem highly attuned to the ways in which racism constrains their lives. As Jake's friend Bob poses the question, "You ever hear of an uncle treating his nephews like Uncle Sam treats us?" (130). More specifically, the group later collectively laments Chicago's practices of housing segregation, overcharging African American tenants, and bombing black families who attempt to change these prevailing patterns (172). By the same token, Jake and his coworkers take pride in African American heroes who symbolically defeat the white world (such as boxing champions Jack Johnson and Joe Louis), providing a way for these working-class black men to say, "[L]et them white folks chew that" (169–71). Yet, Wright seems to suggest that because his protagonist's anger is attuned to issues of race to the exclusion of class consciousness, Jake can formulate no meaningful way of transforming his circumstances. Thus, after a vehement and racially charged argument with a white supervisor, Wright describes Jake's response:

> Out of the corner of his eye Jake saw the inspector standing at the end of the aisle, watching. He bent his head lower and threw his mail faster. *You sonofabitch! It ain't always going to be this way!* His mind went abruptly blank. He could not keep on with that thought, because he did not know where that thought led. He did not know of any other way things could be, if not *this* way. Yet he longed for them *not* to be this way. . . . And the feeling that he could do nothing doubled back upon him, fanning the ashes of other dead feelings of not being able to do anything, and he was consumed in a fever of bitterness. (142–43)

Even more, I have argued that, for Wright, extreme race nationalism bore a discomforting resemblance to the fascistic nationalisms that were gaining increasing power in Europe by the mid-1930s. Hence, Jake's thoughts of revenge against his postal supervisor, and white America more generally, take shape as a fantasy of black imperial conquest along the lines of Garveyite symbolism:

> *Yeah, some foreign country ought to whip this Gawddamn country! Some black country ought to do it!* He remembered the parade he had seen that morning. . . . He saw millions of black soldiers marching in black armies; he saw a black battleship flying a black

flag; he himself was standing on the deck of that black battleship surrounded by black generals; he heard a voice commanding: "FIRE!" *Boooooooom!* A black shell screamed through black smoke and he saw the white head of the Statue of Liberty topple, explode, and tumble into the Atlantic Ocean. . . . *Gawddamn right!* (143–44)

In effect, where artist John Wilson chose to render the Statue of Liberty as an icon of deeply conflicted sentiments for African Americans of the early 1940s in his painting *Black Soldier,* Wright's depression-era novel opts to portray a character almost wholly disaffected from this emblem of the promise of a democratically inclusive American society. Clearly, Wright's own political perspective regarding imperialism and fascism would render this fantasy neither practical nor entirely desirable, as much as the author might empathize with the *source* of his protagonist's frustrations. Again, then, one finds a case wherein a social realist artist and writer sharing similar political sensibilities opt for subtly, but significantly different portraits of the African American working class—with graphic artists such as Wilson gravitating toward portrayals of this group as deeply conflicted but resolute in their aims to strive for a more just society, while novelists like Wright tended to represent a vast majority of this group as teetering on the brink of utter disillusionment.

Given the fact that Wright himself first entered the literary circle of the John Reed Club through friendships that he established with white radical fellow writers like Abe Aaron at the Chicago post office, one might expect him to dramatize this type of interaction in *Lawd Today!* In fact, the Windy City's post office earned the nickname of "The University" because of the way in which it enabled many of the city's writers to support themselves and meet fellow intellectuals during the depression (Walker, *Richard Wright* 63). Yet, this intellectual contingent among Chicago's postal employees occupies only a fleeting and none too flattering place in protagonist Jake Jackson's consciousness:

> The white clerks got their hats and coats and hurried up the stairs. Many of them carried books under their arms; most of them were young students who regarded their jobs in the Post Office as something temporary to tide them through the University. Jake scowled as he watched their tense, eager faces. *Them white boys always in a hurry to get somewhere. And soon's they get out of school they's going to be bigshots. But a nigger just stays a nigger.* (117)

Moreover, one African American postal worker asserts, "Unions ain't nothing but a gyp game," while another notes, "Most Unions don't want no black members nohow" (132). Far from mirroring Wright's own politically empowering experience, then, Jake pursues a drastically different set of objectives: furthering his own material prosperity and social status; enjoying himself with bridge games, alcohol, and the pursuit of women; and physically and psychologically exerting a tyrannical authority over his wife, Lil. In striking contrast to the romantic workerism that I have described as typical of certain strains of depression-era visual art and poetry, Jake experiences his work routine as both mentally tedious and physically excruciating. Suggestively enough, Wright titles the section that describes Jake's work experience "Squirrel Cage," and his working title for the novel was *Cesspool* (Rampersad, "Foreword" v). Moreover, Jake seems to regard his unpleasant work routine with a sense of fatalism, as a torture to be endured rather than a situation capable of being transformed by the collective action of workers.

In comparison to the work of Attaway and Wright, Ann Petry's *The Street* (1946) offers a more complex portrait of class consciousness in Lutie Johnson, who recognizes the traps and hypocrisies of American Dream ideology and, yet, often embraces its seductive logic. Whereas Wright's Jake Jackson never manages to grasp the significance of his dream of running up an unending flight of stairs to answer the calling of "that guy who had a voice just like his boss" as a metaphor for the illusory promises of upward mobility (5–6), Petry's Lutie Johnson consciously wrestles with her conflicted sentiments regarding the rhetoric of meritocracy. While working as a domestic for the wealthy, white Chandler family in Lyme, Connecticut, "Lutie absorbed some of the same spirit. The belief that anybody could be rich if he wanted to and worked hard enough. . . . She and Jim could do the same thing, and she thought she saw what had been wrong with them before—they hadn't tried hard enough, worked long enough, saved enough" (43). After returning to New York, where she takes a job in a steam laundry to support herself and her son Bub while going to night school, Lutie applies this ethic to her own life with a vengeance: "Every time it seemed she couldn't possibly summon the energy to go on with the course, she would remind herself of all the people who had got somewhere in spite of the odds against them. She would think of the Chandlers and their young friends—'It's the richest damn country in the world'" (55). At one point, Lutie even goes so far as to identify with one of the preeminent icons of entrepreneurial self-help among the nation's so-called founding fathers: "She couldn't help thinking that if Ben Franklin could live on a little bit of money and could prosper, then so could she" (64).[54] Clearly, Franklin is not a figure who turns up in the historical imagery of many social realist murals, which bears remarking in that it suggests a fundamental difference in strategies between social realists operating in these two divergent media. Muralists tended to memorialize historical instances of oppression and resistance as allegories for contemporary sociopolitical struggle; novelists, by contrast, operated via an intense scrutiny of the interior consciousness of contemporary poor and working-class individuals—often essaying a quite critical appraisal, as in Petry's portrait of Lutie Johnson.

At certain moments, Lutie turns a more cynical and bitterly ironic eye on Franklinesque uplift ideology, as when she reflects on the type of housing available to working-class African Americans: "Dirty, dark, filthy traps. . . . Click goes the trap when you pay the first month's rent. Walk right in. *It's a free country.* Dark little hallways. Stinking toilets" (73, my emphasis). On another occasion, in imagery reminiscent of Wright's *Lawd Today!* Lutie senses her struggle to climb the socioeconomic ladder as comparable to "running around a small circle, around and around like a squirrel in a cage," and reflects that, "Streets like the one she lived on were no accident. They were the North's lynch mobs" (323). Likewise, to musician Boots Smith's callous assertion that "[t]here's plenty of money to be made in Harlem if you know how," Lutie replies sarcastically, "Sure. . . . It's on the trees and bushes. All you have to do is shake them" (154). Yet, despite these and other moments in which Lutie recognizes the ways in which factors of race, class, and gender constrain one's ability to access America's promises of upward mobility, her thinking does not undergo a linear progression toward class consciousness. Rather, Petry suggests that a principal flaw of her protagonist is the way in which Lutie inconsistently oscillates between critique and acceptance of the rhetoric of American meritocracy, ultimately tending to return to some variation of this same seductive bootstraps optimism. Consequently, Lutie repeatedly chastises *herself* and her own family for her impoverished circumstances. Even late in the novel, the reader finds, "Lutie thought of the Chandlers and their friends in Lyme. They were right about people being able to make money, but it took hard, grinding work to do it—hard work and self-sacrifice. She was capable of both, she concluded" (315). Notably, her zealous adherence to this ethic also leads her to berate her small son Bub for creating extra strain on their budget in minor acts such as leaving on a light or leaving soap in a bowl of water (317)—as if only such "extravagant" behavior prevented them from saving enough money to move to a safer, more affluent neighborhood.

One should note, of course, that if Lutie remains somewhat invested in the American ideology of meritocracy, one of Petry's primary ambitions as author clearly is to debunk the hollowness of this rhetoric. Indeed, Petry stresses Lutie's adherence to this rhetoric precisely in order to show that even a talented and hard-working person cannot always overcome the confluence of prohibitive environmental, racial, and class constraints that confronts most urban, working-class African Americans (Ivy 48–49). Significantly, too, even though Lutie is an ambitious woman with admirable goals—such as finding a safe, supportive place in which her son can grow up—her plans do not encompass anything resembling a collective working-class context.

Clearly, neither Attaway's Moss brothers, Wright's Jake Jackson, nor even Petry's Lutie Johnson exactly fits the mold of radical, class-conscious proletarians. However, there are exceptions on this front, and the most notable instance in the period under study is Lloyd Brown's *Iron City*, with its CP-led campaign to save the life of Lonnie James. Still, one should note that even Brown, a CP member and an editor of *Masses and Mainstream* at the time of the novel's publication, does not depict a uniformly progressive working-class prison population. In one poignant scene, CP member Paul Harper smuggles out information through a coded conversation with his wife, even as Brown juxtaposes the Harpers' conversation with fragments of a vituperative quarrel between an anonymous white prisoner and his mother (170–72). So too, the prison certainly has its snitches and other forms of corruption, as exemplified by the rangeman who attempts to bully and swindle his fellow inmates until he receives a severe beating at their hands. Ultimately, though, the apparent success of the Lonnie James campaign depends not only on CP members (and their wives and friends outside the prison) but also on the progressive impulses and cooperation of noncommunist prisoners like Slim Gaither, who risks his own impending release to aid Lonnie's cause. Thus, while Brown joins his peers in suggesting the fallibility of the CP, he parts company with a majority of his contemporaries by depicting the party as being composed primarily of sincere and self-reflexive working-class members.

In a similar vein, Motley's hopes about the relative political progressiveness of America's ethnic minorities and working classes is evident in the fact that the last jury members to concede the guilty verdict that sends *Knock on Any Door*'s Nick Romano to the electric chair are a Jewish social worker and a white truck driver. By comparison, the middle-class and professional members of this jury appear decidedly more conservative. Equally notable are the heroic strikers of Motley's *We Fished All Night:* Jim Norris in his more noble moments, as well as minor characters like the "rebel girl" and working mother, Edna, and the dyed-in-the-wool union supporter, O'Keefe. On the whole, however, Motley, Attaway, Petry, and Wright tend to portray America's poor and working classes, both black and white, as far from being on the verge of the type of interracial, collective social movement anticipated by many depression-era radical theorists, social realist poets, and a novel such as Lloyd Brown's *Iron City*.

The overarching question raised by these ambivalent representations, then, is why each of these writers, whose own political sensibilities were certainly leftist, chose to depict America's poor and working classes in decidedly less than optimistic terms—especially given that the vision of an interracially unified and politically mobilized working class was dramatized in many contemporaneous works of social realist theater, poetry, and visual art. One partial explanation might reside in an issue of media, for while iconic imagery may at times prove effective in visual media or poetry, such symbolically and morally weighted modes of characterization (for example, the wholly heroic worker, the irredeemably evil capitalist) do not lend themselves in the same way to a novelistic narrative, which typically must sustain the activities of a particular set of characters over time. Or, at least one might argue that such an iconic approach to characterization has seldom resulted in compelling fiction. Whatever the full range of reasons why this trend evolved, African American novelists of the social realist school obviously were more interested in displaying members of the working classes as they perceived them in the present moment, flaws and virtues alike, than in attempting to delineate a prophetic vision of "wish-fulfillment," to use Rideout's term. Specifically, it is by now clear that these authors offered at least an implicit critique of: (1) the failure of leftists to attain in practice the full democratic inclusiveness promised in their rhetoric and/or to effectively communicate their message to America's working classes; and (2) the insufficiently radicalized—indeed, sometimes reactionary—character of working-class consciousness among many African Americans and their peers.

It is also clear that African American authors were hardly unique in revising the doctrinaire prescriptions espoused in certain of the more infamous theoretical statements issued by the John Reed Clubs, *New Masses*, and other leftist organs. In fact, one might argue that this quality of ambivalence toward communist politics and workerist proletarian formulas—shared with influential authors such as John Steinbeck, John Dos Passos, and even Jack Conroy to an extent—positions the social realist novels of these African American authors firmly *within* an evolving literary tradition of U.S. social realism. After all, while each of these authors substantially explored the lives of working-class protagonists in his or her writing, none of them simply grafted an economic or political theory onto the lives of two-dimensional protagonists in a routine or entirely predictable way. Rather, these novelists were very much in tune with the spirit of poet Sterling Brown's injunction to cultural workers at the second annual meeting of the National Negro Congress in 1937:

> Those artists who are struggling to portray a changing world and, in their own way, to speed that change—are having no easy time. The misery, and tragedy that they must include in their portrait of the real America, are unwelcome to the many readers who want as slick a reality as the paper of the magazine they read. . . . The Negro social realist, like his brothers, will be confronted by these problems. But the Negro artist who will be worth his salt must join with those who are recording a world of injustice and exploitation, a world that must be changed. ("Problems" n.p.)

However unwelcome, African American novelists proved willing to confront readers not only with the "misery and tragedy" referenced by Brown but also with even more disquieting doubts regarding the tenability of the social realist project itself. Contrary to the assertions of subsequent cold war–inflected critiques like

Rideout's, African American social realists took up their important cultural work with eyes squarely trained on the considerable gulf that separated their visionary ideals from contemporary American realities. Whether works of literature or more direct activist engagement could ultimately bridge this divide most African American authors left open to question, but what their novels did seem to suggest is that an intensive self-critique of the left and of America's working classes themselves would prove an essential first step to any such transformations.

Coda:
The Legacy of African American Social Realism

In mural paintings, graphic arts, poetry, and novels, African American cultural workers operating between the onset of the depression and the cold war years of the early 1950s sustained profound engagements with both black cultural traditions and social realism. Indeed, they not only derived inspiration from social realism but also actively helped to *shape* the thematic and aesthetic contours of this movement. It seems certain, for instance, that the theme of racial justice occupied such a central place in U.S. social realist art and literature due in no small part to the activity of the cultural workers documented in this study. Even more, of course, African American artists and writers contributed to social realism by exploring issues such as poverty, legal injustice, labor organizing, and the politics of antifascism. To overlook the full range of this body of cultural work is to render an inadequate portrait of both U.S. social realism and African American cultural history. Conversely, to rediscover the type of work discussed here is, of necessity, to expand both the chronological and thematic parameters of American social realism and to recapture a vital chapter in the history of African American arts and letters.

Among the lessons offered by the preceding study of African American social realism, three bear special emphasis. First, one contribution of this study has been to document the ways in which African American artists and writers sustained an engagement with the themes and aesthetics of social realism well beyond the conventional periodization of this movement as a phenomenon more or less limited to the depression decade. In fact, readers versed in African American art and literature might even question my rationale for bounding the endpoint of this study with the rather untidy date of 1953. And well they should. My choice of this date stems in no small part from a practical concern: that is, to ac-

302

commodate texts and works of art from the early 1950s that I consider crucial to driving home a fundamental point regarding the endurance of African American social realism into the very heart of the cold war period. Still, I do not feel particularly invested in making any special claims for this as a definitive periodization of African American social realism. And I say this not simply to abscond from the task of analyzing the unraveling of the movement. After all, I do set the parameters of my study in this manner due to a sense that by midcentury the sheer volume and relative visibility of social realist cultural work was diminishing appreciably. The rise to prominence of poetry such as *Annie Allen* (1949) by Gwendolyn Brooks, the first African American winner of a Pulitzer prize, and a novel such as *Invisible Man* (1952) by Ralph Ellison, the recipient of a National Book Award, as well as the increasing shift toward abstraction by artists of social realism such as Charles Alston and Hale Woodruff collectively serve as signposts that African American literature and visual art *were* gravitating in a qualitatively new direction—one still vastly understudied but clearly stemming from a heightened engagement with American high modernism and "universalist" impulses.

That said, however, I feel it important to stress that ultimately my periodization remains as arbitrary as any other. One could well make a case, for example, that this sort of project should include discussion of works such as Frank London Brown's *Trumbull Park,* a novel not published until 1959. Likewise, even with regard to the figures whom I do feature in this study, Willard Motley went on to publish two further novels—*Let No Man Write My Epitaph* (1958) and *Let Noon Be Fair* (1966)—stylistically consistent with the texts that I do include here; Frank Marshall Davis continued his activist role in poetry and especially journalism following his 1948 move to Hawaii via the *Honolulu Record,* a newspaper sponsored by the local chapter of the Longshoreman's Union; Langston Hughes's posthumously published *The Panther and the Lash* (1967) reprised many of his radical poems of the depression era with a new articulation to the political concerns of the 1960s; John Wilson returned to the United States from Mexico in 1956 and completed several graphics for labor-oriented publications like the *Packinghouse Worker;* John Biggers completed a mural for the local Longshoreman's Union of Houston, Texas, in 1956–57; and Elizabeth Catlett has continued to produce radical lithographs and linocuts into the present moment. So too, figures such as Catlett, Davis, and Charles White helped to influence many of those African American cultural workers who forged the Black Arts Movement of the 1960s and early 1970s in ways that have yet to be fully examined.

As should be apparent from the preceding chapters, my sense is that what matters more than the precise dates by which one marks African American engagement with social realism is establishing a clearer understanding of how and why the movement emerged when it did, *and* how and why so many African American cultural workers maintained a steadfast allegiance to this brand of art and literature to a significantly greater degree than the majority of their peers. To explore these matters is, at least implicitly, to make a broader point that should by now be axiomatic: scholars and teachers need to move away from "one movement at a time" models, which permit only one major player onto the field of American culture for a given period—often marked conveniently by decades in the study of twentieth-century visual arts and literature (i.e., the Harlem Renaissance as a movement neatly bounded within the "Roaring Twenties," social realism as a phenomenon of the depression decade, and so forth). Although we know the fallacies of such neatly drawn chronologies as a matter of fact, in actual scholarly and pedagogic practice such models nonetheless often prove remarkably seductive. So although I concentrate here on social realism as a predominant focus of African American art and literature of the 1930s and 1940s, it bears emphasizing that this should in no way obscure the importance of work by writers such as Zora Neale Hurston and artists such as Romare Bearden, the vast majority of whose work during the period does not fall under even a broadly construed notion of social realism. It is to the credit of a scholar like William Maxwell, for example, that he draws attention to the *connections* between the novels of Hurston and the early fiction of Richard Wright, without gainsaying the oft-noted rhetorical antagonism between these two literary giants. By the same token, John Edgar Tidwell aptly notes that social realist verse comprises only one facet of the wide-ranging poetry of Frank Marshall Davis, whose broader corpus also includes jazz poetry, social satire, and lyric and love poetry ("Introduction" xxiii). One could well make a similar point with respect to a majority of the figures considered in this study. Further, scholarship such as Michael Denning's *The Cultural Front* provides a useful reminder of the diversity of issues and aesthetic styles that occupied the pages of even left-leaning periodicals such as *Art Front* and *New Masses* during the period under study. Put simply, these and most other leftist publications proved extremely supportive of social realism but eschewed championing it as the *exclusive* direction to which all politically engaged artists and writers should subscribe. Vigilance on this point, I would suggest, is worth our while. As this study has demonstrated, perhaps nowhere does the "one movement at a time" brand of academic common sense distort the historical record more than in the case of social realism in African American art and literature—acting, as it does, to obfuscate an entire decade of social realist cultural production that stretches roughly from the U.S. entry into World War II to the early 1950s.

A second overarching point that I hope emerges from this study is that social realist cultural workers created a shared movement that extended beyond conventional disciplinary boundaries. Recognizing the way in which common themes such as racial justice, labor organizing, and antifascism surface consistently in mural paintings, graphic arts, poetry, and novels should encourage scholars to pay more attention to both the similarities *and* the nuanced differences in how cultural workers address such themes across divergent media. Identifying the sheer pervasiveness of lynching imagery in works of graphic art and poetry, for example, should open up possibilities for better understanding not only why but also *how* cultural workers of this period deployed the iconography of racial violence to articulate a wide range of social and political concerns—not least, the instrumental use of racism as a tool of class control and the perils of an incipient fascism taking shape on the U.S. home front. At the same time, the differences between, say, the "Double V" style call to arms voiced in Langston Hughes's poem "Freedom Road" and the bitter disillusionment visualized in John Biggers's *Dying Soldier* mural can help to broaden our picture of the range of responses articulated by U.S. citizens with respect to the prospect of African American soldiers' participation in World War II and the vexing societal hypocrisies attendant to this watershed historical moment. Moreover, I would hope that this study invites further interdisciplinary research that will address the work being done in African American film, drama, and music of the 1930s and 1940s in relation to the artistic and literary media that I have discussed here.

As a necessary corollary to such interdisciplinary work, it is essential to recognize that African American social realists did not attempt to realize their objectives of forging a politically progressive "people's culture" by operating as individuals in isolation from one another. Quite to the contrary, direct personal contacts and concrete institutional networks catalyzed the initial flourishing of U.S. social realism during the 1930s and proved essential to its continued vitality among African American cultural workers during the 1940s and early 1950s. Even with all of the reasons that African Americans had to sustain a cultural critique with respect to matters of economic and racial justice throughout the 1940s, social realist artists and writers would have proven much less successful in accessing an audience for their work were it not for enabling agents such as the Rosenwald Foundation; the Harlem and South Side Community Art Centers; sympathetic colleges and universities like Talladega and Hampton; little magazines such as *Negro Story, Common Ground,* and *Masses and Mainstream;* and the Esmeralda and Taller de Gráfica Popular in Mexico City. Ultimately the labor of crafting visual art and literature tends to be a task completed by individuals, and this proved true with most works of social realism as well. Yet, it is also clearly the case that African American cultural workers initiated and sustained their respective engagements with social realism in terms of a genuine sense of shared purpose that extended well beyond mere lip service to a collectivist ethic. In shared exhibition spaces, in the pages of progressive little magazines, and occasionally in picket lines, African American social realists did, in a concrete sense, stand shoulder to shoulder with their fellow cultural workers and with members of America's poor and working classes more broadly. Nor are such patterns historically unique to social realism, for one could readily document the vital role played by similar institutional matrices and cross-disciplinary influences among those artists and writers of the 1960s and 1970s who together drew inspiration from and contributed to the multifaceted social struggles for African American civil rights, for women's liberation, and to end U.S. involvement in the Vietnam War—to say nothing of the revival of mural painting in several U.S. cities during this same period.

Finally, it should be apparent that—like both their Harlem Renaissance forebears and their descendants in the Black Arts Movement—African American social realists believed intensely that *cultural work does matter.* As White articulated his credo in a 1955 essay for *Masses and Mainstream,* "My major concern is to get my work before common, ordinary people, for me to be accepted as a spokesman for my people, for my work to portray them better, and to be rich and meaningful to them. A work of art was meant to belong to the people, not to be a single person's private possession. Art should take its place as one of the necessities of life, like food, clothing and shelter" ("Path" 36). Driven by a similar ethic, Elizabeth Catlett was still urging fellow artists in 1961, "Let us take our paintings and prints and sculpture not only to Atlanta University, to the art galleries, and to patrons of the arts who have money to buy them; let us exhibit where Negro people meet—in the churches, in the schools and universities, in the associations and clubs and trade unions" (Samella Lewis 99). Indeed, artists and writers engaged with the Black Arts Movement, the women's movement, and the antiwar movement during the 1960s and 1970s quite often did precisely this. That, of course, is another story. Here, I simply want to suggest that the conviction expressed by White, Catlett, and so many of their contemporaries with regard to the *crucial* societal importance of artistic and literary expression may ultimately comprise the most significant legacy of African American social realism. And it is not mere rhapsodizing to point out that the accomplishments of the cultural workers discussed in this study continue to inspire numerous novelists, poets, visual artists, dramatists, dancers, musicians, and students, reminding us that the social realist art and literature produced by African Americans between 1930 and the early 1950s can continue to perform important cultural work in our own day.

Notes

Chapter 1. Expressing the Life and Cause of the Masses: Ideologies and Institutions

1. For a representative statement of this position, see Allen, *Negro*.

2. See, for example, Record, *Negro;* Howe and Coser, *American Communist Party;* Aaron, *Writers;* and Cruse, *Crisis*. For a concise rejoinder to such texts, see Foley 15–29.

3. All citations of Cunard's anthology are from the 1970 reprint edition of *Negro;* although reduced in size from the original volume, this is the version most likely to be available to contemporary readers.

4. The Tom Mooney and Scottsboro cases both became celebrated causes on the American left during the depression. Mooney was a labor organizer who had been framed for a 1916 San Francisco bombing. He was imprisoned for more than twenty years, until his pardon in the late 1930s by progressive California governor Culbert Olsen (Denning 18). The nine "Scottsboro Boys" were arrested and convicted for the alleged rape of two white prostitutes in Alabama under highly dubious circumstances in 1933. Both the Communist Party and the NAACP took up this latter case as a blatant example of racial inequality in the American justice system through a protracted series of legal appeals. For more on the Scottsboro Boys, see D. Carter.

5. The latter exhibit was cosponsored by, among other CP organizations, the League of Struggle for Negro Rights, of which Langston Hughes was the president (Park 322–24, 338–50).

6. An African American cause célèbre among depression-era leftists second only to the trials of the Scottsboro Boys, Angelo Herndon was sentenced to death under a nineteenth-century Georgia antisedition law for "incitement to riot" before a celebrated appeal secured his release. Herndon himself became a prominent member of the Communist Party following his trial.

7. For a fuller story of the New Deal programs in visual art, see McKinzie and Marling.

8. Charles Alston, interview by Harlan Phillips, Archives of American Art, September 28, 1965.

9. Ibid.

10. Charles White, interview by Betty Hoag, Archives of American Art, March 9, 1965.

11. For more on the Federal Writers' Project, see Mangione.

12. One can find documentation of specific American Artists' Congress campaigns of this sort in the pages of *The American Artist,* a quarterly news bulletin published beginning in 1937. For a detailed account of the kinds of activities carried out by politically engaged writers during this period, see Folsom.

13. Minutes of the 1937 American Artists' Congress, AAC papers, Archives of American Art; "A League of American Artists," *Art Front* 2, no. 5 (April 1936): 3.

14. The IWO originally emerged from a subculture of Jewish socialism, but by 1940 it had evolved into a multiethnic fraternal benefit society of some 165,000 members (Denning 74–75).

15. Nicola Sacco and Bartolomeo Vanzetti were Italian-born anarchists and labor activists who were tried and convicted on what many took to be trumped up charges of armed robbery and murder. (Judge Thayer, who presided over their trial, openly told the press— as the trial was ongoing—that he would not rest until Sacco and Vanzetti were put to death.) Their trial drew substantial protests and national notoriety, but nonetheless they were sentenced to death in the electric chair in 1927.

16. Margaret Burroughs, interviews by Anna Tyler, Archives of American Art, November 11 and December 5, 1988.

17. In 1943, White was drafted and subsequently served eighteen months in the U.S. Army, where he was assigned to a series of decidedly unaesthetic tasks in the army's camouflage division in Missouri. During the planning stages of a mural for his station's mess hall—his first truly artistic endeavor in the military—White became ill while working with fellow soldiers to combat a flood, which led to his contracting tuberculosis and being given a medical discharge. Complications from the tuberculosis resulted in the loss of one of his lungs.

18. *Contemporary American Art* exhibition brochure, Charles White papers, Archives of American Art. Directed by Herman Baron and operated on a collective basis, the ACA Gallery hosted many important exhibitions and sales for Artists' Union members and other politically engaged artists from its founding in 1931 onward (Horowitz 20; Shapiro 26).

19. The Charles White papers at the Archives of American Art document these and other activities from White's Soviet travels.

20. Other Rosenwald Fellowship recipients between 1932 and the fund's discontinuation in 1948 included Charles Alston, Hale Woodruff, Langston Hughes, Sterling Brown, Margaret Walker, Robert Hayden, Chester Himes, Arna Bontemps, Owen Dodson, Zora Neale Hurston, Ralph Ellison, James Baldwin, Jacob Lawrence, and Gordon Parks, as well as dancers Pearl Primus and Katherine Dunham (Bone 457–60).

21. As scholarship, novels, and even a feature film have reminded audiences in recent

years, the *Amistad* was a slave ship overtaken in a revolt by its captives in 1839. When the ship came to port in the United States a trial ensued, the end result of which was the emancipation of the *Amistad* slaves and an arrangement for their "return" to Sierra Leone in 1841. For Woodruff's own summary of the *Amistad* incident, see Locke, *Negro in Art*.

22. Thompson served as an organizer and officer of the IWO beginning in 1933 (see also Thompson 327–28). In 1940, she was elected a vice president of the organization, as documented by a notice appearing in the September 1940 issue of the *Crisis*.

23. Charles Alston, interview by Harlan Phillips, Archives of American Art, September 28, 1965.

24. For statements about the Harlem Artists' Guild and the Harlem Community Art Center from participating artists, see G. Bennett 20; "Harlem Artists' Guild" 4–5; and Hayes 210–12.

25. Among Woodruff's more noted Atlanta students were Wilmer Jennings, Vernon Winslow, Robert Neal, and Frederick Flemister. With the aid of fellow teachers such as Elizabeth Prophet, Woodruff thus helped to train a new generation of art teachers who went on to serve as instructors at some fifteen schools, including Dillard, Tuskegee, Bennett, and Jackson College.

26. The connections between African American and Mexican visual art are documented most extensively in LeFalle-Collins and Goldman and Herzog.

27. The Ingram case stemmed from an incident in which a white farmer threatened the widow Ingram with a shotgun. In defense of their mother, Mrs. Ingram's teenage sons, Wallace and Sammie, fought with the farmer, who died from a blow sustained to the head. An all-white jury quickly sentenced Mrs. Ingram and her sons to the electric chair in 1947 (E. Nelson 16–19). For more on the Trenton Six, see the discussion of related graphic artwork by Charles White in chapter 3.

28. One can find a reproduction of this work in the Charles Alston papers, Archives of American Art.

29. This poem appeared in the spring 1942 issue of *Negro Quarterly*, 40. Eugene Talmadge was first elected governor of Georgia in 1932 and proved an outspoken opponent of Roosevelt's New Deal, trade unions, and racial integration. He was reelected to office three more times before his death in 1946; in the course of his final election campaign, Talmadge encouraged rampant Ku Klux Klan terrorism to deter African American voters from going to the polls.

30. For discussion of the "living newspapers" and similarly innovative Federal Theatre Project productions, see Flanagan.

31. Although the details surrounding the Rockefeller Center incident are far from clear, the crux of the controversy centered around the Rockefeller family's decision to curtail—and later destroy—Rivera's mural because it included a heroic image of Lenin joining the hands of a multiracial cast of American workers. For a more detailed account of the *Man at the Crossroads* controversy, see Hurlburt 162–68.

32. Gwendolyn Brooks enjoyed success in this regard as well, of course, following her first publication, *A Street in Bronzeville*, in 1945.

33. Although *Lawd Today!* was published only posthumously in 1963, Arnold Ram-

persad concludes that Wright completed this first novel by 1935 ("Foreword" xiii). I will refer to the 1940 edition of Wright's *Uncle Tom's Children*, as it includes the important novella *Bright and Morning Star*, which was not a part of the earlier 1938 edition.

Among other novels of note that could merit consideration in this study are George Washington Lee's *River George* (1937); Chester Himes's *If He Hollers Let Him Go* (1945), *Lonely Crusade* (1947), and *Cast the First Stone* (1952); William Gardner Smith's *Last of the Conquerors* (1948) and *Anger at Innocence* (1950); William Demby's *Beetlecreek* (1950); Frank London Brown's *Trumbull Park* (1959); and, perhaps most notably, Wright's *Native Son*. Most of these I have omitted simply to keep the scale of this study manageable. In the case of *Native Son*, I have opted to focus attention on the two less frequently discussed Wright texts noted above, rather than simply retrace ground already well covered by the vast amount of extant scholarship on this novel.

Chapter 2. Articulating History to the Radical Present: Murals

1. George Biddle, interview by Harlan Phillips, Archives of American Art, 1963.

2. Charles Alston, interview by Harlan Phillips, Archives of American Art, September 28, 1965.

3. One can find a reproduction of Benton's *Politics and Agriculture* in Dennis 46.

4. For further discussion of the Coit Tower murals, see McKinzie 24–32, Contreras 44–46, and Marling 45–49. For a gloss of Guston's Scottsboro-themed murals, see Park 359. For details regarding Ishigaki's Harlem Courthouse murals, see McKinzie 111 and Kalaidjian 181–82.

5. One can find a reproduction of Rivera's reconstructed version of the *Man at the Crossroads* mural, *Man, Controller of the Universe* (painted for the Palacio de Bella Artes in Mexico City 1934), in Rochfort 134–35.

6. *General Report of the Mexican Delegation to the American Artists' Congress*, published as a pamphlet by the ACA Gallery in 1936: AAC papers, Archives of American Art. See also "The Mexican Congress Reports," *Art Front* 3, nos. 3–4 (April–May 1937): 13–14.

7. One can find reproductions of both Rivera murals mentioned here in LeFalle-Collins and Goldman 106, 108.

8. One can find a reproduction of Siqueiros's *Portrait of the Bourgeoisie* mural in the color plates gathered at the front of Hurlburt.

9. For a detailed scholarly account of the *Portrait of America* murals and the circumstances of their production, see Hurlburt 175–93. One can find reproductions of most of the murals from this series, including *The New Freedom*, in Rivera and Wolfe.

10. Notes for a lecture titled "Role of Negro Art in the Negro Liberation movement" (c. 1945), John Wilson papers, Archives of American Art.

11. Charles White, interview by Betty Hoag, Archives of American Art, March 9, 1965.

12. Ibid. See also Motley, "Negro Art" 22.

13. As LeFalle-Collins writes of this pamphlet, "The language and writing style in this booklet suggest that it may have been 'ghost written' by a more mature member of the

Communist Party and attributed to White" ("Contributions" 41). The basic point regarding White's party participation remains valid in either case.

14. Charles White, interview by Betty Hoag.

15. Ibid.

16. See White's autobiographical notes for an unidentified fellowship application (c. 1946), Charles White papers, Archives of American Art.

17. Horowitz 14–15; Charles White, interview by Betty Hoag.

18. Siporin, in fact, had worked on murals with Orozco and Rivera (LeFalle-Collins and Goldman 55). One can find a reproduction of *Susan B. Anthony* from Millman's *Women's Contribution to American Progress* mural series in Contreras 185.

19. In a 1994 article, Anna Tyler lists Archibald Motley Jr. as a charter member of this group (31), but I have found no mention of Motley in this context in the recollections of either Charles White or Margaret Burroughs.

20. Margaret Burroughs, interviews by Anna Tyler, Archives of American Art, November 11 and December 5, 1988; Charles White, interview by Karl Fortess, Archives of American Art, April 8, 1969; Charles White, interview by Betty Hoag; Locke, "Chicago's New Southside" 372–73.

21. In keeping with established policy, the FAP paid salaries and related expenses to staff the center once the community itself arranged for the purchase of an appropriate building. Ironically, the trend of "white flight" from Chicago's expanding black neighborhoods of the South Side enabled artists to purchase the SSCAC facility for a remarkably low price (Tyler 31–35). See also Charles White, interview by Betty Hoag.

22. See especially Mullen's chapter "Artists in Uniform: The South Side Community Art Center and the Defense of Culture," 75–105.

23. Margaret Burroughs, interviews by Anna Tyler; Fitzgerald 159.

24. One can find a reproduction of White's *There Were No Crops This Year* in Locke, *Negro in Art* 121.

25. Charles White, interview by Betty Hoag.

26. "Art Today," *Daily Worker*, August 28, 1943.

27. Charles White, interview by Betty Hoag. See also autobiographical notes for an unidentified fellowship application (c. 1946), Charles White papers.

28. One can find a reproduction of White's *Five Great American Negroes* in the exhibition catalog *To Conserve a Legacy* (1999), where Powell and Reynolds present the mural with the title *Progress of the American Negro* (44). As this catalog documents, the recently restored mural currently belongs to the collection of the Howard University Art Gallery.

29. Charles White, interview by Betty Hoag.

30. Sidney Finkelstein, untitled essay for a German exhibition catalog, Charles White papers. One can find a reproduction of White's *History of the Negro Press* in Mullen ii–iii.

31. Interestingly, court officials protested that Ishigaki either alter or remove what they deemed the "Negroid features" of the artist's original Abraham Lincoln (McKinzie 111).

32. The Art Students' League also was where Catlett received her most important early training in lithography in 1944. She had studied graphic media with James Lasesne

Wells at Howard University, but this training had consisted primarily of work in linocuts and woodblock prints.

33. Charles White, interview by Karl Fortess, Archives of American Art, April 8, 1969. See also Charles White, interview by Betty Hoag.

34. Charles White, interview by Betty Hoag.

35. Ibid. See also Horowitz 18.

36. For example, a June 1940 *Crisis* notice on the American Negro Exposition in Chicago highlighted a project, under the supervision of William E. Scott, that aimed to produce a series of twenty-four murals depicting historical events and figures, such as the death of Crispus Attucks; Matthew Henson's trip to the north pole; a black boat pilot who accompanied Columbus; the building of the Sphinx and pyramids; early iron smelting in Africa; and seven murals depicting the participation of black soldiers in American wars. As a participant in the exposition, White almost certainly viewed these works—if, indeed, he did not actively participate in the project in some regard.

37. Although this may, in fact, not have been the case with Attucks, the popular history conception of Attucks as heroic martyr clearly is the one upon which White draws here.

38. One can find reproductions of Rivera's *Detroit Industry* murals in the color plates gathered at the front of Hurlburt.

39. One can find a reproduction of Orozco's *Allegory of Science, Labor, and Art* mural in LeFalle-Collins 102. A color study for Fogel's mural appears in Melosh (color plate 7, following p. 146).

40. Fran White's notes in the subject files of the Charles White papers at the Archives of American Art affirm her husband's long-standing interest in the music of Leadbelly.

41. Although *Contribution of the Negro to Democracy in America* was the last extant social realist mural White would complete in the period under study, he did work on a mural project with Ernest Crichlow for the Paul Robeson Recreational Center at Camp Wo-Chi-Ca (a leftist Workers' Children's Camp affiliated with the IWO) during the summer of 1947, but to date I have managed to locate only partially obscured photographs of one still-incomplete mural.

42. In addition to these firsthand experiences, five of White's own relatives—"2 uncles and 3 cousins over a long span of years," as he once explained—were lynched in Mississippi. And White himself was beaten by racists in Greenwich Village during the 1940s. Charles White, interview by Betty Hoag.

43. Charles Alston, interview by Harlan Phillips.

44. Ibid.

45. One can find a reproduction and discussion of Hayes's mural in Kalaidjian 181–82. One can find a reproduction of Seabrooke's *Recreation in Harlem* mural from this same project—which includes several city scenes emblematic of a spirit of interracial harmony—in Prigoff and Dunitz 50–51.

46. In addition, Alston's mural designs were exhibited publicly, along with the work of some thirty other Harlem Artists' Guild members, in Harlem's Dorrance Brooks Square. See "Art in Harlem."

47. Charles Alston, interview by Harlan Phillips.

48. Undated open letter by Alston, Charles Alston papers.

49. Charles Alston, interview by Harlan Phillips.

50. Charles Alston, interview by Albert Murray, Archives of American Art, October 19, 1968.

51. My comments regarding Locke's influence on Alston owe a significant debt to Gylbert Coker's essay "Charles Alston: The Legacy" in the Kenkeleba Gallery's exhibition catalog, *Charles Alston: Artist and Teacher* (1990). As Coker notes, the Fang reliquary figure also turns up in works such as Palmer Hayden's still-life painting *Fetiche et Fleurs* (1926) and Wilmer Jennings's 1937 wood engraving *Still Life* (10–11).

52. Charles Alston, interview by Albert Murray.

53. In writings and interview statements from the mid-1940s onward, Alston often rejected the label of "black art" as a segregationist and empirically fallacious concept.

54. Information on the historical figures and events depicted in Alston and Woodruff's Golden State murals derives from the artists' notes, Charles Alston papers, Archives of American Art.

55. Undated slide lecture notes regarding Wilson's mural *Incident,* John Wilson papers.

56. Notably, the second meeting of the National Negro Congress in 1937 passed a resolution to mount formal protests of derogatory representations of African Americans in Hollywood movies, radio, drama, and newspaper cartoon strips ("Cultural Session Resolutions").

57. Woodruff's papers at the Archives of American Art include extensive technical notes on fresco techniques dating from his period of study with Diego Rivera in 1936, as well as numerous sketches of distinctively Mexican people and landscapes.

58. For more on the *Amistad* case, see chapter 1, note 21.

59. Hale Woodruff, interview by Esther Rolick, Archives of American Art, November 10, 1970.

60. Specifically, Woodruff's *Amistad* murals were reproduced as a special color insert in *Phylon* 2, no. 1 (first quarter, 1941): 5–6. One also can find reproductions of Woodruff's *Amistad* murals in LeFalle-Collins and Goldman 171–73.

61. One can find reproductions of Woodruff's *Building the Library* and *Underground Railroad* in McDaniel 4, 9.

62. One can find a reproduction of Benton's *City Building* in Dennis 25.

63. After being drafted into the navy for an unpleasant stint of service between 1943 and 1945, Biggers went to Pennsylvania State in large part to rejoin his Hampton Institute mentor, Viktor Lowenfeld (Wardlaw, *Art* 33–34). One can find reproductions of *Harvest Song* and *Night of the Poor* in Wardlaw, *Art* 38, 119.

64. Biggers also executed an etching titled *Cotton Pickers* in the early 1950s that closely echoes the form of this tableau.

65. One can find a reproduction of Dix's *War* in Lucie-Smith 28.

66. Biggers's preliminary graphite sketches for the mural include a scene of two white soldiers committing a brutal rape against an African American woman. Although he chose

not to incorporate this sketch into the final mural, through this image Biggers seems to have intended to demystify the nobility of American soldiers and to reverse the rhetoric of white racist ideology regarding the alleged propensity of black men for raping white women. One can find a reproduction of Biggers's *Rape* sketch in Wardlaw, *Art* 130.

67. John Wilson, interviews by Robert Brown, Archives of American Art, March 11, 1993–August 16, 1994.

68. Ibid. See also Fax, *Seventeen* 45.

69. One can find a reproduction of Wilson's *Incident* in a photo insert between pages 82 and 83 in Fax, *Seventeen*.

70. Notes for a January 1990 talk at Tufts University, John Wilson papers.

Chapter 3. Chronicling the Contemporary Crisis: Graphic Art

1. Lee-Smith notes that critical attempts to categorize his work typically have employed terms such as "romantic realist," "magic realist," or "neo-surrealist." Hughie Lee-Smith, interview by Karl Fortess, Archives of American Art, February 14, 1973.

2. Charles Alston, interview by Albert Murray, Archives of American Art, October 19, 1968.

3. American Artists' Group statement of purpose, Louis Lozowick papers, Archives of American Art.

4. Margaret Burroughs, interviews by Anna Tyler, Archives of American Art, November 11 and December 5, 1988.

5. For more on Daumier, see Howard Vincent's richly illustrated *Daumier and His World* (1968).

6. One can find reproductions of Goya's *Disasters of War* series in the Dover Publications book of the same title.

7. Reproductions of these and other relevant works by Kollwitz are available in Nagel.

8. Charles White, interview by Betty Hoag, Archives of American Art, March 9, 1965.

9. Alston's cartoons appeared not only in leftist little magazines but also in publications such as *Redbook, Collier's,* the *New Yorker,* and *Fortune.* In fact, such commercial artwork enabled Alston to support himself financially, whereas he was typically able to sell only one or two of his works of fine art per year, for much more meager returns. Charles Alston, interview by Albert Murray.

10. Although the artists affiliated with *The Masses* generally allowed editors to attach captions to their graphics in the early years of the magazine, a desire to curtail this practice seems to have been part of the motive leading artists like John Sloan and Stuart Davis to distance themselves from the magazine by 1916 (Zurier 53–57).

11. White, letter to Sophie Gropper (c. 1977), Charles White papers, Archives of American Art.

12. Cary Nelson's rich archival work in *Repression and Recovery* (1989) remains the quintessential scholarly work on this topic.

13. John Wilson, interviews by Robert Brown, Archives of American Art, March 11, 1993–August 16, 1994. Unless otherwise noted, all ensuing quotations and information from Wilson in this chapter derive from this lengthy series of untranscribed interviews.

14. Wilson did not serve in the military because he was classified IV-F by his draft board in January 1943 due to a heart murmur.

15. Remarks prepared on the occasion of Crite's receiving the first Edward Mitchell Bannister Award from Boston's National Center of Afro-American Artists on March 21, 1976. See also Crite, letter to Wilson, March 1943, John Wilson papers, Archives of American Art.

16. Wilson, letter to Kay Cremin, 1946, Wilson papers. Cremin, a writer for *Ebony* magazine, had written to Wilson inquiring about the situation of black artists in the Boston area.

17. Notes for a lecture titled "Role of Negro Art in the Negro Liberation Movement" (c. 1945), Wilson papers.

18. In a 1945 letter, Locke thanks Wilson for the gift of an unspecified print and notes his hope of seeing Wilson on an upcoming trip to Boston. Alain Locke, letter to John Wilson, March 6, 1945, Wilson papers.

19. Winslow, letter to Wilson, August 17, 1955, Wilson papers. For a complete listing of Wilson's numerous awards from the Atlanta University shows, see Richard A. Long's exhibition catalog *Highlights from the Atlanta University Collection of Afro-American Art* (1973). During the period under study alone, Wilson received seven prizes from the Atlanta University annuals.

20. Untitled autobiographical sketch (1990), Wilson papers.

21. Barbara Melosh's *Engendering Culture* explores this issue at length with regard to New Deal theater and visual art.

22. It bears mentioning that Roosevelt issued this directive only after African American labor leader A. Philip Randolph promised to mobilize a massive "March on Washington" of one hundred thousand black workers on July 1, 1941, in protest of such segregation.

23. One can find a reproduction of Wilson's *Adolescence* in Reese 212.

24. Wilson, letter to Reese, October 26, 1947, Wilson papers.

25. Undated notes on work, Wilson papers.

26. Remarks prepared on the occasion of Crite's receiving the first Edward Mitchell Bannister Award from Boston's National Center of Afro-American Artists on March 21, 1976, Wilson papers.

27. *One Hundred Twentieth Century Prints* exhibition brochure, Wilson papers.

28. One can find reproductions of several of the murals from Orozco's *Epic of Civilization* in Mello and Miliotes 142–85; this same text also includes a 1933 version of the artist's *Hanging Negroes* lithograph (87).

29. One can find a reproduction of Wilson's *Native Son* in LeFalle-Collins and Goldman 161.

30. Virginia Shull (managing editor of *New Masses*), letter to John Wilson, December 13, 1944, Wilson papers.

31. Undated statement regarding "War Machine," Wilson papers.

32. One can find a reproduction of this Harrington illustration in Inge xxiv.

33. One can find a reproduction of Orozco's *The Rich Banquet While the Workers Fight* in Rochfort 43.

34. Barbara Foley points out that many proletarian novelists of the 1930s employed similar physical features to stress the moral corruption of villainous capitalists (345–46, 383–84, 391–92).

35. Charles Keller (art editor of *New Masses*), letter to John Wilson, July 12, 1946, Wilson papers. Incidentally, the winner of the *New Masses* contest was Charles White's Art Students' League mentor, Harry Sternberg.

36. Wilson also received a B.S. in Education from Tufts University in 1947 through a joint program between Tufts and the Museum School.

37. Smith, letter to Wilson, July 27, 1948, Wilson papers. See also Fax, "John Wilson" 94.

38. Untitled autobiographical sketch (1990), Wilson papers. See also Faxon 4-A.

39. Untitled autobiographical sketch (1990), Wilson papers. *Blvd. de Strasbourg* was featured in the exhibit *Alone in a Crowd* but did not appear in the accompanying catalog.

40. John Wilson, interview by Phyllis Reddick, Archives of American Art, July 15, 1978.

41. Untitled autobiographical sketch (1990), Wilson papers.

42. One can find a reproduction of Wilson's *Trabajador* in LeFalle-Collins and Goldman 164.

43. Wilson has recalled that his mentor at the Boston Museum School, Karl Zerbe, would sometimes show him the work of prestigious social realists of the day—including works by Gwathmey in particular—and tell him, "[Y]ou could do this."

44. All of the Wilson quotations regarding *The Trial* derive from the artist's notes for a January 1990 talk at Tufts University, Wilson papers.

45. Winslow, letter to Wilson, August 17, 1955, Wilson papers.

46. "Ten Months of Action: A Report on the National and Regional Activities of the Independent Citizens Committee of the Arts, Sciences and Professions." Jo Davidson, correspondence to John Wilson, May 16, 1945, Wilson papers.

47. Exhibition brochure, Prentiss Taylor papers, Archives of American Art. One can find a reproduction of Taylor's *Scottsboro Limited* in Haskell 275.

48. Bellows originally crafted this lithograph to accompany a short story by Mary Johnston titled "Nemesis" in *Century Magazine,* specifically the text that read, "One of the four men lighted the pile, the cane blazed up, and the night turned red and horribly loud—like hell" (Park 319–21; Vendryes 166–67). For a brief overview of the Ashcan School, see Haskell 61–93.

49. It is worth noting that the John Reed Clubs, Louise Thompson's Vanguard group, and other CP-affiliated organizations cosponsored a rival exhibition titled *The Struggle for Negro Rights*, for which Charles Alston served as one of the sponsors (Park 338, 361). Yet, in terms of participation by African American artists and relative impact in the art world, the NAACP exhibit seems to have been decidedly more significant.

50. One can find reproductions of these and several other works from the *Art Commentary on Lynching* exhibit in Park and Vendryes.

51. One can find a reproduction of Woodruff's *Giddap* in Locke's *The Negro in Art* 57.

52. One can find a reproduction of Catlett's *And a special fear for my loved ones* in Herzog 64.

53. One can find reproductions of Catlett's *Mother and Child* and White's *Hope for the Future* in Williams and Williams 24–25.

54. White certainly would have been well acquainted with this work, since it served as the frontispiece to Alain Locke's *The New Negro*, a book White credited on various occasions as a formative influence on his evolving racial consciousness as a youth.

55. One can find a reproduction of Lange's *Migrant Mother*, as well as a thematically related Lange photograph titled *Drought Refugees from Oklahoma Camping by Road* (1936), in Peeler 114–15.

56. One can find a reproduction of Spruance's *Souvenir of Lidice* in Landau 111.

57. For more on Leo Frank, see Leonard Dinnerstein's *The Leo Frank Case*.

58. One can find a reproduction of Crichlow's *Lovers* in Williams and Williams 8.

59. For more on the Ingram case, see chapter 1, note 27. See also E. Nelson 16–19. This article is accompanied by a graphic from White that depicts the Ingram family standing directly against the bars of their jail cell, as if demanding their freedom. White even renders Mrs. Ingram with a prominent clenched fist, emblematic of leftist labor militancy.

60. The *Dixie Comes to New York* pamphlet is available in the Charles White papers, Archives of American Art.

61. Sidney Finkelstein, untitled essay for a German exhibition catalog, White papers.

62. White employed a similar motif in a graphic titled *Five Years Is Too Long!* with regard to the aforementioned Ingram case. This work portrays a heroic Rosa Lee Ingram tearing down the barbed wire that imprisons her and her sons. It appeared as a cover illustration for Robeson's *Freedom* and on the February 1953 cover of *Sing Out!*

63. One can find a reproduction of Catlett's *I have special reservations* in Samella Lewis 171.

64. One can find a reproduction of Catlett's Harriet Tubman and Sojourner Truth linocuts in Herzog 62–63.

65. Catlett originally planned for the *Negro Woman* series to be exhibited in black colleges and community centers, particularly in the southern United States. Although Catlett's original exhibition plans were not realized, the Barnett Aden Gallery in Washington, D.C., exhibited the series between December 1947 and January 1948, and several of the linocuts appeared in the Taller de Gráfica's 1949 catalog *Doce Años de Obra Artística Colectiva* (Herzog 20, 59).

66. Exhibition brochure, White papers.

67. Charles White, interview by Karl Fortess, Archives of American Art, April 8, 1969.

68. Foreword, in a 1940 brochure for the fourth annual AAC exhibition, AAC papers, Archives of American Art.

69. One can find a reproduction of White's *Our War* in LeFalle-Collins and Goldman 153.

70. Clearly, Schuyler had not, at this point, completed his rather circuitous evolution into the prototypical black neoconservative.

71. This advertisement appeared, among other places, in the *Crisis* beginning in August 1942. Bill Mullen's recent work in *Popular Fronts* demonstrates that the paper had

considerable justification in touting itself as a defender of vanguard politics during the war years—see especially chapter 2.

72. One can find a reproduction of Benton's *Strike* in Robertson 13.

73. Especially noteworthy in this regard are Gellert's prints for the 1934 publication *Capital in Lithographs*. Several relevant examples of Gellert's graphic art from this volume appear in Kalaidjian 135–46.

74. In literature, one might note that in the early 1940s Richard Wright worked on an unpublished novel, *Little Sister*, about the experiences of domestic workers. In fact, he spoke often and eagerly about this book as "a sort of feminine counterpart of *Native Son*" in interviews, and read from this work in progress as part of the 1940–41 League of American Writers lecture series (Kinnamon and Fabre 28–37; Fabre 188–90; Denning 224).

75. One can find a reproduction of Catlett's *I have always worked hard in America* in Herzog 60.

76. Letter from Steth and Perry, May 3, 1945, Raymond Steth papers, Archives of American Art.

77. Raymond Steth, interview by Margaret Kline, Archives of American Art, April 28, 1990.

78. One can find a reproduction of Catlett's *War Worker* in Herzog 43. Bloch's *Sheet Metal Worker* appears in Landau 17.

79. One can find a reproduction of *Skinny Depressed* in Locke's *The Negro in Art* 124.

80. One can find a reproduction of Jacobi's *The New Deal—Pro and Con* in Park and Markowitz 90.

81. One can find a reproduction of Biggers's *Despair* in Wardlaw, *Art* 135. Blackburn's *Toil* appears in Foner and Schultz 58.

82. One can find reproductions of both Blackburn's *Upper New York* and Lee-Smith's *Desolation* in Locke's *The Negro in Art* 126.

83. One can find a reproduction of Rothstein's *Farmer and Sons Walking in the Face of a Dust Storm* in Peeler 137.

84. One can find a reproduction of Woodruff's *View of Atlanta* in Williams and Williams 31.

Chapter 4. Forging a Language of Radical Exhortation: Poetry

1. All citations of Rampersad in this chapter refer to *The Collected Poems of Langston Hughes* (1994).

2. Kreymborg was a radical white poet who published numerous works on laborist and black themes in journals such as *New Masses* and *Negro Quarterly* over the course of the 1930s and early 1940s.

3. Gold published essays such as "Towards Proletarian Art" in the *Liberator* as early as 1921 (C. Nelson 103).

4. This poem appeared in the February 1935 issue of *Midland Left* (Fabre 115).

5. This poem appeared in the May 12, 1936, issue of *New Masses*, 14.

6. For a fuller discussion of Fearing's work in this regard, see Kalaidjian 200–206.

7. Olsen's poem appeared in the March 1934 issue of *Partisan* and is reprinted in Nekola and Rabinowitz 179–81. Gold's poem was anthologized in Freeman 160.

8. One can find recordings of these two songs, among other places, on the 1997 Rounder album *Coal Mining Women*.

9. Bill Mullen makes a similar case for the appeal of the short story genre within Chicago's Popular Front circles of the 1930s and 1940s. See especially his chapter "Genre Politics/Cultural Politics: The Short Story and the New Black Fiction Market" (126–47).

10. One can find Hughes's *Don't You Want to Be Free?* in Hatch and Shine 266–83.

11. Unless otherwise indicated, all biographical information on Davis derives from his memoirs, *Livin' the Blues* (1993). For simplicity's sake, I cite specific page numbers from this book only in the case of direct quotations.

12. Davis remarked: "I found no appeal at all in Fenton Johnson's traditional, rhymed work. I felt that content was more important than technique. That is probably why I could not get into Countee Cullen" (Tidwell, "Interview" 106).

13. Three years later, Locke had soured somewhat on Davis, much as he expressed his lack of enthusiasm for Hughes's shift to more overtly political poetry during the depression: "Both of these writers are vehemently poets of social protest now; so much so indeed that they have twangy lyres" (Stewart 276).

14. Interestingly, Davis later recalled that the main criticism of this poem from Wright—then still a CP member—was what he termed "its 'hopeless bitterness' and 'lack of a positive resolution for the plight of black people'" (*Livin' the Blues* 240).

15. Like Langston Hughes, Davis used his prestige and contacts to help further the careers of several young black writers. For instance, Davis arranged the publication of early social realist short fiction—what Davis described as "grim and realistic short stories about discrimination"—by Frank Yerby in Conroy's *New Anvil*. Davis also published short stories by Chester Himes, then in prison, while he worked on the *Atlanta World* during the 1930s (*Livin' the Blues* 249).

16. Among numerous other activities, Davis also served on the board of directors and taught courses at Chicago's Abraham Lincoln School, as did figures like Jack Conroy (*Livin' the Blues* 278). Like the George Washington Carver School of New York City, this school came under attack during the anticommunist hysteria that was set in motion by the Dies Committee in the late 1930s (Wixson 455; Denning 70).

17. This poem appeared in the August 27, 1935, issue of *New Masses*, 13.

18. This poem appeared in the February 1935 issue of *Crisis*, 44. Davis was a reader of Monroe Work's series of *Negro Yearbooks*, which served as his primary source of information on black history. Davis also was familiar with the work of black historians such as Du Bois, Carter G. Woodson, and J. A. Rogers (*Livin' the Blues* 65; see also Tidwell, "Reliving" xxi).

19. For instance, Davis subtitles the poem "Lynched" (c. 1935) a "Symphonic Interlude for Twenty-one Selected Instruments" and includes relatively detailed margin notes describing the appropriate instrumentation, tone, and tempo for various sections of the poem. In a similar fashion, when Langston Hughes's "Three Songs about Lynching" appeared in the May 1936 issue of *Opportunity*, each of the three "songs" was labeled for

instrumentation, while annotations in the margins provided specific suggestions for the style and tone for the musical accompaniment (Rampersad 648–49).

20. For examples of imagery of a smooth integration of man and machine in New Deal art, see Melosh 113–26. Notably, this type of enthusiasm for the productive potentialities of industrial innovation even surfaces, albeit with some measure of qualification, in the 1933 *Detroit Industry* murals of Marxist painter Diego Rivera (see Kozloff 216–29).

21. Before its appearance in *47th Street*, this poem was featured in the February 1944 issue of the leftist international magazine *Free World* (*Livin' the Blues* 304).

22. One should note that this is also almost surely a jab at white critical reception of politicized themes in African American cultural work.

23. One important exception, of course, was Angelo Herndon. Significantly, Davis supported Herndon through his newspaper columns in the *Atlanta World* and became friends with Herndon upon the latter's release from prison (*Livin' the Blues* 194–95).

24. This poem, titled "Steel Mills," appeared in the February 1925 issue of the *Messenger*, 103 (Rampersad 625).

25. Scott employs the term "hidden transcripts" to describe discourse by oppressed peoples "that takes place 'offstage', beyond direct observation by powerholders" (4–5).

26. This poem appeared, along with three other "Madam" poems by Hughes, in the summer 1943 issue of *Common Ground*, 88–90.

Alice Childress, a dramatist who came of age as part of the leftist cultural scene in New York City, would in the 1950s publish a series of prose "conversations" in which the protagonist, Mildred, recounts actually voicing such sentiments to her employers. First published in the *Baltimore Afro-American* and Paul Robeson's *Freedom*, the conversations were collected for publication in the book *Like One of the Family: Conversations from a Domestic's Life* in 1956 (T. Harris xxiv–xxv).

27. This poem appeared in the December 1944–January 1945 issue of *Negro Story*, 50.

28. In drama of the period, one of the more intriguing treatments of John Henry in a proletarian manner is Theodore Browne's Federal Theatre Project work *Natural Man* (1937), which appears in Hatch and Shine 342–63.

29. Angelo Herndon recognized precisely this connection in a 1943 editorial commentary for *Negro Quarterly*, although he was quick to argue that such a stage of consciousness was ultimately insufficient for progressive political transformation (296).

For a more thorough discussion of the badman's place in African American folklore, see chapter 5 of Roberts.

30. "Old Lem" appeared in the fall 1937 issue of *New Challenge*, 46–48. Bodenheim's poem appeared in the March 2, 1937, issue of *New Masses*, 18.

31. See Brown's scathing review of *I'll Take My Stand*: "A Romantic Defense," in *Opportunity* (April 1931): 118.

32. This poem appeared in the February 1939 issue of *Opportunity*, 54.

33. This poem appeared in the fall 1937 issue of *New Challenge*, 49–50.

34. This poem appeared in the April 10, 1934, issue of *New Masses*, 21.

35. Griffin astutely discusses the difficulties confronting African American migrants once they arrived in the urban North—see especially chapters 2 and 3.

36. This poem appeared in the January 1, 1935, issue of *New Masses.*

37. This poem appeared in the July–August 1935 issue of *Partisan Review* (Fabre 123).

38. This poem appeared in the January 21, 1936, issue of *New Masses,* 10.

39. Here, one also might consider poems such as Marcus Christian's "Martyrs of the Rope Brigade" (*Opportunity,* May 1934), James E. Andrews's "Burnt Offering" (*Opportunity,* March 1939), and T. Thomas Fortune's "That Other Golgotha" (Cunard 261).

40. This poem appeared in the *Daily Worker* in October 1933 and again in November 1934 (C. Nelson 207–8).

41. This poem appeared in the June 28, 1938, issue of *Daily Worker,* 7.

42. This poem appeared in the December 1931 issue of *Opportunity,* 379.

43. This poem appeared in the June 12, 1934, issue of *New Masses,* 20.

44. "Chant for Tom Mooney" appeared in the September 1932 issue of *New Masses,* 16.

45. Robeson, of course, became a martyr with the escalation of the cold war later in the decade but was not generally regarded in this way when White painted his mural in 1943.

46. This poem appeared in the December 30, 1944, issue of the *Chicago Defender.*

47. This poem appeared in the December 31, 1946, issue of *New Masses,* 11. Here, one also might note Orson Welles's series of five CBS radio broadcasts about Woodward. Significantly, this radio drama, which Welles narrated in the persona of a detective tracking down the men responsible for the crime, directly compared "the justice of Dachau and Oswiekem" to that of Aiken, South Carolina (Denning 399–400).

48. Benton Spruance's *Souvenir of Lidice,* a prizewinning lithograph in the 1943 *Artists for Victory* exhibit, used a crucifixion motif to comment on this same Czech travesty (Landau 110–11).

49. As League of American Writers memoirist Franklin Folsom details, several leftist American writers opted for military service in the Spanish conflict by enlisting in the Abraham Lincoln Brigades (38).

50. In this regard, one also might consider Hughes's "One More 'S' in the U.S.A.," a poem he originally composed for the occasion of the eighth Communist Party convention in Cleveland in 1934 (Berry 205–7).

51. Here, one also might consider Frank Marshall Davis's "To the Red Army," a previously unpublished poem included in John Edgar Tidwell's recent collection of Davis's poetry, *Black Moods* (169–71).

52. For an account of roughly comparable experiences authored by a member of the Alabama Sharecroppers Union, see Jackson 13.

53. This poem appeared in the April 13, 1937, issue of *New Masses,* 14.

54. This poem appeared in the April 28, 1936, issue of *New Masses,* 16.

55. This poem appeared in the June 26, 1934, issue of *New Masses,* 16. Wright's "Spread Your Sunrise" is even more explicit in its call for a Soviet-style transformation of the United States, urging a "bushy-haired giant child . . . / With great big muscles bursting through his clothes!" to "red-wash the whole world." This latter poem appeared in the July 2, 1935, issue of *New Masses,* 26.

56. The version of the ballad quoted here was collected by proletarian novelist Grace

Lumpkin from a National Textile Workers Union Hall in Charlotte, North Carolina, and published as "A Southern Cotton Mill Rhyme" in the May 1930 issue of *New Masses*, 8.

57. This poem appeared in the October 1928 issue of *New Masses*.

Chapter 5. Fractured American Dreams and Revolutionary Skepticism: Novels

1. As Michael Denning notes, Crichton published this essay under the nom de plume of Robert Forsythe (241).

2. Regarding the disparity between the time frame of *Lawd Today!*'s writing and its subsequent publication, as well as the distinctions between the 1938 and 1940 editions of *Uncle Tom's Children*, see chapter 1, note 33. For a list of other novels that could merit consideration in this study, again see chapter 1, note 33.

3. This was, of course, one of Wright's ongoing points of contention with the Communist Party, which contributed to his final break with the CP around 1942.

4. John Wilson, interviews by Robert Brown, Archives of American Art, March 11, 1993–August 16, 1994.

5. Transcript of June Baker radio program, Willard Motley Collection, Northern Illinois University. Hereafter, I cite documents from this collection as WMC-NIU.

6. Sharon Lee-Shapiro, letter to Motley, April 20, 1950; H. W. Couenhoven, letter to Dana Ferrin (of Appleton-Century Publishers), May 6, 1947, WMC-NIU.

7. "Knock on Any Door," *Chicago Times*, April 29, 1945.

8. Untitled publicity materials for *Knock on Any Door*, WMC-NIU; see also Fleming 61. Interestingly, before the novel went on to enjoy this commercial success, Motley said that an editor from Harper's rejected the book because "he thought that the day of the realistic novel was over" ("Education" 26).

9. For a more in-depth discussion of naturalist fiction, see Mitchell, and Pizer.

10. The novels of Chester Himes, William Gardner Smith, and William Demby from the 1940s and early 1950s also support this point.

11. One notable exception was *American Stuff* (1937), an anthology of fiction and personal essays by employees of the Federal Writers' Project, which included Wright's essay "The Ethics of Living Jim Crow" (Fabre 152).

12. In addition to Cayton and Drake's *Black Metropolis*, other influential social science books from the period under study include Sterling D. Spero and Abram Harris's *The Black Worker* (1931), Horace Cayton and George S. Mitchell's *Black Workers and the New Unions* (1935), and Gunnar Myrdal's *An American Dilemma* (1942).

13. John Steinbeck, Josephine Herbst, Jack Conroy, Theodore Dreiser, and John Dos Passos were only a few of the most visible white authors to undertake similar types of documentary journalism projects.

14. The displacement of the John Reed Clubs by the League of American Writers, the latter of which placed greater emphasis on attracting established authors, is emblematic of this mid-1930s trend (Rideout 244).

15. Section 2 notes, "Of Night, Perchance of Death" manuscript, Willard Motley

papers, University of Wisconsin. Hereafter, I cite documents from this collection as WMP-UW.

16. For a recent consideration of the special representational burdens imposed on African American artists, see Kobena Mercer's essay "Black Art and the Burden of Representation" in *Welcome* (233–58).

17. Alan Wald also makes note of a flash-forward that demonstrates the perpetuation of racism in the post–World War II era by foretelling the murder of an inmate named Army in Georgia following his honorable service to his country ("Foreword" xxv).

18. Motley grew up believing that Archibald Motley Jr. and Flossie Moore (née Motley) were his siblings and that Mary and Archibald Motley Sr. were his parents. In fact, it was not until Mary's death in 1959 that Willard learned that Flossie was actually his mother. (Evidently, the deceit was contrived due to the fact that Willard was born out of wedlock—although Flossie would later protest the issue of her marital status in a letter to Willard). Archibald Motley, letter to Willard Motley, November 19, 1959; Willard Motley, letter to Archibald Motley, December 12, 1959; Flossie Moore, letter to Willard Motley, December 22, 1959, WMC-NIU. Given that Willard did not publicly trumpet this discovery it seems understandable that most scholars of both Willard and Archibald have tended to perpetuate this misconception regarding the Motley family tree.

19. In addition to a handful of articles, these travels also resulted in a book-length manuscript titled "Adventures and Misadventures." For more on this manuscript, see Wood. For more on the broader topic of "Traveling Reporters in Thirties America," see chapter 2 of Peeler. William Attaway was one contemporary who undertook similar rambles across the midwestern and western states (Garren, "William Attaway" 4).

20. For more on Archibald Motley's art vis-à-vis the politics of racial representation, see Mooney.

21. Motley honed his documentary appreciation not only of Italian American communities but also of Chicago's full kaleidoscope of ethnic cultures through a series of *City Sketches* for the Illinois Writers' Project. The series included titles such as *The Unknown Worker, Cinco de Mayo, Chinatown, Greek Good Friday,* and *The City Cellar* (WMC-NIU). Work on the FWP's Pan-American Unit also granted Motley a chance to immerse himself in Latin and Mexican American cultures (Klinkowitz 177–78)—one of many factors contributing to his later decision to move to Mexico.

22. Conroy had moved from Missouri to Chicago to work on the collection of industrial folklore under the direction of the FWP's National Folklore editor Benjamin Botkin. Motley and Conroy seem to have quickly discovered a shared interest in the "underclass" of Chicago's skid row environs. During the 1940s, Motley gave guest lectures in Conroy's courses at the progressive Abraham Lincoln School (as did Richard Wright and Arna Bontemps), while Conroy read and commented on a draft of *Knock on Any Door.* Earlier, encouraged by Conroy, Motley had submitted a story titled "The Beer Drinkers" to the *New Anvil,* although the story was not published (Fleming 31).

23. Motley, letter to MacMillan editor Mary Thompson, July 11, 1944, WMC-NIU.

24. Petry concludes her first novel, *The Street,* with the somewhat more poetic but essentially similar closing sentence, "*And it could have been any street in the city,* for the snow

laid a delicate film over the sidewalk, over the brick of the tired, old buildings; gently obscuring the grime and the garbage and the ugliness" (436, my emphasis).

25. As late as 1960, although he had lived in Mexico for nearly ten years by that point, Motley was sketching out plans for a Chicago-based photo-documentary book to be titled *Sunday Afternoon, Skid Row, U.S.A.* Motley, letter to Ted Purdy, October 31, 1960, WMP-UW.

26. In later correspondence, Motley frequently pointed to director Nicholas Ray's lack of interest in undertaking such firsthand immersion as one of the reasons for the unsatisfying form of the final film product. For his most extended critique of the film, see Motley, letter to Ted Pierce, March 8, 1949, Theodore Pierce papers, University of Wisconsin.

27. Transcript of "Latimer-Motley Interview" from the Human Rights Program, WMC-NIU.

28. Motley, letter to Nicholas Ray, July 25, 1948, WMC-NIU.

29. "Of Night, Perchance of Death," Newspaper Research Files, WMC-NIU.

30. Interestingly, Motley originally planned for the bulk of *We Fished All Night* to detail the "environmental influences" of five major characters, much in the manner of *Knock on Any Door* (Notes for Sections 1 and 2, "Of Night, Perchance of Death" manuscript, WMC-NIU). However, he later jettisoned this idea in order to give greater attention to the impact of the war on the featured characters *after* their respective tours of duty.

31. Preparatory notes for "Of Night, Perchance of Death," WMC-NIU.

32. Motley, letter to Ted Pierce, September 30, 1943, Theodore Pierce Papers, University of Wisconsin.

33. Motley, letter to Purdy, March 21, 1947, WMC-NIU.

34. "I Discover I'm a Negro," undated essay c. 1942–43, WMC-NIU.

35. In his original character sketches, Motley indicates that Dave would be a conscientious objector on *both* philosophical and racial grounds (WMC-NIU). A draft of an early chapter (ultimately unused) describes Dave bidding his farewells to his family and turning himself in to a police station when his time to be drafted arises. Chapter 3, "Of Night, Perchance of Death" manuscript, WMP-UW.

36. Draft of untitled remarks and flyer for "Humanity versus the H Bomb" symposium and "ballad drama, living newspaper style," scheduled for May 3, 1950, WMC-NIU.

37. Like so many of his social realist peers, Motley himself was a Progressive Party supporter who backed the Henry Wallace campaign in 1948.

38. Again, Motley collected several articles pertaining to precisely this kind of incident (WMC-NIU).

39. One can find a color reproduction of Evergood's painting in Foner and Schultz 69.

40. Motley, letter to Ted Purdy, March 21, 1947, WMC-NIU.

41. For a definitive study in this regard, see Lipsitz, *Rainbow*.

42. This, of course, is only a partial explanation of why Motley chose to move to Mexico. While he did feel a "push" out of the United States due to the factors mentioned here, Motley also felt a considerable "pull" toward the folk cultures of Mexico as well. In fact, he developed an abiding interest in Mexican and Mexican American lifeways by at least

the late 1930s, as evidenced by the 1938 article "Calle Olvera—America's Most Picturesque Street," based on a visit to Los Angeles.

43. Attaway, meanwhile, essentially seems to have ceased writing fiction following *Blood on the Forge*. Thus, of the 1930s and 1940s veterans of the social realist movement, only Petry and Brown continued to produce cultural work in the novel medium from within the United States by the early 1950s.

44. Neoslave narratives, such as Arna Bontemps's *Black Thunder: Gabriel's Revolt: Virginia 1800* (1936) and Margaret Walker's *Jubilee* (not published until 1966, but initiated during the period under study), provide intriguing analogues with the use of historical allegories by social realist mural painters. And clearly both Bontemps and Walker were very much a part of the social realist milieu during the 1930s and 1940s. My decision to forgo consideration of these works simply owes to concerns of keeping the scope of this chapter's discussion manageable.

45. Wright also added "The Ethics of Living Jim Crow: An Autobiographical Sketch" as a preface to the 1940 edition of *Uncle Tom's Children*, an essay that seems to further foreground the primacy of race over class factors in the shaping of African American lives.

46. "I Discover I'm a Negro," unpublished essay c. 1942–43, WMC-NIU.

47. The full text of this speech, "Not My People's War," was reprinted in the June 17, 1941, issue of *New Masses* (8–9, 12).

48. Alan Wald offers several insightful observations on the way in which Hananiah Harari's cover art for Brown's *Iron City* works to elaborate this metaphor of American society as a prison ("Foreword" xxxiv–xxxv).

49. As noted in chapter 4, this poem appeared in the June 26, 1934, issue of *New Masses*, 16.

50. Similarly, in a 1958 interview with *Ebony* magazine, Motley remarked that "bums are more honest, more tolerant than middle class people" ("Return" 85).

51. Likewise, Robert Stepto's seminal study of patterns in African American narrative, *From Behind the Veil* (1979), provides numerous compelling examples in which black authors symbolically configure a journey northward as what Stepto terms a "narrative of ascent" (67).

52. For statistics on African American emigration from Kentucky and immigration to western Pennsylvania's industrial centers, see Epstein 7–10, 19–20 and Dickerson 17, 27–28, 37–39.

53. Among the most engaging discussions of this issue in relation to depression-era fiction are Hapke, and Foley's chapter "Women and the Left in the 1930s" in *Radical Representations*.

54. In Wright's *Lawd Today!* Jake Jackson and his fellow workers appear to fully embrace these same mythologies of meritocracy and class mobility (even at the height of the depression), referring to "how all great men started out poor" and citing as examples of self-help uplift Benjamin Franklin, Abe Lincoln, and "old Rockefeller" (166).

Bibliography

Aaron, Daniel. *Writers on the Left: Episodes in American Literary Communism.* New York: Harcourt, Brace and World, 1961.

Alexander, Stephen. "Art." *New Masses* March 19, 1935: 29.

Allen, James. *The Negro Question in the United States.* New York: International Publishers, 1936.

Alston, Charles. *The Drawings of Charles Alston.* Washington, D.C.: The National Archives Trust Fund Board, 1980.

Anderson, Jervis. *A. Philip Randolph: A Biographical Portrait.* New York: Harcourt, Brace, and Jovanovich, 1974.

Aptheker, Herbert, ed. *American Negro Slave Revolts.* New York: Columbia University Press, 1943.

———. *Writings in Periodicals Edited by W. E. B. Du Bois: Selections from The Crisis, volume 2, 1926–1934.* Millwood, N.Y.: Kraus-Thomson, 1983.

Arnow, Harriette. *The Dollmaker.* 1954. New York: Avon, 1972.

"Art Exhibit Against Lynching, An." *Crisis* April 1935: 106.

"Art in Harlem." *Art Front* 2.8 (July–August 1936): 11–12.

"Art Today." *Daily Worker* August 28, 1943.

Attaway, William. *Blood on the Forge.* 1941. New York: Monthly Review Press, 1987.

———. *Let Me Breathe Thunder.* Garden City, N.Y.: Doubleday, Doran and Co., 1939.

Baigell, Matthew. *The American Scene: American Painting of the 1930s.* New York: Praeger, 1974.

Baigell, Matthew, and Julia Williams, eds. *Artists against War and Fascism: Papers of the First American Artists' Congress.* New Brunswick, N.J.: Rutgers University Press, 1986.

Baker, Houston A., Jr. *Blues, Ideology, and Afro-American Literature: A Vernacular Theory.* Chicago: University of Chicago Press, 1984.

Baker, James H., Jr. "Art Comes to the People of Harlem." *Crisis* March 1939: 78–80.

Bayliss, John F. "Nick Romano: Father and Son." *Negro American Literature Forum* 3.1 (spring 1969): 18–21, 32.

Bearden, Romare, and Harry Henderson. *A History of African-American Artists: From 1792 to the Present.* New York: Pantheon Books, 1993.

Beauchamp-Byrd, Mora J., and Floyd Coleman. *Struggle and Serenity: The Visionary Art of Elizabeth Catlett.* New York: Caribbean Cultural Center, 1996.

Bellamy, Edward. *Looking Backward: 2000–1887.* 1887. Boston: Bedford Books, 1995.

Benjamin, Walter. *Illuminations.* New York: Schocken Books, 1968.

Bennett, Gwendolyn. "The Harlem Artists' Guild." *Art Front* 3 (May 1937): 20.

Bennett, Lerone, Jr. "'They Loved Him, the People Did.'" *Freedomways* 20.3 (fall 1980): 203–5.

Berry, Faith. *Langston Hughes, before and beyond Harlem.* 1983. New York: Wings Books, 1992.

Biggers, John, and Carroll Simms. *Black Art in Houston: The Texas Southern University Experience.* College Station: Texas A and M University Press, 1978.

Biles, Roger. *A New Deal for the American People.* DeKalb: Northern Illinois University Press, 1991.

Blair, Fred Bassett. "Poetry and the People." *New Masses* July 31, 1945: 19–20.

Bone, Robert. "Richard Wright and the Chicago Renaissance." *Callaloo* 9.3 (1986): 446–68.

Bontemps, Arna. *Black Thunder: Gabriel's Revolt: Virginia 1800.* New York: MacMillan, 1936.

"Book Union, The." *New Masses* April 23, 1935: 56.

Bordwell, David, and Kristin Thompson. *Film Art: An Introduction.* 1979. New York: Mc-Graw-Hill, 1993.

Bradford, Roark. *John Henry.* New York: Harper, 1939.

Brennan, Ray. "Best Seller Author Tells Eight Years' Work." *Chicago Times* May 27, 1947: 4–5.

Brooks, Gwendolyn. *A Street in Bronzeville.* New York: Harper and Brothers, 1945.

Brown, Frank London. *Trumbull Park.* Chicago: Regnery, 1959.

Brown, Lloyd L. "Death to the Lynchers!" *New Masses* August 6, 1946: 3.

———. *Iron City.* 1951. Boston: Northeastern University Press, 1994.

———. "What about It, United Nations?" *New Masses* July 16, 1946: 14.

———. "Which Way for the Negro Writer?" *Masses and Mainstream* March 1951: 53–63.

Brown, Sterling A. "A New Trend." *Opportunity* February 1933: 56.

———. "The Problems of the Negro Writer." *Official Proceedings of the Second National Negro Congress, October 15–17, 1937.* Philadelphia: Metropolitan Opera House, 1937.

———. "A Romantic Defense." *Opportunity* April 1931: 118.

———. "A Son's Return: 'Oh, Didn't He Ramble.'" In Sanders, *Son's Return* 1–21.

———. *Southern Road.* New York: Harcourt, Brace, 1932.

———. "Two Negro Poets." *Opportunity* July 1936: 216, 220.

Burck, Jacob. "Sectarianism in Art." *New Masses* March 1933: 26–27. Reprinted in Shapiro, 69–73.

Burroughs, Margaret G. "He Will Always Be a Chicago Artist to Me." *Freedomways* 20.3 (fall 1980): 151–54.

Calmer, Alan, ed. *Get Organized: Stories and Poems about Trade Union People.* New York: International Publishers, 1939.

Cannon, David Wadsworth, Jr. *Black Labor Chant and Other Poems.* New York: National Council on Religion in Higher Education, 1939.

Cantwell, Robert. *Land of Plenty.* 1934. Carbondale: Southern Illinois University Press, 1971.

Carter, Dan T. *Scottsboro: A Tragedy of the American South.* Baton Rouge: Louisiana State University Press, 1969.

Carter, William. "The Art Notebook." *Chicago Sunday Bee* May 26, 1940.

Catlett, Elizabeth. "The Negro Artist in America." *American Contemporary Art* April 1944: 3–6.

Cayton, Horace R. "The Known City." *New Republic* May 12, 1947: 30–31.

Cayton, Horace R., and St. Clair Drake. *Black Metropolis: A Study of Negro Life in a Northern City.* 1945. Rev. Ed. New York: Harper and Row, 1962.

Cayton, Horace R., and George S. Mitchell. *Black Workers and the New Unions.* Chapel Hill: University of North Carolina Press, 1939.

Childress, Alice. *Like One of the Family: Conversations from a Domestic's Life.* 1956. Boston: Beacon Press, 1986.

Coal Mining Women. Rounder Records, 1997.

Coker, Gylbert Garvin, ed. *Charles Alston: Artist and Teacher.* New York: Kenkeleba Gallery, 1990.

"Communists and the Negroes: A Symposium, The." *New Masses* March 28, 1944: 15–16.

Conroy, Jack. *The Disinherited.* New York: Covici-Friede, 1933.

Contreras, Belisario R. *Tradition and Innovation in New Deal Art.* Lewisburg: Bucknell University Press, 1983.

Cruse, Harold. *The Crisis of the Negro Intellectual.* 1963. New York: Quill, 1984.

Cullen, Countee. *The Black Christ and Other Poems.* New York: Harper and Brothers, 1929.

"Cultural Session Resolutions." *Official Proceedings of the Second National Negro Congress, October 15–17, 1937.* Philadelphia: Metropolitan Opera House, 1937.

Cunard, Nancy, ed. *Negro: An Anthology.* 1934. New York: Continuum, 1996.

Davis, Frank Marshall. *Black Man's Verse.* 1935. Ann Arbor: University Microfilms, 1979.

———. *Black Moods: Collected Poems.* Ed. John Edgar Tidwell. Urbana: University of Illinois Press, 2002.

———. *47th Street.* 1948. Ann Arbor: University Microfilms, 1975.

———. *I Am the American Negro.* 1937. Freeport, N.Y.: Books for Libraries Press, 1971.

———. *Livin' the Blues: Memoirs of a Black Journalist and Poet.* Ed. John Edgar Tidwell. Madison: University of Wisconsin Press, 1993.

———. *Through Sepia Eyes.* Chicago: Black Cat Press, 1938.

Davis, Robert A. "The Art Notebook." *Chicago Sunday Bee* October 6, 1940.

Demby, William. *Beetlecreek.* 1950. Jackson: University Press of Mississippi, 1998.

Denning, Michael. *The Cultural Front: The Laboring of American Culture in the Twentieth Century.* London: Verso, 1997.

Dennis, James M. *Renegade Regionalists: The Modern Independence of Grant Wood, Thomas Hart Benton, and John Steuart Curry.* Madison: University of Wisconsin Press, 1998.

Dickerson, Dennis C. *Out of the Crucible: Black Steelworkers in Western Pennsylvania, 1875–1980.* Albany: State University of New York Press, 1986.

Dinnerstein, Leonard. *The Leo Frank Case.* 1966. New York: Columbia University Press, 1968.

Dos Passos, John. *U.S.A.* 1937. Boston: Houghton Mifflin, 1960.

"'Double V' Campaign, The." *Common Ground* 2.4 (summer 1942): 114–15.

Du Bois, W. E. B. *Black Reconstruction: An Essay toward a History of the Part Which Black Folk Played in the Attempt to Reconstruct Democracy in America, 1860–1880.* New York: Harcourt, Brace, and Company, 1935.

———. *Dusk of Dawn: An Essay toward an Autobiography of a Race Concept.* New York: Shocken Books, 1940.

Ellison, Ralph. *Invisible Man.* New York: Penguin Books, 1952.

Epstein, Abraham. *The Negro Migrant in Pittsburgh.* 1918. New York: Arno Press, 1969.

Ervin, Hazel Arnett. *Ann Petry: A Bio-Bibliography.* New York: G. K. Hall, 1993.

Fabre, Michel. *The Unfinished Quest of Richard Wright.* 1973. Urbana: University of Illinois Press, 1993.

Farrell, James T. *Studs Lonigan: A Trilogy.* New York: Vanguard Press, 1935.

Fax, Elton. "John Wilson." *Artist and Influence* 5 (1987): 92–97.

———. *Seventeen Black Artists.* New York: Dodd, Mead, and Company, 1971.

Faxon, Alicia. "John Wilson: Reality Is Not a Fad." *Boston Sunday Globe* September 5, 1971: 4-A.

Federal Writers' Project. *American Stuff: An Anthology of Prose and Verse by Members of the Federal Writers' Project.* New York: Viking Press, 1937.

Fitzgerald, Sharon G. "Charles White in Person." *Freedomways* 20.3 (fall 1980): 158–62.

Flanagan, Hallie. *Arena: The History of the Federal Theatre.* 1940. New York: Benjamin Blom, 1965.

Fleming, Robert E. *Willard Motley.* Boston: Twayne, 1978.

Flynn, Elizabeth Gurley. "The Feminine Ferment." *New Masses* May 13, 1947: 6–7.

Foley, Barbara. *Radical Representations: Politics and Form in U.S. Proletarian Fiction, 1929–1941.* Durham: Duke University Press, 1993.

Folsom, Franklin. *Days of Anger, Days of Hope: A Memoir of the League of American Writers.* Niwot: University Press of Colorado, 1994.

Foner, Philip S., and Reinhard Schultz. *The Other America: Art and the Labour Movement in the United States.* London: Journeyman Press, 1985.

Ford, Nick Aaron. "Four Popular Negro Novelists." *Phylon* 15 (1954): 29–39.

Forhman, Larry. "Portrait of an Artist: Morris Topchevsky (1899–1947)." *New Masses* July 22, 1947: 9–10.

Forsythe, Robert [Kyle Crichton]. "Down with the Novel." *New Masses* April 16, 1935: 29–30.

Freeman, Joseph, ed. *Proletarian Literature in the United States.* New York: International Publishers, 1935.

Gabbin, Joanne V. *Sterling Brown: Building the Black Aesthetic Tradition.* Westport, Conn.: Greenwood Press, 1985.

Gaither, Edmund Barry. "John Biggers: A Perspective." In Wardlaw, *Art* 76–95.

Gallagher, Buell G. "Talladega Library: Weapon against Caste." *Crisis* April 1939: 110–11, 126.

Garman, Bryan K. *A Race of Singers: Whitman's Working-Class Hero from Guthrie to Springsteen.* Chapel Hill: University of North Carolina Press, 2000.

Garren, Samuel B. "Playing the Wishing Game: Folkloric Elements in William Attaway's *Blood on the Forge.*" *CLA Journal* 32.1 (September 1988): 10–22.

———. "William Attaway." In *Afro-American Writers, 1940–1955. Dictionary of Literary Biography.* Ed. Trudier Harris and Thadious M. Davis. Vol. 76. Detroit: Gale Research, 1988. 3–7.

Gates, Henry Louis, Jr. "The Face and Voice of Blackness." In *Facing History: The Black Image in American Art, 1710–1940.* Ed. Guy C. McElroy. Washington, D.C.: Bedford Arts, in association with the Corcoran Gallery of Art, 1990. xxviii–xlvi.

Gelfant, Blanche Houseman. *The American City Novel.* Norman: University of Oklahoma Press, 1954.

Gellert. Lawrence. *"Me and My Captain" (Chain Gang Songs): Negro Songs of Protest.* New York: Hours Press, 1939.

Glicksburg, Charles. "The Alienation of Negro Literature." *Phylon* 11.1 (March 1950): 49–58.

Gloster, Hugh. "Race and the Negro Writer." *Phylon* 11.4 (December 1950): 369–71.

Gold, Michael. Foreword. *New Masses* July 1926: 19.

———. *Jews without Money.* New York: H. Liveright, 1930.

———. "The Masses Tradition." *Masses and Mainstream* 4.8 (August 1951): 45–56.

———. "Towards Proletarian Art." *Liberator* 1921. Reprinted in *The Mike Gold Reader.* Ed. Samuel Sillen. New York: International Publishers, 1954.

Goldman, Shifra M. *Dimensions of the Americas: Art and Social Change in Latin America and the United States.* Chicago: University of Chicago Press, 1994.

Gone with the Wind. Dir. Victor Fleming. Selznick International Pictures and MGM, 1939.

Gordon, Edmund W. "First and Foremost, an Artist." *Freedomways* 20.3 (fall 1980): 134–40.

Goya, Francisco. *Disasters of War.* New York: Dover Publications, 1967.

Greene, Alison de Lima. "John Biggers: American Muralist." In Wardlaw, *Art* 96–107.

Griffin, Farah Jasmine. *"Who Set You Flowin'?": The African-American Migration Narrative.* New York: Oxford University Press, 1995.

Grimes, William. "The Art of Black Printmakers: Making Life Real." *New York Times* December 21, 1992: C11, C16.

Hapke, Laura. *Daughters of the Great Depression: Women, Work, and Fiction in the American 1930s.* Athens: University of Georgia Press, 1995.

"Harlem Artists' Guild: A Statement." *Art Front* 2.8 (July–August 1936): 4–5.

"Harlem Hospital Murals." *Art Front* 2 (April 1936): 3.

Harper, Michael S., ed. *The Collected Poems of Sterling A. Brown.* Chicago: TriQuarterly Books, 1983.

Harris, Jonathan. "Art, Histories and Politics: The New Deal Art Projects and American Modernism." *Ideas and Production* 5 (spring 1986): 104–19.

Harris, Trudier. Introduction. In Childress, xi–xxxiv.

Hart, Henry, ed. *American Writers' Congress.* New York: International Publishers, 1935.

Haskell, Barbara. *The American Century: Art and Culture, 1900–1950.* New York: Whitney Museum of American Art and W. W. Norton and Company, 1999.

Hatch, James V., and Ted Shine. *Black Theatre USA: Plays by African Americans: The Early Period, 1847–1938.* New York: The Free Press, 1996.

Hayden, Robert E. *Heart-Shape in the Dust.* Detroit: Falcon Press, 1940.

Hayes, Vertis. "The Negro Artist Today." In O'Connor, 210–12.

Hayward, DuBose. *Porgy.* Dunwoody, Ga.: Norman S. Berg, 1925.

Herndon, Angelo. "Editorial Comment." *Negro Quarterly* 1.4 (winter–spring 1943): 295–302.

Herzog, Melanie Anne. *Elizabeth Catlett: An American Artist in Mexico.* Seattle: University of Washington Press, 2000.

Hills, Patricia. *Modern Art in the USA: Issues and Controversies.* Upper Saddle River, N.J.: Prentice Hall, 2001.

———. *Social Concern and Urban Realism: American Painting of the 1930s.* Boston: Boston University Art Center, 1983.

Himes, Chester. *Cast the First Stone.* New York: Coward-McCann, 1952.

———. *If He Hollers Let Him Go.* Garden City, N.Y.: Doubleday, Doran, and Company, 1945.

———. *Lonely Crusade.* New York: Alfred A. Knopf, 1947.

Holladay, Hilary. *Ann Petry.* New York: Twayne Publishers, 1996.

Holmes, Eugene C. "Problems Facing the Negro Writer Today." *New Challenge* 2.2 (fall 1937): 69–75.

Horowitz, Benjamin, ed. *Images of Dignity: The Drawings of Charles White.* Los Angeles: Ward Ritchie Press, 1967.

Howe, Irving, and Lewis Coser. *The American Communist Party: A Critical History (1919–1957).* Boston: Beacon Press, 1957.

Hughes, Langston. *The Big Sea.* 1940. New York: Thunder's Mouth Press, 1991.

———. "A Fine New Poet." *Opportunity* fall 1945: 222.

———. *Good Morning Revolution: Uncollected Writings of Social Protest.* Ed. Faith Berry. Secaucus, N.J.: Carol Publishing Group, 1992.

———. *The Negro Mother and Other Dramatic Recitations.* New York: Golden Stair Press, 1931.

———. *A New Song.* New York: International Workers' Order, 1938.

———. *One-Way Ticket.* New York: Alfred A. Knopf, 1949.

———. *Scottsboro Limited.* New York: Golden Stair Press, 1932.

———. *Shakespeare in Harlem.* New York: Alfred A. Knopf, 1942.

Bibliography

————. "To Negro Writers." In Hart, 139–41.

Hurlburt, Laurance P. *The Mexican Muralists in the United States.* Albuquerque: University of New Mexico Press, 1989.

Hurston, Zora Neale. "The 'Pet' Negro System." [1943]. Reprinted in *I Love Myself When I Am Laughing . . . And Then Again When I Am Looking Mean and Impressive: A Zora Neale Hurston Reader.* Ed. Alice Walker. New York: The Feminist Press, 1979. 156–62.

————. *Their Eyes Were Watching God.* Philadelphia: J. B. Lippincott Company, 1937.

Hutchinson, George. *The Harlem Renaissance in Black and White.* Cambridge: The Belknap Press of Harvard University Press, 1995.

Inge, M. Thomas. *Dark Laughter: The Satiric Art of Oliver W. Harrington.* Jackson: University Press of Mississippi, 1993.

Ivy, James W. "Ann Petry Talks about Her First Novel." *Crisis* 53 (1946): 48–49.

Jackson, Albert. "Alabama's Blood-Smeared Cotton." *New Masses* September 24, 1935: 13.

James, C. L. R. *The Black Jacobins: Toussaint L'Ouverture and the San Domingo Revolution.* New York: Dial Press, 1938.

Jarrett, Thomas D. "Sociology and Imagery in a Great American Novel." *English Journal* 38 (November 1949): 518–20.

Jemison, Noah. *Bob Blackburn's Printmaking Workshop: Artists of Color.* Brookville, N.Y.: Hillwood Art Museum, 1991.

Johnson, Abby Arthur, and Ronald Maberry Johnson. *Propaganda and Aesthetics: The Literary Politics of Afro-American Magazines in the Twentieth Century.* Amherst: University of Massachusetts Press, 1979.

Johnson, James Weldon, ed. *The Book of American Negro Poetry.* 1922. New York: Harcourt, Brace and Company, 1931.

Johnson, Josephine W. *Jordanstown: A Novel.* New York: Simon and Schuster, 1937.

Judge Priest. Dir. John Ford. Fox Film Corporation, 1934.

Kalaidjian, Walter. *American Culture between the Wars: Revisionary Modernism and Postmodern Critique.* New York: Columbia University Press, 1993.

Kelley, Robin D. G. *Hammer and Hoe: Alabama Communists during the Great Depression.* Chapel Hill: University of North Carolina Press, 1990.

Killens, John Oliver. "He Took His Art More Seriously Than He Did Himself." *Freedomways* 20.3 (fall 1980): 192–94.

Kinnamon, Kenneth, and Michel Fabre, eds. *Conversations with Richard Wright.* Jackson: University of Mississippi Press, 1993.

Klinkowitz, Jerome, ed. *The Diaries of Willard Motley.* Ames: Iowa State University Press, 1979.

Klinkowitz, Jerome, and Karen Wood. "The Making and Unmaking of *Knock on Any Door.*" *Proof* 3 (1973): 121–37.

Kogan, Herman. "Motley Learned the Hard Way: His Fiction Realistic? He Even Went to Jail to Obtain Background." *Chicago Sun* June 22, 1947: n.p.

Kozloff, Max. "The Rivera Frescoes of the Detroit Institute of Fine Arts: Proletarian Art under Capitalist Patronage." In *Art and Architecture in the Service of Politics.* Ed. Henry A. Millon and Linda Nochlin. Cambridge: MIT Press, 1978. 216–29.

Kwait, John. "John Reed Club Art Exhibition." *New Masses* February 1933: 23–24. Reprinted in Shapiro, 66–68.

LaCour, Jean. "NM's Art." *New Masses* October 8, 1946: 21.

Landau, Ellen G. *Artists for Victory: An Exhibition Catalog.* Washington, D.C.: Library of Congress, 1983.

Larsen, Edward. "Theatre in a Suitcase." *Opportunity* December 1938: 360.

"League of American Artists, A." *Art Front* 2.4 (March 1936): 13.

League of American Writers. *Writers Take Sides: Letters about the War in Spain from 418 American Authors.* New York: The League of American Writers, 1938.

Lee, George Washington. *River George.* New York: Macaulay, 1937.

Lee, Ulysses. "Two Poets in Wartime." *Opportunity* December 1942: 379–80.

LeFalle-Collins, Lizzetta. "'Contributions of the American Negro to Democracy': A History Painting by Charles White." *International Review of African American Art* 12.4 (1995): 38–41.

LeFalle-Collins, Lizzetta, and Shifra M. Goldman. *In the Spirit of Resistance: African-American Modernists and the Mexican Muralist School.* New York: American Federation of Arts, 1996.

Léger, Fernand. "The New Realism Goes On." *Art Front* 3.1 (February 1937): 7–8.

Levine, Lawrence W. *Black Culture and Black Consciousness: Afro-American Folk Thought from Slavery to Freedom.* Oxford: Oxford University Press, 1977.

Lewis, David Levering. *When Harlem Was in Vogue.* 1981. New York: Oxford University Press, 1989.

Lewis, Samella. *The Art of Elizabeth Catlett.* Claremont, Calif.: Hancraft Studios, 1984.

Lewis, Sinclair. *It Can't Happen Here.* Garden City, N.Y.: Doubleday, Doran and Company, 1935.

Life and Times of Rosie the Riveter, The. Dir. Connie Field. First Run Features, 1980.

Lipsitz, George. *A Life in the Struggle: Ivory Perry and the Culture of Opposition.* Philadelphia: Temple University Press, 1988.

———. *Rainbow at Midnight: Labor and Culture in the 1940s.* Urbana: University of Illinois Press, 1994.

Locke, Alain. "Chicago's New Southside Art Center." *Magazine of Art* August 1941: 370–74.

———. *The Negro in Art: A Pictorial Record of the Negro Artist and of the Negro Theme in Art.* 1940. New York: Hacker Art Books, 1979.

———. "Resume of Talk and Discussion." *Official Proceedings of the Second National Negro Congress, October 15–17, 1937.* Philadelphia: Metropolitan Opera House, 1937.

———, ed. *The New Negro: Voices of the Harlem Renaissance.* 1925. New York: Atheneum, 1992.

London, Jack. *The Iron Heel.* 1908. London: Arco, 1966.

Long, Richard A. *Highlights from the Atlanta University Collection of Afro-American Art.* Atlanta: High Museum of Art, 1973.

Lucie-Smith, Edward. *Art of the 1930s: The Age of Anxiety.* London: Weidenfeld and Nicolson, 1985.

Lumpkin, Grace. *A Sign for Cain*. New York: Lee Furman, 1935.

———. "A Southern Cotton Mill Rhyme." *New Masses* May 1930: 8.

Mangione, Jerre. *The Dream and the Deal: The Federal Writers' Project, 1935–1943*. Philadelphia: University of Pennsylvania Press, 1983.

Margolies, Edward. *Native Sons: A Critical Study of Twentieth-Century Black American Authors*. Philadelphia: J. B. Lippincott Company, 1968.

Marling, Karal Ann. *Wall-to-Wall America: A Cultural History of Post-Office Murals in the Great Depression*. Minneapolis: University of Minnesota Press, 1982.

Marx, Karl, and Hugo Gellert. *Capital in Lithographs*. New York: Ray Long and Richard R. Smith, 1934.

Maxwell, William J. *New Negro, Old Left: African-American Writing and Communism between the Wars*. New York: Columbia University Press, 1999.

McCoy, Garnett. "The Rise and Fall of the American Artists' Congress." *Prospects: An Annual of American Cultural Studies* 13 (1988): 325–40.

McDaniel, M. A. "Reexamining Hale Woodruff's Talladega College and Atlanta University Murals." *International Review of African American Art* 12.4 (1995): 4–17.

McKay, Claude. *Harlem Shadows*. New York: Harcourt, Brace, and Company, 1922.

McKinzie, Richard D. *The New Deal for Artists*. Princeton: Princeton University Press, 1973.

Mello, Renato González, and Diane Miliotes, eds. *José Clemente Orozco in the United States, 1927–1934*. New York: Hood Museum of Art and W. W. Norton and Company, 2002.

Melosh, Barbara. *Engendering Culture: Manhood and Womanhood in New Deal Public Art and Theater*. Washington, D.C.: Smithsonian Institution Press, 1991.

Mercer, Kobena. *Welcome to the Jungle: New Positions in Black Cultural Studies*. New York: Routledge, 1994.

"Mexican Congress Reports, The." *Art Front* 3.3–4 (April–May 1937): 13–14.

Minus, Marian. "Present Trends of Negro Literature." *Challenge* 2.1 (April 1937): 9–11.

"Miscellany." *Common Ground* 4.2 (winter 1944): 108–9.

Mitchell, Lee Clark. *Determined Fictions: American Literary Naturalism*. New York: Columbia University Press, 1989.

Mooney, Amy M. "Representing Race: Disjunctures in the Work of Archibald J. Motley, Jr." *Museum Studies* 24.2 (1999): 162–79, 262–65.

Motley, Willard Francis. "Calle Olvera—America's Most Picturesque Street." *Highway Traveler* 10.4 (August–September 1938): 14–15, 41–46.

———. "The Education of a Writer." *New Idea: Magazine of Student Thought and Writing* winter 1960: 11–28. [University of Wisconsin student publication.]

———. "Handfuls." *Hull-House Magazine* 1.3 (January 1940): 9–11.

———. *Knock on Any Door*. New York: Appleton-Century-Crofts, 1947.

———. "Let No Man Write Epitaph of Hate for His Chicago." *Chicago Sunday Sun-Times* August 11, 1963: sec. 2: 1–4.

———. "Negro Art in Chicago." *Opportunity* January 1940: 19–22, 28–31.

———. "Pavement Portraits." *Hull-House Magazine* 1.2 (December 1939): 2–6.

———. *We Fished All Night*. New York: Appleton-Century-Crofts, 1951.

Mullen, Bill V. *Popular Fronts: Chicago and African-American Cultural Politics, 1935–46.* Urbana: University of Illinois Press, 1999.

Murphy, James F. *The Proletarian Moment: The Controversy over Leftism in Literature.* Urbana: University of Illinois Press, 1991.

Murray, Albert. "An Interview with Hale Woodruff." In *Hale Woodruff: 50 Years of His Art.* Ed. Helen Shannon. New York: Studio Museum in Harlem, 1979. 71–88.

Myrdal, Gunnar. *An American Dilemma: The Negro Problem and Modern Democracy.* New York: Harper and Brothers, 1944.

Nagel, Otto. *Käthe Kollwitz.* Greenwich, Conn.: New York Graphic Society, 1971.

Naison, Mark. *Communists in Harlem during the Depression.* Urbana: University of Illinois Press, 1983.

"National Negro Congress." *Art Front* 2.4 (March 1936): 3.

Nekola, Charlotte, and Paula Rabinowitz. *Writing Red: An Anthology of American Women Writers, 1930–1940.* New York: Feminist Press, 1987.

Nelson, Cary. *Repression and Recovery: Modern American Poetry and the Politics of Cultural Memory, 1910–1945.* Madison: University of Wisconsin Press, 1989.

Nelson, Edward L. "Two Members Work for Ingram Family's Freedom." *Fraternal Outlook* October–November 1949: 16–19.

New York Artists' Union Executive Committee. "The Artists' Union: Builders of a Democratic Culture." *Art Front* 3.3–4 (April–May 1937): 3.

Norris, Frank. *The Octopus: A Story of California.* 1901. New York: New American Library, 1981.

O'Brien, John. "Interview with Ann Petry." In Ervin, 72–77.

O'Connor, Francis V., ed. *Art for the Millions: Essays from the 1930s by Artists and Administrators of the Works Progress Administration Federal Art Project.* Greenwich: New York Graphic Society, 1977.

Odum, Howard W. *Rainbow round My Shoulder: The Blue Trail of Black Ulysses.* Indianapolis: The Bobbs-Merrill Company, 1928.

Olds, Elizabeth. "Prints for Mass Production." In O'Connor, 142–44.

Oles, James. *South of the Border: Mexico in the American Imagination.* Washington, D.C.: Smithsonian Institution Press, 1993.

Olsen, Tillie. *Yonnondio: From the Thirties.* 1974. New York: Delta, 1989.

Ottley, Roi. "The Good-Neighbor Policy—At Home." *Common Ground* 2.4 (summer 1942): 51–56.

Page, Myra. *Gathering Storm: A Story of the Black Belt.* New York: International Publishers, 1932.

Park, Marlene. "Lynching and Antilynching: Art and Politics in the 1930s." *Prospects: An Annual of American Cultural Studies* 18 (1993): 311–65.

Park, Marlene, and Gerald E. Markowitz. *New Deal for Art: The Government Art Projects of the 1930s with Examples from New York City and State.* Hamilton, N.Y.: Gallery Association of New York State, 1977.

Peeler, David P. *Hope among Us Yet: Social Criticism and Social Solace in Depression America.* Athens: University of Georgia Press, 1987.

Pells, Richard. *Radical Visions and American Dreams: Culture and Social Thought during the Depression Years.* New York: Harper and Row, 1973.

Petry, Ann. *The Street.* Boston: Houghton Mifflin, 1946.

Phillips, Lisa. *The American Century: Art and Culture, 1950–2000.* New York: Whitney Museum of American Art and W. W. Norton and Company, 1999.

Pittman, John. "Charles White's Exciting 'Negro Woman' Show at A.C.A. Gallery." *Daily Worker* February 26, 1951.

Pizer, Donald. *The Theory and Practice of American Literary Naturalism: Selected Essays and Reviews.* Carbondale: Southern Illinois University Press, 1993.

Porter, James A. *Modern Negro Art.* 1943. Washington, D.C.: Howard University Press, 1992.

Powell, Richard J. "*I Too, Am America,* Protest, and Black Power: Philosophical Continuities in Prints by Black Americans." *Black Art* 2.3 (spring 1978): 4–25.

Powell, Richard J., and Jock Reynolds. *James Lesesne Wells: Sixty Years in Art.* Washington, D.C.: Washington Project for the Arts, 1986.

———. *To Conserve a Legacy: American Art from Historically Black Colleges and Universities.* Andover, Mass., and New York: Addison Gallery of American Art and The Studio Museum in Harlem, 1999.

Prigoff, James, and Robin J. Dunitz. *Walls of Heritage / Walls of Pride: African American Murals.* San Francisco: Pomegranate, 2000.

Rampersad, Arnold. Foreword. In *Lawd Today!* v–xi.

———, ed. *The Collected Poems of Langston Hughes.* New York: Vintage Books, 1994.

Randall, Dudley. "The Black Aesthetic in the Thirties, Forties, and Fifties." In *The Black Aesthetic.* Ed. Addison Gayle. Garden City, N.Y.: Doubleday, 1971. 224–34.

———. "'Mystery' Poet: An Interview with Frank Marshall Davis." *Black World* 23.3 (January 1974): 37–48.

Rayson, Ann L. "Prototypes for Nick Romano of *Knock on Any Door:* From the Diaries in the Collected Manuscripts of the Willard Motley Estate." *Negro American Literature Forum* 8.3 (fall 1974): 248–51.

Record, Wilson. *The Negro and the Communist Party.* Chapel Hill: University of North Carolina Press, 1951.

Reese, Albert. *American Prize Prints of the Twentieth Century.* New York: American Artists Group, 1949.

"Return of Willard Motley, The." *Ebony* 13 (December 1958): 84–90.

Rideout, Walter B. *The Radical Novel in the United States, 1900–1954: Some Interrelations of Literature and Society.* 1956. New York: Columbia University Press, 1992.

Rivera, Diego, and Bertram D. Wolfe. *Portrait of America.* New York: Covici, Friede, 1934.

Roberts, John W. *From Trickster to Badman: The Black Folk Hero in Slavery and Freedom.* Philadelphia: University of Pennsylvania Press, 1989.

Robertson, Bruce. *Representing America: The Ken Trevey Collection of American Realist Prints.* Santa Barbara: University Art Museum (University of California), 1995.

Rochfort, Desmond. *Mexican Muralists: Orozco, Rivera, Siqueiros.* New York: Universe, 1993.

Rollins, William. *The Shadow Before.* 1934. New York: A. M. S. Press, 1998.

Rowell, Charles H. "'Let Me Be with Ole Jazzbo': An Interview with Sterling A. Brown." *Callaloo* 14.4 (fall 1991): 795–815.

Salzman, Jack, and David Ray. *The Jack Conroy Reader.* New York: Burt Franklin and Co., 1979.

Sanders, Mark A. *Afro-Modernist Aesthetics and the Poetry of Sterling A. Brown.* Athens: University of Georgia Press, 1999.

———, ed. *A Son's Return: Selected Essays of Sterling A. Brown.* Boston: Northeastern University Press, 1996.

Savage, Kirk. *Standing Soldiers, Kneeling Slaves: Race, War, and Monument in Nineteenth-Century America.* Princeton: Princeton University Press, 1997.

Saxton, Alexander. *Grand Crossing.* New York: Harper and Brothers, 1943.

Schatz, Philip. "Songs of the Negro Worker." *New Masses* May 1930: 6–8.

Scott, James C. *Domination and the Arts of Resistance: Hidden Transcripts.* New Haven: Yale University Press, 1990.

Shapiro, David, ed. *Social Realism: Art as a Weapon.* New York: Frederick Unger Publishing Co., 1973.

Shapiro, David, and Cecile Shapiro. "The Artists' Union in America." In Foner and Schultz, 93–94.

Simama, Jabari. "Black Writers Experience Communism: An Interdisciplinary Study of Imaginative Writers, Their Critics, and the CPUSA." Diss. Emory University, 1978.

Sinclair, Upton. *The Jungle.* 1906. Urbana: University of Illinois Press, 1988.

Smethurst, James Edward. *The New Red Negro: The Literary Left and African American Poetry, 1930–1946.* New York: Oxford University Press, 1999.

Smith, William Gardner. *Anger at Innocence.* New York: Farrar, Straus, and Company, 1950.

———. *Last of the Conquerors.* New York: Farrar, Straus, and Company, 1948.

Songs of Citizen CIO. Asch Records, 1944.

Spero, Sterling D., and Abram Harris. *The Black Worker: The Negro and the Labor Movement.* 1931. Port Washington, N.Y.: Kennikat Press, 1966.

Stavenitz, Alex, ed. *Graphic Works of the American Thirties.* 1936. New York: De Capo Press, 1977.

Steinbeck, John. *The Grapes of Wrath.* New York: Modern Library, 1939.

Stepto, Robert B. *From behind the Veil: A Study of Afro-American Narrative.* Urbana: University of Illinois Press, 1979.

Stewart, Jeffrey C., ed. *The Critical Temper of Alain Locke: A Selection of His Essays on Art and Culture.* New York: Garland, 1983.

Stoelting, Winifred L. "Hale Woodruff, Artist and Teacher: Through the Georgia Years." Diss. Emory University, 1978.

Stott, William. *Documentary Expression and Thirties America.* New York: Oxford University Press, 1973.

Tarr, Amy. "A Capital Career: Artist John Wilson Expresses the Spirit of Black Americans." *Boston Phoenix* March 12, 1993.

Thomas, Norman. "Can America Go Fascist?" *Crisis* January 1934: 10–11.

Thompson, Louise. "Southern Terror." *Crisis* November 1934: 327–28.

Thurman, Wallace. *Infants of the Spring.* 1932. Freeport, N.Y.: Books for Libraries Press, 1972.

Tidwell, John Edgar. "Frank Marshall Davis." In *Afro-American Writers from the Harlem Renaissance to 1940.* Vol. 51 of *Dictionary of Literary Biography.* Ed. Trudier Harris and Thadious M. Davis. Detroit: Gale Research, 1987. 60–66.

———. "An Interview with Frank Marshall Davis." *Black American Literature Forum* 19 (fall 1985): 105–8.

———. "Introduction: Weaving Jagged Words into Song." In F. M. Davis, *Black Moods* xxi–lxv.

———. "Reliving the Blues: Frank Marshall Davis and the Crafting of a Self." In F. M. Davis, *Livin' the Blues* xiii–xxvii.

Tolson, Melvin. *Rendezvous with America.* New York: Dodd, Mead, and Company, 1944.

Tompkins, Grace. "Justice Wears Dark Glasses." *Negro Story* 1.2 (July–August 1944): 10–14.

Turner, Elizabeth Hutton, ed. *Jacob Lawrence: The Migration Series.* Washington, D.C.: Rappahannock Press, 1993.

Tyler, Anna M. "Planting and Maintaining a 'Perennial Garden': Chicago's South Side Community Art Center." *International Review of African American Art* 11.4 (1994): 31–37.

Untermeyer, Louis. *Modern American Poetry: A Critical Anthology.* New York: Harcourt, Brace, and Company, 1921.

Van Vechten, Carl. *Nigger Heaven.* New York: Alfred A. Knopf, 1926.

Vaughan, Philip H. "From Pastoralism to Industrial Antipathy in William Attaway's *Blood on the Forge.*" *Phylon* 36 (December 1975): 422–25.

Vendryes, Margaret Rose. "Hanging on Their Walls: *An Art Commentary on Lynching,* the Forgotten 1935 Art Exhibition." In *Race Consciousness: African-American Studies for the New Century.* Ed. Judith Jackson Fossett and Jeffrey A. Tucker. New York: New York University Press, 1997. 153–76.

Vincent, Howard P. *Daumier and His World.* Evanston: Northwestern University Press, 1968.

Wald, Alan M. *Exiles from a Future Time: The Forging of the Mid-Twentieth-Century Literary Left.* Chapel Hill: University of North Carolina Press, 2002.

———. Foreword. In L. Brown, *Iron City* vii–xxxvii.

Walker, Margaret A. *For My People.* New Haven: Yale University Press, 1942.

———. *Jubilee.* Boston: Houghton Mifflin, 1966.

———. "New Poets." *Phylon* 11.4 (December 1950): 345–54.

———. *Richard Wright, Daemonic Genius: A Portrait of the Man, a Critical Look at His Work.* New York: Warner Books, 1988.

Wardlaw, Alvia J. *The Art of John Biggers: View from the Upper Room.* New York: Harry N. Abrams, 1995.

———. "Strength, Tears, and Will: John Biggers' 'Contribution of the Negro Woman to American Life and Education.'" *Callaloo* 2.5 (February 1979): 135–43.

Weiss, Henry George. "Poetry and Revolution." *New Masses* October 1929: 9.

Wheat, Ellen Harkins. *Jacob Lawrence: American Painter.* Seattle: University of Washington Press, 1986.

White, Charles. "Path of a Negro Artist." *Masses and Mainstream* April 1955: 33–44.

White, Josh. *Southern Exposure: An Album of Jim Crow Blues.* Keynote Records, 1941.

White, Walter. *Rope and Faggot: A Biography of Judge Lynch.* New York: Alfred A. Knopf, 1929.

Whiting, Cécile. *Antifacism in American Art.* New Haven: Yale University Press, 1989.

Williams, Reba, and Dave Williams. *Alone in a Crowd: Prints of the 1930s–40s by African American Artists.* New York: American Federation of Arts, 1993.

Wixson, Douglas. *Worker-Writer in America: Jack Conroy and the Tradition of Midwestern Literary Radicalism, 1898–1990.* Urbana: University of Illinois Press, 1994.

Wood, Charles. "The Adventure Manuscript: New Light on Willard Motley's Naturalism." *Negro American Literature Forum* 6.2 (summer 1972): 35–38.

Woodson, Carter G. *The Rural Negro.* Washington, D.C.: The Association for the Study of Negro Life and History, 1930.

Wright, Richard. *American Hunger.* New York: Harper and Row, 1977.

———. "Blueprint for Negro Writing." *New Challenge* 2.2 (fall 1937): 53–65.

———. *Lawd Today!* 1963. Boston: Northeastern University Press, 1993.

———. *Native Son.* New York: Harper and Brothers, 1940.

———. "Not My People's War." *New Masses* June 17, 1941: 8–9, 12.

———. *Twelve Million Black Voices: A Folk History of the Negro in the United States.* New York: Viking Press, 1941.

———. *Uncle Tom's Children.* 1938. New York: HarperPerennial, 1993.

Yarborough, Richard. Afterword. In Attaway, *Blood* 295–312.

Yoseloff, Thomas, ed. *Seven Poets in Search of an Answer.* New York: B. Ackerman, 1944.

Young, James O. *Black Writers of the Thirties.* Baton Rouge: Louisiana State University Press, 1973.

Zeidler, Jeanne. "John Biggers: Hampton Murals." *International Review of African American Art* 12.4 (1995): 51–57.

Zurier, Rebecca. *Art for the Masses: A Radical Magazine and Its Graphics, 1911–1917.* Philadelphia: Temple University Press, 1988.

Index

Brown, Lloyd, 19, 129, 240, 251, 325 (n. 43); *Iron City*, 21, 244, 245–46, 252–54, 276, 279–80, 282–83, 293, 299, 323 (n. 17), 325 (n. 48); response to Richard Wright's fiction, 253; work with *New Masses/Masses and Mainstream*, 27, 36, 245, 299

Brown, Sterling, 4, 31, 70, 93, 185, 206, 236, 238, 248, 249, 282; critical reception of, 7, 182; as cultural critic, 213, 300; and Federal Writers' Project, 15, 245; interest of, in African American folklore, 212, 253. Works: "Cabaret," 173, 176; "Call for Barnum," 221; "Odyssey of Big Boy," 213; "Old King Cotton," 213–16; "Old Lem," 178, 214–16; "Revelations," 217; "Sharecroppers," 233–34, 279; "Side by Side," 232–34; "Southern Road," 179–81, 210, 213; "Street Car Gang," 209

Browne, Theodore, 320 (n. 28)

"Brown Girl's Sacrament" (Hayden), 221–22

Brown Madonna, The (Reiss), 146

Building the Library (Woodruff), 89–90

Burke, Fielding, 241

Burroughs, Margaret, 22, 50, 51–54, 61, 101, 109, 138, 151, 188–89

Bury the Dead (Shaw), 53

By Parties Unknown (Woodruff), 142–44, 170, 183

"Cabaret" (Sterling Brown), 173, 176

Cadmus, Paul, 141

Caldwell, Erskine, 141

"Call for Barnum" (Sterling Brown), 221

"Call to Creation" (Hughes), 171–72

Campbell, E. Simms, 27, 30, 142; *I Passed along This Way*, 146–47

Cannon, David, Jr., 209–10

Cantwell, Robert, 240

Capitalists: as subject in graphic art, 110–12, 126, 130–31, 200; as subject in murals, 60; as subject in novels, 218, 251, 268–69, 272–73, 283, 287, 292, 299–300, 316 (n. 34), 325 (n. 54); as subject in poetry, 172, 176, 194–96, 198–202, 205, 209, 219, 231–33, 235–36

Carver, George Washington, as subject in cultural work, 56, 65, 71, 197

Catlett, Elizabeth, 17, 19, 31, 61–63, 112, 117, 134, 138, 142–46, 303, 306, 311–12 (n. 32); activities of, at Dillard University, 61, 144; activities of, in Mexico, 33, 150–51, 275. Works: *And a special fear for my loved ones*, 144; *I have always worked hard in America*,

159; *I have special reservations*, 150, 159–60; *In Harriet Tubman, I helped hundreds to freedom*, 150–51; *Mother and Child*, 144–46; *My right is a future of equality with other Americans*, 151, 202; *My role has been important in the struggle to organize the unorganized*, 157–59, 233; *The Negro Woman* series, 26, 150–51, 157–60, 202, 212, 317 (n. 65); *War Worker*, 164, 170

Cayton, Horace, 157, 246–47; *Black Metropolis*, 247, 284

Chain gangs, as subject in cultural work, 12, 170, 179–80, 193, 213–14, 218

Challenge, 7, 13, 20–21, 27–28, 182, 247–48, 276, 282.

"Chant for Tom Mooney" (Hughes), 224

Chicago: American Negro Exposition (1940) in, 54, 56, 188, 312 (n. 36); as a center of social realism, 3, 14, 22, 28–29, 50–57, 61, 184–89, 206, 246–47, 256–58, 261, 323 (n. 22)

Chicago Defender, 27–28, 55–57, 101, 155–56, 211, 255, 286–87, 317–18 (n. 71)

Childress, Alice, 320 (n. 26)

"Christ in Alabama" (Hughes), 222

Christ in Alabama (Taylor), 140, 147

"Christ Is a Dixie Nigger" (Davis), 221–22, 232

CIO (Congress of Industrial Organizations), 28, 41, 70, 86, 208; African American social realists' support of, 24, 157, 175, 192, 232–33, 274; as model for cultural workers, 17–18; as patron of cultural work, 101, 277

City Building (Benton), 90

Civil War murals (Ishigaki), 44, 59–60, 311 (n. 31)

Cleveland, as a center of social realism, 6, 31, 165

Coit Tower murals, 44, 73

Cold war: impact of, on social realism, 21–22, 33–34, 78, 96, 155, 267, 274–75, 321 (n. 45), 325 (n. 43); influence of, on critical evaluation of social realism, 9, 151, 156, 292, 300–301; social realists' persistence in face of, 24–25, 34–35, 47, 53, 133, 138–39, 303; as subject in cultural work, 266–67, 269, 274, 282–83

"Coleman" (Hayden), 227

"Colored Soldier, The" (Hughes), 224, 227

Committee for the Negro in the Arts, 23

Common Ground, 27, 113, 165, 209, 211, 225, 305

Communist Party (CPUSA), 2, 4, 35, 232; and African American artists, 8, 49, 310–11

Union, 9. Works: *The Negro in Art*, 6, 89, 117; *The New Negro* (editor), 11–12, 49–50, 77, 146, 317 (n. 54)

London, Jack, 49, 257; *The Iron Heel*, 243

Long Black Song (Wright), 277, 289

Looking Backward (Bellamy), 243

Lovers (Crichlow), 147–48, 170

Lowenfeld, Viktor, 63–64, 65, 94, 97–98, 101, 313 (n. 63)

Lumpkin, Grace, 321–22 (n. 56); *A Sign for Cain*, 11–12

"Lynched" (Davis), 319–20 (n. 19)

Lynching, 128–29, 137, 201, 282, 312 (n. 42); campaigns against, 14, 17, 19, 140–44; as general subject in social realism, 5, 13, 18, 305; likened to crucifixion, 100, 146–47, 221–22, 228, 233; as subject in graphic art, 62, 102, 122, 126–30, 140–47, 149, 170, 183, 196, 221; as subject in novels, 250, 284, 298; as subject in poetry, 172, 182–83, 193, 195–96, 203, 205, 209–10, 215, 218–23, 228, 232–33, 235, 238, 319–20 (n. 19)

Machine politics, as subject in art, 60, 266, 268–69

"Madam and Her Madam" (Hughes), 211–12

Madonna and child imagery, 146

Magic and Medicine (Alston), 73–78, 312 (n. 46)

Malcolm X, 205

Man at the Crossroads (Rivera), 32, 38, 45–47, 309 (n. 31)

"'Mancipation Day" (Davis), 204–5, 282

Marcus, Raymond, 227

Marinetti, F. T., 199, 230

Marsh, Reginald, 141, 221

Marxist ideology: as expressed in cultural criticism, 6, 8–9, 147, 212; as expressed in graphic art, 130–31, 156–57, 194; as expressed in murals, 47, 58, 60; as expressed in novels, 253, 270, 277–80, 284, 292, 300; as expressed in poetry, 171, 194–96, 207–8, 209, 219, 227, 232, 235; influence of, on social realists, 8, 9–10, 14, 27, 44–45, 54, 124–26, 133, 190–91

Masks (Gwathmey), 137

Massachusetts Fifty-fourth regiment, as subject in cultural work, 65–69

Mass chant, 174–76, 206, 223

Masses, 110, 112–13, 130, 147, 314 (n. 10)

Masses and Mainstream, 23, 27, 62, 103, 139, 305–6

Masters, Edgar Lee, 185

Matthews, Miriam, 79, 83

McDaniel, Hattie, 86

McKay, Claude, 4, 9, 11, 30, 185, 248; "If We Must Die," 173; as subject in cultural work, 197

Méndez, Leopoldo, 33

Meritocracy, 124; as subject in cultural work, 194, 197, 250, 259, 270, 297–98, 325 (n. 54)

Messenger, 3, 11, 104, 174

Mexican mural painting: African American social realists' exposure to, 32, 46–47, 63–64, 76, 87–88, 102–3, 122–23, 134–35; influence of, on U.S. art, 32, 38–39, 44–48, 51, 57, 65–68, 79, 94, 98, 130–32

Mexico City, as a center of social realism, 32–33, 87, 102–4, 135, 138–39, 150–51, 275, 305

Mexico through the Centuries murals (Rivera), 45–46

Migrant labor, as subject in cultural work, 146, 170, 205, 240–41, 252, 285–86

Migrant Mother (Lange), 146, 170

Migration. *See* Great Migration

Migration of the Negro series (Lawrence), 287

Militant self-defense, as subject in cultural work, 58–60, 69, 82, 87, 88–90, 94–95, 102–4, 204, 212, 273–75

Miller, Dorie, 152–54; as subject in cultural work, 152–54, 197, 225–26

Millman, Edward, 50–51, 256

Minor, Robert, 112–13; *In Georgia*, 147

Minus, Marian, 13, 28, 247, 276

Modernism, 36, 217; social realists' critiques of, 183, 271; social realists' engagement with, in art, 63, 78, 122, 132–35, 303; —, in novels, 248–54, 270–72, 274, 281, 303, 323 (n. 17); —, in poetry, 175–77, 185, 199, 303, 319–20 (n. 19); as subject in cultural work, 270

"Modern Man—the Superman" (Davis), 198–202, 230, 267, 283

Monus, Olga, 182

Mooney, Tom, 11, 307 (n. 4); as subject in cultural work, 46, 195, 224

"Moonlight in Valencia" (Hughes), 228–29

Mother and Child (Catlett), 144–46

Motley, Archibald, Jr., 52, 151, 255, 311 (n. 19), 323 (n. 18)

Motley, Willard, 4–5, 21, 52, 53, 240, 244, 251, 254–75, 324 (n. 26), 325 (n. 50); activities of, in Chicago, 254–58, 261–63, 267, 323 (nn. 21–22); —, in Mexico, 33, 275, 324

122–24, 132–34, 141; *Allegory of Science, Labor, and Art*, 69; *Dive Bomber and Tank*, 32; *The Epic of Civilization* murals, 122; *Hanging Negroes*, 122; *The Rich Banquet While the Workers Fight*, 130

Our War (Charles White), 155

Page, Myra, 11–12
Panther and the Lash, The (Hughes), 303
Parks, Gordon, 29, 54, 57, 189
Passing Scene, The (Wilson), 164, 167
"Peace Quiz for America" (Davis), 192, 197
Petry, Ann, 21, 240, 261, 293, 325 (n. 43); popular reception of, 242; *The Street*, 121, 242, 244, 245–46, 251, 276, 280–81, 291, 297–99, 323–24 (n. 24)
Phylon, 6, 31, 89
"Poem to a Dead Soldier" (Hughes), 224
Police, 144, 266; as subject in graphic art, 107, 126, 149, 156; as subject in novels, 260, 264–65, 268, 273–74, 279, 285–86, 324 (n. 35); as subject in painting, 60, 71, 195, 274; as subject in poetry, 204–5, 215, 233
Political cartooning, 68, 102, 104, 109, 110–11, 129–31, 157, 194, 200, 228, 314 (n. 9); influence of, on social realism, 112–13, 130
Politics and Agriculture (Benton), 43–44, 82–83, 90
Pollock, Jackson, 22
Popel, Esther, 182–83
Popular culture, 110, 133, 221; images of African Americans in, 49, 83, 86, 89, 159, 178, 245, 249, 313 (n. 56); social realists' use of, 178–79, 183–84, 262, 324 (n. 26); as subject in cultural work, 240, 249–50
Popular Front, 22, 57, 70, 179; appeal of, to social realists, 17–18, 20, 181, 189; defined, 10–11; as expressed in cultural work, 10–11, 68–71, 129–30, 138, 183–84, 196–98, 227
Porgy (Heyward), 12
Porter, James, 31, 61, 165, 183
Portrait of America murals (Rivera), 46–47
Portrait of the Bourgeoisie (Siqueiros), 46
"Postcard from Spain" (Hughes), 228
Poverty, 325 (n. 50); as general subject in social realism, 4, 179, 302; social realists' experiences with, 4–5, 14–15, 48–49, 186, 255–56; as subject in graphic art, 31, 54, 111, 118–22, 165–70; as subject in novels, 243–47, 255, 258–65, 277–78; as subject in painting, 57–60, 90–93, 96–97, 116, 214; as subject in photography, 92, 169–70, 324 (n. 25); as subject

in poetry, 172, 177, 186, 194–96, 214, 216–17, 235
Poverty and Fatigue (William E. Smith), 165
Prison: as general subject in social realism, 12; social realists' experiences with, 245, 255; as subject in graphic art, 128, 150, 317 (nn. 59, 62), 325 (n. 48); as subject in novels, 245–46, 252–53, 259–61, 263, 264–65, 266, 279–80, 282–83, 299; as subject in poetry, 177, 179–80, 182, 205, 218, 222, 282–83
"Progress, the" (Brooks), 226
Progressive Party: and social realists' support of 1948 Wallace campaign, 134, 192, 324 (n. 37); as subject in cultural work, 202, 268–70
Public Works of Art Project (PWAP), 14–16, 42–43, 44, 87

Quirt, Walter, 76

Race riots, 161, 254; as subject in cultural work, 29, 149, 161
Racism, 34–36, 83, 86, 140, 161, 178, 309 (n. 29); equated with fascism, in cultural work, 36, 102, 126–30, 148, 150, 200–202, 227–28, 281–82, 284, 321 (n. 47); —, in leftist commentary, 10, 36, 68, 128–29, 138, 155–56, 282; as general subject in social realism, 21, 179, 305; protests against, 10, 11–12, 14, 17; social realists' encounters with, 11, 49, 50, 52, 72, 103–4, 137–38, 144, 254, 282, 312 (n. 42); as subject in graphic art, 102, 126–31, 135–37, 194, 223; as subject in murals, 44, 47, 57, 103, 313–14 (n. 66); as subject in novels, 11–12, 240–41, 251–52, 263, 266, 269–70, 272, 277–79, 281–82, 285, 294–95, 323 (n. 17); as subject in poetry, 24, 36, 172, 175, 183, 190–91, 193–94, 200–205, 217–19, 222–28, 235, 238. *See also* Jim Crow (segregation); Legal injustice; Lynching
Rainey, Ma, 181
Randolph, A. Philip, 18, 315 (n. 22); and *Messenger*, 3, 11, 104, 174
Rape, as subject in cultural work, 111, 147–48, 203, 222, 251, 271–72, 289, 313–14 (n. 66)
Raymond, Harry, 149
Rebel Poet, 27, 182
Recreation in Harlem (Seabrooke), 312 (n. 45)
"Red Clay Blues" (Hughes and Wright), 219
"Red Flag over Tuskegee" (Hughes), 208
Reece, Florence, 179, 235
Refregier, Anton, 23, 78

American history, 50, 56; military service of, 154, 308 (n. 17); and *New Masses/Masses and Mainstream*, 23, 27, 48, 62, 72; participation of, in leftist networks, 31, 49, 51, 52–54, 134, 138, 151, 188–89, 312 (n. 41); popular reception of, 19; and South Side Community Art Center, 52–54, 56; visit of, to Soviet Union, 23–24, 72. Works: *The Contribution of the Negro to Democracy in America*, 26, 64–72, 102, 105, 193–94, 224; *Dixie Comes to New York* (with Raymond), 149; *Five Great American Negroes*, 55–56, 94; *History of the Negro Press*, 56–57; *Hope for the Future*, 144–46; *Laborers*, 49; *The Living Douglass*, 150, 224; *Native Son No. 2*, 123–24; *Our War*, 155; Rosa Lee Ingram graphics, 317 (nn. 59, 62); *Technique to Serve the Struggle*, 57–61, 72, 105; *There Were No Crops This Year*, 54, 60

White, Josh, 18, 70, 179, 183–84; *Southern Exposure*, 183

White, Walter, 29, 30; as organizer of *An Art Commentary on Lynching* exhibit, 140–42, 147; *Rope and Faggot*, 140

Whitman, Walt, 172–73, 207, 208, 244

Who Likes War? or *Justice at Wartime* (Alston), 152

"Will V-Day Be Me-Day Too?" (Hughes), 227

Wilson, John, 21, 47, 114–39, 148, 183, 201, 225, 241, 315 (nn. 14, 18); activities of, in France, 132–34; —, in Mexico, 32, 102–4, 134–39, 275; —, in New York City, 134; and Atlanta University annual exhibitions, 31, 114, 116, 117, 315 (n. 19); and Boston Museum School, 102, 116, 118, 122, 123, 132; critical reception of, 117–18; early life of, 118; view of, on Marxist ideology, 8–9, 124–26, 131; —, on Mexican artists, 47, 102, 122, 124, 131–32. Works: *Adolescence*, 119–22, 133; *Black Soldier*, 114–17, 296; *Blvd. de Strasbourg*, 133–35; *Breadwinner*, 118–22, 135; *Deliver Us from Evil*, 126–31, 137, 139, 164, 170, 193–94, 200–201, 282; *Incident*, 102–4; *Native Son*, 123–24; *The Passing Scene*, 164, 167; *The Straphanger*, 139, 167; *Trabajador*, 135; *The Trial*, 135–37

Winslow, Vernon, 117, 137–38

Wood, Grant, 61, 168

Woodruff, Hale, 15–16, 31–32, 42–43, 52, 64, 112, 113, 303; and the Atlanta University "Outhouse School," 31, 167–68, 309 (n. 25); critical reception of, 89; influence on, by

Mexican art, 32, 313 (n. 57). Works: *Amistad* murals, 26, 87–90; *Building the Library*, 89–90; *By Parties Unknown*, 142–44, 170, 183; *Giddap*, 142, 221; *Negro in American Life* murals, 87; *The Negro in California History: Settlement and Development*, 27, 78–87, 95–96, 158; *Underground Railroad*, 89–90; *View of Atlanta*, 170

"Words This Spring" (Hayden), 229–30

Working class: artists' efforts to serve, 30, 59–61, 69–71, 72, 106–9, 132–35, 138, 151, 160–61; novelists' efforts to serve, 248, 255–56, 263, 271, 299–301; poets' efforts to serve, 40, 172–75, 177–78, 181, 192–93, 201–2, 207–8, 215, 228, 230–38; social realists' general efforts to serve, 2, 4–5, 13, 18–20, 33–34, 37–38, 305–6; as subject in graphic art, 31, 39, 49, 106, 111–12, 121–23, 126, 130–32, 133–35, 139, 150–51, 156–57; as subject in murals, 27, 32, 45, 56, 57–61, 62, 65, 69–71, 82–86, 89–90, 94–97, 100; as subject in novels, 12, 41, 243–47, 250–54, 256–57, 263, 268, 270–75, 278–80, 283–91, 293–301; as subject in poetry, 40, 172–75, 177–81, 186, 195–96, 203–5, 207–15, 218–19, 227, 228, 230–38, 321 (n. 55)

Work songs, 64, 214; as subject in cultural work, 179–81, 209–10

World War I, as subject in cultural work, 98–102, 183, 224, 227, 280, 294

World War II: impact of, on social realism, 21, 35–36, 68–69, 98, 111, 139, 154, 191, 274; social realists' ambivalence toward, as expressed in graphic art, 35, 102, 154–55, 161–64; —, as expressed in novels, 265–68, 280–82, 324 (n. 35); —, as expressed in painting, 98–102, 114–16, 305; —, as expressed in poetry, 35–36, 183–84, 200–201, 224–28; social realists' experiences with, 101, 154, 160–61, 308 (n. 17), 313 (n. 63), 315 (n. 14); as subject in cultural work, 35, 114–17, 152–55, 183, 197, 205, 224–28, 231, 266–74, 280–82, 305, 324 (n. 30)

WPA (Works Progress Administration), 4, 14–16, 20, 29, 44, 52, 72–73, 74, 78, 244. *See also* Federal Art Project (FAP); Federal Theatre Project (FTP); Federal Writers' Project (FWP)

Wright, Richard, 25, 93, 201, 225, 244, 249, 251, 261, 285, 304; activities of, in Chicago, 53, 229, 246–47, 296, 323 (n. 22); —, in New York City, 29, 30, 70, 183; and Communist Party, 8, 126, 191, 234, 245, 278, 322 (n. 3);

Wright, Richard (*continued*)
as cultural critic, 7–8, 181, 247–48, 281–82, 289, 319 (n. 14); and Federal Writers' Project, 16, 189, 244, 257; and John Reed Clubs, 13, 206, 234, 296; popular reception of, 123–24, 241–42; and South Side Writers' Group, 13, 18, 28–29, 188; travels of, 33, 138, 275. Works: "Between the World and Me," 220–21; *Big Boy Leaves Home,* 249, 277; "Blueprint for Negro Writing," 7–8, 10, 20, 71, 248, 277–78; *Bright and Morning Star,* 278–80, 293; *Down by the Riverside,* 277; "The Ethics of Living Jim Crow," 322 (n. 11), 325 (n. 45); *Fire and Cloud,* 277–78, 293; "Hearst Headline Blues," 177; "I Have Seen Black Hands," 235–36, 278, 282–83; "King Joe," 184; *Lawd Today!,* 239–40, 250–51, 258, 283–84, 289, 295–97, 298–99, 325 (n. 54); *Little Sister,* 318 (n. 74); *Long Black Song,* 277, 289; *Native Son,* 29, 121, 123, 241–42, 247, 253, 258, 265; "Red Clay Blues," 219; "Rise and Live," 174–75; "Spread Your Sunrise," 321 (n. 55); *Twelve Million Black Voices,* 241, 247, 287; *Uncle Tom's Children,* 123–24, 249, 276–80, 289, 293, 325 (n. 45); "We of the Streets," 234–35, 278

Yerby, Frank, 248, 319 (n. 15)
Yonnondio (Olsen), 288

Zerbe, Karl, 102, 316 (n. 43)
Zola, Émile, 243